# Music and Medicine

Anton Neumayr

# Music and Medicine

*Haydn*
*Mozart*
*Beethoven*
*Schubert*

Notes on Their Lives, Works,
and Medical Histories

Translated by Bruce Cooper Clarke

The original edition of this work, *Musik und Medizin, Am Beispiel der Wiener Klassik*, by Anton Neumayr, has been published by J&V Edition Wien Dachs-Verlag Ges.m.b.H.

Library of Congress Cataloging-in-Publication Data:
Neumayr, Anton.
        [Musik und Medizin.  English]
        Music and medicine / Anton Neumayr.
        v. cm.
        Translation of:  Musik und Medizin.
        Includes bibliographical references and index.
        Contents:  [1] Haydn, Mozart, Beethoven, Schubert : notes on
their lives, works, and medical histories.
        ISBN 0-936741-05-8 (v.  1)
        1.  Composers--Medical care.  2.  Composers--Health and hy-
giene.  3.  Music--18th century--History and criticism.  I.  Title.
ML390.N38513   1994
780'.92'2--dc20                                               94-21413
                                                                CIP
                                                                MN

MEDI-ED PRESS
Constitution Place, Suite A
716 East Empire Street
Bloomington, Illinois 61701
1-800-500-8205

# Contents

*An asterisk (\*) within the text indicates medical editor's notes on pages 431-434, presenting supplemental medical information.*

# Preface to
# the English Edition

We are pleased to have the privilege of offering *Music and Medicine* to English-speaking audiences with an interest in classical music, the Vienna classical composers, and historical medical treatment of the 18th and 19th centuries. Originally published in Austria in the German language, the task of translating *Musik & Medizin* was indeed challenging. The German language with its complex, lengthy sentences, full of descriptive prepositional phrases, requires patience and skill. We believe that this series of volumes is worth that effort, since it conveys the results of more than twenty years of original research by the author. The final English version is possible only as a result of the individual efforts and subsequent teamwork of many. Our common goal was to portray the original text as accurately as possible. Our thanks to the author Anton Neumayr, the Austrian publisher Jugend & Volk, the translator Bruce Cooper Clarke, the medical editor Harold O. Conn, M.D., the general editor Emily P. McNamara, and many others.

# Biographical Comments on the Author

Dr. Anton Neumayr was born in 1920 in Hallein, near Salzburg, Austria, into an academic family. In 1938, he was graduated with honors from the Realgymnasium in Salzburg. Following a period of military duty, he began the study of medicine at the Friedrich Wilhelm University in Berlin and finished it, after several interruptions caused by the war, at the university in Vienna in 1944. He wrote his doctoral dissertation on the subject of "Acute Necrosis of the Pancreas." After serving a brief residency at the provincial hospital in Salzburg, he became resident physician in the Second Medical University in Vienna in December 1945, under the direction first of Prof. Dr. Nikolaus von Jagic and later of Prof. Dr. Karl Fellinger. During his internship there, he spent half a year at the medical university in Stockholm for instruction in special gastroenterological techniques.

In 1956, Dr. Neumayr passed the examinations qualifying him as a university lecturer with his thesis on "Investigations into Hepatoportal Circulation in Humans." He became associate professor in 1963. Dr. Neumayr's research and scientific activities have resulted in some two hundred fifty publications, including many contributions to books. The subjects of his scientific works are drawn principally from the fields of gastroenterology and hepatology. In recent years he has also produced professional works in the field of clinical geriatrics and on the application of nuclear medical diagnostics to problems of internal medicine. Dr. Neumayr has been invited to give more than one hundred twenty lectures both in Austria and in other countries. Of special distinction was the Searle Lecture in 1963 to the annual congress of the American Association for the Study of Liver Disease in Chicago. He was invited to give this lecture as recognition for his development of a new method for continuously monitoring the circulation of blood in the human liver as well as a new process to determine arterial and portal venous blood flow in the liver.

In April 1964, Dr. Neumayr assumed direction of the medical department of the Kaiserin Elisabeth Hospital in Vienna. When the newly established Rudolfsstiftung Hospital was opened in September 1975, Dr. Neumayr became the director of its medical department. While serving in that capacity from 1975 to 1988, he established a gastrointestinal endoscopic center in the department. In addition, a nuclear medicine service was set up with the most modern equipment available, and a special central oncological service was created where cancer patients could be treated and followed by specialists employing internationally established methods.

Since 1979, Dr. Neumayr has been president of the International Geriatrics Congresses held in Bad Hofgastein. Since 1985, he has been editor of the newly founded German-language journal, *Moderne Geriatrie (Modern Geriatrics)*. He has been Director of Research for Clinical Geriatrics at the Ludwig Boltzmann Institute since 1986.

Dr. Neumayr is a member of numerous societies in Austria and elsewhere, including the Austrian Society for Internal Medicine (member of the Board of Directors), the German Society of Internal Medicine, the German Society for Alimentary and Metabolic Diseases, the Swiss Society for Gastroenterology, the International European Association for the Study of Liver Diseases (founding member), president of the Austrian Society for Health Care Economics, chairman of the Vienna Sanitary Commission, president of the Commission on Ethics of the City of Vienna, and member of the board of the Austrian Society for Geriatrics and Gerontology.

In recognition of Dr. Neumayr's scientific achievements, he was awarded the Cross of Honor for Arts and Science (first degree) in November 1980 and the Cross of Honor in gold (first degree) from Vienna and Salzburg in 1986 and 1988 respectively.

Aside from being a doctor of rare distinction, Dr. Neumayr has been active in the realm of music from his earliest years. He was only six years old when he gave his first public performance on the piano. At the age of seven, he began ten years of piano studies at the renowned Salzburg Conservatory of Music, the Mozarteum, where he frequently appeared as pianist in evening concerts. In 1945 in Vienna, he formed close musical ties with members of the Vienna Philharmonic. Since then, many members of this distinguished orchestra have accompanied Dr. Neumayr in evenings devoted to chamber music and in innumerable festive medical-musical presentations in Austria and other countries. In 1971, the Vienna Philharmonic Orchestra awarded Dr. Neumayr the Franz Schalk Medal in recognition of his long association with the orchestra.

Dr. Neumayr has devoted the last twenty-five years or so to the study of medical-historical aspects of the diseases and deaths of famous composers. He presented the results of his studies in a series of unusual public lectures, in which he both spoke and provided musical interpretations on the piano, accompanied by members of the Vienna Philharmonic. These presentations were exceptionally well received in Austria and abroad. Five of them were broadcast on Austrian television. Dr. Neumayr subsequently published the findings of his research in three volumes under the general rubric of *Music and Medicine.*

Since 1988, Dr. Neumayr has been the moderator of a regular series on Austrian television called *Diagnosis*, devoted to themes of popular medical interest and concern. In the last five years, some thirty different disorders and topics have been examined and discussed on these programs.

—This minibiography was first published in the *Wiener klinische Wochenschrift*, 102. Jahrgang, Heft 24 (1990), Springer Verlag (Vienna, New York), and has been updated and modified by Dr. Neumayr.

# *Preface to the Original Edition*

The art of music and the science of medicine have had an irresistible attraction for one another since time immemorial. The two appear together consistently throughout history. Among physicians in every country, a striking number express their active love of music through performance in public concerts. In addition, many doctors devote themselves with particular zeal to music-making at home and with friends, to say nothing of the numbers who, although they have no skill as performers, are among the most appreciative members of the audiences in the concert halls. Why is it that so many medical doctors have such a special love and feeling for music? The reason, I believe, is that the physician confronted constantly with sickness, suffering, and death, has a more urgent longing, a more pressing need, for music's restorative, beneficent effect than persons in other professions.

Doctors do not merely enjoy a direct involvement with music and music-making; their deep attachment often reaches far beyond that of most people and leads them to study and write about musical matters, whether in the reviews of musical events or in books on substantive musical subjects. For example, the standard textbook on violin playing was written by the famous physiologist Dr. Trendelenburg. Doctors have also been the authors of important books on major musicians, for example, Dr. Aloys Greither's books on Mozart and Dr. Albert Schweitzer's masterly aesthetic biography of Johann Sebastian Bach. But naturally the most obvious temptation for a doctor is to investigate the physical illnesses of famous composers and evidence of their emotional suffering and to try to unearth the latent relationship of musical creativity to particular pathological and psychological findings.

Every biography of a composer should take into consideration the psychological problems and physical illnesses of its central subject, for otherwise many of the behavioral patterns and individual characteristics in the artist's creative achievements cannot properly be evaluated or understood. But most biographers are not physicians and so they choose either to ignore medical aspects or, at best, to incorporate, more or less uncritically, the conclusions of others in their text. In this way, the most ridiculous hypotheses have often been widely disseminated, right down to today. We need only think about the rampant growth, nourished by ignorance and superstition, of scurrilous poisoning legends surrounding the death of Wolfgang Mozart. Many of Beethoven's illnesses and the death of Schubert are also still being completely misrepresented today and presented in ways inconsistent with the facts. Such portrayals are due to either ignorance or deliberate bias. They are not only regrettable but utterly reprehensible when the author, because of his mindset about, say, syphilis in connection with a major composer, has no scruples in imputing such a diagnosis to that person. This charge also applies, unfortunately, to many pathological studies that have flowed from the pens of doctors.

Only in relatively recent times has there been a serious and dispassionate effort to clarify the confused and complicated presentations and contentious analyses and—by calling upon documentation that has become more inaccessible over the years—to undertake factual, objective investigations of the illnesses of famous composers of the last two centuries and the causes of their deaths. Both Gerhard Böhme and especially Hermann Franken deserve special mention for having applied themselves to the medical-historical aspects of the problem, something of the greatest importance in making critical interpretations of obsolete technical terms or of long-outdated views about the origin, diagnosis, and management of various illnesses.

As both doctor and musician, I have presented the results of my research on the lives of composers in words and music in many concert halls, in Austria and elsewhere. Now, in response to the wishes of many friends and colleagues, I gather my lecture notes together to give them broader distribution in the form of a book, even though many relevant pathological studies already exist. I do so essentially for three reasons. After years spent studying the primary sources, I hold the view that the observations of persons who lived closest to the composers during their periods of illness have seldom been analyzed with sufficient care or precision and have often been subjected, deliberately or not, to biased ways of thinking. In addition, after studying the medical literature contemporary with the composers themselves, I am convinced that the powers of observation of the composers' doctors and their experience with the often fatal course of illnesses (no effective treatment then existed) have been underestimated time and again, leading inevitably to failures of interpretation. More than two hundred years ago, the doctors of the Vienna school of medicine were already able, for example, to make an acute distinction between the swellings associated with severe rheumatoid arthritis and those caused by kidney disease. Finally, it is my impression that in many pathological studies too little attention has been given to those circumstances that exerted a decisive influence on the formation of the composer's character and psyche. For artists who do indeed live on the edge of neurosis and whose nervous systems are known to be sensitive and labile, it is especially true that psychological stresses and strains can inevitably affect their creative endeavors.

These viewpoints seemed to me to justify a retrospective effort to diagnose as accurately as possible the illnesses of our great composers of the Vienna classical era, drawing on all sources still available today and relating the state of 18th and early 19th century medicine to modern medical science, and to spell out, objectively and without speculation, the causes of their deaths. In addition, as a physician intensively concerned with problems of internal medicine for more than fifty years and, at the same time, as a practicing musician active for more than seventy years, I could not resist the temptation, while writing up the pathologies of Haydn, Mozart, Beethoven, and Schubert, to go into the interesting (and devilish) matter of the association between creativity and affliction. I realize, of course, that an all-too-subjective approach to this question can easily result in errors of judgment. Faustian misinterpretation of music is all too easy because of our inclination to read various things into it according to the kind of music it is. We falsely assume that our feelings and thoughts on hearing it are similar to those of the composer who wrote it, and that we therefore have insight into his inner being.

Yet, on the other hand, we know that every fundamental creative impulse of a composer reflects emotional tensions seeking relief. There should certainly be some reflection of the composer's psychological and physical tribulations in many of his compositions, or parts of them at least. Relationships of this kind can in fact be found between states of depression or emotional crises and particular compositions or passages. In my discussions of Haydn, Mozart, Beethoven, and Schubert, I have attempted to show that such connections of cause and effect can also be discovered in the record left by the composers themselves, "autobiographically" as it were.

We hear time and again that the search for such cross connections between creativity and affliction is fruitless and moreover is of no particular interest. On the contrary, it seems to me that it is not only interesting but personally moving for each music-lover to learn the history of physical affliction or emotional turbulence that underlies the origin of many of the great masters' works. When we know of such connections, the works themselves take on new meaning. Even leaving aside their passages of lightness and grace and apparently untroubled cheerfulness, we are not able to tell from listening to the overwhelming majority of works in what painful conditions of illness and affliction they may have been born, or that they were sometimes virtually wrested from death itself. Where the sources allowed it, I have taken these aspects into account. Through such examples, the creative spirit of our great musical geniuses, which as a rule functioned independently of external circumstances, shines all the brighter.

In closing, I would like to thank those who contributed to the preparation of this book: Professor Grasberger, who performed invaluable service in providing me with source materials found in the Austrian National Library in Vienna; Dr. Biba, archivist in the Vienna Gesellschaft der Musikfreunde; Dr. Sablik and Dr. Stellamor of the Institute for Medical History at the "Josephinum" of the University of Vienna; and my wife Nina, whose patience and encouragement made the work on the book possible.

Prof. Dr. Anton Neumayr

Vienna, Austria

# Music and Medicine:
## Reflections on the Historical Relationship

"By cultivating music, we learn inner harmony." The significance of music for human beings can hardly be better characterized than it is in these words of Confucius (551-479 B. C.). Since humanity implies nothing less than the harmonious development of all those moral and intellectual qualities that invest persons with their essential humanness, we could also say: "By cultivating music, we achieve the education leading to true humanity." And in fact, among the arts, only music seems to have the faculty of bringing together all the fundamental values—ethical, moral, and aesthetic—as does religion and of creating the harmony that expresses the inner spiritual order so necessary for the uplifting of mankind.

Even for St. Augustine, this attainment of a higher order was the essence of the musical experience. As he put it, "Only through [music] do we experience the joy of bringing to the soul that measure of importance it enjoys in the universal scheme of things." This view was widely accepted in the Middle Ages and corresponded fully to the concepts of Pythagoras and Plato, who held that music is the audible expression and sounding medium of universal numerical relationships. Thus, even in ancient Greece, music was felt to be not only something magical but also, in a higher sense, a fundamental element in the makeup of the cosmos. For Plato (427-347 B. C.), the world was a unity of music divided in three parts, a "musica mundana," the music of the spheres or cosmic harmony, a "musica humana," the psychic harmony unifying body and soul, and the "musica instrumentalis," the audible musical sounds made by voices and instruments. This concept, which was adopted later by Boethius (480-524), a Roman philosopher and the ill-fated minister to the Emperor Theodoric, saw the same harmonic and rhythmic relationships prevailing in the body and soul of mankind as are found in the movements of celestial bodies and in the intervals of the musical scale.

Before the onset of the Age of Enlightenment, the concept was given its most elegant formulation by the famous astronomer Johannes Kepler (1571-1630), who became mathematician to the states of Upper Austria in 1612. Like the ancients before him, Kepler gave a musical interpretation to the harmony of outer space. In his work *Harmonices mundi* (*Harmony of the Spheres*), the significance of which was soon broadly recognized, he found evidence for a cosmic symphony in the rhythmic behavior of the planets. More in the spirit of an artist than of a scientist perhaps, Kepler made harmonic transpositions of the various orbits of the planets to arrive at basic tonalities, scales, and melodies, which enabled him ultimately to reach his goal of depicting how the primal polyphonic harmonies of the planets might have sounded on the first day of creation.

It is surprising and fascinating how these old and somewhat fantastic ideas could in more recent times be translated through Einstein's theory of relativity into the spirit of the 20th century. As Harburger sees it, music is founded on cosmic geometric principles of a multidimensional universe, one in which the diversity of the time-tone dimension that forms the basis for music fits smoothly into the master plan of a geometric universe. It is almost beyond understanding that there are such intimate connections between the sublime world of mathematics and the heart-touching world of music and that, as Ernst Ansermet once expressed it, the very tones we use to make music are ones chosen so deliberately that they constitute a logarithmic system.

Hans Kayser's modern "harmonic conception of the world," which takes the primordial phenomenon of tonal harmonics as the basis for the entire development of the universe, is similarly suffused by the spirit of the Pythagoreans. His "harmonics" is not identical with that of music theory, however, but is a much more all-encompassing term, to some degree a vestige of the ancient theory of the "sound of the earth." He even finds the characteristic three-step of the musical cadence in the earth's geological structure. He bases his case on the observation that seismic waves are refracted from the different zones inside the earth and that the radii of these concentric zones show a remarkable concordance with the overtones of the primary major chord of the harmonic series, itself a natural physical phenomenon. In short, he describes a "triadic structure of the earth's core"—a conception of our planet as one enormous chord, which corresponds perfectly to the ancient view of the "musica mundana."

The ancients first perceived a conception of music—the "musica humana," in essence a principle unifying the body and soul of man as well as parts of his body—in the beating of the human pulse. This conception goes back to the Greek physician Herophilus, who was active in Alexandria 300 years before Christ, and was adopted later in the medicine and musical theory of the Middle Ages. Roger Bacon (1215-1295), the English scholar and scientist, published his *Opus tertium* in 1267, in which he demonstrated that the beats of the pulse follow the same laws and rhythms as music does. He placed his concept of the pulse under the discipline of music and demanded that every well educated doctor have a thorough knowledge of music. Also, the Muslim philosopher and physician Avicenna (980-1037) devoted a chapter in his *Canon of Medicine* to this association between pulse and music. With its translation from Arabic into Latin in the 12th century, this work became the most influential medical textbook of the Middle Ages in Western countries, and through it Herophilus' musical-metrical theory of the human pulse received a fixed place in the teachings of medicine.

In late antiquity, with its neoplatonic and neopythagorean currents, the idea of deriving musical-metrical mathematical relationships from pulsation had already led to the question of whether one who healed did not generally need a special knowledge of musical theory as part of his overall education. Even Galen (129-199) perceived the ideal of a doctor having a comprehensive, liberal education in which music has a special place. This idea was taken over by Cassiodorus (487-583) in the early Middle Ages.

Finally, through a compulsory basic course, the English educator Alcuin (730-804) at Charlemagne's court placed medicine over music as integrated in the study of the seven so-called "liberal arts."

Thus it is not surprising that, by the 10th century, the study of medicine presupposed study of the arts as well, a condition that became a required part of the university curriculum in the 13th century. So, for example, from 1426 on, the medical faculty in Paris made it mandatory that medical students pass examinations in the various liberal arts before receiving their doctor's degree. Moreover, because candidates for a master's degree in the arts were required to take a course in music, we can assume that, from the late 14th century on, each medical student also had to complete a course in music theory. The textbook of Johannes de Muris (1290-1351), which was based on the musical treatise of Boethius, was regarded as the principal source for these music courses.

Rooted in this close, centuries-old connection between music and medicine is the striking fact that greater-than-average numbers of medical doctors have had a special fondness for music and music-making down through the ages. The Italian scholar and physician Marsilio Ficino (1433-1499), whom Cosimo de' Medici chose to head the Platonic Academy in Florence, regarded the practice of both arts—music and medicine—by the same person as the most natural thing in the world. Speaking of his own experience, Ficino said that, during his medical studies, he often turned to music "to dispel the burdens of body and soul and lift the spirit to higher things." Many similar examples could be given down to the present time. The embodiment of both arts in one person is most notable in the Viennese doctor Theodore Billroth, whose close friendship with Johannes Brahms is well known and who earned his place in history not only as a surgeon of worldwide renown but also as an outstanding music theorist who was both a practicing musician and a composer.

With the work of Leonardo da Vinci (1452-1519), the first to undertake the systematic timed measurement of the human pulse, the 16th century saw the beginning of a new chapter in the connection of the pulse with music. Attempts were made to clarify the association between pulse and music with the help of musical mensural notation as a kind of "pulse-script." This approach of using musical notation in the medical study of the pulse lasted into the beginning of the 19th century. The epoch-making work of the French physician René Laennec (1781-1826) on auscultation sought to illustrate the different pathological sounds through the arteries with the assistance of notated musical examples.

Around the beginning of the 17th century, music ceased to be a scientifically based discipline in medical universities and was dropped as a required course of study. In the 18th century, the long tradition of the "musica humana" came slowly to an end, only to undergo a kind of renaissance in this century, specifically through the musical concepts of the Swiss theoretician Ernst Kurth (1886-1946). For him, the audible, inner music we experience as a force of nature represents a "musica humana" transposed, so to speak, from the harmonic into the dynamic, wherein he sees "all that sounds in music as but the outward-flung radiation of primal events whose energies encircle the inaudible inner world." Its original, formative states, according to Kurth, are psychic conditions of stress, straining to become active and to convert their energies into sensorially perceptible musical sound. Such a concept of the internal harmonic process transforms music from a symphony of sound into a symphony of psychic energy—in short, a new world arising out of the concept of the "musica humana"!

This brief review of the Platonic concept of music as an element in the creation of the universe enables us to see in a new light man's place in the cosmic scheme of things, and especially his deep, abiding relationship to the "musica instrumentalis," the audible music that we play and sing. As a result, we may understand better why, even at the dawn of human history, people called upon the magical power of music (which E. T. A. Hoffmann once termed "a Sanskrit of nature expressed in sound") to heal the sick.

The first beginnings of music's inclusion in medical thought and practice, when music and the art of healing were still inseparably joined, are lost in the mists of history. In this connection, the so-called hymn of healing appears to have played an important role. Homer, for example, describes Odysseus being healed by the song of the sons of Autolykus after being wounded by a boar while hunting, and tells in the *Iliad* of a special form of healing hymn, the paean, which was called on to prevent epidemic disease. This mystical notion of the healing power of music is expressed in an account from 665 B. C. that tells how Thaletas, who came to Sparta from Crete at the bidding of the Delphic oracle, freed the people of Lacedaemon from the plague by his song.

Antiquity's use of music in healing included, in addition to song, two instruments—the aulos (a reed instrument similar to an oboe) and the kithara (a small harp, or lyre). Its basis was the doctrine of the ethos of music, that is, the idea that a certain instrument with its characteristic sound, or a particular tempo and especially a particular rhythm, was what in each case lent music a distinctive ethos, which in turn was able to evoke different emotional and ethical attitudes in the persons hearing the music. Asclepiades (124-60 B. C.), for example, used the exciting effect of the aulos to bring persons suffering from depression out of their melancholy. The favorite instrument, however, was the lyre. With its gentle sound and introspective music, it was said to purge the soul of its residue of lust and passion. Thus people came to speak of the catharsis of music.

Strangely enough, doctors in classical times made only sporadic therapeutic use of this doctrine of the ethos of music. Music as an integral part of medicine was introduced by doctors in Arabic countries in the 9th century. Their view that music could heal the unwell body by way of the soul was gradually absorbed into medical thinking in Western lands once the writings of Avicenna became known. By the 13th century, music was included as one of the most important medical measures for slowing the decline brought on by the aging process. Roger Bacon was the first to call attention to the "delay of aging's symptoms" through music. Gabriele Zerbi's *Gerontocomia* (1489)—the first published work on gerontology—explained this life-prolonging effect on the grounds that, through its mathematical regularity, music is especially related to mankind's inner harmony. This view was also put forward by Franchinus Ranchinus (1561-1641) in his *Gerocomia*, published in 1627.

In addition to its gerontological use, music as a means of healing achieved its greatest significance in the treatment of mental diseases, again in connection with melancholia as pointed out by Raymund Minderer in his work *Threnodia medica*, published in 1619. In this connection, a Dane, Olaus Borrichius (1626-1690), commented that music was not invented simply "...to drive away illnesses, but more importantly to have an effect on the soul of mankind." This statement was apparently prompted by the purely theoretical, often downright childish notions of music's effects that had been prevalent throughout western Europe in the Middle Ages. For example, in his *Musurgia universalis* (1684), the Jesuit priest Athanasius Kircher explained that music opens the "air holes"—that is, the pores—of the body, thus enabling the evil spirits that cause sickness to escape.

It was not until the Age of Enlightenment that music's effect on the mind and soul finally was raised to a more realistic position in medical thought. For this evolution we must give particular thanks to Johann Peter Frank (1745-1821), the founder of the science of public hygiene and a friend of Beethoven. Frank was convinced of music's importance in maintaining public health. In his nine-volume work, *A Plan for a Comprehensive Public Policy on Medicine*, the first volume of which appeared in 1779, he wrote:

> The program must not leave out this major source
> of encouragement....But we must be thoughtful
> in using the power of this divine means of arous-
> ing the emotions....Doctors have recorded many
> cases of illnesses that have been cured through
> the magic of music, and its effect on sensitive nerves
> is so effective that the circulation...can be quickly
> restored to order, to the great relief of our body.

In 1807, the Viennese physician Dr. Lichtenthal published a book on this subject with the title, *The Musical Doctor, or an Essay on the Influence of Music on the Body and Its Use for Certain Illnesses*. It described the way that music is able to influence the psyche and thus indirectly the body itself.

Only with the development of modern scientific medicine, however, was music's effect on the human body addressed on a more objective basis. The knowledge we have today is due in no small part to the impressive results of the investigations undertaken by Herbert von Karajan during his work as conductor. We know that with soft, flowing melodies and calmer, more gentle rhythms the parasympathetic (peaceful) components of our autonomic nervous system become predominant, whereas dissonances, brisk tempos, and strongly stressed rhythms set off largely sympathetic (aggressive) impulses. According to the latest findings, various polypeptides and hormones play a major role in these effects, either by calming certain centers in the brain or by stimulating the emergency integration centers in the brainstem. In the latter case, emotional feelings are unleashed which, in the extreme, can cause aggressive tendencies and even wanton destructiveness. Thus we see the classical doctrine of the ethos of music finding parallels and scientific affirmation in our century. The modern definition of the music-therapeutic healing process given by Aleks Pontvik is substantially at one with the classical Platonic-Pythagorean concept in saying that "...the curative musical experience is rooted in the acoustic representation of archetypal harmonies, through which the unity of body and soul returns to reflect the laws of natural balance."

Indeed, music is seen today as an indispensable adjunct to the treatment of mental problems and psychological disturbances. Cases of depression can be helped more readily if the patient listens, completely relaxed, to the right sort of music. When crises occur in life that seem to defy either analysis or solution, we can often achieve remarkable success in treating them with music therapy. Examples abound in both ancient history and more recent times: King Saul found relief from depression when he heard David play on his harp; the Russian Grand Duke Constantine's terrible fits of rage were cured by listening to the then ten-year-·old Frédéric Chopin play the piano. The most noteworthy example, however, is perhaps that of the sad King of Spain, Philip V. Only through the use of music could he be persuaded to leave his bed and tend to affairs of state. His queen engaged the services of the famous Italian castrato Farinelli to present a concert every evening at the court in Madrid—and he did so for ten long years, until Philip died in 1746.

A particular aspect of music that is receiving increasing attention these days is its sociological significance. The harmonious
effect of music on people's feelings makes contact between them
easier and enhances interpersonal communication, something
many hospitals have already taken into consideration. The anxiety patients feel on being hospitalized, a matter often discussed
by sociologists, can undoubtedly be mitigated by using music as
a harmonious element in the clinical atmosphere to bring diversion and relaxation. This does not mean, of course, that a commitment to personal medical care that centers on the individual
needs of the patient can be met simply by having music constantly playing in the background. But undoubtedly, music in the
hospital does make patients feel more confident and cheerful,
and this must be why Muslim hospitals in the Middle Ages made
such unparalleled use of music.

Music can do more, however; it can activate people and help
release those afflicted in mind and spirit from their involuntary
lassitude. For this reason, music is being introduced increasingly
into geriatric clinics and homes for the care of the elderly, where
it helps to reduce the patients' tendency to isolate themselves.
Thus, the age-old interweaving of music and medicine can, when
integrated with modern scientific understanding, prove to be ad-
vantageous to today's doctors in their therapeutic approach. As
the medical historian Berendes so aptly said:

> It has forever been the wish of the physician to be
> not only a guide to man along his biological path-
> way but a sympathetic and helpful advisor in his
> quest for life's meaning as well. Man's inborn spiri-
> tual realm lies apart from the material world, and
> in this realm a treasure trove exists which is filled
> with lovely music and whose gates will open to
> each who eagerly seeks to find it.

Music's ability to bring about concord applies not only to
persons as individuals, but to the greater human community as
well, a sociopolitical effect of growing significance. Our steadily
increasing access to a variety of cultural events, as manifested in
the boom in music festivals in Europe, is impressive testimony to
their popular success. At the beginning of the century, music in

the concert hall was reserved almost exclusively for the privileged few, but today it is equally available to all levels of society.
Music festivals, in keeping with their ancient festive significance,
have become a vital force in society as a whole. Even if such
music festivals cannot contribute directly to the solution of political and social problems, they provide better proof than science
can of our fundamental unity. They are better able to shape and
raise the human spirit than any course of learning. As A. Lernet-
Holenia once said of the music of Johann Sebastian Bach: "...he
who listens to his music becomes truly human and buries all
feelings of enmity while hearing it. It does not show us for what
we are—it shows us what we should be." In fact, we know that
during the Olympic games in ancient Greece—which had much
higher cultural worth than the games do today, by the way—all
hostilities were set aside for the duration of the celebrations.

Even though music has become increasingly the expression
of an individual composer's personal inspiration and unique qualities and thus has lost much of its fundamental primal power, a
kind of universal music still exists, one that is understandable to
all. No mother could do without a lullaby to calm her child and
bring it to sleep. And we all know how music with a strong
rhythmic beat can spark the performance of persons at work, or
how a brisk march can instill new energy into even the weariest
of soldiers. Napoleon personally experienced the exhilarating
effect of *La Marseillaise* during the French Revolution, and he
knew well what he was doing when he had his military bands
play under the windows of the hospitals where his soldiers lay
wounded.

This ability of music to stimulate or to suppress activity acts
through the motor responses of the brain, responses that we are
subject to in the concert hall as well. Each of us is familiar with
involuntary, unconscious rhythmic movements of the hand or head,
movements not always looked on with favor by the person in the
next seat. How greatly such movements can be stimulated by a
given tempo played in a certain rhythm is shown by examples
from the past to the present. The Greeks' ecstatic playing on the
aulos reached its climax in the cult of Dionysus as well as in the
so-called Corybantic orgies during the festival celebrations of the

Phrygian cult of Cybele, the Great Mother of the Gods, which were usually accompanied by wild music and dancing. Perhaps the best known example from more recent times is the dancing mania of tarantism, which came out of Apulia in Italy in the 13th century. The persons involved were whipped into a virtual frenzy by the music and literally danced until they dropped. Tarantism was only one form of dance mania to hit Europe in those times, as we learn from reports about actual dance psychoses that arose from a form of religious hysteria. In 1374, for example, a crowd of dance-crazed persons went from the Rheinland in western Germany to the Netherlands. In 1418, a procession of people went leaping and jumping from Strasbourg to Rothenstein, where a chapel dedicated to St. Vitus was located—an event preserved to this day in the common description of a form of epilepsy known as St. Vitus dance.

Such motor-driven ecstatic mass behavior occurs even today, as we can see in fans at rock concerts. The aggressive and destructive tendencies mentioned previously can mount to the point that the fans go on a rampage. In Berendes' view, such persons are first brought by the music to a primitive level of consciousness and then, with the loss of their individuality, fused into a restless, wildly moving mass. This effect may also explain why persons with rather primitive personality structures are more readily susceptible to such agitated, ecstatic mass behavior.

Plato was not without his reasons, therefore, when he pointed out that music is capable not only of improving social customs but of corrupting them as well and that in the realm of social behavior, nothing does so much harm as turning away from music that is ethically and politically "right." The early Christian missionaries in the 2nd century may have been driven by similar considerations when they took steps against the use of worldly songs that were crudely stirring up the populace. The young church was very much aware of the power music exerted over the hearts of believers, which is why St. John Chrysostom (c. 347-407) expressly recommended the singing of psalms as a useful way "to bring the Holy Word nearer to weak and impressionable souls."

Music has an even greater effect on persons who take an active part in its making than on those who only listen to it. The therapeutic value of active music-making was aptly characterized by the physician Heinrich Hanselmann in these words: "Music frees us from the prison of our self-preoccupation. In performing with others, we constantly practice anew that leading and being led which most contribute to the betterment of human society, whether in a marriage or in the League of Nations. True music-making makes social beings of us all." We have probably too often overlooked this important sociopolitical aspect of music.

All these considerations apply with particular force to the musician who is active creatively, for whom music can be, in essence, a kind of self-therapy. Because artists tend to live at the very edge of neurosis, the creation of their art is often the outlet they need to overcome their neuroses and maintain their emotional balance. Moreover, because their music liberates them from tensions pressing for release, it will be marked to some degree by whatever emotional conflicts and sufferings they experience. At the same time, the creative act often enables the artist to succeed in surmounting pain and even the fear of death itself—which brings music, from a metaphysical point of view, close to theology.

From ancient times to the present, the manifold interweavings of music and medicine show us that there is no realm of the liberal arts in which the spirit of *humanitas* is so evident as in the realm of music, nor any science to which music has a closer historical and idealistic connection than it does to medicine.

# Joseph Haydn
## (1732 - 1809)

In June of 1804, at Joseph Haydn's suggestion, Johann Nepomuk Hummel was appointed Konzertmeister for the court of young Prince Nikolaus II von Esterhazy, in Eisenstadt. Hummel dedicated his recently completed Piano Sonata op. 13 to Haydn, his fatherly friend and benefactor, with the following words:

> Most beloved Papa!
> Confident that, as an obedient son, I can rely on the kind indulgence of my great father of music, I have been so bold as to dedicate this modest little work to you....I was led to do so by the great feelings of gratitude, esteem, and sincere admiration I owe you. If you would continue to honor me with your generous confidence and goodwill, then nothing could be more pleasing to your most devoted son, Johann Nepomuk Hummel.

Wolfgang Amadé Mozart also expressed his boundless admiration for his paternal friend Haydn in much the same way in the words of dedication that accompanied his six "Haydn" string quartets (KV 387, 421, 428, 458, 464, 465):

> To my dear friend Haydn!
> A father who has decided to send his children out into the big world believes he should entrust them to the care and guidance of a celebrated man, one who, by happy chance, is also his best friend. Here they are, my six children, O famous one and dearest

friend!...You yourself bespoke your satisfaction with them, dearest friend, on your last visit with us here in the city. The approval you voiced especially emboldens me to recommend them to you and lets me hope they will not seem entirely unworthy of your favor....

These two examples alone show how Haydn's contemporaries were much more aware of his brilliance and appreciated his achievements than the generations that followed. When he died in 1809, Haydn was still the most famous composer of his time. Yet a relatively short time later his music had been so overshadowed by the immortal works of Mozart and Beethoven that, in 1841, even so perceptive a composer and musical commentator as Robert Schumann could dismiss the significance of Haydn's music with the words: "But he no longer has a deeper interest for us today...." This attitude would be common among most music "experts" for another hundred years. Only one seemed to have an inkling that Haydn's music was destined to undergo a rebirth without parallel: Johannes Brahms. As the Austrian music critic Richard Heuberger recalls it, Brahms was complaining in 1896 that Haydn's importance had been grossly underestimated. In that connection, he expressed the opinion that, with the centennial celebrations of the composition of the oratorios, *The Creation* and *The Seasons*, Haydn was bound to emerge into prominence for a second time.

As late as 1945, little more than a tenth of Haydn's works had been published; a generation later, however, the gigantic project of publishing his complete works had been finished and today the importance of Haydn's artistic accomplishments is universally recognized and acclaimed. Still, relatively little attention has been given to his life and to the kind of man he was, or to the fact that, despite the endless anecdotes as to how healthy and robust he was, Haydn was indeed very ill for the last ten years of his life. From 1803 on, he was unable to compose another note and lived fully retired in his house in Gumpendorf, on the edge of Vienna.

# The Early Years

"That so great a man was born in such a simple cottage!" was the emotional reaction of Beethoven shortly before he died when he was shown a picture of Haydn's birthplace in the Austrian village of Rohrau. It was in a plain and modest house that the second child of Mathias and Anna Maria Haydn first saw the light of day on 31 March 1732. Unlike Mozart, Joseph Haydn was not born into a family of artists but rather into a family whose forebears had been farmers and artificers. Haydn's father was a farmer and a master wheelwright and had been made a village official as the result of his industry and honest character. The young Haydn's only musical experience came in the evenings when his father would play on a harp he had made and his mother would sing. Eager to participate, the youngster made a kind of imitation violin out of pieces of wood on which he would keep rhythm with remarkable sensitivity. Soon he began to accompany his mother's singing with a lovely voice of his own.

Although his affection for music may have delighted his parents, the young Haydn was anything but the prodigy of whom Goethe and Konrad Zelter spoke in an essay as "the new Wunderkind who came poor into the world." Musicologists have shown that Haydn used many Slavic tunes in his works, particularly as dance themes in the last movements of quartets and symphonies. They echoed his childhood memories of the mostly Slavic children's songs his mother sang to him. Haydn later told his biographer, Georg August Griesinger, about his parents. In his account, Griesinger confirms the lasting influence these songs must have had on the young Haydn:

> ...the five-year-old Haydn sat beside his parents and ran a stick back and forth across his arm as though he were accompanying on the violin. It struck the school teacher that the lad was able to keep time so carefully; he concluded from this that he must have a good aptitude for music....The melodies of these songs were so fixed in Joseph Haydn's memory that he could recall them still even in his old age.

The school teacher was Johann Mathias Franck, a distant relative of the Haydns who lived in the nearby town of Hainburg. He suggested to Haydn's parents that they entrust the lad to him for his education. And so it was that, at a very early age, young Haydn went to live away from home. His mother "...had from the beginning given him the most tender care," as he later told another of his biographers, Albert Christoph Dies, but he got "more whippings than food" at the home of schoolmaster Franck. Nevertheless, the education he received in Hainburg was very important for the young man, for there he was introduced to many musical instruments, in addition to being taught reading, writing, arithmetic, and singing. Only a year later he was already "brashly showing the choir how to sing some of the masses and playing a little on the piano and the violin," as he put it in a letter on 6 July 1776.

Religious instruction also had an important place in the curriculum, and Haydn's mother would have been pleased if he had taken holy orders. The possibilities that opened up to the youth by virtue of the education he was receiving more than compensated for the disadvantages of living with the Franck family, as Haydn himself would acknowledge in later life when he remembered his schoolmaster with gratitude and said: "I owe it still to this man now long in his grave that he introduced me to so many things."

It was a happy chance of fate that, in 1739, the "slight but pleasant" voice of the seven-year-old Haydn was brought to the attention of Georg Reutter the younger, then Kapellmeister at St. Stephen's Cathedral in Vienna and later Kapellmeister to the court, who was visiting the parish priest in Hainburg. After a brief audition, all were agreed, including his parents, that young Haydn would be accepted as a choirboy at St. Stephen's as soon as he was eight years old. In the following nine years that the lad spent at the cathedral, the schooling he received was probably not the best imaginable. Reutter seemed to be more interested in the twelve hundred gulden he received each year for the upkeep of his six pupils than in their intellectual improvement. As Dies reports about this period:

As soon as Joseph had received as much instruction as he needed in his new position to fulfill the duties of a choirboy, the teaching came to a complete stop....It seemed as though one was intent on allowing the spirit to hunger along with the body. Joseph's stomach had to accustom itself to constant fasting.

The choirboys at St. Stephen's were certainly physically over-taxed by the heavy program of church services they were called upon to perform, and no one really looked after their general state of well-being. In any event, the well-being of the healthy, robust farmboy does not seem to have suffered. Haydn, like the people in his birthplace of Rohrau in Burgenland, was not delicate physically. We have no reports, either from his parents or his relatives, of his bout with smallpox, then one of the most frequent infectious diseases from which not even young Haydn was spared. From Dies, we have a description of the marks it left: "...his hawk's nose...was, like the rest of his face, strongly pitted with pockmarks, indeed the nose itself with smallpox scars such that each nostril had a slightly different form." Incidentally, even Haydn was wont occasionally to allude wryly to this souvenir from his attack of smallpox. For example, he wrote the Vienna merchant F. J. van der Null on 25 March 1796, saying: "May I take the liberty of asking most respectfully for a loan of one hundred gulden against my pockmarked face."

Griesinger reports that while young Haydn was living in the choir school, he considered undergoing castration because of his beautiful soprano voice. Just what credence we can place in this story is hard to say, although Haydn is supposed to have mentioned it to various people, including the composer Ignaz Pleyel. In his biographical notes, Griesinger writes:

> In those days there were still many castratos engaged at court and in the churches of Vienna and the choirmaster at the boarding school undoubtedly believed young Haydn's fortune would be made when he conceived the idea of making a castrato out of him and actually sought the

> agreement of Haydn's father. The father completely
> disapproved and set off for Vienna as fast as he
> could go. Apprehensive that the operation could
> already have taken place, he burst into his son's
> room and cried: "Does it hurt, lad? Can you walk?"
> Overjoyed to find that his son was still whole, he
> protested strongly against any further bizarre ideas
> of this sort.

It was a great bit of luck for Haydn that the plans to make him an
adult soprano never came to pass. If there is one thing all his
biographers agree on, it is that he was very fond of the ladies
throughout his life.

Haydn's formal schooling certainly left much to be desired, as
is evident from his lifelong difficulties with proper spelling. But
the choirboys obviously did not receive any instruction in music
theory either, for Haydn later could remember "having received
only two lessons on the subject from the good Reutter." Reutter
did encourage him, however, to improvise freely on the liturgical
music sung at the cathedral, something that brought him to musical ideas of his own. A *missa brevis* in G and one in F, two of
Haydn's earliest conventional works which he himself later dated
to the year 1749, originated in his choirboy days.

Although Haydn spent the formative years of his youth separated from his mother, for whom he felt a special love and attachment, his experience led to the early development of a healthy
degree of self-confidence. This trait is shown by an episode in
November 1749 when his service as a St. Stephen's choirboy
abruptly came to an end. His biographer Dies reports that Haydn,
apparently out of high spirits

> ...and mischievousness, cut off the pigtail of one
> of the other choirboys who, contrary to the cus-
> tom among the boys at the time, plaited his long
> hair and made a tail of it. This was reported to
> Reutter, who sentenced Haydn to flogging with
> strokes on the flat of the hand. The moment for
> carrying out the punishment arrived. Haydn sought
> every way he could to avoid it, finally declaring

he would rather not be a choirboy any longer and
was ready to quit immediately if he would not be
punished. "That won't help!" responded Reutter,
"First you'll be punished and then out you go!"

Haydn's defiant offer to quit the boarding school of his own
free will in fact suited Reutter just fine, because Haydn's voice
had already begun to change and was no longer up to singing
soprano parts. Reutter would almost certainly have dismissed
him from the choir sooner or later in any event, especially since
the empress shortly before had remarked that "the choirboy
Joseph Haydn does not sing, he screeches like a pheasant."

With his ejection from the choir, difficult times began for
Joseph Haydn. "Without money or means, having but three old
shirts and a worn-out coat, the nineteen-year-old went out into a
world he did not know," as he put it later to his biographers. In
a letter of 6 July 1776, he was still complaining that for eight years
he was compelled to eke out a miserable existence: "Many persons of talent are ruined by such a hard life, for they lack the time
to study." By giving lessons and playing at the Brothers of Mercy
in the Leopoldstadt suburb of Vienna (which earned him only
sixty gulden a year), he was finally able in 1751 to afford quarters
in the Michaelerhaus in Vienna's inner city. His cubbyhole of a
room in the unheated top story leaked rain in the summer and
snow in the winter. But not even these meager circumstances
could keep Haydn from working steadfastly to improve himself,
thanks to his rugged constitution, his irrepressible sense of humor, and his positive, self-confident attitude toward life. "When I
sat at my old, worm-eaten piano, I envied no king his fortune,"
he said later.

Despite the cold and the hunger, Haydn began to throw himself eagerly into the study of music theory which had been so
neglected at the choir school. Probably the greatest encouragement to do so he owed to the works of the Viennese Kapellmeister
Johann Joseph Fux, especially his treatise on counterpoint, *Gradus
ad Parnassum*, and to *Der vollkommene Kapellmeister (The Perfect Kapellmeister)* by the German composer and theorist Johann
Mattheson.

In addition to pursuing his self-imposed curriculum of study of music theory in these times, he became familiar with the piano sonatas of Carl Philipp Emanuel Bach, which were particularly important to his subsequent artistic development. Where before he had known only the lively and rather superficial world of the musical rococo, suddenly he was confronted with music of feeling and personal expression and it impressed him deeply. In later years he described his experience in this way: "I played them [Bach's piano sonatas] over and over again to my own delight, particularly when I felt discouraged or burdened down by cares, and I always came away from the piano feeling cheered up and in a good mood." Just how deeply the "Berlin Bach" came to influence his musical development is confirmed by Haydn himself: "Anyone who really knows me must perceive that I owe Emanuel Bach a great deal, that I studied him carefully and understood him."

## Haydn on the Way to Success

While living in the Michaelerhaus, Haydn made the acquaintance of two personalities who would turn out to be important for his further artistic growth: the court poet Pietro Metastasio, to whom he owed his knowledge of the Italian language, and the opera composer and singing teacher Nicola Porpora, from whom he received the basic essentials for composing his Italian operas. "I used to write carefully but not always soundly until finally I was privileged to learn the true fundamentals of composing from the famous Herr Porpora," he acknowledged to his biographers in later years.

Around 1756, Haydn was able to move to better quarters and his compositions were engraved and published for the first time. One was his double concerto for organ and violin, which he conducted on 12 May 1756 on the occasion of Josepha Therese Keller's taking the veil; Haydn had been in love with her and, to his misfortune, she had elected to enter a convent. Apparently out of gratitude for the support given to him by her father, Johann Peter Keller, in the early years after his dismissal from the choir school, Haydn acquiesced to the father's wish that he marry the oldest daughter, Maria Anna (1729-1800). The wedding took place at St. Stephen's Cathedral on 26 November 1760. Haydn later came to regret the marriage very much, for it was soon obvious to him that this union with an uneducated, wasteful, and religiously bigoted woman, who could not seem to summon up the least understanding for her husband's talents, held little promise. Furthermore, Maria Anna proved to be "incapable of bearing children," which must have been a bitter disappointment to Haydn. For the last ten years of their marriage, before Maria Anna died in 1800, the couple lived apart most of the time.

The fact that Haydn was able to give his bride one thousand gulden as the bridegroom's traditional gift is explained by the favorable developments in his professional activities as a musician. A Viennese physician, Dr. Franz Weber, had been elevated to the ranks of the nobility by Emperor Charles VI in recognition of his medical services and subsequently was known as Lord Karl Joseph von Fürnberg. In the summer of 1755, Fürnberg invited the still impoverished Haydn to his summer residence, Schloss Weinzierl, in the vicinity of Melk on the Danube, to take part in nightly chamber music concerts that included the local pastor playing the violin, a steward on viola, and a cellist named Albrechtsberger. (Whether this was the later teacher of Beethoven, Johann George Albrechtsberger, or his brother Anton Johann is something we can not ascertain.) Thus, Haydn received his first, albeit short-lived, position, and because it involved a quartet of players, Fürnberg asked Haydn for compositions for this extended circle of musical amateurs. Haydn surprised Fürnberg a short time later with a four-part movement for strings. So began Joseph Haydn's career as a composer of string quartets. He composed some seventy-five in the course of his life.

These early quartets quickly brought Haydn broad recognition and were the first of his works to be published in other countries. With Fürnberg's recommendation, Haydn was appointed Kapellmeister to Count Maximilian Franz Morzin in 1758, with room and board and a yearly income of two hundred gulden. Moreover, at the country estate in Lukavec, near Pilsen in Bohemia, where the count's family spent their summers, Haydn had a complete orchestra at his disposal for the first time. During this period he composed his first symphonies. They were highly successful and soon showed that, along with the string quartet, Haydn had begun to create a new form for the symphony, one that would greatly influence its future development.

From these happy times with Count Morzin, we know of only one medically relevant event, an apparently insignificant accident in 1759 in which Haydn fell from a horse. Its only discernible lasting effect was Haydn's firm resolution never to get on a horse again. Haydn himself later reported another "accident" that occurred as he was at the piano, accompanying the lady of the house as she sang. On this occasion it happened

> ...that as he was seated at the piano and the beautiful Countess Morzin leaned over him to see the notes, the scarf at her neck came undone. "It was the very first time," Haydn recounted later, "that I beheld such a sight; it flustered me, my playing came to a halt, my fingers stopped on the keys."— "What is it, Haydn, what are you doing?" the Countess asked; with great deference, I answered: "But Your Grace, who wouldn't lose his place at this point?"

Count Morzin suffered financial reverses and disbanded his orchestra at the beginning of 1761. Haydn would have found himself once more standing in the street if he had not been engaged by the rich and influential Esterhazy family. As he and his wife took their leave of Vienna and moved to Eisenstadt, Haydn could not have known that he would spend the next thirty years of his life in his new home.

Haydn's first contract with Prince Paul Anton Esterhazy was dated 1 May 1761. In it, Haydn was expressly obliged "not to tell anyone about new compositions, much less allow them to be copied, but to reserve them solely for His Highness alone." In 1765, he was further directed to send the prince a neat and accurately copied score of all new compositions before they were to be performed. This instruction, together with the new regulation of church music in Eisenstadt, led to Haydn's being assigned the copyist services of Joseph Elssler (grandfather of Fanny Elssler, a famous dancer in the first half of the 19th century) for reproducing the scores and parts needed and for preparing a catalogue of Haydn's works.

Throughout three decades of productive musical creativity at the court of the Esterhazy family, Haydn was seldom ill, as far as the record shows. He fell seriously ill for the first time in 1764, as we learn from a written response of the prince to a letter from Haydn requesting permission to charge the cost of his apparently expensive medicines to the prince's establishment. In this connection, it is worth noting that Prince Paul Anton, despite being a grandseigneur of the rococo period—and even more his brother Nikolaus I, who succeeded him as reigning prince on his death in March 1762—was a man of tolerance and generosity, marked by humanity and enlightenment. For example, he extended his personal protection to the Jews in Eisenstadt and arranged to provide welfare for the poor and the sick. In 1760, Prince Paul Anton had founded the Hospital of the Brothers of Mercy and a pharmacy in Eisenstadt, where seriously ill patients were treated at his expense. And when the house that Haydn had purchased for one thousand gulden in Eisenstadt in 1766 was damaged by a fire in 1768, it was Prince Nikolaus who paid the reconstruction costs of three hundred gulden.

Some time around 1770, Haydn apparently had to take to his bed with an acute fever, an illness that must have robbed him of his strength. In Griesinger's biography, the following account appears:

> Shortly afterward [the doctor having strongly forbidden him to have anything to do with music], Haydn's wife went off to church, after first ordering the maid to keep her eye on her husband to make sure he did not go to the piano. Haydn lay in bed and pretended not to have heard anything of this instruction; as soon as his wife had gone, he sent the maid out of the house on an errand. Then he quickly swung over to the piano; with the first chords, the inspiration for a whole sonata came to him and the first part was completed while his wife was at church. When he heard her coming back, he swiftly threw himself back in bed

and there he composed the remainder of the sonata, one that Haydn could no longer describe to
me accurately other than to say it had five sharps.

We know nothing more about the exact nature of this sickness, but surely the swampy region surrounding Schloss Eszterháza
was one that tended to promote the outbreak of fever-ridden
infectious illnesses. Baron Riesbeck suggested as much in his
1784 article on Schloss Eszterháza in Cramer's *Magazin der Musik*.
Baron Riesbeck called the place the "Hungarian Versailles."
With one hundred twenty-six rooms and a sumptuous opera
theater, it was the most splendid privately erected establishment
in the entire Austro-Hungarian Empire:

> The castle is enormously large and filled with
> every item of opulence to the point of extrava-
> gance. The grounds contain everything that hu-
> man imagination has devised for beautification....
> What intensifies the splendor of the place tremen-
> dously is the way plantings divide it from the sur-
> rounding area. You cannot imagine anything more
> desolate or depressing. The Neusiedler Lake,
> which is not far from the castle, creates bogs that
> run for miles and threaten in time to swallow the
> countryside right up to the prince's residence....
> The inhabitants of these adjoining lands look for
> the most part like ghosts and are plagued with
> attacks of chills and shivering fits almost every
> spring....And yet, as unhealthy as the location is,
> especially in spring and fall, and as often as the
> prince himself falls victim to the chills, neverthe-
> less he is convinced there is no healthier nor more
> pleasant region anywhere else in the world.

In this fairytale castle in the swamps, whose construction was
possible only after dams and canals had been laid to drain the
marshes around Neusiedler Lake, Joseph Haydn spent at least
twenty years of his life. It says something for the sturdy constitution he inherited from his Burgenland ancestors that he did not
suffer more often than he did from the notorious chills. On the

other hand, of course, he led a privileged life at Schloss Eszterháza, just as, for example, the prince's personal physician did. His apartment with its three large rooms was kept heated by servants, and both a manservant and a maid looked after his well-being.

Despite the comforts, the extended periods of almost total isolation at Schloss Eszterháza came to weigh on Haydn's spirits more and more as the years passed. "I was cut off from the world," Haydn remarked later to Griesinger; "There was no one around who could confuse me or bother me, so I was forced to be original." These were indeed Haydn's *Sturm und Drang* years when he was introducing new approaches to music, ones that were not understood by many of his contemporaries because they were judged in part too modern and in part too difficult technically. A characteristic product of this period was the Piano Sonata no. 20 in C Minor. Haydn found it hard to understand why works such as this met with disapproval, as he wrote in a letter on 6 July 1776: "...I only wonder why it is that the otherwise so intelligent...gentlemen have no middle ground in their criticism of my compositions, for in one weekly they raise me to the stars, in another they hammer me 60 fathoms into the ground, and all that without explaining why."

Perhaps this is one reason why Haydn again began to change his style and turned more in the direction of what was light and lively and pleasing. Possibly the change of style can also be traced to a hint from the prince that works which were too difficult for normal music lovers, such as the numerous aristocratic guests at the opera house at Eszterháza, would inevitably remain unappreciated. The Concerto for Piano in D composed in 1784 counts among those "bright and pleasant" works that made an important contribution to Haydn's rapidly growing popularity. This piano concerto, as well as his later piano sonatas, undoubtedly was a major source of inspiration to Beethoven in his works for the piano. For example, we can see a similarity between the gypsy rondo of the last movement of the D-major Piano Concerto and Beethoven's piece, "*Wut über den verlorenen Groschen.*"

From 1776 on, musical events at Eszterháza began to focus increasingly on opera, with performances that were up to international standards. On 1 September 1773, when Prince Nikolaus (known to all as "the Magnificent") had invited Empress Maria Theresa to Schloss Eszterháza for the first time, she had made the flattering but unquestionably appropriate remark: "When I want to hear a fine opera, then I go to Eszterháza." The opera performed on that occasion was merely a slight, two-act piece of Haydn's, *L'infedeltà delusa*; by 1784, however, Haydn had produced fifteen complete opera compositions of various sorts. This period of concentration on the creation of operatic works was also the high point of Haydn's romantic attachment to the opera singer Luigia Polzelli, who had been engaged for the opera at Eszterháza in 1779 when she was twenty-nine, together with her sickly and much older husband. Because the prince was not particularly taken with their artistic abilities, the Polzellis were supposed to have been dismissed right away. At Haydn's intercession, however, this decision was cancelled and Luigia Polzelli stayed on with the prince's court until 1790 as Haydn's mistress, even though Haydn could hardly have failed to notice that she tried to take full advantage of him financially.

Underlying Haydn's generosity certainly was his deep love of children. Being childless himself, he bestowed all his paternal affection on Luigia's young son, Petruccio. On one occasion when Luigia was spending some time in Italy, he wrote, asking her to send her son to him: "I will see he is dressed well and will do everything for him....He will get everything he needs. My Petruccio will always be with me." The lad died of tuberculosis in 1796 at the age of nineteen and Haydn mourned his passing deeply. When Luigia had borne a second son in 1783, no one had the slightest doubt that the father was Joseph Haydn. Nor could he have made any attempt to conceal the fact, as is evident in a letter that has been preserved which begins with the salutation, "my dear son." Thus the bond of love to Luigia became ever stronger, and in 1792, in a letter from London, Haydn declared: "Perhaps never again will I enjoy those good feelings I just took for granted when I was together with you. Oh, my dearest Polzelli: you are always in my heart!"

After his illness in 1770, Haydn appears to have been in the best of health, apart from a seemingly insignificant sprain of his left leg in July 1782 as the result of an unlucky fall. In a letter to his publisher Artaria in Vienna, he said: "On the very day that I received yours of the 2d, I had the misfortune of falling and injuring my left leg so severely that I have not been able to go out of the house since then; as a result, the strict regimen of care is the cause for the delay in the answer I owe you." We hear nothing further of possible consequences of this accident and it could well have been that the severity of the injury described in the letter was somewhat exaggerated.

Haydn told Artaria in some detail about other illnesses as well. For example, he wrote on 27 January 1783: "...do not be angry with me, for on arriving home, I had to stay in bed for 14 days because of a wonder of a catarrh," and not long afterward he spoke of a "catarrh so severe that I was useless for three whole weeks." Six years later he apologized to the same publisher in the same way again for the delayed delivery of manuscripts he had promised, because an intense catarrh had once again put him out of action for three weeks. These recurrent illnesses could have been caused by viral infections that occasionally affected his upper respiratory tract for extended periods. In those times, people usually spoke of a "rheumatisches Kopffieber" (literally, a "rheumatic head-fever") or "rheumatic pains in the head" or simply a "head-fever." Originally, this condition could have been related to a nasal polyp Haydn inherited from his mother. Such polyps tend to foster low-grade infections in the paranasal sinuses and the bronchial tubes; today we would speak of a sinubronchial syndrome. Haydn mentioned the nasal polyp for the first time in a letter to the Artaria publishing house on 8 April 1783:

> My constantly unhappy situation, to be specific, the present operation on a polyp in my nose, is the reason why I have been utterly incapable of doing any work up to now; because of my pains, you must have patience for another 8 or at the most 14 days until my poor weakened head, with God's help, regains its former strength.

We know from Griesinger that time and again Haydn's breathing was greatly impeded by this nasal polyp because of the size of the growth. The polyp often had to be tied off with a ligature.

Surgeons at the Hospital of the Brothers of Mercy in Eisenstadt operated on it three times. On one occasion, the operation was conducted by no less a personage than the chief surgeon of the Austrian army, Dr. J. A. Brambilla. This attempt by the military doctor was evidently carried out with such vigor that Haydn lost part of his nasal bone, but it did not prevent the nasal polyp from soon growing back to its original size. We probably should not charge Brambilla with a therapeutic failure, however, for even today there is a relatively high recurrence rate after the removal of such polyps.

Like Mozart, Haydn became a Freemason and on 11 February 1785 was admitted to the Viennese lodge, Zur wahren Eintracht (True Concord). The *Funeral-Cantata* for the Prussian King Friedrich Wilhelm II who died on 17 August 1786, as well as the *Paris Symphonies* which Haydn wrote for the Parisian lodge, Loge Olympique, are testimony to his membership in the Masons, which enabled him to associate as an equal with gentlemen of culture. In these times, the number of Haydn's friends and admirers in Vienna was steadily growing. They came less from circles directly involved in the Viennese court, which was still rather disdainful of Haydn, than from members of the lesser nobility and the well-to-do middle class who were increasingly influential in Vienna's musical activities. The two daughters of the famous physician Dr. Joseph Leopold von Auenbrugger (founder of the percussion method of physical examination, most commonly used on the chest and back for examination of the heart and lungs) were among Haydn's most devoted admirers. Haydn dedicated six piano sonatas to them, saying in a letter to Artaria on 25 February 1780: "The approval of the two Misses von Auenbrugger is most important to me, for their performing skills and their insight into music compare with the greatest masters."

Haydn also developed a close relationship with the family of another prominent doctor, the gynecologist Dr. Peter L. von Genzinger, who had served as personal physician to the princely Esterhazy family for many years. The relationship extended in particular to the doctor's wife, Marianna Sabina, whom Haydn first met in 1789. The letters that subsequently passed between Haydn and Marianna von Genzinger are certainly the most personal documents that have survived from Haydn. For the first time in his life, he felt free to speak of his innermost feelings, disappointments, and moods. The completely natural and somewhat unconventional way he wrote conveys a realistic impression of just how he must have spoken in everyday life. A typical example is found in an excerpt from a letter of 9 February 1790, written to Marianna after his return to the solitude of Eszterháza after enjoying the warm and comfortable atmosphere of the Genzinger household:

> So—here I am, sitting in the wilderness—abandoned—like a wretched orphan—practically devoid of human society—forlorn—full of thoughts of rare days now gone by—yes, alas, gone by—and who knows when such pleasant days will come again? such lovely company? where the whole circle is in one heart and soul—all those beautiful evenings of music—which live only in the memory and cannot be described—where are all those moments of rapture and enthusiasm?—they are gone, and they have been gone a long, long time. Your Grace should not wonder that I have taken so long to write my letter of thanks! On my return, I found everything here in chaos, 3 days long I didn't know if I was a Kapell-Meister or a Kapell-drudge, nothing was able to console me, my entire lodgings were a mess, even my piano which I normally love was fractious and disobedient, it served more to provoke than to comfort me....

Just as Haydn's love for Luigia Polzelli inspired him to compose masterful opera arias, so his feelings of love and devotion for Marianna von Genzinger turned him into a master in composing for the piano, the instrument uniquely capable of giving the perfect illusion of an entire orchestra. Where before Haydn's sonatas reminded one of the technically brilliant but impersonal, often empty piano works of a Muzio Clementi, now his composing for the piano reached its absolute summit. The Sonata in E-flat no. 49, which Haydn dedicated to Marianna von Genzinger,

presages the perfection of the piano sonatas of Beethoven and
Schubert. When Haydn sent this work in June 1790 to Marianna,
who was herself an excellent pianist, she voiced a gentle request
in her otherwise enthusiastic letter of thanks: "I like the sonata
very, very much; only I wish one thing might be changed...there,
you see, in the second part of the adagio where one hand must
play over the other one; because I am not used to that, I find it
hard to do." But it was precisely this cross-hands passage, with
its symbolically intended merging of two into one, that Haydn
meant to suggest his close emotional attachment, something also
seen in his words of dedication: "This adagio...which I most
warmly commend to Your Grace...means many things, which I
will spell out for Your Grace at the next opportunity."

A question has often been raised about whether something
more than mere friendship existed between the two. Study of the
letters they exchanged suggests the answer is no. For her part,
Frau von Genzinger seems to have weighed each word very carefully so as not to express anything more than her personal esteem
for the obviously infatuated Haydn. He, on the other hand, was
not quite so reserved, as his letter of 20 June 1790 reveals: "I
would have so much to tell Your Grace and so much to confess
which no one but Your Grace alone could absolve me from." Yet
in another passage he stressed how exalted and irreproachable
his feelings for her were:

> Your Grace can therefore be completely free of
> concern not only for the past but also in the fu-
> ture, because my friendship and high regard for
> Your Grace (as heartfelt as they may be) will never
> be culpable, for I constantly keep in mind my re-
> spect for the noble virtues of Your Grace, which
> not only I but everyone who knows Your Grace
> must admire; therefore do not let Your Grace be
> deterred from comforting me from time to time
> with such a pleasant exchange of letters, which is
> so necessary for bringing cheer into my loneli-
> ness, to my often deeply troubled heart; oh, if I
> only could breathe the solace of a quarter hour
> with Your Grace, then I could overcome the many

annoyances of our present regime which I must
suffer here in silence; the only consolation I have
is that I am healthy, thank God, and am keenly
interested in my work…so, God be praised; these
times will also pass and those will come again
when I shall have the infinite pleasure of sitting at
the piano with Your Grace.…

But why should Haydn have such an urgent need to be cheered
up in his loneliness and in his "deeply troubled heart"? The explanation almost certainly can be found in the drastic turn of
events that had taken place in the court at Eszterháza. When on
25 February 1790 Prince Nikolaus lost his wife, Maria Elisabeth,
after fifty-three years of marriage, he fell into a profound depression and lost all interest in his surroundings. In vain, Haydn "did
everything I could to rouse the prince from his melancholy," as
he wrote later. The prince's black mood inevitably affected everyone around him. "Now yet again it means I have to stay here,"
Haydn wrote on 27 June 1790 to Marianna von Genzinger, "and
what I lose by that is something Your Grace can imagine. It is
really sad always being a slave: but Providence wants it so, and
I am just a poor creature!"

From these words, we see clearly that Haydn no longer felt
happy to be in Eszterháza and, now almost sixty years old, could
no longer stand the constraints on his freedom of action. Prince
Nikolaus survived the death of his beloved wife by only a few
months and died on 28 September 1790. His son and successor,
Prince Anton, had little interest in music and only a few days after
his father's death dismissed the entire orchestra. Haydn, who had
received a lifetime pension of one thousand gulden (which later
was even increased) in the testament of Prince Nikolaus, was no
longer tied to Eszterháza. Leaving behind almost all he owned,
he moved as fast as he could to Vienna, where he would soon
receive offers that were tempting indeed.

## Haydn Goes to London

As early as 1782, efforts had been made to invite Haydn to
England but at the time he felt obligated to Prince Nikolaus to

remain in Eszterháza.  Now, however, it was 1790 and he was enjoying "sweet freedom" for the first time.  When a stranger introduced himself with the words, "I am Salomon from London and I have come to get you.  We will sign the contract tomorrow," Haydn threw himself into the greatest adventure of his life with enormous zeal and creativity.  Johann Peter Salomon came from Bonn am Rhein in Germany, where his father had once lived in the same house with Beethoven's father.  He had established himself in London in 1781, first as a virtuoso on the violin and later as a successful concert impresario.  He offered Haydn such attractive conditions to come to London for a concert season that Haydn accepted immediately.  Salomon had to deposit a guaranty of five thousand gulden in advance in the bank of Count Moritz von Fries; the bank was in what is today the Palais Pallavicini in Vienna, a town estate where Beethoven later gave many concerts.

Haydn's friends attempted to dissuade him from undertaking such an arduous journey, for he was almost sixty years old and had never traveled much beyond Vienna, Pressburg, Eisenstadt, and Schloss Eszterháza.  But Haydn felt strong and in good health and was determined to embark on the venture.  When his friend Mozart objected on the grounds that he did not speak a word of English, Haydn is supposed to have replied: "My language is one the whole world understands."  Mozart, who had agreed the day before to accept a similar proposal from Salomon to go to London after Haydn returned, took his leave of Haydn on 15 December 1790 with tears in his eyes, saying:  "We are surely saying adieu to one another for the last time in this life!," little suspecting that it would be he, the younger man, who would be dead in a year's time.

After traveling by way of Munich, Bonn, and Calais, Haydn crossed the English Channel, arriving in Dover on 1 January 1791.  The fact that he endured the wearisome trip with no complaints, especially the stormy crossing of the Channel, speaks well for the remarkable physical condition of the sixty-year-old Haydn.

Writing to Frau von Genzinger on 8 January, Haydn described crossing the Channel from Calais to Dover:

> Would therefore report that on the first of the
> month, that is, on New Year's day, I went on board

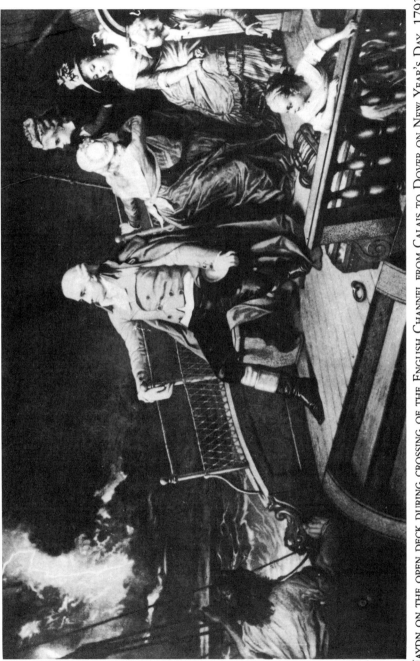

49

Haydn on the open deck during crossing of the English Channel from Calais to Dover on New Year's Day, 1791.

ship at 7:30 in the morning after attending mass
and at 5 in the afternoon arrived, thanks to the
Almighty, safe and sound and in good health in
Dover. At first, we had hardly any wind for 4 whole
hours, and the ship went so slowly we didn't make
more than one English mile in these 4 hours, out
of the 24 [miles] there are from Calais to Dover. In
a most foul mood, our ship's captain said if the
wind didn't change, we might have to spend the
whole night at sea, but luckily around 11:30 such
a favorable wind arose that by 4 o'clock we had
covered 22 miles, but because with the ebb tide
setting in we could not reach the shore with our
large ship, from far off two smaller ships set out in
our direction, into which we transferred with all
our baggage, and finally landed happily in the midst
of a little windstorm...some of the passengers remained [on the larger ship] because they were afraid
of getting in the smaller ones, but I went with the
crowd; during the entire crossing I remained on
the open deck to see my fill of the enormous ex-
panse of ocean; as long as the wind was calm, I
wasn't afraid, but finally because steadily stronger
winds came up and I saw the high, wild, beating
waves, a bit of anxiety came over me and, with it,
a little feeling of seasickness, but I overcame it all
and fortunately reached shore without—hail
Mary—throwing up. Most of the others were sick
and looked like ghosts...it was only after arriving
in London that I first felt the rigors of the trip and
I needed 2 days to rest up; now however I am fit
as a fiddle again...

Haydn was quickly swept up into London's social life. In the
same letter of 8 January to Frau von Genzinger, he reported: "My
arrival caused a big stir throughout the city, for three days I was
spread around in all the newspapers; everyone is eager to meet
me." From the very beginning of his stay in London, he recorded
his impressions and his personal experiences in his "London

diaries," to which—along with daily reports in the London press—
we are indebted for most of the details about his London visit.

It apparently was hard for Haydn to learn English, even though
he "went walking in the woods every morning in the spring accompanied only by his English grammar book." An account from
the annals of the Musical Graduates Society suggests how little
progress he made. It says that eighteen months later, just before
Haydn's return to Vienna, Salomon had to be invited to the farewell banquet "in part because he was Mr. Haydn's intimate friend
and in part to act as interpreter because Dr. Haydn had not made
sufficient progress in learning English."

The first of the subscription concerts was announced for
19 February 1791 but was postponed twice and finally took place
on 11 March. The format of the program reflected the approach
that would apply to all subsequent ones. From his initial experiences with London's "nobility and gentry," Haydn had expressly
demanded that any newly composed symphony which he was
under contract to provide would be given in the second half of
the Salomon concerts, and for good reason, as his biographer
Dies would later report:

> With the very first musical concerts, Haydn ob-
> served that he had done the right thing to insist
> the performance of his works come in the second
> half. The first half was customarily disturbed in
> various ways by the noise of those listeners arriving
> late. Not an inconsiderable number of persons
> came directly from well-laid tables (where the
> gentlemen...were served strong spirits to drink),
> took a comfortable seat in the concert hall, and
> were so overwhelmed by the glories of the music
> that they fell fast asleep. Now just imagine whether
> in a concert hall where not only a few but many
> people, some of them wheezing, others snoring
> or nodding, offer the alert listeners something to
> comment on or even laugh at, whether that is a
> place tranquillity can prevail?

Even the first concert made such a strong impression that the
*Morning Chronicle* ended its review with this sentence: "Let us

hope that the leading musical genius of our times might now see himself led to make his home permanently in England."

The success of Haydn's first concert season—it ended on 3 June 1792 with the twelfth subscription concert—was so immense that in July he was granted the honorary degree of Doctor of Music at Oxford University. He devoted only a short, dry comment to this occasion in his diary: "For the pealing of the bells at Oxford because of the Doctor's degree, I had to pay 1 1/2 guineas and for the gown, 1/2 guinea." It could have been that, because of his difficulties with the English language, he did not feel entirely comfortable with the solemn proceedings, but he obviously did not let the august gathering of learned gentlemen disconcert him. After the investiture, when he was asked to perform something of his own composing, he walked calmly to the organ—according to Dies—and turned to the worthy assemblage. Every eye was on him; Haydn opened his doctoral robes, then closed them again, and said in a loud, clear voice: "I thank you." The gathering obviously understood the gesture perfectly and responded in all British politeness: "You speak English very well." Haydn's waggish and straightforward behavior on this occasion shows once again how essentially down-to-earth and natural he had remained, despite the fame he had enjoyed in London. "I have mixed with emperors and kings and many great persons and heard many flattering things from them; but I would not want to live on close terms with such people," he said later.

Throughout 1791 while he was in London, we know of only a single occasion when Haydn was ill and that was with so-called "English rheumatism." As we learn from a letter to Frau von Genzinger on 20 November 1791, it was a simple case of lumbago: "Up to now, thank God, I was always well, but then a week ago was struck by English rheumatism so sharp I sometimes have to cry aloud. But I hope to get over it soon for I have completely wrapped myself from top to bottom in flannel, as is the custom here"—a method of treatment not much different from that of today. Haydn was having enormous artistic and financial success and was in an excellent frame of mind. His high spirits are reflected in his music, such as the "rondo all'Ongarese" of his Piano Trio in G Major, and his roguish sense of humor is shown by a sly bit of verse written for his concert manager Salomon and for the tenor Giacomo David, who frequently took part in his concerts:

> David and Salomon lived lusty lives,
> Made many children, had many wives.
> But now they're old and can't make heirs,
> So one makes songs, the other, prayers.

Naturally there were times, too, when Haydn was sad, as a letter of 4 August 1791 to his beloved Luigia Polzelli, who had recently lost her husband, lets us see:

> My dear Polzelli!
> Perhaps, just perhaps the time we have longed for
> so often is coming when four eyes will have closed.
> Two of them are closed now, the other two—well,
> enough of that, God's will be done! I urge you to
> look after your health, and write back soon, for I
> have been full of despondency for a long time,
> without knowing why. Your letters comfort me,
> even when they are sad.

The depressed mood that shows up from time to time in Haydn's letters may have been associated with the unfamiliar lifestyle he experienced in London, and perhaps also with the vagaries of the English weather. Take, for instance, an example from his diary describing the reception following the installation of the Mayor of London, with the British prime minister William Pitt also in attendance:

> 5 November 1791...I was a guest at the midday
> festivities for the Lord Mayor...following the ban-
> quet, all the highest society retired to a special
> room set aside for them...but we other guests were
> taken to an adjoining room....I wandered from
> there into another room, which was more like an
> underground cave, because there a drum was play-
> ing along, which covered up the sins of the violin
> players...the remaining tables all filled up once
> again with men who stoutly swilled away as usual

all night long....It's worthy of note that the Lord
Mayor didn't need to have a knife at the table, for
he had a fellow...who cut up everything for
him....But taken altogether, it was a mess."

His diary contained another notation about the peculiarities of
the climate: "The fog was so thick on the 5th of December that
you could have spread it on your bread. To be able to write, I
had to light the lamps at 11:00 in the morning."

The major factor in his swings of mood, however, could have
been the news of the unexpected death of his friend Wolfgang
Mozart. It left him deeply shaken. "Mozart died the 5th of December 1791" is the sole entry written across two pages of his
diary. In January 1792, in a letter to Michael Puchberg, Mozart's
friend who had helped him in many times of need, Haydn wrote:
"For a long time I was stunned by his death and simply could not
believe that Providence would so quickly claim such an indispensable man for the netherworld." Given such a deep-seated
mood, we can understand, too, his remarks in a letter of 14 January 1792 to Luigia Polzelli: "...My state of health is really all right;
but I have English moods most of the time, and they are melancholy."

However, Haydn drew diversion from various ladies of
London's society and was able to take home with him many vivid
personal recollections of his first visit to England. For instance, in
September 1791 he found himself very attracted to the famous
soprano Elizabeth Billington, whom the Irish tenor Michael Kelly
praised as "an angel of beauty and the Saint Cecilia of song." He
encountered other ladies as well in the homes of London's society whom he would later describe in his diaries as "the loveliest
woman I've seen in my life" or "the most beautiful woman I've
ever seen." A special attraction developed between Haydn and
Rebecca Schroeter, the wealthy widow of the late German pianist
Johann Samuel Schroeter. He later told Dies that "...although she
would shortly have been sixty years old, she was still a lovely and
charming woman whom, if I had been single at the time, I would
quite readily have married."

Haydn was inspired in a special way by (and probably a little
bit in love with) Mrs. Anne Hunter, the wife of the well-known

surgeon John Hunter. With her help, he undertook to set English
lyrics to music, despite his imperfect understanding of the language. His acquaintance with this family is also of interest for
medical reasons. John Hunter, the prominent surgeon general of
the Royal Army, called Haydn's attention to the possible adverse
effects of the polyp in his nose. He particularly pointed out that
the polyp "disfigured Haydn's face and was repugnant to the ladies"—a point of view which Haydn, given his success with the
fair sex up to that time, was of course hardly prepared to share.
Despite his previous unhappy experience with Dr. Brambilla,
Haydn may have given consideration, however reluctantly, to
having an operation performed once again. Probably as the result of misunderstandings due to his incomplete knowledge of
English, he then stumbled into a sort of "doctor's trap," as he later
reported in his own witty manner to his biographer Dies, who
recorded this final event before Haydn's departure from London:

> Haydn had already submitted to surgery several
> times before and had had the bad luck, at the hands
> of the famous Brambilla himself, to lose part of his
> nasal bone without being rid completely of the
> polyps. In London Haydn came to be acquainted
> with the prominent surgeon John Hunter..., "a
> man," Haydn said, "who undertook surgical op-
> erations almost every day and always successfully.
> He examined my polyp and offered to get rid of
> the miserable thing for me. I had halfway agreed
> to do it, but the operation kept being delayed,
> and finally I gave it no more thought. Shortly
> before my departure, Mr. H. requested me to come
> see him in connection with some urgent business.
> I went there. After an initial exchange of compli-
> ments, some sturdy lads came in the room, grabbed
> me, and wanted to pin me to a chair. I shouted,
> hit them black and blue, and kicked with my feet
> so long that I was finally able to get free and make
> Mr. H. understand, who was standing there with
> his instruments at the ready, that I did not want to

be operated on. He was amazed at my insisting
on this and he pitied me, it seemed, that I did not
want to enjoy the good fortune of testing his skill."

Of course, in those days, anesthetics were unknown and strong
assistants forcibly held the patient in the desired position during
surgery. Because of the pain Haydn had experienced in the
earlier operation on the polyp in his nose, and perhaps also because complications could occur in the form of pus discharges or
blood poisoning caused by the use of unsterile instruments, he
did not want to undergo surgery again. In his old age, he jokingly remarked about his nasal polyp: "I'll just have to let the
rascal rot in the grave; my mother also suffered from this nui-
sance without having died from it."

When Haydn arrived in Vienna on 24 July 1792, the composer
who had enjoyed so many honors in England was surprised that
no one seemed to take any particular notice of his return to his
homeland. Even the court in Vienna attributed no significance to
the arrival of the composer who had contributed so much to
Austria's renown abroad. But then, many personal relationships
in Vienna were no longer the same. For Haydn, the death of
Mozart meant not only the loss of a true friend but also an irre-
placeable loss for the whole world of music. Even in Mozart's
lifetime, Haydn had shown no envy in recognizing Mozart's unique
qualities and, shortly after his death, had declared to a music
dealer in England: "Friends often flatter me that I have some
talent, but he stood far above me." Perhaps he never quite got
over Mozart's untimely death, for even in 1807 he broke out in
tears at the mention of Mozart's name and excused himself, saying: "Forgive me, but I always have to cry when I hear the name
of my Mozart."

Soon Haydn was to suffer another heavy blow. His only soul
mate, Marianna von Genzinger, died on 20 January 1793; she was
not yet forty-three years old. This musically accomplished and
spirited Viennese society lady with whom Haydn carried on such
an intense correspondence had done much to reawaken his interest in composing for the piano. In view of the close emotional
bond between them, the renowned Haydn scholar H. C. Robbins
Landon could well be right when he suggests that the inception

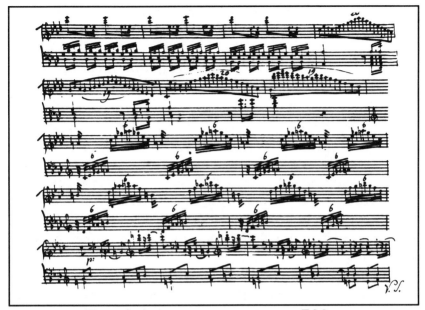

A PAGE FROM HAYDN'S ANDANTE CON VARIAZIONI IN F MINOR, COMPOSED IN 1793, PERHAPS IN RESPONSE TO THE UNTIMELY DEATH OF HIS NOBLE LADY FRIEND, MARIANNA VON GENZINGER. (NOT HAYDN'S HANDWRITING, BUT THAT OF HIS ASSISTANT AND COPYIST, JOHANN ELSSLER.)

of one of Haydn's most important piano compositions—Variations in F Minor—was influenced by the tragic death of this lady. In this piece, with the pathos of its principal theme, as though it were a funeral march, and the consoling nature of its F-major trio, we can begin to glimpse the emergence of the Romantic era. The stormy character of the mighty coda prefigures Beethoven's style in his early and middle periods.

Haydn created this work, by the way, during the short span of time when the young Beethoven was one of his students. Beethoven, then twenty-two years old, had come to Vienna on 10 November 1792 to study with Haydn, to whom he had been introduced in Bonn during Haydn's return trip to Vienna from London. Because Beethoven had no personal means, Maximilian Franz, the Elector of Cologne (who had his court in Bonn), provided financial support for the young man, who had served as second Kapellmeister to the elector's court. But serious artistic differences soon arose between Haydn and his student, although "the jovial older gentleman did his best to tame the demonic young man." Haydn evidently did not take his duties as instructor very seriously. Nevertheless, this intermittent instruction (none, in effect) lasted for a year. Although Beethoven's intensely personal approach to music was diametrically opposite to Haydn's universal approach, Haydn, in a letter of 23 November 1793 to the elector in Bonn, spoke of the young Beethoven's great talents about which "both those who know music and those who do not had equally to agree that in time he will occupy the position as one of the greatest composers in Europe." This perception of Beethoven did not, of course, keep Haydn from teasing his student for his prickly sense of personal pride or from referring to him in fun as the "great mogul."

In June 1793, Haydn hinted for the first time at a certain falling off in his productivity. Writing from Eisenstadt in response to a request for money from Luigia Polzelli, he said among other things: "...keep in mind that I can no longer exert myself as I used to in recent years, for I am beginning to get old and my memory is slowly, slowly starting to fade." With these discreet words, Haydn may have intended primarily to provide a reason for cutting back on his financial assistance to her. The fact is that we find no indications in his compositions, either at this time or in the years that remained before the close of the century, of any diminution at all in his powers of creativity.

Purely out of politeness to Prince Paul Anton, Haydn spent the summer months of 1793 at Eisenstadt. He was able to use this time to prepare for his second trip to England, which like the first was not universally endorsed. In this time, he also signed the contract to buy the "pretty little one-story house with a small yard in the [Viennese] suburb of Gumpendorf" that his wife had found while he was in England the first time and whose quiet location pleased him very much. During his second stay in London, another floor was added to the house and he would later live there until he died.

On 19 January 1794, Haydn set off for the second journey to England in a "comfortable carriage" provided by Gottfried van Swieten. He was accompanied by his copyist and assistant,

Johann Elssler (the son of his first copyist, Joseph Elssler). As before, his contract with Salomon required him to compose six new symphonies for London. Having in mind the demands on him during his first stay in London, he had already cleverly composed them in large part in Vienna before he left. The first of the subscription concerts took place in London on 10 February and was the occasion for the first performance of Symphony no. 99. Haydn's predominant artistic position was uncontested and acknowledged by all, and reviews of his concerts vied with one another in their enthusiasm. Along with his social contacts among the British aristocracy, a closer relationship to the royal family had developed; the king and queen apparently tried very hard to keep Haydn permanently in England.

However, Prince Paul Anton had died in January 1794 and his successor, Prince Nikolaus II, reestablished the orchestra and called on Haydn to take over as Kapellmeister once again. The conviction that the prince needed him, together with the fact that friends and a new house were waiting for him in Vienna, finally persuaded him to start the trip back to Austria on 15 August 1795. In early September 1795—after eighteen months in London—Haydn returned to Vienna, a famous and wealthy man.

## Once Again in Eisenstadt

Back in his role as princely Kapellmeister, Haydn was by now too self-assured and proud to allow himself to be treated like a lackey by Prince Nikolaus II, a young man in his early thirties, impulsive, arrogant, and vain, and still stuck in feudal times. Once when the prince attempted to interfere in the work going on in a rehearsal Haydn was leading, Haydn is said by members of the orchestra to have called out in an irritated voice: "Serene Highness, taking care of this is my business," whereupon the prince reputedly never interfered again. Similarly, the prince came to accept that his Kapellmeister, Joseph Haydn, who stood in personal contact with the King of England and the Emperor of Austria, was no longer to be seated at the table with other officers of the court but at the family table of the prince. This was evidently in response to Haydn's wish and influenced no doubt by Nikolaus' wife, Princess Maria Hermenegild.   Moreover, apart from an annual stay during the summer months in Eisenstadt, where an apartment in one of the buildings adjoining the castle was available to him, Haydn thereafter lived in Vienna most of the time. The year 1796 was an exceptionally productive one for Haydn. In addition to doing an arrangement of *The Seven Last Words*— the work composed earlier for the cathedral in Cadiz on *The Seven Last Words of Our Saviour on the Cross (Die sieben letzten Worte unseres Erlösers am Kreuz)*—and completing the *Heiligmesse* and various other compositions, he did the first sketches for his oratorio, *The Creation (Die Schöpfung)*.   His activities on behalf of the prince himself, apart from the obligation to compose an occasional new mass, were not at all extensive, probably in part because of the prince's lack of music appreciation.

One example of how elegantly Haydn circumvented the instructions of his prince is the story told in connection with the piano trio known as *Jacob's Dream*.   This work composed in 1795 is one of Haydn's most interesting chamber music pieces. The fact that, in comparison with earlier works of this sort, it is particularly demanding for the piano is probably attributable to Haydn's familiarity with the pianos developed in England, which were clearly superior both technically and in dynamic expression to the instruments produced in Vienna.   One day—so the story goes—the prince wrote from Paris to instruct his Kapellmeister to write a piano sonata for a Parisian lady named Moreau who was very fond of music.   Haydn respectfully declined and, instead of a single sonata, sent a collection of sonatas already published, complete with a personal dedication to Madame.   This response did not satisfy the prince at all and he insisted on his original request.   Whereupon Haydn decided simply to drop the cello part from his *Jacob's Dream* piano trio, which had been published long before, and to offer the work as a piano sonata with violin accompaniment, one composed especially for Madame Moreau.   The ruse succeeded and the unmusical prince did not recognize Haydn's trio.

The first performance of *The Creation* was on 30 April 1798 and undoubtedly marked for Haydn the crowning of his entire musical achievement.   Haydn had brought the text back with him from his second trip to England. An English poet had put the story of the creation, as it is found in the book of Genesis, in verse form. Apparently, it was this text, as Salomon told the story, that had once been offered to Georg Friedrich Handel, who decided not to use it. At first, Haydn did not want to take on this theme either. Only when his friend Gottfried van Swieten, at the time director of the court library, encouraged him to do so and offered "to festoon the English verse with German garments" did the two of them begin to tackle this enormous work together. When we look at the unusually large number of sketches Haydn made, particularly those for the orchestral "Representation of Chaos," we can see that he worked long and hard on the oratorio's various elements. When he doubted his power to go on, the pious man would seek to reinvigorate himself with prayer, as he once told Griesinger: "Never was I so devout as during the time I was working on *The Creation*. I fell on my knees every day and asked God to lend me the strength for successful completion of this work." Curiously enough, because of alleged traits of Freemasonry in the text, both the emperor and the Church once forbade the performance of this glorious work in a Catholic church.

## A Time of Trial and Tribulation

The period in which Joseph Haydn composed his second oratorio, *The Seasons (Die Jahreszeiten)*, is critical to his medical history. The work took considerable pain and effort to compose and finish. An initial indication of Haydn's condition comes from the composer himself in a letter of 12 June 1799 to the Breitkopf publishing house in Leipzig:

> I am indeed ashamed to think, with my long delayed reply, I may have offended a man who has so often favored me with his letters in a most honorable way beyond my deserving; negligence is not to blame, but rather the number of things to do which grows by the day the older I get; I only regret that, due to my increasing age and with my (unfortunately) decreasing mental powers, I can take care of but the smallest part of them; true, the

world gives me many compliments every day for the fire in my latest works, yet no one can conceive what toil and exertion it costs me to search it out, for on many days I am so crushed by poor memory and failing nerves that I sink into the most miserable state and for many days afterward am incapable of finding a single idea, until finally, buoyed up by Providence, I seat myself at the piano once more and can begin to scratch away— but enough of that.

And in fact, during the two years when he often labored to the point of exhaustion to finish the oratorio, Haydn became an old man; as he would tell his friends: "The Seasons broke my back."

Even while composing *The Seasons*, Haydn became aware that his creative powers were dwindling. Writing to the German music lexicographer Ernst Ludwig Gerber on 23 September 1799, he said: "In spite of all, I will, with the help of Providence, gather my strength and, after it is completed, avail myself of some rest for my weak nerves, so that I can complete my latest work involving vocal quartets..." To make matters worse, he fell seriously ill in the spring of 1800, but we have no details as to the exact nature of the disease. In Hugo Botstiber's biography, we find only this cryptic note: "Haydn was not able personally to lead the performances [of *The Creation*] at Prince Schwarzenberg's on 12 and 13 April 1800. He was suffering from a 'rheumatic head-fever' and lay sick in bed, and Joseph Weigl conducted in his place." It probably was once again an upper respiratory infection accompanied by inflammation of the sinuses abetted by the polyp in his nose. This illness often brings headaches that can impair a person's ability to function. As Haydn mentioned in a letter written in May 1800: "It's certainly correct about those 4 Seasons: I have just done Summer and hope, in spite of the fact that I was very sick a short while ago, that I'll be finished with it by the end of the coming Winter."

The fact that Haydn was obviously having great difficulties completing the oratorio was not lost on his contemporaries. The Swedish writer F. S. Silverstolpe reported to Stockholm in the spring of 1801:

Haydn's The Seasons is finished, of course; but an illness Haydn has been suffering from has caused such a long delay in the matter that I believe the performance will be planned for next year. Too bad, for who can guarantee that the Master will then be able to present his work himself? He is old.

In fact, the premiere took place on 24 April 1801, and soon thereafter, on 29 May, the first public performance of *The Seasons* followed in the grand Redoutensaal of the Hofburg in Vienna with Haydn conducting, albeit looking visibly older. Perhaps there is a gentle foreboding of approaching death in the music of this oratorio. In the orchestral lead-in to "Winter," Robbins Landon sees signs that Haydn might have intended, with this deeply moving passage, to signal his farewell to music.

Haydn's physical decline which was already evident at the first performance of *The Seasons* was partly the result of a new illness, again alluded to as a "head-fever," that had occurred shortly before. On 21 February 1801, Griesinger wrote the publishers Breitkopf and Härtel in connection with publication of *The Seven Last Words*: "Papa Haydn cannot write to you; he is bedridden again with 'head-fever'," and said it was the composer's "greatest torment that his fantasies are unceasingly preoccupied with notes and music." This "rheumatic head-fever," which probably corresponded to inflammatory and perhaps even suppurating sinusitis, could well have occurred with increasing frequency after every influenza infection of the throat and upper respiratory tract as Haydn got older. Again in the fall of 1801, Haydn caught a bad cold that forced him to take to his bed. As so often before, he complained anew about severe "rheumatic pains in the head." Because he got out of bed too soon, he suffered repeated attacks of fever that continued into December and prevented him from taking winter lodgings in Vienna's inner city as he had planned. Griesinger reported on 19 November 1801: "Haydn is not going to move into the city this winter as he usually does, but rather remain in his house in one of the farthest suburbs. Here he lives without being bothered, but every visit to see him entails a small journey."

Still, the aging composer had recovered so well that, on 22 and 23 December 1801, he was again able to conduct performances of *The Seasons* himself. The repeat performances were as successful as the premiere in spring, even though this oratorio was not so rapturously received by the public as *The Creation* had been. This reception of the work was quite in accord with Haydn's own critical and objective attitude toward it; he once wrote his friend Giuseppe Carpani: "I'm sure you will recognize too that it is no second 'Creation.' I sense that and you will sense it also. But the reason of course is this: in the one, the characters are angels, in the other, they are peasants."

Haydn was convinced that the decline in his physical and mental powers which perceptibly hindered the task of composing *The Seasons* was attributable to his overwork and superhuman exertions in setting to music the stiff and ungainly verse that van Swieten had derived from the English original. Years later he was still complaining that it was only this overexertion that had undermined his health. Once during a visit of his biographer Dies in 1806, when Haydn had made a vain effort to play something for him on the piano, the composer said bitterly: "You can hear yourself that it doesn't work anymore; eight years ago it was different, but The Seasons inflicted this misery on me, I shouldn't have written it; I overdid." And when the poet August Wilhelm Iffland extolled the marvelous depiction of nature in the music of this oratorio during a visit with Haydn in 1809, Haydn interrupted him, saying:

> The Seasons—ah, yes, The Seasons! The Seasons
> did me in. I wanted to do it of course—but the
> words were not up to it! No, they were really
> impossible, days at a time I had to toil over a single
> passage and then—then—no, you can't imagine
> how I tortured myself…yes, yes, it's all over with
> me as you can see and The Seasons are to blame.

For a long time, people were inclined to believe the reason for the diminution of Haydn's powers while he was composing *The Seasons* was that he could not come to terms with the subject of the oratorio and thus had literally to drive himself to work on it. But the text, which is based on James Thomson's popular epic of the same name and had been adapted by van Swieten just as had the libretto of *The Creation*, is not really so "stiff" as it has been portrayed. The reason Haydn's distaste for it grew by the day apparently lies in another direction, as Max Friedländer suggests from examining van Swieten's rediscovered original manuscript. While setting the text, Haydn frequently complained about "having to compose something like that!" The despotic Baron van Swieten was giving him "imperative instructions in a commanding tone of voice" on just how he was to set various passages in the libretto to music; even the kind of instrumentation was in part dictated to him. Haydn took particular umbrage at the "pictorial apeings" of the sounds of nature that were demanded of him and rebelled against such a trivialization of his artistry. This is reflected in a note he made while correcting the piano arrangement: "This whole passage imitating a frog did not just flow from my pen; I was forced to write down this silly rubbish."

In short, it was not work on *The Seasons* as such that caused the deterioration in Haydn's intellectual powers. Rather, it was that during the composition of this oratorio the first symptoms appeared of infirmities that would increasingly hamper his efforts to compose and ultimately render them impossible. The state of Haydn's health seems to have improved for a while after he finished *The Seasons*. He continued to take part in various charity concerts, directing his oratorios until the end of 1803. Haydn's final public appearance was in a performance of *The Seven Last Words* in its second version at the Redoutensaal for the benefit of the destitute at St. Mark's Hospital on 26 December 1803. Haydn's last two masses—the *Schöpfungsmesse* composed in 1801 and the *Harmoniemesse* of 1802—can also be taken as evidence of a temporary improvement in his health. In this familiar and beloved sacred music, the full extent of his all-encompassing genius was displayed once again before it gave out, finally and forever.

Haydn continued to be offered commissions of all kinds, such as for leading concerts in other countries and composing new works. In particular, the court in Vienna considered the idea of having him undertake a concluding third oratorio, *The Last Judgment*, as his crowning achievement. While Haydn refused most of these commissions with the excuse that, as an "ailing old boy of seventy years," he no longer felt up to such tasks, he appeared to be enthusiastic at the thought of a third oratorio. And because it would be the realization of a favorite idea of the devout empress, he would be that much more inclined to work on it *con amore*. The German poet Christoph Martin Wieland seemed to Haydn the man best suited to composing an appropriate text. Wieland, however, declared that he was not prepared to do it, and ultimately the whole project came to naught.

As it happened, this was probably a piece of luck for Haydn, for he would scarcely have survived the exertions of composing a third oratorio. He even had doubts as to the success of his last two masses, as he suggested in a note to Prince Nikolaus II on 14 June 1802: "...I was exceedingly painstaking, yet at the same time fearful whether I would still be able to win some applause [with them]."

## 1803: An End to Composing's Delights

In 1803, Haydn laid down his duties as Kapellmeister to the prince because of age; on 31 March, he was seventy-one years old. From that year on, aside from a few fragmentary efforts, his creative powers as a composer were at an end. The last string quartet remained unfinished and was in effect his swan song. Griesinger tells us about its inception:

> The Quartet in D Minor no. 83...is the last of his compositions. "It is my last child," Haydn said at the time, "but still it really does look like me." The quartet consists of only an andante and a minuet, both completed in 1803. Haydn kept waiting into 1806 for a resurgence in his strength...to be able to add an allegro. But in vain.

On 21 August 1805, Griesinger wrote to Breitkopf and Härtel: "Unfortunately, his body is increasingly fragile and every raw breeze that blows takes a lot out of him. He has himself given up hope of ever being able to complete the half-done quartet." In place of the two missing movements, Haydn enclosed a calling card with the score. On it the following text appeared:

> Gone is all the strength I had,
> Old am I, and weak.

This is the opening of a text Haydn had earlier set to music. The origin of the calling card—so typical of Haydn's sense of humor—is given by Griesinger:

> Around 1803, Haydn let Breitkopf and Härtel pub-
> lish his three- and four-part vocal works with
> piano accompaniment....Haydn had the opening
> lines of one of the songs, entitled "Der Greis" ["The
> Old Fellow"], engraved with his name in the form
> of a calling card and would send it to friends who
> asked after his health.

Now that Haydn was clearly no longer capable of completing the string quartet he had begun three years before, Griesinger included the following written statement at Haydn's wish on sending the incomplete quartet to the publisher: "As an apology that the quartet is incomplete, Haydn is sending you his personal calling card; wherever this quartet may be heard, people will immediately learn from these few words why it is unfinished and be moved to sympathize thereby."

A year before composing this last quartet, Haydn drew up his will for the first time, one he would change frequently later on. One day when Baron van Swieten paid a visit, he found Haydn—according to an account by Sigismund Neukomm—busy with the fourth or fifth revision of his will. "That's right," van Swieten said, "at our age you must be mindful of setting your house in order." Haydn had indeed set his house in order. It is touching, as the biographer Karl Geiringer notes, "that in the last will and testament of this world-famous composer, it is mostly humble people who are remembered"—seamstresses, cobblers, blacksmiths, lacemakers, the widow of a harnessmaker, four factory workers, and various other hard-working simple souls, and of course his faithful assistant, Johann Elssler. The money left to Elssler was turned to good use, for with it he was able to prepare his daughter Fanny for her career as one of the greatest dancers of all time, the "prima ballerina of two hemispheres," as Heinrich Heine once described her.

Despite his steady physical and mental decline, Haydn continued to hope for some recovery; only from 1803 on did he accept the fact that his condition would not improve. He gave voice to his despair over this situation in a letter of 22 January 1803 to his beloved brother, the composer Michael Haydn, who was in the service of the Archbishop in Salzburg: "For the last five months, I have been totally incapable of undertaking anything because my nerves are getting weaker and weaker; how painful and overwhelming I find this sudden change, you can easily imagine." He said to Dies on 19 February 1806, "Musical ideas usually pursue me to the point of torture, I simply can't get rid of them. If it's an allegro that's hounding me, then my pulse beats faster and I can hardly sleep. If it's an adagio, then I notice my pulse beats slowly. My fantasies play on me as if I were a piano....I really am a living piano."

From then on, Haydn withdrew more and more into his house in the Vienna suburb of Gumpendorf, hardly ever leaving it in the last years of his life. About these times, Griesinger reports:

> It was only through rest, careful attention to his health, and maintaining a strict daily routine that he was able to husband what remained of his strength. He could hardly walk because his legs were swollen and often he would not leave one room for another for months at a time. Here he passed the time in prayer and in thinking back on earlier days, particularly on the stay in England, as well as in reading the newspaper and going over the household expenses; on the long winter evenings, he talked with his neighbors and servants about the events of the day, and would play cards with them occasionally and be amused at the pleasure they got from winning even a single kreutzer.

It was a particular joy and diversion for him when people came by. Carl Maria von Weber, who visited Haydn in 1804 with the hope of taking lessons from him, gave the following picture:

In 1805, when Haydn was seventy-three, he had this calling card prepared, with the text "Hin ist alle meine Kraft, alt und schwach bin ich"—"Gone is all the strength I had, old am I, and weak."

"I was at Haydn's a number of times. Except for the infirmities of age, he is always cheerful and spirited, likes very much discussing things that interest him, and especially enjoys talking with young up-and-coming artists....It is touching to see grown men approach him, how they call him Papa and kiss his hand." With particular pride, Haydn would show his visitors the many honors and medals conferred upon him throughout his life. In this connection, Haydn is quoted in C. F. Pohl's biography as saying:

"I felt great pleasure at having received these signs of favor and I still enjoy looking at them occasionally with my friends. You will say, they are an old man's playthings! But for me, it is more than that—they take me back in time and for some moments, I am young again."

He maintained his neat and orderly living habits to the very end. Dies comments about them:

> In the warmer times of the year, Haydn would get up at 6:30 and shave himself right away, something he allowed no one else to do until he reached his seventy-third year. Then he got fully dressed....At eight o'clock he had breakfast....The hour from two to three was set aside for his midday meal....Around ten at night he would have supper. It was law with him to enjoy only wine and bread in the evening....At 11:30 he would go to bed; toward the end, even later. Generally speaking, the winter months made no difference in his routine, except that Haydn would get up a half-hour later in the morning; everything else remained as it was in the summer....In the morning immediately after rising, he would dress completely, so that he would only have to ask for his hat and cane to be able to show up any place; this was a habit he had come by in his early years when his prince would often send for him without warning. If he was expecting a visit, he would put on a diamond ring and adorn his suit with the red band holding his medals....

Writing in April 1805, Dies gives a further description of Haydn's living habits in these last years:

> Although he had been sick for a long time and his legs were swollen, Haydn came to meet me.... Haydn was completely dressed—the powdered wig and, notwithstanding the swelling, the boots and gloves he was wearing banished every thought of illness....I had feared his feeble condition might

HAYDN'S MEDICINE SPOON RESTING ON A BOX OF PINS.

not allow him to talk for a longer period of time...
and I left anyway because it was almost time for
his afternoon's nap. They told me that Haydn
undressed completely for his rest, put on a night-
gown and dressing robe, and then went to bed.
He kept very punctually to the time from 4:30 to
5, summer and winter, and never slept more than
half an hour. Following his rest, he would dress
completely once again.

Despite seeming extremely frail, the old master was most fas-
tidious about his appearance, as the composer Wenzel Johann
Tomaschek recounted after a visit with Haydn:

Haydn was sitting in his easy chair, all dressed up.
A powdered wig curled on either side, a white
collar with a golden clasp, a richly embroidered
vest of heavy silk resplendent with an elegant ja-
bot in between, a festive morning coat of fine cof-
fee-brown cloth, embroidered cuffs, black silk
knee-length trousers, white silk stockings, shoes
with large silver buckles bent over the instep, and
on the little table nearby beside his hat, a pair of
white leather gloves, these were the things that
made up his attire.

In 1805, working with his copyist Johann Elssler, Haydn was still sufficiently alert mentally to start a detailed inventory of his library and a listing of his compositions that was intended to be as comprehensive as possible. "There are children here who turned out well and some who turned out bad, and here and there an impostor has crept in," Haydn told Griesinger one day. To Elssler, he dictated his "catalog of all those compositions which I generally recall having completed from my 18th into my 73d year." That was the last intellectual activity of which he was capable. The rate at which his physical and mental powers were declining is evident in a note Dies made in April 1805: "It must be a great blessing in advanced years that the feeling of declining physical strength is in most cases lessened by equally declining memory and the loss of one's powers of imagination. That is the case with Haydn. He knows himself his mind is weak. He cannot think, cannot feel feelings, cannot compose, cannot even listen to music!"

In addition to the symptoms of being generally feeble physically, of increasing forgetfulness, headaches, and giddiness, visitors began to notice a new one—Haydn's spells of involuntary weeping. On quite ordinary occasions, tears would suddenly roll down his withered cheeks, or sometimes he would just burst out in sobs. During a visit from August Wilhelm Iffland, Haydn lamented over this state of affairs, saying: "When something makes me happy, I start to cry. I don't want to, but I can't help it." In his biography, Dies also says that Haydn became inclined to depression as he aged:

> In his loneliness, Haydn may chance to open the
> drawers of his desk. The things lying there bring
> the past home to him....This awakens his spirits
> and for some minutes the strength of his youth
> courses through his worn-out body....His over-
> strained heart seeks relief and finds it in outbursts
> of tears....The persons taking care of Haydn must
> attempt to prevent such scenes by appropriate di-
> versions and amusements; for once he inclines to
> be melancholy, then it is not very easy to make
> him cheerful again.

What particularly tormented Haydn was his forgetfulness. Dies tells us that he was once asked by Haydn to come see him in February 1806 for the sole purpose of telling him the name of an erudite friend and Kapellmeister in Berlin, which Haydn had forgotten. As soon as Dies said Konrad Zelter's name, Haydn was visibly relieved and apologized with the words: "I didn't know what else to do, for it vexes me terribly when my memory deserts me." Slowly, with the years, this master of music, who numbers among the greatest of the composers, became a weak, pitiable old man who could neither write his own letters, nor correctly strike a few chords on the piano. And on top of that, he suffered time and again from colds that sapped his strength. Dies reports that Haydn was sick twice between June and November 1805. On 23 February 1807, he delivered a similar report:

> Our good Haydn has once again overcome being sick. It has only been a few days since returning strength enabled him to leave his bed. Nevertheless, he denied himself the easy comfort of just wearing a house robe and I found him, as usual, all dressed up. He told me about the sufferings he had survived and I saw that zest for life in his face again which I had been missing for some time. Haydn joked that he wasn't dead yet. The pains in his bones reminded him only too well that he was still among the living.

Along with his decreasing strength, his sentimental weeping, and his tormenting inability to remember things, Haydn had, since 1805, developed ever more pronounced swelling of the legs as the result of increasing cardiac insufficiency. In both 1807 and 1808, he made a pilgrimage on the 27th of April, the holy name day of St. Peregrinus, to the chapel dedicated to the saint in the Servite monastery in the Rossau district just outside Vienna's inner city, hoping for help through the intercession of the "saint of those with suffering legs." His religion brought Haydn great comfort in his afflictions and visitors in these years often found him with rosary beads in hand.

## Rumors of Haydn's Death

Prompted by Haydn's steadily worsening state of health, a rumor spread in early 1805 that he was dead. In January 1805, the English *Gentleman's Magazine* noted in its obituary column that the famous composer Joseph Haydn had died in Vienna at the age of ninety-seven (sic!). In Paris, there was even a memorial service with Mozart's *Requiem*, and Luigi Cherubini, who earlier had presented Haydn with a diploma making him an honorary member of the Paris Conservatory, composed a funeral cantata on his death. When the February issue of the English magazine carried a retraction of its earlier report and Haydn learned of the ceremonies that had taken place in Paris on the occasion of his reported death, he commented with amusement: "The splendid gentlemen! I am really grateful to them for the unsuspected honor. If I had only known about the ceremony, I would have gone to be there myself and conduct the masses in person." The good relationship between Haydn and Cherubini was not affected by this incident and in February 1806 Haydn made him a present of the original score of his Symphony no. 103, complete with a dedication.

As a patient, Haydn was quite demanding. His personal physician, Dr. Hohenholz, had to come by to see him almost every day in the last years and frequently was summoned in the night as well. The costs for the doctor's treatment and the purchase of medicines amounted to a heavy financial burden on Haydn. Accordingly, he advised Princess Maria Hermenegild, who was concerned for him and looked after him, that he would very much welcome an increase in the stipend he received from the prince. Prince Nikolaus II responded promptly:

> Dear Kapellmeister Haydn!
> My wife, the Princess Maria, has told me of your wish to receive six hundred gulden from me in addition to the emoluments you already enjoy, with the observation that fulfillment of this wish would very much relieve and satisfy you. I hasten to take this opportunity to convey our esteem and friendship for you and to inform you of my

guarantee, whereby you are to receive three hundred gulden every six months from my disbursing office, which will be notified of this. I send my wishes for continuing good health, and remain your obliging Prince Esterhazy.

In contrast to many portrayals of him, this letter of 26 November 1806 shows the generous and high-minded character of the prince, who subsequently was prepared to assume the entire expenditures for doctors' fees and medicine, which had mounted up to two thousand gulden in the meantime. But the prince and his family also endeavored to be solicitous of Haydn's personal needs. Dies writes:

> ...Haydn often receives presents of Malaga wine from the prince's estate, and he attributes the preservation of his life first of all to this wine. Some years ago, the prince, wanting to provide for Haydn's comfort, offered to make a carriage available to him. But Haydn requested the prince to reconsider his offer, and to turn the carriage into wine. Since then, Haydn gets the wine of a prince, as much as he needs.

Meanwhile, Haydn's decline went inexorably on. He tried time and again to address himself to problems of composing, in spite of his infirmities, depression, and difficulty in concentrating, but without success. He was no longer able even to organize his early works for a printed edition. On his seventy-fourth birthday in March 1806, he remarked in a resigned tone of voice that although he often had ideas in mind "by which my art could be advanced still farther, my physical strength no longer allows me to work them out." But the greatest tragedy was that he was fully aware of his mental and physical breakdown. He often alluded to it to his friends. In 1807, he said to Griesinger: "I would never have thought a person could cave in as much as I now feel I have. My memory is gone, I sometimes still have good ideas at the piano but I weep that I am not even able to repeat them and write them down." The composer Johann Friedrich Reichardt made a similar report, after a meeting with Haydn in the autumn of

1808, in his *Confidential Letters* which he published in 1810: "Three or four times, Haydn slowly ran his gaunt hand over both my cheeks....He gazed at me for some time with emotion and then said: 'so fresh still; alas, I demanded too much of my mind and now I'm nothing but a child' and wept bitter tears." Over and over again, to Wenzel Tomaschek and others, Haydn weepingly bewailed his fading memory which forced him increasingly to give up all intellectual activity. All the letters from these years that have been preserved were in fact written at his dictation by Elssler and other copyists, and Haydn's shaky signature shows us it was hard for him even to sign them.

At the end, Haydn could not even play music. The man who earlier had been an outstanding performer on the piano and the organ was hardly able to play a few chords one after the other. Dies reported in 1806 that in an effort to play something, Haydn "constantly hit wrong notes, which he clumsily tried to correct." Later he would suffer spells of giddiness simply from listening to music.

In the last years of his life, the gifted composer, who once had been capable of dealing self-confidently and assuredly with monarchs and the most exalted personages and who had managed his affairs with various publishing houses in the most clever and businesslike way, had become a helpless old man. As the years rolled by, he could only pass the time in his easy chair, mulling over memories of great times, or in bed during his frequent illnesses with colds and their attendant complications. On a visit as early as April 1805, Camille Pleyel, son of the well-known Parisian composer and builder of pianos Ignaz Pleyel, found Haydn to be exhausted and frail and described him in a letter to his family on 16 June 1805 as: "a man in his seventies, but looking as though he were over 80 and praying constantly, rosary in hand."

By 1808, Haydn had not been able to leave the house for a long time. The last time he went out in public was to attend a performance of his oratorio *The Creation* given in the auditorium of the old university to mark his seventy-sixth birthday. The performance was conducted by Antonio Salieri and the event has been captured in a watercolor painting by Balthasar Wigand. Everyone who was anyone in Vienna was present for the occasion—one of the greatest birthdays Haydn would experience. Griesinger says of this memorable event:

> I expressed to him my wonderment at his having been able to decide, despite his infirmities, to attend the festivities in the university hall on 27 March 1808. He replied: "Concern for my health could not hold me back; it wasn't the first time Haydn had been honored and I wanted to show them that I was still up to it." To the accompaniment of enormous applause, Haydn was carried into the hall in a sedan chair. All the aristocracy was present and Haydn and Salieri embraced. Even Beethoven was there, tears running down his cheeks as he emotionally kissed the hand of his former teacher.

On 5 April 1808, Dies provided additional details:

> People were very concerned lest the feeble old gentleman catch cold; for this reason, they made him keep his hat on....Haydn thought he felt a slight draft, which persons sitting nearest him noticed. Princess Esterhazy took her scarf and put it around him. Several other ladies then did the same and in a few moments, Haydn was covered with ladies' scarves. After a while, he no longer could control his feelings; his heart, overflowing with emotion, sought and found relief in a stream of tears. He had to take a sip of wine to revive his weakened spirits. But it did not help and his mood remained so nostalgic and melancholy that finally, after the end of the first section, he had to leave. The farewell did him in completely: he could scarcely speak and was able to express his gratitude and very best wishes for the good health of all those gathered there as well as for the artists and art itself only with weak and halting words and gestures. Every face was deeply touched and eyes welling with tears followed him as he was carried away to his coach.

Haydn's friend and biographer Giuseppe Carpani, who was also present, recounts that, in that overwhelming moment when the passage "*Und es ward Licht*" ("And It Was Light") began, Haydn "...raised his trembling arms to heaven as though praying to the God of Music." Everyone sensed that Haydn was among them for the last time. Carpani went on to say that as Haydn, still seated in the sedan chair, reached the exit, he ordered the bearers to stop. "The two bearers complied and turned him to the audience. He made appropriate gestures of thanks and then, lifting his face to heaven and with tears in his eyes, he made the sign of blessing on all his children."

Haydn had become so weak that, on the advice of his doctor, he exchanged his grand piano for another that was smaller and easier to play. Finally the doctor forbade him to play music at all because it wearied him so. Still, he was constantly drawn to the piano even though he could no longer play anything but a few simple songs and, especially, his *Volkslied*. Even this was often interrupted because he felt weak or overcome with emotion. The *Volkslied—Gott erhalte Franz, den Kaiser (God Save Our Emperor Francis)*—was composed in 1797 at the instigation of Baron van Swieten and Count Saurau as a sort of companion piece to the English hymn *God Save the King*, and later served as the emperor's anthem. In view of the bad news coming from the battlefields at the time, the emperor desperately needed something to strengthen the people's faith in their sovereign. Dies is surely right in his view that this *Volkslied* did more to make the emperor popular with the people than any of his more-than-questionable govern-mental measures. The *Emperor's Hymn*, by the way, is based on an old folksong melody, one that Haydn had incorporated into the variation movement of the *Emperor's String Quartet* which originated in the same year.

Just how great the decline in Haydn's mental and physical faculties had become with time can be seen from the portrayal by August Wilhelm Iffland. He wrote on 8 September 1808 after being introduced to Haydn by the director of the Eisenstadt theater, Heinrich Schmidt:

> He made a move as though to stand. The servant
> helped him up and thus he made...a few short

SCORE OF HAYDN'S *VOLKSLIED* (*GOD SAVE OUR EMPEROR FRANCIS*), COMPOSED IN 1797 AFTER THE EXAMPLE OF THE BRITISH ANTHEM, *GOD SAVE THE KING*.

steps in our direction, arduously pulling one leg after the other along the floor in an effort to walk quickly. In the course of the conversation, Haydn asked: "Do you want to hear something of mine? Of course, I can do little more—you should hear my last composition. I made it even as the French army was approaching Vienna....The song is called: 'Gott erhalte Franz, den Kaiser!'...I can't help it, I have to play it once every day. When I play it, I feel so well then and for a while afterward."

In another passage, Iffland describes Haydn's extreme forgetfulness and his inability to recall even something he had just heard. Haydn was tremendously pleased with the great success of a charity performance of his oratorio *The Creation*, in Berlin. When he learned that the religious foundation had cleared over 2,000 taler, he said to Elssler: "Over 2,000 taler for the poor! Over 2,000 taler! Did you hear that? My 'Creation' made over 2,000 taler in Berlin for the poor! That's wonderful, that's heart-warming....How much was it that the 'The Creation' brought the poor? Make a note of it, I'll enjoy it so much." Even as he was repeating the news, he had already forgotten how much the concert had earned. Because of

Haydn's rapidly diminishing memory and his difficulty in concentrating, Dies began to doubt the wisdom of continuing his talks with Haydn to gather biographical information, for "...Haydn's extraordinary weakness kept him from thinking about the past. He was not even clear about the present. His memory was no longer sharp, but of course it had not yet gone so far with him that one could have called him childish in his weakened state. He would probably only have come to that when he was even older."

The events surrounding the war between France and Austria in 1809 also affected the state of Haydn's physical and mental well-being. Two dear friends were forced to flee imperial Vienna for political reasons—his beloved student Sigismund Neukomm on 16 February and his biographer Georg August Griesinger on 3 May. When an artillery shell with grapeshot landed in the immediate vicinity of Haydn's house on the morning of 10 May, the venerable composer, who was in the act of getting dressed, was so frightened that he "would have fallen on the floor without the quick assistance of his servants." Dies writes that:

> ...he was seized by a terrible fit of trembling. Unhappily there followed shortly three more shells one right after the other, causing Haydn's convulsive trembling to increase and leading to a general worsening of his dreadful condition. Nevertheless, the old man gathered up all his powers and, straining his voice to the utmost, called out: "Don't be afraid, my children! Where Haydn is, there nothing can happen!" The servants put him back in bed and saw to it that the doctor was called, who came and sought to moderate the worst with the appropriate medicine, which succeeded to the point that Haydn was able to get up again the same day and continue his usual routine....Still, one could see he was gloomy and depressed, a mood that did not leave him in the days that followed. He seemed to want to forget his woes by playing the piano. Every day toward noon, he

would seat himself at the instrument and let his
favorite piece, the *Volkslied*, ring out.

At one o'clock in the afternoon of 26 May 1809, Haydn had
his servants take him to the little piano in his living room for the
last time. He played *Gott erhalte Franz, den Kaiser* three times in
quick succession and with such expression that even he was
amazed at it, according to Elssler. An hour later he enjoyed a
final surprise. An officer of the French army asked to be admitted
and as Elssler, trembling with fear, showed him in, the stranger
turned out to be a passionate admirer of Haydn and his music.
He asked if he might be allowed to sing the aria from *The Creation*, "*Mit Wurd und Hoheit angetan*," to his idol. The sick old
man was lifted from his bed and taken, with just a robe to cover
his naked legs, to the piano in the living room. The Frenchman,
who introduced himself as Clément Souléy, had scarcely finished
singing the aria when Haydn asked to embrace him; "impetu-
ously, Haydn pulled him down and covered him with numerous
kisses," as we learn from Dies.

## 31 May 1809: Haydn's Death

In the evening of the same day, Haydn suffered headaches
and a chill. His attendants put him to bed earlier than usual and
on the following day (27 May), when he was unable to rise, they
requested the family physician, Dr. Hohenholz, to call in a second doctor—a Dr. Böhmer—for consultation. As was to be expected, there was nothing the two doctors could do for Haydn.
He faded slowly away, remaining conscious to the end. If someone would ask him how he was, his calm and composed answer
was always the same: "Be of good cheer, dear ones, I'm doing
fine." Four hours before he died he spoke his last words, and in
the first hour of 31 May he pressed the hand of his faithful old
cook Nannerl in gratitude minutes before the end came. The
death certificate in the Gumpendorf parish church gave "exhaustion" as the cause of death. His assistant of many years, Johann
Elssler, wrote a detailed report on Haydn's last days and hours to
Griesinger on 31 May, closing with these words: "Our good Papa
was born on 31 March 1732 and the 31st of May 1809 was the

saddest day of death for us all. Thus our good Papa reached 77 years and 61 days in his old age....May God soon help us out of our unhappiness." And in a postscript, he added: "I made a plaster of paris cast of my good Papa."

Concerning Haydn's funeral, Joseph Carl Rosenbaum, a friend of Haydn's and the son-in-law of Haydn's former colleague, the late composer Florian Leopold Gassmann, wrote in his diary:

> Corpus Christi Day, 1 June. A hot day, suffocating dust....He was dressed in black and lay in the main room, face not disfigured at all, at his feet were the seven medals of honor from Paris, Russia, Sweden, as well as the local citizen's medal. After five o'clock, Haydn was conducted in an oaken coffin to the Gumpendorf church, was carried around the church three times, then consecrated and conveyed to the cemetery at the Hundsturm line. Not <u>one</u> Kapellmeister from Vienna accompanied his remains.

(This is not the last we hear of Herr Rosenbaum; we shall meet him again shortly.)

Many years later, on 11 April 1827, Anton Schindler, Beethoven's secretary and biographer, wrote about the paltry attendance at Haydn's funeral to the pianist and composer Ignaz Moscheles: "Today, at any rate, we know that the reason for this state of affairs lay in the regulations of the [French] occupying forces and the fact that news of Haydn's death did not reach his best friends until the funeral was over." The famous Viennese builder of pianos Andreas Streicher, who had passed the sad news on to Griesinger, also sought to excuse the ill-attended funeral with these words: "If the circumstances at the time had not been what they were, Haydn's funeral service would have been a memorial celebration such as Vienna had never seen before."

Haydn's remarkable personal fortune consisted of cash, stocks and bonds, jewelry, silverware, and many precious objects of all kinds as well as his house in Gumpendorf. The auction sale alone brought twenty-three thousand gulden. His house was appraised at twenty-five thousand gulden and Prince Nikolaus II,

DRAWING OF THE TOMBSTONE ERECTED IN 1814 AT HAYDN'S FIRST RESTING
PLACE IN THE HUNDSTURM CEMETERY OUTSIDE VIENNA.

to whom a large part of the compositions left by Haydn actually
belonged by virtue of contract, paid forty-five thousand gulden
for the musical works. When he died, Haydn was, in comparison
with other major composers of his time, an exceptionally well-to-
do citizen. He was so famous that, to quote the *Allgemeine Musik-
Zeitung*, even "...people from the lower classes fought and sparred

with one another to own something from Haydn, just as if it was a matter of the holy relics of a saint."

From the symptoms involved in Joseph Haydn's physical and intellectual breakdown, a diagnosis of the clinical picture that had been emerging since 1799 can be reconstructed reasonably well. If we overlook the frequent spells of illness in his last decades, which were certainly fostered by his difficulty in breathing as a result of his nasal polyp and which probably involved the sinuses as well, two different diseases stand out as having contributed— but only in part, of course—to the overall change in his condition, that is, to a general case of arteriosclerosis or "hardening of the arteries."

Calcareous degeneration of the coronary vessels—today known as coronary sclerosis—led to degenerative changes in the cardiac muscles over several years' time, ultimately causing increasing weakness of the heart. At the latest from 1805 on, the developing myocardial insufficiency became evident through the appearance of edema, that is, swelling in the legs. Along with the difficulty in breathing repeatedly mentioned by Dies, swelling in his legs increasingly affected Haydn's mobility. He often did not leave his room for months at a time and later found it difficult, even with the help of his servants, to make his way from bed to easy chair or piano.

Whether Haydn's prolonged sitting in his armchair led to leg ulcers as a result of venous insufficiency caused by retardation of blood flow in the veins of his swollen legs is a question we cannot answer definitively for lack of direct information from his biographers or reports of his contemporaries. An indirect and tentative indication of this possibility is the fact that Haydn made pilgrimages in 1807 and 1808 to the chapel of St. Peregrinus, who was represented in the traditional picture on the altar as having a large varicose ulcer on his lower leg.

Nor do the available sources allow us to determine whether hypertension (high blood pressure) could have contributed to the arteriosclerotic changes in the coronary vessels that went along with aging. With our present knowledge, we would place hypertension first among the risk factors. One indirect suggestion of such a possibility is Haydn's "reddish facial complexion," as Dies described it, together with the frequent headaches and spells of dizziness.

Even more dramatic and heartrending for us today than his heart disease, however, is the disintegration of Haydn's person–ality that began to manifest itself from 1801 on. It is virtually certain that here, too, arteriosclerosis played a causal role, affect-ing the blood vessels in the brain. Degeneration of the nerve cells themselves appears to have been even more important, for that process usually underlies such a dwindling away of the men-tal faculties. The earliest sign of evolving personality disintegra-tion, something that normally takes years to develop fully, is a drop in personal initiative and general intellectual vigor together with, most particularly, decreasing ability to remember things. Typical in this kind of forgetfulness is a reduced capacity to com-prehend and integrate new information, which is why more re-cent memories are much more strongly affected than older ones, such as those stemming from one's youth. We speak of this con-dition today as Korsakoff's psychosis. In this syndrome, of all the functions of the brain, memory is more strongly affected than any other component of a person's thought and behavior. So it was with Haydn in his last years.

In Haydn's medical history, however, other characteristic symp-toms of an ongoing, degenerative disease of the nerve cells in the brain can also be found: his inability to continue his accustomed professional activities, the perseveration in his speech and in various actions—for instance, the showing off of his medals and awards—and, most notably, his altered emotional state. An inor-dinate emotional instability, marked by outbreaks of weeping at the slightest provocation, and a state of depression are common in persons with this disease, especially those who are fully aware of their diminishing mental capacities—as was the case with Haydn. Their locomotive powers also are affected. They have motor disorders in walking, tend to stand in a bent-forward position, and take little, tentative steps—all symptoms of Haydn described by his visitors in the last years. Finally, the venerable Haydn's striking and almost exaggerated compulsion for order and his insistence on maintaining fixed daily routines are typical of the ways by which such patients unconsciously seek to compensate for their failing memory.

In sum, Joseph Haydn died of a disease that developed slowly over the span of his last decades, one that in our present society, with its substantially longer life expectancies, is among the most frequent causes of death: arteriosclerosis of the coronary vessels and the arteries of the brain, with degeneration of the nerve cells of the brain playing a decisive role.

## Haydn's Burial: The Aftermath

Disgraceful is the word for what happened after Haydn had been buried in the Hundsturm cemetery.

Joseph Carl Rosenbaum, who had once been secretary to Prince Nikolaus II and was a member of Haydn's innermost circle of friends, and Johann Nepomuk Peter, an acquaintance of Rosenbaum's who was an official in the provincial jail of Lower Austria, were both fanatic adherents of Franz Joseph Gall's science of craniology. Gall held that intellectual characteristics are defined by the size, shape, and proportions of the skull, a notion considered very modern in those days. Accordingly, Rosenbaum and Peter decided to take the skull of the composer they venerated so highly and to give it solemn keeping. As an excuse for their dreadful outrage, they later claimed that they could not in good conscience accept that the bony seat of intellect of such a magnificent spirit should be eaten away by maggots and worms. By bribing the gravedigger, they in fact succeeded in opening Haydn's grave at night and in getting the head cut off the body of the corpse. Macabre as it may seem, Rosenbaum duly recorded this nefarious deed in his diary in excruciating detail:

> After the grave had been closed, I spoke to our good Jakob Demuth, an Austrian, a rather well-liked, large, and jovial fellow who had been plundered by the French soldiers, about the removal of this head so worthy of honor in every respect and got everything perfectly arranged...Sunday, the 4th [of June 1809]...we drove to the Hundsturm line, I got out and received Joseph Haydn's

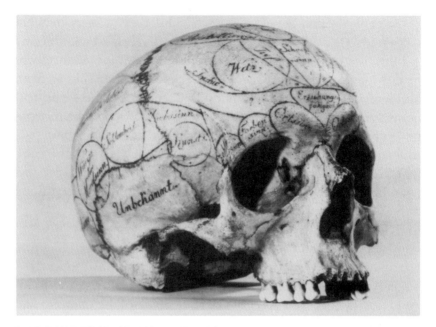

WHO BELIEVED THAT NATURAL TALENTS AND ABILITIES COULD BE DISCERNED FROM THE SHAPE OF THE SKULL. ADHERENTS OF GALL'S IDEAS ROBBED HAYDN'S GRAVE IN 1809 TO GET HIS SKULL.

invaluable relic from Jakob Demuth. It smelled terrible. Once I had the package in the coach, I had to throw up. The stench was too much for me. We drove to the General Hospital, I stayed for the dissection, the head was already rather green but still easily recognizable. The impression this sight made on me will stay with me forever....

One wonders still how the two grave robbers carrying the head of Joseph Haydn were able to go calmly to the General Hospital for its postmortem examination and preservation without later being prosecuted. The explanation is to be found in the legal situation at the time, which Rosenbaum and Peter cited in exoneration of their deed in these words: "Because this great man had been committed to be consumed by the earth in the burial grounds beyond the Hundsturm line and was thereby free to anyone, there was therefore no legal obstacle to appropriating what had been abandoned."

Peter, however, gave a somewhat different version of what happened. He said the gravedigger had been bribed with money and the plotters, who included a certain Michel Jungmann from the city magistrate's assessment bureau and an Ignaz Ullman from the Vienna city treasury in addition to Rosenbaum and Peter, had themselves opened the grave and removed Haydn's head from the body. Peter is said to have macerated it and bleached the skull later by himself. This story could well be closer to the truth than that of Rosenbaum, who claimed that the gravedigger had given him Haydn's head and that the maceration had been done in the General Hospital.

The well-known Viennese professor of anatomy Julius Tandler, who later subjected Haydn's skull to more detailed examination, determined that Rosenbaum's allegation that the postmortem examination had shown "the size of the brain [to be] very great" could not have been correct because the vault of the cranium had not been removed. Thus no view into the inside of the skull had been possible. Perhaps Rosenbaum was ashamed of his participation in desecrating Haydn's grave and therefore wrote a somewhat less incriminating version of the gruesome proceedings in his diary. Peter, on the other hand, as a zealous disciple of Gall's craniology, told with pride of believing he had been able, in the course of the so-called examination of Haydn's skull, to establish proof of "the seat of hearing, just as it is given in the preface to Gall's book."

After this "examination," the precious relic was given safekeeping at Rosenbaum's house in, as he put it, a most reverent fashion: the skull rested on a cushion covered with white silk and draped with black satin inside a black wooden cabinet that was modeled after a Roman sarcophagus and decorated with a golden lyre. To emphasize still more the sanctity of its care, Rosenbaum built a mausoleum for displaying the small wooden sarcophagus in his yard, where privileged visitors were able to view the invaluable possession. The utter tastelessness of the whole matter is compounded by the fact that Frau Rosenbaum—who was Florian Gassmann's daughter—sang Michael Haydn's *Requiem* for the dead composer at the Gumpendorf church on the day after Haydn's burial just as her husband was setting into motion the plan for seizing Haydn's skull.

Prince Nikolaus II had planned to have Haydn's remains brought to Eisenstadt and ceremonially laid to eternal rest in the Franciscan vault there. In fact, he had already had an iron casket made earlier in 1809 and had secured the approval of the Lower Austrian provincial authorities for the intended transfer of the body. But in the turbulence attending the political disorders of 1809, the prince was so occupied with other matters that he quite forgot his former Kapellmeister lying in the Hundsturm cemetery. Fortunately, Haydn's pupil Sigismund Neukomm, who had become a member of French Minister Tallyrand's diplomatic staff, came to Vienna in 1814 to take part in the Congress of Vienna. He interested himself immediately in the grave of his beloved former teacher and marked Haydn's last resting place before the gates of Vienna by mounting a modest tablet on the site. Had he not done so, Haydn's grave, like Mozart's, might have been threatened with oblivion. It would be many years before the prince was reminded of his plan to transfer Haydn's corpse to Eisenstadt. In the meantime, the iron coffin that had been ordered in 1809 for Haydn's remains stood stored in the vicinity of the kitchen in the prince's town estate in Vienna, despite the fact that one of the prince's household managers had inquired of him in 1811, "What is to be done with that iron casket intended for the dead Kapellmeister Haydn and which is now only standing in the way by the kitchen?"

The robbing of Haydn's grave did not come to light until eleven years later in 1820. In September of that year, Duke Frederick of Cambridge paid a visit to Eisenstadt where, among other things, he enjoyed a performance of *The Creation*. Deeply moved by this musical experience, the noble guest from England recalled Haydn's triumphs in London in the course of his after-dinner remarks and ended his toast with the words: "How fortunate is the man who possessed Haydn while he lived and who possesses still his earthly remains." Abruptly reminded of his earlier plan by this embarrassing pronouncement, the prince immediately ordered that Haydn's remains be exhumed and transferred to Eisenstadt. When the coffin was opened and only Haydn's wig was found in place of his head, the shock was enormous. Beside himself with rage and driven by concern that he would be the laughingstock of Vienna when the desecration became known, the prince demanded that Count Sedlnitzky, the chief of Vienna's police department, promptly find and punish the perpetrators. The prince could hardly have dreamed that there were people in the police department who, through their friendly relationships with the Rosenbaum and Peter families, had known for a long time where Haydn's skull was stored. Thus, the perpetrators were identified immediately.

First to be questioned was the administrator of the Lower Austrian provincial jail, Herr Peter, whose passion for collecting dead persons' skulls was well known. Peter, however, asserted that he had left Haydn's skull with his friend Rosenbaum and had turned it over to him to be properly preserved, with the innocent claim that thus the two of them "had rescued a palace of music from destruction." A search of Rosenbaum's house was ordered immediately. To their consternation, the legal authorities came up with nothing, even though they were certain beyond doubt that Haydn's skull must be in the house. Frau Rosenbaum, it seems, had hidden the precious relic under the mattress of her bed as soon as the police arrived and then quickly lay down, explaining to the officials that unfortunately, because it was "the wrong time of the month," she had to keep to her bed.

Frustrated in these attempts to find the skull, the prince then decided to send his personal doctor to the grave robbers and offer them a substantial award for revealing its location. But even after this "ransom" had been paid, Rosenbaum succeeded once again in defrauding his former employer—perhaps as belated revenge for having been discharged without grounds from the prince's service many years before. He first handed over the skull of a twenty-year-old man and then, when this trick was discovered, that of an old man, all the while retaining the true skull of Haydn for himself. Thus, on 4 December 1820, the skull of a stranger was added to Haydn's remains in Eisenstadt in the belief that an honest deal had been made. But in fact, Rosenbaum handed on the genuine skull only when he was on his deathbed and then to his friend and accomplice, Peter. After Peter's death in 1839, his widow bequeathed it to her husband's physician,

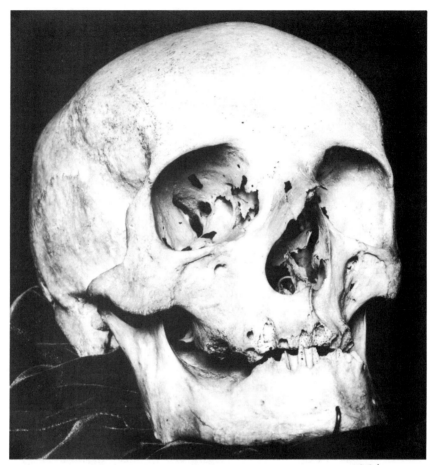

HAYDN'S SKULL WAS RETURNED TO THE REST OF HIS BODY IN 1954 AT HIS PERMANENT BURIAL PLACE IN EISENSTADT.

Dr. Karl Haller. He in turn entrusted it to the famous Viennese pathologist Professor Carl von Rokitansky in 1852, who stored it in the museum of the Pathological-Anatomical Institute of the University of Vienna, where it remained until his successor, Professor Hans Kundrat—under the impression that the skull had been the private property of his predecessor—gave it to Rokitansky's sons. Finally, they presented it to Vienna's pre–eminent musical society, the Gesellschaft der Musikfreunde, where it remained until 1954.

In 1954 the ceremonial transfer of Haydn's skull to the government of the province of Burgenland took place, in keeping with a plan for the skull to be interred in Haydn's coffin in the Bergkirche in Eisenstadt.  A commemorative article from Burgenland in 1959 states that "on Saturday, 5 June 1954, the skull was placed in an urn decorated with a golden laurel wreath surrounded by red and white peonies in the grand hall of the Musikverein in Vienna.  The Cardinal Archbishop of Vienna conducted the consecration."  With the invaluable relic in its glass-covered case covered by a black cloth, a procession of over a hundred automobiles drove first to Haydn's birthplace in Rohrau, where it paused briefly before the archway to his parents' house while one of Haydn's string quartets was played and the bells of the church pealed.  Then it proceeded on to Eisenstadt, where Haydn's skull was finally and forever joined with his remains in the sarcophagus in the Bergkirche to the playing of soft music on the organ.  So—some one hundred and fifty years after he died—Haydn at last received the first-class funeral service he had expressly requested in his will and which had been denied him at the time of his burial in the Hundsturm cemetery because of the unsettled political situation in 1809.

At Haydn's grave is a tablet on which we can read these words:

> DOCTOR OXONIENSIS.  VIR PIUS, PROBUS, MANSUETUS.
> FUGANDI CURAS ARTIFEX, MULCENDI PECTORA PRIMUS.

Doctor of Oxford.  A devout, honest, and peaceful man.  An artist in banishing cares, a master in enchanting the heart.

With these words chiselled in stone, we are reminded once more of music's healing effect, as personified by the ancient Apollo, god of medicine and music, and recognized and experienced over the millennia.  And we are moved by the appropriateness of these words on the tablet that speak of the covenant Haydn had made with the Almighty:

> STERBEN WERD' ICH NICHT, SONDERN LEBEN
> UND ERZÄHLEN DIE WERKE DES HERRN.

I shall not die, but live
and proclaim the works of the Lord.

## Haydn's Doctor

### *Dr. Johann Alexander von Brambilla (1728-1800)*

Born in the Lombardy region of northern Italy, Dr. Brambilla made his career as a military surgeon, earning the particular confidence of Emperor Joseph II and his soldiers. From 1780 on, as surgeon general, he was in charge of all matters of health and hygiene for the army. As a confidant of the emperor, he was present at the Hotel Dieu in Paris when Joseph II first inspected the model for the new General Hospital to be built in Vienna. Dr. Brambilla took a personal interest in improving the standing not only of military doctors but of surgeons as a whole, who in those days often were held in little more esteem than the barbers performing surgery in the streets.

A noteworthy contribution made by Dr. Brambilla was the establishment in 1785 of the imperial medical-surgical academy of Joseph II, known as the "Josephinum," for the schooling of military doctors. That institution was quickly acclaimed for the wealth of its instructional material, including an extensive library with more than six thousand volumes of the medical works then most highly regarded, and in particular its anatomical-pathological museum. The wax models and exhibits on display there, prepared by Fontana in Florence and transported to Vienna in 1785 on the backs of twenty mules at the order of the emperor, excite the admiration and amazement of visitors to this remarkable institute even today.

Dr. Brambilla once attempted to excise Haydn's nasal polyp after previous attempts at the hospital of the Brothers of Mercy in Eisenstadt had failed. Unfortunately this attempt also failed. After this last unsuccessful surgical effort, which cost him part of his nasal bone, Haydn never let a surgeon work on his nose again.

# Wolfgang Amadé Mozart
## (1756-1791)

The changes in the perception of Mozart that have occurred over the past two hundred years are due almost entirely to the uniqueness of his musical genius. Hardly any other major composer has evoked such widely varying views. Mozart is "something beyond all reach in the realm of music," Goethe once said in a letter to his friend Johann Peter Eckermann, "he is one of those figures the Furies occasionally place among mankind: so beguiling everyone wants to be like them and yet so superior none can reach them." Today we find it hard to imagine that there were contemporaries of Mozart who thought his fame was on the wane even before he died. In truth, just the opposite happened: in some mysterious way, the inexhaustible power of Mozart's creativity has loomed ever larger in the consciousness of succeeding generations. In the Romantic era's transfigured picture, Mozart was idealized as "Apollo," as "music's genius of subtle light and tender love," to use Richard Wagner's effusive phrase. Mozart's powerful G-minor symphony was perceived by Robert Schumann as a work of "Grecian lightness and grace." The rediscovery of Mozart's demonic force came about only with the end of the 19th century in the Mozart renaissance initiated by Richard Strauss and Gustav Mahler. For them, Mozart was "the greatest dramatic genius of the entire 18th century" and, as Felix Mottl said once, "perhaps the most daring innovator in musical composition who ever lived."

Born on the threshold of a new political era and in the midst of the *Sturm und Drang* literary movement, with its bold new visions of mankind, Mozart's eclectic, synthesizing musical style turned out to be a synthesis oriented to future generations. Perhaps that is why, as Tschitscherin once observed, it was reserved to our age to be the first to grasp Mozart fully, that is, to perceive his cosmic reach and his ambivalence as well as his demonic element, and to penetrate the measureless depths of his music. Due to its universality and its ambiguous nature, Mozart's music not only outlived the 19th century, but has also, effortlessly and uncontested, prevailed throughout the 20th.

A new approach is being taken to the biographical interpretation of Mozart, based on his works themselves, not on what the Romantic period has made of them, with its need to reconcile his classical music with his mundane life. It has led to a growing rejection of the biographical and aesthetic ideas of such authors as Otto Jahn, Hermann Abert, Alfred Einstein, and Bernhard Paumgartner, in favor of a more realistic picture of Mozart. Their view that the widely traveled Mozart was oblivious to the major political and social developments of his times, to the American War of Independence, to Rousseau and the French Revolution, to democratic stirrings in England, or to the important personages of the Enlightenment, is simply not credible. On the contrary, we can be certain that Mozart, whose Vienna years (1781—1791) coincided with the reign of Emperor Joseph II, was a keen and close observer of the emperor's Enlightenment-inspired program of reforms. The finality with which he quit his service to the Prince-Archbishop of Salzburg, Hieronymus Colloredo, his unstinting commitment to Freemasonry (something not at all opportune, given its strict surveillance by the imperial authorities), and especially his operas, which contain so much political dynamite it is a wonder they escaped being banned by the censors, all testify eloquently to the man Mozart was. The German author Gunthard Born, whose modern analysis deciphers "the symbols found in Mozart's musical rhetoric" to produce a "key to his life and works," comes to essentially the same conclusion in his book *Mozarts Musiksprache (The Musical Language of Mozart)*:

> The genius who tends to be looked on today primarily as a naïve Wunderkind reveals himself in fact to be a composer who was very much engaged both ideologically and politically, one who

spoke up for the universal truth of the natural order, for the relief of the downtrodden, and even
for the women's [movements] and peace movements of his era.

Thus, at least since the appearance of Wolfgang Hildesheimer's
work in the late 1970s, an entirely new perception of Mozart has
begun to emerge, one that seeks explicitly to distance itself from
cherished predilections of the past. In examining the medical
aspects of Mozart's life, his biographers, especially those who
were not physicians themselves, have been faced with the almost
impossible task of creating a coherent picture from the myriad
polemical and controversial explanations of the nature of his illnesses and the diagnosis of his last illness and the circumstances
that led to its fatal outcome. The treatment of these questions,
even in pathological studies of Mozart by physicians, has been
rather mixed and, given persistent biases, not always profession-
ally sound. The following discussion therefore seeks to correct or
modify some especially egregious interpretations in the light of
modern medical knowledge. All available documents from
Mozart's time are considered, as well as the historical and cultural
circumstances of his era, including the customs and practices of
the first Viennese school of medicine. Despite the difficulties
involved, the influences that Mozart's illnesses may have had on
his personality and his creative activities are examined and an
attempt is made to determine from his compositions whether
personal psychological factors worked to shape his artistic creativity.

## Mozart's Early Years

Leopold Mozart wrote a letter on 9 February 1756 to Jakob
Lotter in Augsburg (the publisher of Leopold's treatise on violin
playing) and added the following lines in closing:

...by the way, I pass on the news that on 27 January at 8 in the evening my loving wife was happily
delivered of a baby boy, but they had to remove
the afterbirth from her. She was terribly weak as a
result. Now, however, both mother and child are

> doing fine, thank God! She sends her respects to
> you both. The boy's names are Joannes Chriso-
> stomos, Wolfgang, Gottlieb.

From these four names, which were entered in the parish register
in Salzburg on 28 January 1756, Mozart later chose Amadé (the
French form of Gottlieb or Theophilus) to go with the first name
of Wolfgang—not Amadeus, as it is usually written today.

Wolfgang was the last of seven children born to his parents
while they lived in the old house (known in records back to
1408) owned by the merchant and grocer Johann Lorenz
Hagenauer in the street called the Getreidegasse in Salzburg. The
only other child to survive to adulthood was his sister, Maria Anna
Walburga, nicknamed "Nannerl," who was almost five years older.
The baby Wolfgang must have had a rugged constitution, for he
evidently suffered no adverse effects from the widely accepted
custom followed by the Mozart family of raising children on
water rather than milk. In the 18th century, it was common not to
breastfeed babies, but to nourish them with a mixture of honey-
water and a gruel of barley or oats, a regimen that Mozart himself
later wanted to follow with his own children, as he mentioned in
a letter on 18 June 1783:

> ...My wife [Constanze]...should never nurse her
> baby. And my baby ought not to be gulping down
> somebody else's milk either—but rather water, like
> my sister and I...except that most of the people
> here have really begged me not to do that... be-
> cause most children here die from using water....
> That has caused me to give in.

His mother's heritage probably played a greater role in shaping Mozart's personality than has generally been assumed. His
gift for the theatrical and for music-making, the wealth of his
fantasy, his earthy, often coarse humor, and his pronounced delight in pranks and horseplay were characteristic traits of his
mother's family, as were his plainspoken candor and his innate
sense of personal pride. Her family, the Pertls, were from the
village of St. Gilgen on the lake at the Wolfgangsee. Mozart's self-
assurance was evident in his early years, as described in an

eyewitness account of his first performance at the imperial court in Vienna on Wednesday, the 13th of October, 1762, at the age of six:

> ...Even then he displayed a trait that was to remain with him, that is, disdain for the praises of his elders and a certain disinclination to play for them if they were not themselves music connoisseurs....So it happened once at the emperor's. As he seated himself at the piano to play a piece, with Emperor Francis I standing beside him, Mozart said, isn't Herr [Georg Christoph] Wagenseil here? He will appreciate it. Wagenseil came and the little virtuoso told him, I'm playing a piece you wrote and you must turn the pages for me.

Later in life, with the nobility of spirit that Mozart felt, he began to rebel against the system of inherited nobility, prompted no doubt by the political developments in England, France, and America. For example, Mozart had a well-known run-in in 1781 with Archbishop Colloredo, whom he came to hate "to the point of frenzy" and to refer to as "the Archboob." After the Archbishop had called him a clod, a rascal, and a miserable lad in the course of one of their sharp exchanges, Mozart fired back at Count Arco (who later sent Mozart flying out of the Archbishop's service with his notorious kick in the composer's pants): "When I see that someone looks down on me and treats me with contempt, then I can be as proud as any prince." His view of the sanctity of his honor and the nobility of the human spirit was expressed even more clearly a week later in a letter written on 20 June 1781: "...It is the soul that makes a noble of a man; and even though I may not be a count, still I have perhaps more honor in me than lots of counts, and whether count or lackey is all the same, the one who insults me, as soon as he does, is a knave."

In coming to grips with his sexual feelings and providing them an intellectual outlet, Mozart greatly enjoyed playing with words and their infinite variety of expression, as we see in an example from the often-mentioned letters to his cousin in Augsburg (whom he called "Bäsle," meaning "little cousin"). Some recent writers have attempted to demythologize Mozart, who was elevated practically to a demigod in the 19th century, and, in the process, to make him out to be an infantile neurotic because of the eccentric language in his letters.  But they obviously have failed to recognize important deep psychological aspects.  As Voser-Hoesli has demonstrated in an analysis well worth reading, the spoken language was, for Mozart, merely another instrument for making music.  He reveled in the sounds of words, in the rhythm of language and the vast number of its phrase variations and word combinations, while often not being particularly concerned with the specific content of the sentences—"just as in his music the link to a perceptible end result often cannot be recognized in advance.  From this perspective, his highly personal writing style turns out to be essentially a continuation of his brain's perpetual preoccupation with musical composition, in which musical patterns emerge and take shape on the pages of his letters just as they do in his scores."  It is true that Mozart's letters often show a certain fondness for crude turns of language, but they must be understood in the context of the customs of his fellow countrymen in Bavaria and Salzburg, who even today are wont to employ certain vigorous anal expressions of annoyance or sociable good humor.

From his father Leopold—an uncommonly well-educated and artistic man of high moral principles—young Mozart received an education without parallel in the history of music.  Andreas Schachtner, a trumpeter at the court in Salzburg and a close friend of the Mozart family, described the five-year-old Mozart as sensitive, frolicsome, and eager to please, with a special bent for arithmetic and number games.  Even in his third and fourth years, there was no play enjoyed more by the lad than amusing himself, in one way or another, with music.  His father became his music teacher in these early years, having already demonstrated significant talents as a music pedagogue with the preparation of his treatise on violin playing.  In the Notenbuch that young Mozart was presented on his name day (31 October 1762) by his father, as was Nannerl in 1759, Leopold had already written: "Wolfgang learned this piece [a scherzo by Wagenseil] in the evening from 9 to 9:30, on the 24th of January 1761, 3 days before his 5th birthday."  Between February and April 1761, the two earliest

ON WOLFGANG'S NAME DAY, 31 OCTOBER 1762, HIS FATHER LEOPOLD
GAVE HIM A MUSIC BOOK WITH THIS DEDICATION: "FOR MY BELOVED SON
WOLFGANG AMADÉ ON HIS SIXTH NAME DAY FROM HIS FATHER LEOPOLD
MOZART, SALZBURG 31 OCT. 1762."

compositions of the young Mozart had already appeared—an
andante and an allegro (which must be counted before the minuet
and trio that later came to receive the first number in the catalog
of Mozart's works, the *Köchel Verzeichnis*)—to which his father
appended the note: "Wolfgang's compositions in the first 3 months
after his fifth birthday."

These initial efforts at the piano and composing were undoubtedly more a matter of play than instruction. Moreover,
Leopold's pedagogy was motivated not simply by a sense of duty
to the task, but by infinite love, one could almost say idolization,
of his son. This explains the boundless devotion of the child in
return. Everyone knows of young Wolfgang's saying: "Right after
God comes Papa." A strict educational regimen probably would
have been unthinkable for such an impressionable and extremely
sensitive child, as suggested by contemporary remarks; Schachtner,
the family friend, said in his recollections of Wolfgang's
childhood in a letter of 24 April 1792 in response to questions
from Mozart's sister:

...regarding your first question: what were the favorite activities of your late brother in his child- hood besides his involvement with music? There is really nothing more to say in reply to this ques- tion, for once he had begun to devote himself to music, all his interests for other matters were as good as dead....Before the time when he began with music, however, he was so receptive for every sort of child's play spiced with a little joke that, while playing, he could forget eating and drinking and everything else....Almost to the time he was ten years old, he had an insurmountable fear of the trumpet...you had only to show him a trumpet and it was as though you had pointed a loaded pistol at his heart. Papa [Mozart] wanted to rid him of such a childish fear and once told me to blow the horn directly at him despite his pro- tests, but my God! I should not have let myself be talked into doing it. Hardly had Wolfgang heard the piercing sound, than he turned pale and be- gan to sink to the ground, and if I had kept it up, he would surely have had a spasm....

Mozart's father has frequently been accused of subjecting his child to serious physical and mental strains, with concert travels throughout Europe that often lasted for years at a time. But it was precisely these travels to the important cultural centers of the day, with the education they provided, that took the lad from the small, culturally backward town of Salzburg, with its petit bourgeois, narrow-minded circumstances, and made a European out of him.

Mozart did, indeed, pay a price for this education, for during these travels he contracted several illnesses that were significant in later years. Because a thorough inquiry into the history of Mozart's illnesses is essential in addressing his fatal illness, infor- mation from the available documents is presented in some detail to provide a preliminary medical history. For this study, the many letters of Leopold Mozart are of the greatest importance.

Toward the end of Mozart's sixth year, he suffered four closely connected illnesses. Leopold took Nannerl and Wolfgang to

Munich in January 1762, where the two young prodigies performed for the Elector of Bavaria Maximilian III Joseph. Then on
18 September the family set out for Vienna, where they were to
remain until 5 January 1763. The trip took them first to Passau
and then, on 26 September, by ship on the Danube River to Linz.
They resumed their trip down the Danube on 4 October. It was
during this leg of the journey that Wolfgang came down with
catarrh, that is, inflammation of the mucous membranes. As
Leopold reported to his friend Lorenz Hagenauer in Salzburg:
"...It constantly rained and was very windy during the trip. In
Linz, Wolfgang had catarrh and, despite all the confusion, the
getting up early and the irregular eating and drinking, the wind
and the rain, he is—thank God—still fit." But Wolfgang's catarrh
was not to be the end of it.

Upon the family's arrival in Vienna on 6 October 1762, a
series of invitations to homes of the nobility arrived in short order
and both Wolfgang and his sister were called upon to play concerts. One of the invitations was from Count Thomas Collalto,
whose palais still stands in Vienna at Am Hof 13. By 13 October,
the family was being received in the imperial residence at Schloss
Schönbrunn by Empress Maria Theresa and Emperor Francis I,
with the composer Wagenseil also present. On 21 October, when
they had been invited once again to Schloss Schönbrunn, Wolfgang came down with a more serious illness. Leopold wrote
about it to Lorenz Hagenauer on 30 October:

> ...How fickle fortune is! I had begun to suspect
> we had been too happy for 14 days in a row.
> Now God has sent us a small cross to bear, and
> we must thank His infinite Grace for the way things
> have turned out. On the 21st at seven in the
> evening, we were again at Her Majesty's, but even
> then our Wolfgang was not feeling as well as usual
> and before we went there and later as he was
> going to bed, he complained about his behind and
> his legs. Once he was in bed, I examined the
> places where he said it hurt and found a number
> of spots the size of a coin that were very red and
> somewhat puffy; when they were touched, it hurt

him. But they were only on his two shins, on both elbows, and a couple on his rump, in other words, very few. He had a fever and we gave him black powder and margrave powder [mixtures of plant and animal substances, some of them quite bizarre]. He was restless in his sleep. The following Friday, we repeated the powders in the morning and at night and found that the spots had grown; that is, they were larger, but not more numerous. We had to send messages to all the nobility by whom we had already been engaged for the next 8 days and, from day to day, cancel out. We continued to administer the margrave powder and on Sunday he began to sweat, something we had been hoping for because up to then his fever had been rather dry.

I ran into the doctor of Countess von Zinzendorf (who happened to be away) and told him the details. He came with me right away. He kindly agreed with what we had done. He said it was a sort of scarlet fever rash. He prescribed the following mixture [ingredients listed]. Then nothing but soups and gruels, as we had been doing; from time to time, some strained barley gruel, or coltsfoot tea with a little milk in it; before going to bed, we gave him a little glass of milk with ground melon seeds and a pinch of poppy seed. Praise God, he is feeling so good now that we hope he will be able to get out of bed in a couple days, if not tomorrow on his name day, and be up for the first time. Along with all this, he has also been getting a molar tooth which has caused his left cheek to swell. The nobles here have not only been so kind as to send around every day to inquire after the lad's condition but they have even eagerly discussed the matter with our doctor, with the result that Doctor Bernhard...couldn't be more concerned than he obviously is. In the meantime, this business has cost me, at a minimum, 50 ducats. Still, I am eternally thankful to God that it has turned out as it has; for these scarlet fever spots which are a prevalent sickness among children here are dangerous; and I hope that Wolfgang has now become acclimated, for it was only the change of air that was the chief cause of it.

For the physician, these passages from the letters are invaluable for undertaking a posthumous diagnosis, however wordy and drawn out they may be in places. In this letter, Leopold provides the classical description of erythema nodosum, a rheumatic nodular eruption. The doctor in attendance, Dr. Bernhard, mistakenly took it to be a kind of scarlet fever rash. This erroneous diagnosis is pardonable, because erythema nodosum was not clinically described until forty-six years later. As Leopold points out in his letter, the nodular eruption, construed as being "spots of scarlet fever," was a dangerous, common disease among children in Vienna. When followed by tuberculosis, it could take a very serious course, with potentially fatal results. Even today it is frequently associated with primary tuberculosis. For Wolfgang Mozart, we can exclude the diagnosis of primary tuberculosis because he was able to go out on 4 November, two weeks after his sickness, and on the following day he played at Dr. Bernhard's to express thanks for his treatment. However, Leopold had no choice but to keep his son away from the homes of the nobility for some time, since the spots were regarded as infectious: "...for here the aristocrats are frightened of pockmarks and all sorts of rash, with the result that the lad's illness has set us back fully 4 weeks," as Leopold wrote to Hagenauer on 24 November 1762.

With Wolfgang, the erythema nodosum was certainly rheumatic in nature and probably was caused by the earlier streptococcal infection in Linz, one that reappeared in a lighter form on 19 November. This conclusion is supported by the fact that, shortly before the return trip to Salzburg, Wolfgang fell ill again of something we now can say was acute rheumatoid arthritis, as described in a much later letter written by Leopold on 15 November 1766: "...and that [the illness of four years before] finally went down into his legs where he complained of pains." As a precaution, the concerned father had written his landlord on 29 December 1762, some days before the trip back to Salzburg, requesting him "to heat the room a couple of days" before they got there.

On 9 June 1763, the Mozart family, accompanied by a servant, boarded a carriage in Salzburg and set off on their grand tour of Europe. They would not return to Salzburg for more than three years. Their first major destination was Paris, where they arrived in the afternoon of 18 November. They had presented concerts in many German cities along the way, and according to contemporary reports and newspaper accounts, the concerts had been received with great enthusiasm. At a concert in Frankfurt on 18 August, Johann Wolfgang Goethe, who was then fourteen years old, was in the audience. As we learn from a letter he wrote to J. P. Eckermann on 3 February 1830: "I saw him when he was a seven-year-old boy and gave a concert as he was passing through. I was about 14 years old at the time and I can still remember quite well the little man with his sword and his done-up hair."

From Leopold Mozart's very informative travel diary, as well as his numerous letters to the Hagenauer family, we learn that Wolfgang suffered an upper respiratory infection, apparently caused by bad weather during a stay in Koblenz am Rhein in September. Leopold reported in a letter on 26 September 1763: "...One of the reasons why I didn't leave Koblenz right away on the 19th or 20th was because Wolfgang had sniffles or a cold that then turned into a regular catarrh the evening of the 22d and in the night." For the rest of his life, Mozart suffered relatively often from such upper respiratory infections, the more serious occasions probably having been caused by tonsillitis.

After the Mozarts' arrival in Paris, we hear nothing of illness or indispositions for some time. On New Year's Day 1764, they were honored to be invited to join King Louis XV and his Queen Maria at the royal table in Versailles. The two children received a variety of gifts after Wolfgang had performed on the organ in the royal chapel. Only the Marquise de Pompadour refused to have anything to do with them. The Mozarts' concerts at court and in the residences of the aristocracy were so successful that the family extended its stay in Paris to five months. But in February 1764,

Wolfgang fell ill once again, this time seriously, as Leopold's letter to Hagenauer on 22 February describes:

> ...Soon thereafter something quite abrupt and un-
> expected caused me some embarrassment. My
> little Wolfgang suddenly suffered a sore throat and
> catarrh that he first noticed early on the 16th and
> that night had such an obstruction in his throat he
> was in danger of choking, only the mucus which
> all at once was loose and which he couldn't bring
> up went down into his stomach. I quickly took
> him out of bed and went back and forth in the
> room with him. His fever was quite astonishing
> and I brought it down slowly with pulvis
> antispasmodicus Hallensis [a preparation appar-
> ently containing saltpeter, potassium sulphate, and
> cinnabar], and God be thanked, four days later, he
> got out of bed and now is feeling better. Just to
> be sure, I wrote to our friend the German doctor
> Herrnschwand, who is physician to the Swiss
> guards. But he did not find it necessary to come
> more than twice. Then I gave him a little aqua
> laxativa Viennensis [a liquid prepared from herbs
> and berries] as a laxative; and now he is fine, thank
> God.

From Leopold's description, a diagnosis of tonsillitis (streptococcal angina) is readily apparent. Unaware of the possible consequences of doing so, Leopold made the child get up and be active again after only four days. And in fact this episode of angina may have had an aftereffect, for Wolfgang experienced similar symptoms only a few months later.

In the same letter, Leopold Mozart gave his opinion of the method of smallpox vaccination that had recently become popu-lar, a method that, in contrast to the cowpox vaccination devel-oped later by Edward Jenner, was still fairly dangerous. His comment: "...do you know what the people here are constantly after? They want to talk me into letting my lad be stuffed with smallpox. So far as I'm concerned, I will leave him to God's mercy. It is up to His holy mercy whether He who put this miracle of nature on the earth wants to keep him here or take him to Himself."

On 10 April 1764, the Mozart family finally took their leave of Paris and proceeded by way of Calais (where they had left their carriage) to London, arriving there on 23 April. A letter of 25 April, the first after their arrival, begins with an account of their safe crossing of the English Channel: "We have, thank God, made it safely over the Maxglan brook [a small stream on the outskirts of Salzburg; Leopold jokingly refers to it as the English Channel] but not without making a generous contribution of vomit, which affected me most of all." Only two days later, on 27 April, they were received by King George III and Queen Sophie Charlotte, and on 19 May a small concert took place at court, which Leopold reported in rhapsodic language to his landlord in Salzburg on 28 May. He summed up young Wolfgang's progress by saying: "...In a word, what he knew when we left Salzburg is but a shadow compared to what he knows now. It transcends all powers of imagination." He did not mention in this letter that Wolfgang had been ill on 20 May, apparently with tonsillitis. This indisposition lasted ten days and was why Wolfgang could not appear before the English public in a concert that had been announced for 22 May 1764. Then his appearance at a concert at the Spring Garden House was announced in the *Public Advertiser* on 31 May and it took place on 5 June. The tonsillitis had abated and again was not taken very seriously. We still cannot say today to what degree the physical well-being of the lad was affected by the repeated throat infections and anginas; the likely aftereffects cannot have been severe, however, or they would hardly have escaped his father's careful attention.

A few years ago a small painting, a haunting and ethereal portrait of a boy of seven or eight, was discovered in Rome. If it is in fact a portrait of Mozart as a child, one can read in it traces of past illnesses. The boy is frail and sensitive, with a searching look of sorrow out of large eyes set in a sickly countenance. Experts believe it may be the first childhood portrait of Mozart and was probably painted by Johann Zoffany, a painter born in Frankfurt but residing primarily in England. The same artist painted

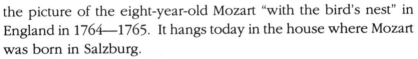

*MOZART WITH THE BIRD'S NEST,*
A PORTRAIT PAINTED IN LONDON
IN 1764—1765 BY JOHANN
JOSEPH ZOFFANY (OR ZAUFFELY)

the picture of the eight-year-old Mozart "with the bird's nest" in England in 1764—1765. It hangs today in the house where Mozart was born in Salzburg.

In Leopold's numerous letters for more than a year, no further illnesses in the Mozart family are mentioned until the autumn of 1765. In addition to his appearances at concerts, Wolfgang was beginning to develop creatively and show evidence of his extraordinary inventiveness. For example, in March 1764, during his stay in Paris, he wrote two sonatas for piano and violin, KV 6 and 7, which he dedicated to Princess Victoire, the second daughter of the King of France. One is amazed by the unusual maturity of the slow movement written by the eight-year-old, which called forth the proud remark by Leopold to his friend Hagenauer: "An andante is included that is exceptionally tasteful." We also find astonishing examples of his unusual gifts in his *London Music Book* and in the six sonatas for piano and violin or flute (KV 10-15) that he dedicated to the Queen of England. After the Queen's sonatas had been performed in Holland, a review appeared in a Dutch newspaper with the following comments:

> ...A composer and musician of some 8 years in age is here who is really a miracle as never before....He plays the cembalo [harpsichord] with unbelievable precision, not only the concertos and sonatas of various masters but also the most difficult improvisations, worthy of being performed by the greatest virtuoso, and all by heart....And if you ask him to play the organ, then he will play a lovely fugue or one of the most difficult compositions....He writes his own compositions, by the way, without the assistance of a cembalo....The whole world must agree that he is an appearance without precedence....

The visit to England lasted longer than expected because Leopold suffered a serious illness in the summer of 1764.  The financial situation of the Mozart family slowly began to worsen and, in addition, the court no longer showed much interest in the young musical wonders.  The family left London on 24 July 1765 for the trip back to Paris, where they had stored some of their luggage.  It was during this trip that Wolfgang was ill again, as Leopold wrote to Salzburg from The Hague on 19 September 1765: "...In Lille, Wolfgang was again overcome by a very strong catarrh and when he was somewhat better after a couple weeks, then it was my turn...."  This sickness apparently was a severe angina, for the Mozart family was forced to remain in Lille for four long weeks.  Finally on 4 September they were able to continue their journey, going by way of Ghent and Antwerp—where they had to leave their carriage—and from Rotterdam by boat to The Hague, arriving there on 11 September.

The very next day, matters took a serious turn.  On 12 September, Nannerl came down with unfamiliar symptoms, initially thought to be catarrh.  After seeming to get better, she developed a high fever on 26 September.  Leopold thought she had pharyngitis (inflammation of the pharynx), but the doctor attending Nannerl, Dr. Heymans, was of the view "that the catarrh must have gone to her lungs and caused an abscess there."  She was bled on 28 September.  Her pulse then improved but the fever continued unchanged and her condition slowly worsened.  She became

delirious and the doctor abandoned all hope for her.    On
21 October, Nannerl was administered the last sacrament while
the unsuspecting Wolfgang "...busied himself with his music in
the next room."

At this desperate point, the Princess von Weilburg offered her
personal physician, Professor Thomas Schwenke, as consultant.
Dr. Schwenke was skeptical of his predecessor's diagnosis and
"demonstrated quite clearly that it wasn't anything except an exceptionally heavy secretional obstruction in the breast." Because
Leopold's descriptions are rather vague, we must assume that the
professor had found a red skin rash along with pneumonia. These
symptoms are all compatible with typhoid fever:  the gradual
onset of the illness with indefinite premonitory symptoms, the
high fever that apparently persisted for several weeks and the
accompanying mental disorientation, the attendant bronchitis, the
presumed presence of roseola-like red spots on the skin and the
slow subsidence of the fever.  Typhoid fever occurred frequently,
indeed it was often endemic, in the large cities of the time with
their deficient hygienic conditions.

By the middle of November, Nannerl had gradually recovered.  But scarcely was she back on her feet when her brother fell
ill.  Writing to Lorenz Hagenauer on 12 December 1765, Leopold
said:

> ...My daughter had hardly been out of bed 8 days
> and learned to walk across the floor of the room
> all by herself when an indisposition overcame
> Wolfgang on 15 November, one that reduced him
> to such a pitiable state for 4 weeks that he was not
> only absolutely unrecognizable but also nothing
> but skin and bones, and now for the last 5 days is
> being lifted out of bed every day to sit in a chair;
> however, yesterday and again today we have
> walked him around the room a couple times so
> that little by little he learns to move his legs again
> and to stand up all by himself.  You would like to
> know what it was?  God only knows.  I am so
> weary of writing about illnesses to you.  It started
> with a fever.  We didn't have any more black

powder so we gave him as usual some margrave
powder three times in a row, but it had no effect.
It seemed a kind of acute fever, and so it was...on
the 30th he was very critical, but on 1 December it
was better and then he lay 8 days without saying a
word...after he had done little for 8 days except
sleep without speaking, then his strength began
finally to return, whereupon he talked day and
night without our knowing what it was. Now however, thank God, things are better. While he was
sick, we had constantly to take care of his tongue
which was dry as wood and so coated that we
had to clean it often; three times his lips shed their
skin, which was hard and black.

Not until the middle of January 1766 did Wolfgang recover
enough to walk without being helped. From Leopold's description of the whole course of the illness, there can be no doubt that
both Wolfgang and his sister had typhoid fever. We are no longer
familiar with untreated cases of typhoid fever today, but a medical textbook on infectious illnesses by Dr. G. Jochmann that appeared in 1914, before the First World War, describes the course
of such a disease:

The clinical picture of the first week of typhoid is
dominated by signs of feverish illness...the feeling of being sick intensifies, lassitude and fatigue
increase by the day, so that the patient must take
to his bed....The tongue is coated and dry....As a
rule, the bowels move normally; diarrhea seldom
occurs in the first week of the illness...the patient
becomes more and more apathetic, indeed, in
severe cases disorientation and loss of consciousness can occur toward the end of the first week....
The disease reaches its zenith with the beginning
of the second week. A fever of around 40 degrees
[104°F.] persists. The mind is strongly affected,
and the characteristic *Status typhosus*, that is, the
clouding of the senses which gave the disease its

name, takes over.  By day the patient lies there, apathetic and indifferent, and does not show the least interest in his surroundings....If one asks him questions, he gives curt replies or simply turns away.  He sleeps a great deal....The night is usually restless and often brings delirium.  The patient mumbles incoherent things to himself...in the most severe cases, the patients lie there deeply unconscious....Now diarrhea may take the place of constipation....In this connection it should be noted, however, that more frequently, even at this stage and throughout the whole course of the ty-phoid, firm bowels predominate and there may even be persistent constipation.  Diagnostically important is the roseola which appears in the form of small, round, pale red spots on the stomach and the lower chest....The tongue is dry and cov-ered with a brown crust.  The bronchitis in the lungs becomes stronger...in the third week, the patient is threatened with the most diverse perils in the form of inflammations of the lungs and many other disorders....By the end of the third week, the fever begins to drop....For several weeks more, the patient remains very weak....In cases where children are affected...toxic symptoms of the brain, hypersomnia, stupefaction, and delirium come very much to the fore.

This description of typhoid fever, from a time when no effec-tive method of treatment was yet known, corresponds so well to Leopold Mozart's account that one really wonders why doctors today would seriously question whether Wolfgang was ever sick with typhoid.  Some authors, such as Katner and Fluker, came to the judgment years ago that both children had typhus abdominalis, that is, typhoid fever.  According to Leopold's detailed account, his daughter first had the general symptoms of catarrh with a suggestion of pharyngitis.  In the course of the next two weeks, the high-fever stage was reached and the consulting physician made the diagnosis that, in addition to signs of bronchitis, all the symptoms of pneumonia were present (to the extent they could be objectively evaluated at the time), indicating the diagnosis of typhoid fever. Today we know that with many serious infectious diseases, and particularly with typhoid fever, bacterial pneumonia can develop. In his interpretation, Franken casts doubt on a diagnosis of typhoid fever and is prepared to accept only that Nannerl had pneumonia and suggests that this was the case for Wolfgang as well. His reasoning turns on the observation that Leopold never mentioned "the onset of diarrhea which is the essential characteristic" of typhoid fever. However, Franken's interpretation overlooks the fact that, in half the cases of typhoid fever, diarrhea does not occur but rather symptoms of constipation may be observed.*

It is characteristic of the creative impulse in the young Wolfgang Mozart—who as a child found music his favorite form of "play"—that even while convalescing from this serious, debilitating, and life-threatening infectious disease, he composed his Symphony in B-flat Major (KV 22). On 22 January 1766, it was performed under his leadership in Amsterdam, where the family had moved some days before. The family, again traveling in their own carriage, finally reached Paris by way of Brussels on 10 May.

On the trip home, which led through the Burgundy region of France, Switzerland, and Bavaria, Wolfgang again fell ill. Writing from Munich on 15 November 1766 to the Hagenauer family in Salzburg, Leopold said: "…I seriously doubt whether we will also go by way of Regensburg because we must first wait for Wolfgang's full recovery and so we don't know how soon we can get moving from here. In the meantime, the weather is growing worse and worse." Then, before continuing with his report on their current situation, he reminded the Hagenauers of its similarity to the circumstances when Wolfgang was ill in December 1762 shortly before returning home from Vienna:

> …It's the same all over again. He can't stand on his legs, can't move a toe or a knee; no one can come near him and for four nights he couldn't sleep. That took a lot out of him, and made us worry all the more because he was constantly hot and feverish, especially in the nights. Today things

are noticeably better: but another week will surely
go by before he is back in shape.

A doctor today could hardly have written a better description
of an acute attack of rheumatic fever. It is hard to understand,
then, why Franken does not accept this second episode of the
illness, commenting that a severe attack of rheumatic fever cannot spontaneously disappear in four days. Apart from the fact
that the acute symptoms of the disease lasted ten days, from 12 to
21 November, one must of course differentiate between rheumatic fever and an acute episode of rheumatoid arthritis.

For us today, it is incomprehensible that Wolfgang—who had
only just recovered from the effects of this illness, and the fever
and pain that go with it—could have been made to appear before
the impatient elector Maximilian III Joseph at his court in Munich
and play the piano on 22 November, one day after leaving his
sickbed.

On 29 November 1766—after being gone more than three
years—the Mozart family arrived back in Salzburg. The Salzburg
cleric Beda Hübner noted in his diary on this date: "I cannot go
on without mentioning that today the famous Herr Leopold Mozart,
the local vice Kapellmeister, arrived back with his wife and two
children, a lad of 10 years and a daughter of 13, to the relief and
joy of the entire city....The boy Wolfgang did not grow much on
the trip but Nannerl is rather tall and is almost marriageable. People
are emphatic in saying moreover that this family of Mozarts will
not remain here very long but will soon be traveling through all
of Scandinavia and Russia and perhaps even to China."

And indeed, the Mozart family set off on their next trip on
11 September 1767, not to China but once again to Vienna. The
trip was not destined to be a lucky one. Leopold Mozart hoped
for concert engagements during the celebrations in honor of the
marriage of King Ferdinand IV of Naples and Sicily to the
seventeen-year-old Archduchess Maria Josepha. These hopes were
abruptly dashed by the death of the young bride. She died of
smallpox on 15 October and with her died the city's mood for
celebrating. The Mozart family itself underwent a severe trial.
Leopold had taken quarters in the house of Gottfried Johann
Schmalecker without knowing that Schmalecker's son had fallen

ill with the smallpox, then raging in Vienna, and had in fact exposed his family to the infection. As soon as Leopold learned of the son's illness, the family fled the city as fast as they could, first to Brünn and then to Olmütz. But it was too late. On 26 October, Wolfgang came down with smallpox. On 10 November, Leopold made a detailed report to Hagenauer:

> Around 10 o'clock, Wolfgang complained about his eyes, but it struck me that his head was warm and his cheeks were hot and very red while his hands, on the contrary, were cold as ice, his pulse wasn't right either. So we gave him some black powder and put him to bed. He had a rather restless night and the hot, dry fever continued through the morning. They gave us two better rooms in the inn, so we wrapped Wolfgang up in furs and hiked over into the other room with him. The fever went up and we dosed him with some margrave powder and some black powder. Toward evening he began to hallucinate, and so it went all night and into the morning of the 28th. After church, I sought out His Excellency Count Podstatsky who received me very courteously; and when I told him that my young son had fallen sick and suspected he could be getting smallpox, he told me he wanted us to come to him, for he didn't fear smallpox at all. Then he called right away for his Hausmeister and ordered him to get two rooms ready, while at the same time sending word to his doctor [a Dr. Joseph Wolff] that he should visit us at the inn. Now it was only a question whether it would be possible to help the child. The doctor said yes! because there was still no rash present and we simply could not yet tell if it was smallpox. At 4 in the afternoon, Wolfgang was packed into chamois skins and furs and carried to the wagon and I traveled with him to the quarters in the cathedral. On the 29th, we saw some small red spots but we were all still uncertain whether it

was smallpox because he no longer felt very sick
and he was taking a little powder only every six
hours. Then on the 30th and 31st (his name day),
out came the smallpox in full force....As soon as
the smallpox emerged, all the fever disappeared,
and thank God! he was feeling better and better.
He was really full of smallpox and, because he
was so incredibly swollen and had such a big nose,
when he saw himself in the mirror, he said: now
I look just like Herr Mayr (he meant Herr Mayr the
musician). Since yesterday, the smallpox have been
coming off here and there, and all the swelling
has been gone for 2 days now.

A short while later Nannerl too came down with smallpox.
Like Wolfgang, she had a relatively light case, as we learn from
Leopold's letter of 29 November: "She was so lucky with smallpox that with her you wouldn't notice it at all, but with Wolfgang
a little." It was great good fortune that the disease took such a
light form in the two children, for in a letter to Hagenauer written
on 7 October prior to their illness, Leopold had spoken with grave
concern of the epidemic then raging with rising intensity in Vienna:
"In Vienna, no one is talking about anything except smallpox.
For every 10 children in the death register, 9 of them died from
smallpox."

By 10 November, Wolfgang had largely recovered his health,
thanks to the attentive care of a young curate at the church and
the medical treatment of Dr. Joseph Wolff. Leopold and the family stayed on in Olmütz until Christmas and thereafter spent a few
days in Brünn. On 10 January 1768 they were once more in
Vienna and a short time later, on 19 January, they were received
by Empress Maria Theresa and her son Joseph II, who had become the new emperor in 1765. Joseph II expressed the wish
that Wolfgang write an Italian opera for Vienna. In the short
period of time from April to June, the twelve-year-old boy composed the opera *La finta semplice* (*The Make-Believe Simpleton*,
KV 51). Presentation of the opera was frustrated, however, by the
new and unscrupulous director of the Burgtheater and the
Kärntnertortheater, Giuseppe Affligio (who ultimately ended up

as a prisoner in Leghorn, Italy). Later, in the autumn of the same year, Wolfgang's one-act comic opera *Bastien und Bastienne* (KV 50) was performed for the first time in the garden theater of the home of the popular physician and pioneer psychotherapist, Dr. Anton Mesmer, in Vienna. Mozart would later create an enduring memorial to this art-loving doctor in the figure of the old philosopher, Don Alfonso, in his opera *Così fan tutte*.

On 5 January 1769, the Mozart family was back in Salzburg. In the same year, on 13 December, father Leopold and son Wolfgang were on their way to Italy, this time just the two of them. The father evidently had two objectives in mind. In addition to using the trip to further Wolfgang's musical education (by acquainting him with the different styles of Italian music), Leopold wanted to use the occasion to show off the boy, now thirteen years old and entering puberty, as a Wunderkind. The Prince-Archbishop in Salzburg, Sigismund Schrattenbach, had lent his support to this journey by bestowing the title of third Konzertmeister of the court orchestra on Wolfgang and giving him six hundred gulden "for the travels in Italy" on 27 November.

It was winter as the trip began and bitter cold, which did not make traveling in a coach exactly pleasant. In a letter of 11 January 1770, after they had reached Mantua, Leopold told his wife in Salzburg: "We are well, thank God! Wolfgang looks like he's been on maneuvers in the field, that is, a little reddish brown, especially around the nose and mouth, from the cold air and the chimney fires. Just as His Majesty the Emperor looks, for example. My beauty, on the other hand, has suffered hardly at all up to now...." On 26 January, Leopold added toward the end of a detailed account of their trip thus far: "I wrote you earlier that Wolfgang had gotten chapped hands and a red face from the cold and the fires, well, now everything is all better. In Mantua, Madame Sartoretti gave him a salve to smear on his hands at night and in 3 days it was better. Now he looks like his old self. We have been, thank God, in good health and the change of air only caused Wolfgang some sniffles which are also long over." Again on 3 February, Leopold emphasized in a letter he wrote to Salzburg that father and son were both fine and "...our hands, especially those of Wolfgang, are completely well again."

Dr. Aloys Greither interprets the "Italian complexion" that Nannerl claims to have observed on her brother after his return from this first journey to Italy as the coloration typical for a person suffering from a chronic kidney disease. But the presumption that Mozart in fact endured inflammation of the kidneys (nephritis) in Italy, which later developed into chronic kidney disease and even led ultimately to an atrophic kidney, is completely unfounded. An attack of acute nephritis has nothing to do with the coloration associated with chronic kidney disease. Moreover, nephritis would have produced such typical symptoms as swelling of the eyelids and edema of the face and the backs of the hands, which surely would not have escaped the notice of the alert and observant father with his passion for playing doctor. In short, the changes mentioned in Leopold's meticulous travel reports undoubtedly should be attributed to a light case of frostbite and possibly somewhat later to the intensity of the southern Italian sun during the summer months; almost certainly they had nothing to do with kidney disease.

In general, father and son stayed well. During the trip through wind and rain, over the rugged Apennine mountains from Bologna to Florence, Wolfgang suffered a headcold, for which he had to be treated on 31 March. But we read in a postscript he added to his father's letter on 14 April: "I, along with my miserable pen, am well, thank God and praise Him, and I kiss Mama and Nannerl a thousand times, or 1,000 if you will." In a letter on 17 November 1770, Leopold mentions that Wolfgang "has had his usual abscessed tooth with a little swelling on one side of his face...." There were no other indications of illnesses during the entire trip. When Wolfgang says to his sister in a letter from Bologna on 4 August, "Italy is a sleepy place, I'm always drowsy," he means nothing more than that the oppressive summer heat in that country affects and slows down all activities. It was just then that the fourteen-year-old composer was heavily engaged in working on his opera *Mitridate, rè di Ponto* (KV 87). Moreover, the travels themselves occasionally turned out to be rather arduous. Consider, for example, the notorious twenty-seven-hour forced march from Naples to Rome, which Leopold and Wolfgang reached the evening of 26 June.

Artistically, this first of three Italian journeys was very successful. Wolfgang received the Papal Order of the Golden Spur from Pope Clement XIV. Christoph Willibald Gluck and Karl Ditters von Dittersdorf had received this same award, but not in the same high degree, which only one other composer, Orlando di Lasso, had been awarded until then. The insignia of the papal order—the golden cross with a red band and the sword and spurs—were bestowed on Wolfgang in the Palazzo Quirinale through the influence of Cardinal Count Lazzaro Opizio Pallavicini. News of this event must have been a particularly pleasant surprise for Wolfgang's mother, because some weeks before she had been anxious lest Wolfgang might have incurred the Pope's disfavor. Wolfgang and his father had been at the Sistine Chapel on Wednesday of Holy Week and there had heard Gregorio Allegri's *Miserere*, which was forbidden to be copied and disseminated on pain of excommunication. After a single hearing, Wolfgang was able to write this polyphonic work from memory with practically no mistakes.

On 28 March 1771, Maundy Thursday of Holy Week, father and son were back home in Salzburg, after an absence of slightly more than fifteen months. Impressed and gratified by the success of the trip, on 19 July Leopold was already letting Count Gian Luca Pallavicini in Bologna know of an upcoming second journey to Italy. Leopold and Wolfgang set off on Tuesday, the 13th of August 1771, for a relatively short trip of four months. Although there are no reports from Leopold about illnesses during this period, Nannerl recalled—some fifty years later, in a letter written on 2 July 1819—that Wolfgang had been very sick while he was on this second Italian excursion. In this she was in error; she almost certainly meant after his return from Italy. In the course of commenting on early portraits of Mozart, she wrote that her brother fell seriously ill soon after completing his Symphony in A (KV 114) and had a sickly and yellow appearance during an apparently prolonged period of convalescence. But Mozart finished the symphony on 30 December 1771, having already returned to Salzburg on 15 December. We must assume, therefore, that Mozart was already home in Salzburg when he became ill, which would also explain why there are no reports of it from

Leopold. There is one from Nannerl, however, in a comment in the July 1819 letter: "After his return from the Italian journey...he was only 16 years old, but because he had just recovered from a very serious illness, his picture looks sickly and very yellow...."

Wolfgang's appearance was almost certainly due to infectious hepatitis, today referred to as acute hepatitis A, a viral disease which he probably contracted in Italy. The incubation period for infectious hepatitis is usually two to four weeks. Because inflammation of the liver caused by the hepatitis A virus rarely has secondary aftereffects, we cannot expect to find any more indications of the disease in later years. It is not possible that the yellow coloration was caused by inflammation of the kidneys. The sallow complexion of a person with chronic nephritis is never so pronounced that it makes the patient "completely unrecognizable." In contrast, jaundice due to inflammation of the liver can cause the facial characteristics to be temporarily greatly changed.

The third Italian trip lasted from October 1772 to March 1773 and, as far as we know, Wolfgang was healthy the whole time. "...We are well," he wrote on 7 November. His father, however, was plagued by a "cursed and confounded rheumatism," one that finally drove him to spend several weeks in bed. For this reason, they did not leave for home until the end of February and they finally arrived back in Salzburg on 13 March 1773. Wolfgang was never to tread on Italian soil again. Although numerous honors had been bestowed on him there, including membership in the famous Accademia Filarmonica of Bologna, and his artistic gifts were greatly enriched in the course of the three journeys, he was never able to obtain an appointment in Italy.

Four months later, on 14 July 1773, father and son were off again, this time to Vienna for a stay of only slightly more than two months. Leopold apparently hoped that after the successful presentation of Wolfgang's opera *Ascanio in Alba*, Empress Maria Theresa might grant his son a well-paid position at court. The opera had been premiered in Milan in October 1771 to celebrate the wedding of Archduke Ferdinand to Princess Maria Beatrice of Modena-Este. Leopold could not have known, of course, that, on 12 December 1771, Empress Maria Theresa had already strongly counseled her son Ferdinand against his proposal to offer

Wolfgang a position with his court in Milan. She urged him not to bother with such useless people, "des gens inutils," as she put it. It is not surprising, therefore, that apart from a ceremonial audience with the empress on 5 August 1773, the trip had little to show for itself. Leopold's disappointment emerges clearly from a report to Salzburg: "The empress was very gracious to us, but that is all there is to say."

The next indication of illness in Wolfgang comes many months later, on 17 December 1774. Since the beginning of December, Leopold and Wolfgang had been in Munich for the rehearsals of his opera, *La finta giardiniera* (*The Make-Believe Gardener*, KV 196), which had been commissioned for the carnival season in 1775. In a playful postscript to one of his father's letters to Salzburg, Wolfgang said, "I have a toothache. johannes chrisostomus Wolfgangus Amadeus Sigismundus Mozartus...." This could well have been a rather unpleasant experience, for on 28 December Leopold was writing: "Wolfgang had to keep to the house for 6 days with a swollen face, the cheeks were swollen inside and out, and the right eye too. For 2 days, he could only eat a bit of broth." But he must have recovered quickly, for the premiere of the opera took place on 13 January 1775, obviously with great success. On the next day, Wolfgang told his mother in a letter: "Praise God! My opera was performed yesterday, the 13th, and they liked it so much it is impossible for me to describe for Mama the noise they made...."

The illnesses Mozart experienced in his youth do not appear to have resulted in any lasting organic damage. All the documentation on the state of his health shows that, after he had recovered from the different illnesses, slight and serious, he felt well again. This is true especially for the period of the three trips to Italy, when Leopold reported more than once on young Wolfgang's robust constitution. Despite years of going from one inn to another, with accommodations that were mostly anything but hygienic and where bad drinking water and vermin were the causes of various infections, and despite changes of climate, strange foods, and the wearying strain of traveling long stretches in a horse-drawn coach, Mozart was not hindered in his musical creativity. Consequently, we need not discuss whether the young Mozart ever suffered from a rheumatic valvular heart defect or from chronic nephritis as a consequence of the sicknesses he endured.

## The First Emotional Conflicts

In the two and a half years that Mozart spent in Salzburg after his return there on 7 March 1775, he composed a hundred or so new works. In these same years, the relationship between the new Prince-Archbishop, Hieronymus Colloredo, and the Mozart family was becoming increasingly strained. When Leopold submitted his petition in August 1777 for leave to undertake a new trip on behalf of his son, the ecclesiastical prince turned it down and dismissed them both instead, noting in his own hand on the petition that "Father and son are hereby permitted, in keeping with the teachings of the gospel, to go seeking their fortune." But shortly afterward, the unexpected dismissal of Leopold was withdrawn and he was reinstated.

Sending Wolfgang off alone on the planned trip to Paris struck his father as entirely too risky given his son's inexperience and youthful naïveté. With great reluctance, Leopold therefore decided to send Wolfgang's mother along on the trip to keep an eye on him. At six o'clock in the morning of 23 September 1777, mother and son were on their way, headed first for Munich.

The journey began on a cheery note, with Wolfgang writing his father from Wasserburg on that very first day that he should "laugh and be gay, and constantly keep in mind, as we do, that the mufti HC [meaning the Archbishop, of course] is an ass, but God, He is compassionate, merciful, and full of love." Wolfgang's confrontation with the raw realities of life would come soon enough. His first soul-wrenching experience occurred when he went to a Munich hospital to visit the talented Czech composer Joseph Myslivecek, whom he had come to know in Bologna. A venereal disease had eaten away the unfortunate man's nose; Mozart was so horrified by Myslivecek's appearance that he could not eat and could hardly sleep that night.

On 11 October, the trip continued on to Augsburg, where Wolfgang made the acquaintance of his younger cousin ("Bäsle") Maria Anna Thekla Mozart, the daughter of his uncle. Maria Anna

was eighteen years old and proved ready to share Wolfgang's
bent for racy language, as is evident from letters he wrote to her
later—the "Bäsle letters" which have since evoked a wealth of
psychological speculation.

Then, on 26 October, mother and son left for Mannheim, arriving there four days later. At the court of Prince Elector Charles
Theodore, the arts were cultivated to an extent hardly matched
by any other principality. The famous Mannheim school of music
was personified especially by the conductor Christian Cannabich,
in whose house Wolfgang was most hospitably received and where
he made friends with members of the renowned orchestra. As a
gesture of gratitude for the kindnesses of the Cannabich family,
he composed a piano sonata (probably KV 309) for the Cannabich
daughter, Theresa Rosina. Unfortunately, here in Mannheim as
earlier in Munich, his hopes of securing an appointment with the
court went unfulfilled, and in December he could report to his
father in Salzburg only that "...at this point, there is nothing going
with the elector."

Wolfgang remained in Mannheim until 14 March 1778 and in
that time appears to have suffered but a single, fleeting illness. In
a letter to his father written 22 February, he said:

> I stayed in for the last 2 days and took anti-
> spasmodic powder and black powder and elder-
> berry tea to make me sweat because I had catarrh,
> a headcold, as well as head-ache, throat-ache, eye-
> ache, and ear-ache; now things are better again,
> thank God, and tomorrow being Sunday, I hope
> to get out again.

Leopold could not understand at first why Wolfgang stayed on
and on in Mannheim despite the evident lack of prospects there
and his repeated urgings to resume the journey to its real goal,
Paris. Only with the receipt of two letters, from 17 January 1778
and 4 February, was it finally clear to the dismayed father that his
son had fallen in love, with a young woman named Aloisia Weber.
The letters that flew back and forth between Salzburg and
Mannheim in these weeks show a growing estrangement between
father and son. This time, however, it took only the peremptory

demand by letter from the distant father— "Get yourself moving on to Paris! and that, in short order...." —to put an end to the son's delaying tactics. After a farewell concert for Wolfgang at the Cannabich home at which Aloisia sang the concert aria *Alcandro, lo confesso* (KV 294), composed by Mozart especially for her, he parted from his beloved, little suspecting that her love for him would already have died by the time he returned from Paris.

After a rather difficult trip, Wolfgang and his mother arrived in the French capital on 23 March 1778. The stay in Paris, which would last until 26 September, was not to be favored by fate. Wolfgang would have to pay for years of being shielded from life's difficulties and conflicts by a father who, however over-anxious he may have been, nevertheless was highly experienced in dealing with worldly affairs.

From the letters of Wolfgang's mother, we learn that she had little to do but sit all day in a dark, disagreeable room that looked out on a narrow inner court and spend her time waiting and waiting. Just after the two had finally moved into better quarters in the middle of June, she came down with a fatal illness. Fever, chills, pains in the head, hoarseness, and soon thereafter diarrhea set in rather suddenly. From the 19th of June on, she could not get out of bed, but still, because she mistrusted French medicine, she refused to allow a doctor to see her. On the 24th—by which time she had lost her hearing—she permitted Dr. Franz Joseph Haina, a German physician known to the Mozarts from the time of their earlier trip to Paris, to be called. Two days later, he informed Wolfgang of his mother's hopeless situation. In a state of feverish delirium, she lapsed into a coma and died at 10:30 on the evening of 3 July 1778.

Dr. Aloys Greither presumes that the death of Mozart's mother was caused by pneumonia; Dr. Peter J. Davies also raises such a possibility, but notes her prolonged coughing spell in December 1777 and therefore does not rule out possible tuberculosis. However, the symptoms Wolfgang reported in his letter of 3 July to his father, which indicate the illness began with fever, followed by diarrhea occurring a few days later, and then later still the onset of total deafness, clearly argue for a diagnosis of typhoid fever, a sickness the two children fortunately had survived at The Hague in 1765. In this connection, it is helpful to review excerpts from this well-known letter by the distraught Mozart. Although his mother had already died, he did not want to tell his father, lest the shock be too great, until he had prepared him for an eventual fatal outcome. He wrote:

> Monsieur mon très cher Père! I have very sad and unhappy news to give you....My dear mother is very ill—she let herself be bled, as she usually did, and it was very necessary too; and it did her good—but then some days afterward, she complained of chills, and of fever at the same time—had diarrhea and headache—at first we only used our home remedies, antispasmodic powder (we would have liked to use black powder too, but we didn't have any)...but because things were steadily worse—she could hardly talk, and lost her hearing so we had to shout, so Baron Grimm sent his doctor here—she is very weak, is feverish and delirious—they say I should have hope, but I don't have much—for a long time now, I have lived day and night between hope and despair—but I have given myself completely over to God's will...no matter how it turns out, I am consoled—for I know that God who ordains all for the best (however obscure it seems to us) will have it so; for I believe (and no one can talk me out of this) no doctor, no person, no misfortune or happenstance can either take a person's life or give it to him, but only God alone...therefore I do not say that my mother shall and must die, that all hope is lost— she can be healthy and active once again, but only if it is God's will—I like to console myself with such thoughts after having prayed to my God with all my heart for the health and life of my dear mother, because afterward I find myself feeling encouraged, calmer, and comforted—and you will easily appreciate how much I need that....

THE LAST LINES OF MOZART'S LETTER OF 3 JULY 1778, WRITTEN FROM PARIS TO THE ABBÉ JOSEPH BULLINGER IN SALZBURG, ASKING HIM TO PREPARE HIS FATHER FOR THE TRAGIC NEWS OF HIS MOTHER'S DEATH.

Wolfgang wrote another letter the very same night to the priest. and old family friend Joseph Bullinger, which shows the extent to which he feared his father's health might be endangered by word of his wife's death. Asking Father Bullinger to prepare his father gently for an imminent report of her death, he said:

> Dearest friend! for you alone. Mourn with me, my friend! this was the saddest day of my life—I am writing you at 2 in the morning—I must tell you that my mother, my beloved mother, is no more! God has called her to Himself—He wanted her with Him, it was clear—and I have accepted the will of God—He gave her to me, and He can take

her from me....All I ask now is your friendship in preparing my poor father, gently and carefully, for the sad news—I have just written him—but only that she is very sick—then I'll wait for his reply, so I know how to proceed.   May God give him strength and courage!...Therefore I beg you, dear friend, take care of my father, strengthen him so he will not take it too hard when he finally hears the worst.  And I send heartfelt wishes to my sister too—please go to them right away—don't tell them yet she is dead, but only get them ready for that— do as you will—whatever is necessary—do it so I can rest easy—and so that I do not have to fear yet another misfortune.  Take care of my dear father for me, and my dear sister too.  Please let me hear from you as soon as possible.

In the letters between father and son, there was often a sharp exchange of words about Wolfgang's relationship with Aloisia Weber, suggesting a certain growing estrangement, with an effort to escape from his father's authority.  In spite of this, there seems to have been no change in Wolfgang's filial affection and respect for his father.  Evidence of these feelings is found, for example, in a letter written by Johann Baptist Becke on 29 December 1778 to Leopold Mozart as Wolfgang stopped in Munich on his way home from Paris:  "...I have had the pleasure of seeing your most affectionate son almost all day long....He is burning with desire to embrace his dearest father...but he practically made me cry too: for an hour I could hardly bring him to dry his tears....I have never seen a child who harbored more affection and love in his bosom for his father than your son does."

Surely it is only through lack of psychological empathy that many Mozart biographers have found his correspondence with his father about his mother's fatal illness to be insensitive and unfeeling.  They allude to his inclusion in the letter of 3 July of reports about his professional successes in Paris, such as:  "...I had to write a symphony to open the concert series.  It was performed on Corpus Christi Day to great acclaim...it was exceptionally well received...."   One need not be a psychoanalyst to recognize that, in reporting on his successful artistic endeavors in Paris, Mozart was seeking to provide his father with an emotional counterweight to the tragic news of his mother's death.

The same applies to the steadfastness and resolution that Wolfgang urged on his father in his letter of 9 July 1778, when he recounted for him the true turn of events:

> Now I hope you are fortified and ready to hear a most sad and painful account...even as I was writing to you, however [a reference to his letter of 3 July], she was already at the gates of heaven....I hope you and my dear sister will forgive me this small and necessary deception...now, however, I hope you both have prepared yourselves to hear the worst and, after the grief and tears that are only natural and fully justified, to give yourselves over to God's will....I had to comfort myself so, and you must too, dear father and sister! Weep, weep till you can weep no more—and finally be consoled—in the thought that the Almighty God wanted it so....

With these words, Wolfgang tried, by referring to his own resigned and steadfast composure, to impart courage and strength to his father and his sister.

During the two weeks of his mother's fatal illness, Mozart became so emotionally spent that "when the threads of his mother's life snapped, his own capacity for suffering did too." This terrible event was a turning point in his life that left its imprint on his artistic creativity, and shaped his fearless and familiar relationship to death itself for the rest of his life. His despair over his mother's death virtually exploded in his Piano Sonata in A Minor (KV 310), Mozart's characteristic key for feelings of hopelessness, particularly in the first movement with its heart-rending expression of emotional anguish. Defiance and determination in the face of destiny give this sonata its special quality. The Sonata in E Minor for piano and violin (KV 304), composed at almost the same time, is its opposite. Here we find deep resignation and subdued grief.

The middle of the second movement of this sonata is like the prayer of one resigned to an irrevocable fate.

No matter how persuaded we may be personally of the connection of these two compositions to the deeply moving experience of the loss of his mother, Mozart himself left us no specific indication of any such association. Wolfgang Hildesheimer has credibly pointed out that it is almost impossible to probe what was going on in the depths of Mozart's soul or to draw conclusions from his music about his emotional state at the time of its composition.

On 26 September 1778, Mozart left Paris after a stay of six months, going by way of Mannheim and Munich (with a prolonged visit in each place), and picking up his "little cousin" (his "Bäsle") for the remainder of the trip home to Salzburg. The two of them arrived there on 15 January 1779. Added to the loss of his mother was Mozart's bitter disappointment in his beloved Aloisia Weber, who had in the meantime been taken on as an opera singer at the court theater in Munich. Having quickly achieved artistic success, the soprano no longer had any interest in an out-of-work musician named Wolfgang Mozart. And beyond the personal grief and disappointment was the fact that the professional accomplishments of the Paris trip had been far short of expectations. Nevertheless, Wolfgang returned from Paris to his father in Salzburg in good health, and his father meanwhile had been able—surely against Wolfgang's inner resistance—to arrange for his son to be reinstated, now as court organist with a fixed salary, in the service of the Prince-Archbishop.

For some time, we hear of no illnesses other than a headcold in November 1780. Contrary to Archbishop Colloredo's usual custom, Mozart was given leave, specifically from 5 November to 16 December, to go to Munich for the rehearsals of his opera *Idomeneo*, which had been commissioned by Prince Elector Charles Theodore for the upcoming carnival season. During his stay in Munich, Mozart made a short health report to his father on 22 November: "…a catarrh, which given this weather is going the rounds; I think and certainly hope it will pass soon, for those two horsemen of the light cavalry, snot and mucus, are going away little by little…." This catarrh may well have gone along with bronchitis that persisted for a while, for on 1 December he was writing to Salzburg:  "At this rehearsal my catarrh got a little worse...today I began to take some violet-syrup and a little almond oil, and I already feel better—and have again stayed inside the last 2 days."  Succeeding rehearsals passed without difficulties and on the 29th of January 1781, the first performance of *Idomeneo* took place with exceptional success.  But again, Mozart received no offer of a permanent appointment.

## The Final Break with Salzburg

While Mozart was working on *Idomeneo* in Munich, the Archbishop of Salzburg had gone to Vienna with his entire staff to be at the side of his sick father, Prince Rudolf Joseph Colloredo. Mozart had already far exceeded the 16 December deadline originally given him to remain in Munich and the archbishop ordered him to come immediately to Vienna.  Mozart left Munich on 12 March 1781 and was taking part in a concert in Vienna on the afternoon of his arrival on 16 March.  It was Mozart's hope, once in Vienna, to remind the emperor's court and the aristocracy of his importance as a musician, but the archbishop would not give him permission to present concerts on his own.  Nevertheless, he did succeed in establishing contact with prominent members of the city's music-loving society, and the enthusiastic reception that greeted him strengthened his conviction that Vienna was "the best place in the world" to pursue his musical career.

This belief is surely what led Mozart to procrastinate when the archbishop ordered him back to Salzburg on some inconsequential business.  His disobedience earned him a sharp rebuke from the archbishop.  And when, during a heated verbal exchange on this memorable occasion, his sovereign came forth with the threatening words, "...there is the door, see, I don't want anything more to do with such a miserable dolt..., " Mozart could no longer put up with such treatment.  He submitted his resignation to the archbishop's official, Count Karl Arco, on 10 May 1781. This stand could well have been encouraged by an awareness of the American Revolution that Mozart had gained during his months in Paris.

The day after his quarrel with the Archbishop, Mozart was still so shaken that he had to leave the opera that evening in the middle of the first act to go home and lie down. According to his own account, he was flushed and hot, shivering from limb to limb, and reeling down the street like a drunkard. Even on the next day, after drinking some tamarind wine, he stayed in bed until noon. At first, after hearing Wolfgang's account of the incident, his father may well have agreed fully with his decision, for on 10 August 1781 Leopold wrote the following in a letter from Salzburg to the publishing firm of Breitkopf & Son in Leipzig:

> ...Concerning my son, he is no longer in service here. He had been summoned by the Prince, who was then in Vienna while we were in Munich, to come to Vienna...Because His Grace the Prince treated my son quite extraordinarily badly while, on the contrary, all the higher nobles were particularly gracious to him, so they were easily able to persuade him to give up his archiepiscopal service with its miserable salary and to remain in Vienna....

As soon became apparent, however, Mozart's decision to remain in Vienna had been influenced also by his renewed acquaintance with the Weber family. When rumors reached Leopold in Salzburg that Wolfgang and Constanze Weber, Aloisia's younger sister, had formed a warm relationship—aided and abetted by Mother Weber—he remonstrated with his son and sought to talk him out of it.

With the great success of his opera *The Abduction from the Harem* (KV 384), first performed in Vienna on 16 July 1782, Mozart felt he could afford to marry. After numerous difficulties, the most emotionally burdensome being the intransigent opposition of his father, he and his beloved Constanze were finally married on 4 August 1782. In a letter of 7 August to his father, who had not been present for the wedding and thus withheld his paternal blessing on the union, Mozart wrote with joy and confidence, still hoping for reconciliation: "...once the knot was tied, both my wife and I began to cry; everyone, even the priest, was moved....I'll

bet you will share in my happiness when you get to know her!"
Leopold finally made the acquaintance of Wolfgang's wife Constanze a year later when the couple made a visit to Salzburg.

A mutual sensual attraction was a vital aspect of the relationship between Wolfgang and Constanze, which is apparent in many
of his letters to her, but we should not overlook the fact that an
emotional commitment growing out of his vast capacity for love
was at the center of their marriage. His love for Constanze, which
grew in intensity over the years, had its origins in feelings of deep
affection. Mozart often had difficulty composing when she was
not with him. His greatest enjoyment was in having her constantly near him; every separation, however short, was painful to
him.

This emotional commitment explains why Mozart never had
even the briefest love affair outside his marriage, despite the speculation we find in various accounts of his life. Even his affection
for Nancy Storace, the beautiful and celebrated soprano who was
the first Susanna in *The Marriage of Figaro*, for example, was as
pure and unsullied as his music. The concert aria he wrote for
her on her departure from Vienna, *Ch'io mi scordi di te?* (KV 505),
with its elaborate piano obbligato part written for Mozart himself,
is in its blending of two voices—Greither says—perhaps "the most
tender wooing by a love-smitten Mozart and, at the same time, its
renunciation."

Just how little we can rely on reports of love affairs ascribed
to Mozart in various writings, especially affairs with women who
were his piano students, is clear from the episode referred to in a
book by Carr. The author says that, of course, there is no certain
evidence that Mozart ever had an intimate love affair with any of
his piano students—with the sole exception of Josepha
Auernhammer, to whom he dedicated six sonatas for piano and
violin. Actually, the daughter of the Auernhammer family, who
were old acquaintances of the Mozart family, had apparently fallen
in love with Mozart, but the "fat Miss Daughter" of his generous
patrons received no affection in return. In a letter to his father in
the summer of 1781 in which he described Josepha as "dirty,
disgusting, and dreadful," Mozart mentioned the young lady's infatuation: "When I noticed it, for she began to take liberties with

me…I felt obliged…to tell her the truth as politely as I could.  But it didn't help, she only fell in love all the more….”  As it turned out, the chubby Viennese maiden continued to be a target for his jibes, but he was loyal to her nonetheless.  He dedicated the “Auernhammer sonatas” to her as a show of gratitude to the family that had done so much for him and which apparently would have been pleased to have him as a son-in-law.

After his marriage, happy and artistically successful times began for Wolfgang Mozart, times that soon brought the young family considerable affluence.  The tender affection which Mozart constantly showed his wife as proof of his love is reflected in some of his compositions.  Along with the slow movement from the Sonata in B-flat (KV 570) written for Constanze, one of his most ingratiating musical professions of love for her is found in the last movement of his String Quartet in D Minor (KV 421).  According to a later statement by Constanze, he composed it on the memorable night from the 16th to the 17th of June 1783 as she was giving birth to their first child.  The recently rediscovered travel diaries of Vincent and Mary Novello, who some forty years after Mozart's death had undertaken “a Mozart pilgrimage” and met with Constanze in Salzburg, report:  “She confirmed the truth…of his writing the Quartet in D Minor while she was in labor with their first child; several passages are indicative of her sufferings, especially the minuet (a part of which she sang to us)….”  Most of the works dedicated to Constanze were never completed, probably because they were written more with her musical interests in mind than with an intent ultimately to publish them.

Mozart mentions illness for the first time in his Vienna years in a reference to having had a seemingly severe case of flu toward the end of May 1783.  Writing to his father on 7 June, he makes the curt report:  “I am back on my feet once again, thank God!  Now my sickness has left me with catarrh as a souvenir; how nice of it!”  This illness was probably a viral infection of the upper respiratory tract, but one from which he recovered relatively quickly.  A much more severe illness struck him in August 1784.  He did not recover until the middle of September and was unable to attend his sister's wedding in St. Gilgen.  A medical reconstruction of this case is difficult because the letter to his father containing his detailed report on the sickness has been lost. The only medically informative document we have is Leopold's written report to his recently married daughter Nannerl in St. Gilgen; it is based on Mozart's letter, but includes too few details for a retrospective diagnostic assessment. However, because this case history has led to various speculations, the relevant passage from Leopold's letter of 14 September to Nannerl is of interest:

> My son in Vienna was very sick—while attending Paisiello's new opera he sweated through his clothes and had to go out into the cold to look for his servant to get his coat because in the meantime the order had been given that no servant would be allowed to enter the theater through the usual exits. As a result, not only he but lots of other people caught a rheumatic fever which, if one didn't do something right away, degenerated into putrid fever. He writes: 4 days in a row at the same time I have gotten painful colics that ended up every time in heavy vomiting; now have to be terribly careful. My doctor is Herr Sigmund Barisani who in the short time he is here was at my place almost every day; he is very well thought of here, is very capable too, and you will see that in no time at all he will go far.

In seeking to explain this sickness, we must not be misled by Leopold's term "rheumatic fever," an expression used, especially by the general public, for a vast range of sicknesses. It had nothing to do with a diagnosis of what we call rheumatic fever today. Dr. Shapiro's presumption that this illness was an acute attack of rheumatic fever must therefore be rejected as unfounded. The proponents of the thesis that Mozart died as the result of kidney failure caused by latent chronic nephritis are inclined to deduce an acute inflammation of the kidney and renal pelvis from the symptoms Leopold described, which they believe resulted in a pyelonephritic atrophic kidney, which possibly could have been triggered by renal colic.

According to a more recent interpretation by Dr. Davies, the sickness in late summer of 1784 could have been a renewed case of streptococcal tonsillitis that led to glomerulonephritis, that is, bilateral nephritis, in the context of Schönlein-Henoch disease. In the latter disease a hypersensitive reaction—frequently to a bacterial antigen—is set off in the blood vessels of the skin, or less often in the vessels of the mucous membranes, which first results in the appearance of small red patches with pinpoint hemorrhaging in the tissues under the skin. This cutaneous eruption is found chiefly on the extensor side of the arms and legs. In about half of the cases, mostly in children, painful swelling of the joints and colic-like abdominal pains also occur. Less frequently, blood in the urine as well as swelling in the face and on the hands and feet can be observed as evidence of an accompanying inflammation of the kidneys. Apart from the fact that the prospects for recovery from this illness are good and only very rarely does it progress to chronic nephritis, none of these symptoms whatsoever is mentioned in Leopold's report. The word "colics" in those days referred almost exclusively to attacks of spasmodic stomach pains. We can assume therefore that Mozart's illness was a gastrointestinal infection accompanied by fever and diarrhea with vomiting, something that even today shows up frequently as "summer diarrhea" or "abdominal flu." This conclusion is underscored by Leopold's note that "...not only he but lots of other people..." exhibited the same symptoms. Moreover, Mozart's words quoted by Leopold—"now [I] have to be terribly careful"—suggest that strict dietary rules were imposed by his attending physician, Dr. Barisani.

An infection by Campylobacter (bacteria implicated in, among other things, acute gastroenteritis) may have been involved, a sickness that begins with unusual catarrhal symptoms and temperatures as high as 40°C. (104°F.), leading typically to severe cramp-like abdominal pains. These pains can be so violent that even today we sometimes consider surgery to rule out other causes, such as appendicitis. Viral enteritis, brought about by the ECHOviruses, is a much less likely diagnosis than an infection caused by either Campylobacter or Yersinia. In the latter disease, diarrhea is prominent, which is not mentioned in Leopold's report, and colicky stomach pains are usually absent.

We can confidently assume that this sickness had no lasting effects. Though Mozart occasionally showed signs of exhaustion in 1784, we must keep in mind that within about two months' time, between the 9th of February and the 12th of April, he not only composed three of his piano concertos (KV 450, 451, and 453) and the Quintet in E-flat for piano and winds (KV 452), but he also appeared as a piano virtuoso in twenty-four concerts. He was moved to comment in a letter of 10 April 1784: "By the way, to tell the truth, I have lately grown tired of it [the piano quintet]—from playing it so often—and it is an honor for me that my audiences never tire of it."

In the four years that followed, Mozart's compositional creativity reached its peak. His father Leopold was obviously very proud of him. In spite of all their differences, the emotional alienation between father and son cannot have been so fundamental and far-reaching as some seek to portray it. One proof among many is Leopold's decision to leave Munich on Shrove Sunday, 6 February 1784, and set off for Vienna to pay a visit to his famous son. Once there, he could see that his daughter-in-law Constanze well knew how to run the household. He was also deeply impressed by the enthusiasm and regard people showed for his son. It was during this visit that Leopold heard Joseph Haydn make his famous statement: "I'll tell you honestly, your son is the greatest composer I know personally or by reputation." And the proud father was surely moved by Wolfgang's great successes in these weeks, with various opera performances and musical concerts. Even on 11 February, the very day he arrived in Vienna, Leopold had the opportunity to hear his son's latest piano concerto (Piano Concerto in D Minor, KV 466) with Wolfgang as soloist.

It was in these creative times that Mozart composed his opera *The Marriage of Figaro*, the work that once prompted Johannes Brahms to remark to his friend Dr. Billroth: "Each number in Mozart's Figaro is a miracle to me; I simply cannot conceive how someone can create something so perfect; it has never been done since, not even by Beethoven." But *The Marriage of Figaro* is not only a masterpiece of music: it is simultaneously a strong and highly topical political statement reflecting the domestic political program of Emperor Joseph II. With its call for the abolition of aristocratic privileges and equality for all citizens before the law, this work was right in line with the emperor's determination to hold up a mirror before the nobility. That is certainly why, despite its provocative content and the call for censorship arising from various aristocratic circles, Joseph II expressly ordered that the opera be presented. The first performance took place in the Vienna Hofburgtheater on 1 May 1786, but the opera was withdrawn from the program on 18 December after its ninth performance, apparently because members of the nobility felt themselves too severely criticized. The situation was different in Prague. Accompanied by Constanze, Mozart arrived there on 8 January 1787 and celebrated a triumphal reception of *Figaro*, leading Prague ultimately to become known as the "Mozartstadt"—"Mozart's city." In a letter to a friend in Vienna on 15 January, Mozart said: "Here no one talks about anything except—Figaro; nothing is played, tootled, sung, or whistled except—Figaro...certainly a great honor for me."

Mozart's health must have been excellent during this period, even though a recorded comment by Mozart to Count Paar in 1786 indicates that he was beset with "headaches and stomach cramps." These troubles probably passed quickly. Then, in 1787, some kind of sickness occurred but we have no details as to what it was or how long it lasted. We only know that again Dr. Barisani looked after Mozart. From an entry Dr. Barisani made in Mozart's guest book on 14 April, we can conclude that Mozart had been ill at some point in the middle of April 1787. In his entry, Dr. Barisani wrote in part:

> ...Do not forget your friend,
> who constantly would be remembered
> with pride and joy, that he
> served you twice as physician
> and saved you for the world's delight....

The illness, whatever it was, may have persisted and may thus explain why the trip Wolfgang meant to make to Salzburg to see his bedridden father never came about and why, after his father died in May 1787, Wolfgang was not present for the burial.

Leopold Mozart had a history of heart trouble, which tended to affect the sixty-eight-year-old musician particularly at times of psychological stress and excitement. It was probably due to arterio-sclerotic constriction of the coronary arteries. Early in 1787 he started to complain of shortness of breath while climbing stairs, and in the middle of March his daughter Nannerl observed symptoms of dropsy. The swelling in his legs was probably caused by a worsening myocardial insufficiency. When Mozart learned of Leopold's state of health, he wrote him a heartfelt letter on 4 April, one that has become well known because in it he obviously wanted to comfort and support his aged and ailing father with his own thoughts on death:

> ...now I hear something that floors me—the more so because from your last letter I gathered you were feeling pretty good; but now however I hear that you're really sick! I don't need to tell you how much I am yearning to see a reassuring report from you yourself; and I'm certainly praying for it too—although I have gotten used to imagining the worst in everything—because death (to be explicit) is the ultimate purpose of our lives, I have made myself so familiar with this truly best friend of mankind over the last couple years that its prospect not only holds nothing for me to dread, but indeed much that is reassuring and comforting! and I thank my God that He has granted me the good luck to have the opportunity (I'm sure you understand) to come to know it as the key to our true happiness.—I never go to bed at night without reflecting that on the next day I (as young as I am) may exist no more—and yet there's not one of all who know me who can say that I am sullen or sad to be around—and for this feeling of joy I thank my Creator every day and wish the same for each of my fellow beings with all my heart. In the letter (sent with Nancy Storace) I already laid out

for you my thoughts on this subject (caused by
the untimely death of my dearest, best friend, Count
von Hatzfeld)—he was just 31 years old, as I am—
I don't grieve for him, but deeply for myself and
everyone who knew him as well as I did. I hope
and pray that even as I write this you are feeling
better; should you, however, despite all hopes, not
be better, then please...[left blank by Mozart him-
self] do not conceal it from me but write me the
whole truth or get someone else do it, so that I can
be at your side as fast as humanly possible; I implore you by all—that is sacred to us both....

Mozart's father died on 28 May 1787, probably as a result of a
myocardial infarction. The attendant severe pains that appeared
caused Dr. Joseph von Barisani, Leopold's physician, to make the
somber diagnosis of a blockage of the spleen, a clinical picture
that is compatible with a diagnosis of "infarction of the spleen" in
today's terminology. From the implied radiating pains, we can
conclude with some confidence that Leopold's death was due to
a posterior wall myocardial infarction.

## Another Parting:  The Death of His Father

After 1778 when he lost his mother, the second important
break in Mozart's life came in 1787 with the death of his two close
friends, Count August Clemens Hatzfeld and Dr. Sigmund Barisani, and most importantly his father. We must keep in mind the
unusual degree of mutual dependency between father and son if
we are to imagine what this loss meant for Mozart's state of mind.
Many Mozart biographers have made a point of saying it was
certainly odd, not to say tactless and unfeeling, that the composition Mozart brought forth only seventeen days after his father's
death was his droll parody, *Ein musikalischer Spaß* (*A Musical
Joke*, KV 522). Whether, as Wolfgang Hildesheimer suggests, this
work was a kind of self-therapy "either to conquer his grief or
else to laugh off his guilt feelings at his lack of sympathy" is
something we shall never be able to determine. (In fact, more
recent research has shown that much of KV 522 was composed

long before Leopold died.) We can be sure, however, that in the weeks when his father was sick in bed, Mozart was anything but cheerful. It is to this forlorn spring of 1787 that we owe Mozart's famous rondo written in the bleak and cheerless key of A minor (KV 511), certainly the most beautiful of all the piano rondos from the Vienna classical epoch.

The pain Mozart felt when confronted by his father's impending death is even more clearly expressed in his well-known String Quintet in G Minor (KV 516), which he completed twelve days before his father died. It is among the most deeply personal of his works. The String Quintet in C (KV 515), in contrast, composed just before the one in G minor, gives the impression of being wholly unburdened by thoughts of death; in it, Mozart reveals the perfect inner harmony of his being. To understand this duality in Mozart, we must reflect on his singular and intensely personal relationship to death as expressed in his last letter to his father. Thoughts of death constantly occupied a remarkable amount of space not only in his life, but also in his operas. His detached attitude about the idea of having to die is reminiscent of the Stoicism of Roman times. "What is death but a crossing over to peace!," as the character Konstanze sings in *The Abduction from the Harem*. We can assume his father's dying put Mozart in a state of mind to see death as no longer anything to dread, and to be concerned less for the world beyond and more for how to incorporate death into life here and now. Aloys Greither once summed up Mozart's psychological outlook: "It is not grace and redemption but rather goodness and wisdom, together with feelings of brotherhood and a life worthily lived in contemplation of death, that represented the ideal toward which Mozart aspired."

Whether or not Mozart was religious in the conventional sense of the Church, the intellectual world of Freemasonry had become increasingly a kind of religious substitute for him. On 14 December 1784, Mozart was admitted into the lodge known as "Zur Wohltätigkeit" ("Beneficence"), which became "Zur gekrönten Hoffnung" ("Crowned Hope") upon merging with other lodges after Joseph II ordered the number of lodges in Vienna to be reduced from eight to two or three. Secret societies, such as the Rosicrucians, were banned by the emperor's order, but the

Freemasons were permitted to continue. Nevertheless, some of the lodges were dissolved altogether and many brothers found it expedient to leave because membership no longer seemed opportune. It speaks for the seriousness of Mozart's commitment to the ideals of Freemasonry that he did not leave his lodge and even nurtured a plan to found a secret society of his own. Mozart counts along with Johann Wolfgang von Goethe and Gotthold Ephraim Lessing as one of the three most significant Masons of the 18th century. He is particularly important to the history of the Craft because one of the greatest musical masterworks of all time, the opera *The Magic Flute*, would not have been possible without the existence of Freemasonry. Its imprint on Mozart's conception of death is clearly felt in another important work, his *Masonic Funeral Music* (KV 477), which was performed on 9 December 1785 at a memorial service for Count Franz Esterhazy.

Whatever Mozart's attitude toward death may have been, with his father's passing he lost not only his dearest and best friend, but also his adviser, organizer, and manager, one whose worldly understanding and unerring sense of the practical had always been there to help him. It is probably no coincidence that the well-known series of letters to his friend and fellow Mason Michael Puchberg asking for financial help began only a few weeks later— letters Erich Valentine sees as "sudden testimonials to a situation divided by harsh reality, radically and disastrously, from all that went before." Whether Mozart intended the figure of the Commendatore in *Don Giovanni* as a memorial to his father is, of course, something about which we can only speculate.

Even as the premiere of the opera *Don Giovanni* took place on 29 October 1787, the Austrian empire was at war with Turkey. Money became scarce, even for the wealthy; the number of servants was cut back, private musical ensembles of the nobility were disbanded, and the frequency of public and private music concerts was markedly reduced. We must keep these historical circumstances in mind to understand the worsening of Mozart's financial situation and the substantial reduction in the number of his concert performances. Many Mozart biographies take the position that, in these years, Mozart fell from favor with his aristocratic patrons, performances of his works in concert were

MOZART'S ENTRY ON 30 MARCH 1787 IN THE GUEST BOOK OF JOHANN GEORG KRONAUER, HIS FRIEND AND A FELLOW MEMBER OF THE MASONIC LODGE, CROWNED HOPE.

boycotted, and finally, penniless and poverty-stricken, he slipped into oblivion. The truth is that Mozart's works, especially his operas, were played with increasing frequency in all the larger cities in Germany, in Prague, and in Holland and England.

By 1791, circumstances were changing as the result of the peacemaking efforts of the new emperor, Leopold II (Joseph II having died in 1790). The middle classes were becoming more involved in Vienna's cultural life. With the renewed cultivation of music and the development of musical patronage among the untitled well-to-do, Mozart began once more to receive commissions for compositions and his creativity overshadowed all that had gone before.

Moreover, his financial situation was anything but that of an impoverished, forgotten musician. Uwe Krämer made a detailed analysis of the sources of Mozart's income in his last four years and came to the surprising conclusion that Mozart was an uncommonly well-off musician. He was earning as much as ten thousand gulden a year at the peak of his career and, even in the last year of his life, had an income of more than three thousand gulden. By comparison, Dr. Sigmund Barisani's income as director of the Vienna General Hospital was three thousand gulden, and Michael Haydn, as a musician for the court of thrifty Archbishop Colloredo in Salzburg, received only fifty gulden a year. Even if Krämer's calculations are perhaps too high, we can probably assume an annual income of four thousand to five thousand gulden for Mozart in these years.

Such income makes it all the more difficult to understand why Mozart seems to have suddenly found himself in financial difficulties after his father died. One of the reasons could have been Constanze's long, drawn-out period of illness which began shortly after Mozart returned on 4 June 1789 from a trip to Berlin. Writing to his friend Michael Puchberg in the second half of July, Mozart reported on his wife's condition and on the doctors' fears that "the bone had been attacked." Constanze's illness, which was diagnosed by Dr. Thomas Franz Closset (who was later to treat Mozart himself), probably was an "open leg," a varicose ulcer as a consequence of recurring phlebitis. Such inflammations of the veins or thrombophlebitis occur frequently in pregnant women, and especially in women who have had numerous pregnancies, and were looked upon in those days as very dangerous. In fact, at that point Constanze had already given birth to four children and was expecting her fifth. The child was born on 16 November 1789 but died of convulsions after only an hour.

Mozart devoted the summer of 1789 to the care of his wife and composed very little. In a postscript to a letter on 17 July 1789 to Puchberg, Mozart wrote: "…how unhappy I am! caught between hope and fear!…" In mid-August, when Constanze was recuperating in nearby Baden, Mozart wrote tenderly from Vienna: "…Dearest wife! I want to tell you from my heart, you have no reason to be unhappy—you have a husband who loves you, who is doing all he can for you—as for your leg, you only need to be patient, it will surely be all better…."

The bills Mozart had to pay for doctors and medicines as well as the costly stay and treatment at the relatively expensive health resort in Baden must have been very high, as we can conclude from one of his letters to Michael Puchberg. On 17 July 1789, he wrote: "…that I wouldn't need [to borrow] such a princely amount if I didn't have such horrendous expenses for my wife's cure

staring me in the face, particularly if she has to go to Baden...."
And in a letter written in December, he said:

> ...despite the big expenses I have every day, I
> would try if I could to hold out until then [Mozart
> refers to his fee for composing the opera *Così fan
> tutte* which he is expecting to receive in January]
> if it wasn't New Year's when I am obliged to pay
> the druggists and the doctors (who are no longer
> needed) if I don't want to ruin my credit;—par-
> ticularly Hundschowsky [one of Mozart's doctors],
> who we've fobbed off (for certain reasons) in a
> rather unfriendly way, which is why I am doubly
> eager to make up with him;...

A passage from a letter of 12 July 1789 informs us of Mozart's
efforts to get together the necessary means not only by borrowing money, but also by additional musical undertakings:

> ...I certainly don't need to tell you again that be-
> cause of this wretched illness I am kept from earn-
> ing any money; only I do have to tell you this, that
> in spite of my miserable situation I decided I would
> give some subscription concerts at my place so I
> could at least meet some of the large and frequent
> current expenses...but even that didn't work;—
> unfortunately, fate is so against me (but only here
> in Vienna) that I can't earn any money even when
> I want to....

Whether it was only the expenses of his wife's illness that led
to the numerous appeals to Puchberg is questionable. These
letters contain allusions suggesting that other matters also could
have contributed materially to Mozart's embarrassing financial situation. For example, Mozart asked Puchberg in late July 1789 "...if
you can, give me your support in that matter you know about."
Even clearer is Mozart's comment to Puchberg in a letter of April
1790 after he had launched an appeal to Emperor Leopold II for a
post as Kapellmeister: "...you know how my present circumstances would damage my petition at the court if they became
known—how important it is that this remains secret; for at the

court they don't judge by the circumstances but unfortunately merely by appearances." A few days later Mozart fervently urged Puchberg, "…if you can and will at least help me out of a temporary embarrassment, then for the love of God, do it."

These allusions to fears for his good reputation give rise to the suspicion that Mozart often had to grapple with large gambling debts. We know that gambling, especially the game of pharao (faro), was widespread in those days. Even Mozart's father was moved to complain once in a letter to his son in Vienna that the young people around the archbishop's court in Salzburg had lost everything they had playing that "damned faro" and how glad he was that the archbishop had finally forbidden it. But gambling for large sums was an everyday affair, particularly for the nobility in Vienna. Because Mozart, who enjoyed playing cards as much as anyone, wanted his aristocratic friends and patrons to treat him as one of them and not like a servant, he almost certainly was not put off by the prospect of playing for high stakes. These people had princely incomes running into hundreds of thousands yearly and could sustain substantial gambling losses without getting into trouble, so we can readily imagine that Mozart was soon unable to keep pace with the level of play. In these circles, a person who was not able to pay his debts promptly was regarded as an outcast. If Mozart did in fact have large gambling losses, his only recourse would have been to pay his debts by borrowing, often in considerable amounts. Otherwise, he would lose his standing in society. In such predicaments, his friend Michael Puchberg helped him out time and again with loans. As chamber music was frequently played at Puchberg's home, Mozart dedicated the lovely Piano Trio in E (KV 542) to him as a sign of gratitude for his friendship.

Mozart also may have tried to find a way out of his financial problems by speculating. A business scheme with the publisher Franz Anton Hoffmeister that was supposed to yield some two thousand gulden while he was in Frankfurt during the coronation of Leopold II in the fall of 1790 seems to have been a source of some concern. Unfortunately, the only evidence we have about such financial dealings is a note for a thousand gulden, predated to 1 October, that Mozart signed to "Heinrich Lackenbacher,

Esquire, Authorized Merchant." Under its terms, Mozart mort-
gaged his entire furnishings as security for the loan and the interest due and offered the fees he expected from his publisher
Hoffmeister toward repayment of the loan. From vague allusions
in various letters, we learn that Mozart had to stay constantly on
the heels of some man (whose identity we never learn) to bring
his business with him to a successful conclusion. This matter
comes out clearly in his letter of 6 July 1791 to Constanze, in
which he mentions the plan of the balloonist François Blanchard
to launch a hot-air balloon on the outskirts of Vienna:

> ...Today I didn't like the brouhaha with Blanchard
> one bit—it's keeping me from finishing my busi-
> ness—N. N. [the name was later obliterated] prom-
> ised to meet me before he went out there, but he
> didn't come—maybe he'll show up when the fun
> is over—I'll wait till 2 o'clock, then I'll throw down
> some food and go all around looking for him.—
> not a very pleasant life at all....

On the very next day, Mozart wrote to Constanze: "...You must
forgive me that you are getting only one letter from me now. The
reason is this: I have to hang on to a certain N. N., don't dare let
him escape—I'm at his place every day at 7 in the morning."

This hectic life, at the time when he was also composing *The
Magic Flute,* may well have overburdened him.

In a letter of 5 July 1791 to his wife, Mozart said:

> ...I hope I can fold you in my arms on Saturday,
> perhaps even before. As soon as my business is
> over, I'll be with you—for I've resolved to rest and
> recover in your embrace; and I need that—be-
> cause the gnawing concerns and irritations and all
> the running around that go with them really take a
> lot out of you....

To make matters worse, because Emperor Leopold II was not
particularly interested in the cultural life of Vienna, Mozart did
not have any great expectations for a position with the Viennese
court in the future. He was evidently not only mentally but also
physically fatigued, a condition that is apparent in various places

in his letters. For example, he wrote to Puchberg on 8 April 1790: "...I would have come to your house myself to speak to you directly, only my head is all bound up with rheumatic pains, which makes me feel my situation all the more...." On 14 August 1790, writing again to Puchberg, he said:

> Yesterday I was feeling so-so, but today I don't feel well at all; pain has kept me from sleeping the whole night long; I must have gotten over-heated yesterday from walking too much and then caught a chill without knowing it; just picture my situation—sick and full of worry and concern—a situation like that definitely keeps you from getting well....

Given all these circumstances in Mozart's last years, it is not necessary to suggest some chronic illness—such as heart disease or a kidney disease—to explain his emotional strains and physical complaints; the incredible burdens he was under are reason enough. Moreover, the letters from this last period of his life show clearly that, until late autumn of 1791, Mozart was in good health. The vigorous creativity of his last year gave us many outstanding works.

## 1791: The Fatal Year

In the summer of 1791, Mozart was under pressure to turn out an almost superhuman amount of work, beginning with the composition of *The Magic Flute* (KV 620). The strange stories told later about the origins of this opera were largely invented by persons deliberately to serve their idiosyncratic points of view. The libretto was adapted by Emanuel Schikaneder from an earlier opera, *Oberon*, by Paul Wranitzky and from excerpts of Christoph Martin Wieland's collection of tales called *Dschinnistan*, with an admixture of notions from Freemasonry. Mozart saw the libretto more as a fairytale than as some mysterious encoded message, and in the beginning he had some problems in setting it to music. As he said himself: "If we have a disaster, then I can't help it, for I've never composed a fairytale opera before." But he soon began working feverishly on the opera, often rising at five in the morning to compose, as disclosed in various letters. For example, in a letter he sent on 11 June 1791 to his wife, who was then in Baden, he said: "...I can't tell you what I would give to be sitting with you in Baden instead of being here.—Out of sheer boredom, I composed an aria for the opera today—I was already out of bed and up at 4:30...!"

On 14 July 1791, the intensive work on *The Magic Flute* was interrupted by an urgent commission from Prague. Emperor Leopold II was to be crowned King of Bohemia there in September and Mozart was supposed to compose the opera *La clemenza di Tito* (*The Clemency of Titus*, KV 621) for the occasion. The pressure was enormous. Mozart composed the opera in only three weeks, working on it even during the trip to Prague with Constanze and his student Franz Xaver Süssmayr at the end of August. Because time was short, Süssmayr wrote the unaccompanied recitatives for the opera; parts of it may also have originated earlier, such as one of Vitellia's arias. Mozart began to have health problems, not only from the strain of finishing the opera in time for the festivities—the first performance took place on 6 September with Mozart himself conducting—but also from having to cope with personal animosities and intrigues. The Prague composer Leopold Kozeluch, in particular, tried to interfere with the opera, which ultimately was one reason the performance of *Titus* met with limited success during the coronation festivities in Prague. For Empress Maria Louise, it was "una porcheria tedesca"— "German junk."

As Mozart and his wife were leaving Prague in the middle of September, their friends observed that he seemed pale and depressed. Writing in 1808 in the second edition of his biography of Mozart, Franz Xaver Niemetschek said:

> Even while he was still in Prague, Mozart began feeling sick and dosed himself constantly with medicines; he was pale and woebegone even though his lively sense of humor often unleashed a torrent of merry jokes when he was in the company of his friends. On taking leave of his group of friends, he was so melancholy that tears poured forth. Forebodings of an early death seemed to

> have brought on his dejected mood—for he al-
> ready bore within himself the germ of disease that
> would shortly carry him away.

The last sentence of this report is a good example of linking a cause to an event that the author knew in retrospect was coming—hardly an objective portrayal of the situation. Niemetschek may have believed that Mozart was overworked, weary, and in poor health in September 1791, and his description undoubtedly fits the facts. However, the cause does not lie in the germ of Mozart's final illness, but rather in his mental and physical exertions during the preceding weeks and months and probably also in a catarrhal sickness—an influenza infection, as we would say today—that he apparently picked up during the trip to Prague. He was still laboring under it at the beginning of September, as suggested by a passage from the *Prague Coronation Journal* of 1791: "The composition [the opera *Titus*] is by the famous Mozart and does him honor even though he had but little time to write it and besides illness overtook him while he was finishing the last part." The illness can hardly have been serious because, according to the biography of Mozart by Georg von Nissen (the second husband of Constanze, who helped him with its preparation), Mozart kept up a full schedule of activities and diversions during his stay in Prague. He conducted performances of *Don Giovanni* and *La clemenza di Tito*, paid visits to the Prague lodge "Zur Wahrheit und Einigheit" ("Truth and Unity") where his cantata *Die Maurerfreude* (KV 471) was performed, and spent some hours almost every day playing billiards with his friends. If Mozart had been suffering from some chronic sickness at the time, such a program of activities, especially while recovering from an infection, would have been inconceivable.

As soon as he was back in Vienna, Mozart got to work finishing *The Magic Flute*. Its premiere performance was in the Theater auf der Wieden, the so-called Freihaus Theater, on 30 September 1791 under Mozart's baton. The opera was a ringing success and was presented some twenty times in October alone—an extraordinary run even for that theater. If Mozart had in fact been depressed in Prague because of unhappy circumstances surrounding the coronation festivities (in contrast to Niemetschek, by the way,

Nissen does not speak of a "dejected mood" but simply of a "nervous irritability"), nothing more was seen of such a feeling after his arrival back in Vienna. On the contrary, the marked success of *The Magic Flute* in Vienna and, at last, of *Titus* in Prague put Mozart in a buoyant and confident frame of mind, as we can see from a report he made to Constanze, who had again been in Baden taking the waters since the beginning of October. On 7 and 8 October, he wrote:

> I've just come from the opera [*The Magic Flute*]; it was just as full as ever…you really can see how this opera is steadily getting bigger…and the most remarkable thing about it is that on the evening when my new opera was first performed to so much acclaim, on that very evening in Prague *Titus* was being presented for the last time and also to extraordinary applause….Now to the story of my life; right after you sailed away, I played two games of billiards with Herr von Mozart (the one who wrote that opera at Schickaneder's). then I sold the old nag for 14 ducats. then I had Joseph the First [Mozart's joking title for a waiter at a nearby tavern, Joseph Deiner; the emperor, of course, had only been Joseph *the Second*] summoned and sent him for some black coffee, all the while puffing on a fine pipe of tobacco; then I orchestrated almost the entire rondo for Stadler [a reference to the last movement of the clarinet concerto, KV 622, Mozart was composing for his friend Anton Stadler]…around 5:30 I walked out of the Stubentor and took my favorite stroll along the glacis to the theater—oh, oh, what do I see before me? what do I smell? it is The First with the pork chops! Che gusto! now I eat to your good health—it has just struck 11 o'clock, perhaps you're already sleeping?…

The letter contains not a hint of a psychologically depressed Mozart, to say nothing of a Mozart seriously ill—quite the contrary. Mozart's good mood often broke out in high spirits, as is evident in the frequently cited letter of 8 October to Constanze reporting on a performance of *The Magic Flute*:

> ...I have just feasted on a delicious piece of fish which The First (my good and faithful servant) brought me and because my appetite is rather large today, I have dispatched him forth yet again to bring me something more, if possible.—...this morning I was composing so diligently that I ran late and it was already 1:30—so I hurried over to Hofer's [Mozart's brother-in-law] (so as not to have to eat alone) where I also ran into Mama. Right after eating I went back home and wrote until it was time for the opera...but with the aria of Papageno's with the glockenspiel, I went into the back of the theater because I felt such an urge today to play it myself.—then I had some fun when Schickaneder had a pause once and I played an arpeggio—he jumped, looked into the wings and saw me—but when it was supposed to come a second time, I didn't play it—he stopped and didn't want to go on—I guessed what he was thinking and played another chord, so he hit the glockenspiel and said shut up—at that everyone laughed—from this bit of fun, I think many people realized for the first time that he didn't play the instrument himself....7 o'clock Sunday morning. I slept well, hope you also have slept well. I have just sumptuously enjoyed half a chicken that my friend Number One brought me later on....

Every line of this letter sketches for us a Mozart who not only had an excellent appetite, but was feeling good and composing from dawn till dusk. The clarinet concerto that he completed in these times is probably the most beautiful of its kind and is further testimony to how high his spirits were. It is really hard to imagine that taking up work on the *Requiem* (KV 626) should have abruptly changed his outlook to one of deep depression.

The *Requiem* had been commissioned by Count Franz Wallsegg through his estate manager Franz Anton Leitgeb—probably with the intercession of Michael Puchberg—as a memorial to his wife who had recently died. The commission was accompanied by a substantial down-payment. In discussing the *Requiem*, most biographers appear to accept Niemetschek's account, which he based almost entirely on what Constanze said later:

> ...The story of his last work, the Requiem just mentioned, is as mysterious as it is strange. Shortly before the coronation of Emperor Leopold II, even before Mozart had received the commission to go to Prague, he was handed an unsigned letter by an unknown messenger which, along with numerous flattering remarks, contained the question whether Mozart was interested in writing a requiem mass. If so, for what price and inside what span of time could he deliver it? Mozart, who never undertook anything without taking his wife into his confidence, told her about the unusual commission, at the same time expressing his desire to try his hand at this kind of composition once again, especially since the exalted style of church music was very much in keeping with his talents. She advised him to accept the proposal. Thereupon, Mozart wrote back to the anonymous initiator, saying he would prepare the Requiem for a certain fee, that he could not determine exactly how long it would take to complete, and that he wished to know where to deliver the work when it was finished. A short time later, the same messenger reappeared, bringing not only the stipulated initial payment but also the promise that, because Mozart had been so modest in his price, he would receive a substantial amount in addition when the work was handed over. He should, moreover, compose as the spirit moved him, but without expending any effort to learn who had ordered the work for that would certainly be in vain.

In the meantime, Mozart had been honored to receive the lucrative offer to write the opera, La clemenza di Tito, for the coronation of Emperor Leopold in Prague. To go to Prague once more and write for his beloved Bohemians, that had far too much charm for him to turn down! In the very moment that Mozart and his wife were climbing into the carriage, the messenger materialized from out of nowhere, tugged on his wife's skirt, and asked: "How is it coming along with the Requiem?" Mozart apologized for having to make the trip and for not being able to inform the unknown gentleman about it; the Requiem would have first priority on his return and so it was only up to the anonymous person if he wanted to wait so long. And the messenger was satisfied with that....

As soon as he was back in Vienna, he busied himself with the requiem mass and worked on it very hard and with great interest; but his generally weakened condition visibly grew worse and put him in a dark and melancholy mood. His wife observed all this with distress. One day as she went with him in the park at the Prater to afford him some distraction and cheer him up, and the two of them were sitting alone, Mozart began to speak of death and asserted he was composing the Requiem for himself. Tears stood in the eyes of the deeply affected man. "I know it all too well," he continued, "it will not last long with me: I'm sure of it, someone has poisoned me! I cannot get this thought out of my mind.—"

These words fell heavily on the heart of his wife; she was hardly able to comfort him and to show him how groundless his morbid thoughts were. Being convinced that a sickness was coming and that the Requiem was too much of a strain for his

THE LAST PAGE IN MOZART'S HAND FROM THE AUTOGRAPH SCORE OF THE
*REQUIEM*: "LACRYMOSA..."

sensitive nerves, she called the doctor and took
away the score he had been composing. And indeed, his condition improved somewhat and he
was able to finish a short cantata that had been
ordered by a society for a ceremony. The good
performance of the cantata and the generous applause it received gave his spirits renewed strength.
Now he was feeling somewhat better and asked
repeatedly to get on with the Requiem and finish
it. His wife could find no excuse not to give him
the score once again....

Right after he died, the messenger turned up and
asked to have the work, even though it was not
finished, and took it with him. From that moment
on, the widow never saw him again, nor did she
ever learn the least thing either about the requiem
mass or about the one who ordered it....

Today we know that this account from the second edition of
Niemetschek's biography of Mozart written in 1808 is in many
respects contrary to the facts. The "anonymous" patron was Count
Wallsegg, who lived in the Schloss Stuppach south of Vienna and
owned the house in Vienna in which Mozart's good friend, Michael
Puchberg, lived. The count invited guests to his place for chamber music concerts and apparently enjoyed making them guess
who had composed the works they heard there. Whether he
would occasionally pass himself off as the composer is not completely documented. When the *Requiem* was performed as a
memorial to his late wife, he may well have left the people present
in uncertainty as to who had composed it without explicitly putting himself forward as its creator. Perhaps for the same reason—
to keep his acquaintances guessing—he charged his estate manager
Leitgeb, who was the go-between with Mozart, with the utmost
discretion.

The relatively large fee for the commission that was promised
and in part advanced can also be easily explained. Michael
Puchberg, who is viewed as the possible intermediary in the matter, could have called the attention of his landlord, Count Wallsegg,
to Mozart's precarious financial situation. This connection must
have been known to Constanze because even the Abbé Maximilian Stadler, who was a close friend of the Mozart family, testified
later "...that Count Wallsegg had ordered the *Requiem* from Mozart,
I knew right after his death..." and we also know today that the
Count subsequently was again in contact with Constanze. Finally, the piece was not in fact handed over in an uncompleted
state, but only after Franz Xaver Süssmayr had supplied the missing movements and instrumentation following Joseph Eybler's
refusal of Constanze's request that he do the job. With the remarkable discovery of a leaf of sketches for the *Requiem* in Mozart's
hand that we can date to the September-October period of 1791,
Prof. Wolfgang Plath has provided proof that the *Requiem* had
essentially been completed in sketches by Mozart himself.
Süssmayr had only to complete the instrumentation or, as Constanze put it to Vincent and Mary Novello much later, do "what
anyone could have done."

The chronology of events suggests that Mozart began in July and August with the conception of the *Requiem*, and set to work on it as soon as he could after his return in October from Prague and the completion of *The Magic Flute*. In his letters to Constanze during the two weeks before she returned from Baden, Mozart describes feeling fine and even feisty. Why he should suddenly have chosen to speak of deep feelings of grief and even presentiments of death in the course of a walk with her in the Prater is totally incomprehensible. Depression and grief do not comport with the external circumstances at all, for it was just at this time that his financial circumstances were starting to improve. The demand for his works in Vienna was growing, elsewhere in Europe his operas were being performed ever more frequently, and the first lucrative financial offers, such as one from London, were arriving. In the autumn of 1791, members of the Hungarian nobility offered him the prospect of an annual stipend of one thousand gulden, and "from Amsterdam came the notice of a still higher yearly sum, for which he was obliged to compose only a few pieces exclusively for the subscribers." Why, then, should Mozart have abruptly fallen into a depression just in the weeks prior to Constanze's return, as graphologists have sought deduce from his handwriting in his last letters to her (where the lines constantly fall off to the right)? Modern psychoanalysts, such as Langegger, postulate that Mozart suffered from a true psychosis toward the end of his life, caused either by fear of dying or by apprehension of having been poisoned, but such conclusions are based ultimately on Niemetschek's reproduction of Constanze's sometimes questionable representation of events.

Finally, even if a composer's thoughts might turn constantly to the subject of death while he is writing a requiem, and even if this may not leave his psyche entirely unaffected, we cannot ascribe forebodings of death to the composer himself.

## The Last Weeks

From Mozart's behavior in the last weeks of his life, the thought of dying hardly appears to have been the only thing on his mind. If Mozart had in fact suffered from depression with paranoid delusions of persecution at this time, we should be able to find some evidence of the most significant symptoms of such a psychosis: lack of appetite with concurrent loss of weight, difficulty in sleeping, biorhythmic reversal with lassitude and listlessness in the early morning hours, as well as a depressive frame of mind. However, in the letters he wrote to Constanze in October 1791, we read of a good appetite, sleeping well, an eagerness to get to work at an early hour, a cheerful mood, and a readiness to play jokes.

In spite of this evidence, the view is put forward time and again, even by doctors today, that Mozart suffered a morbid depression in this period. One psychoanalyst has claimed in recent times that Mozart failed to develop into a mature personality because of the isolation he experienced as the result of being educated solely by his father. Consequently, he is supposed to have reacted with particular sensitivity to the loss of love objects. The death of his mother in Paris as well as the illness suffered by Constanze in July 1789 are cited as examples of events that could have brought on such "reactive" episodes of depression. As if every reasonably normal person would not react to such occurrences with pain and grief!

The extremes such medical speculations have reached, usually because of insufficient familiarity with the literature, are shown by an article published in a medical journal in 1956. It is based on references to recurring attacks of violent headaches and short periods of unconsciousness in Mozart's medical history and seeks to conclude therefrom that Mozart is to be placed in the ranks of famous men who suffered from actual or incipient epilepsy. The author evidently draws on passages from Mozart biographies in both the English and German languages that contain accounts of repeated episodes of unconsciousness. When we look for the source of such allegations, we find a remark in the *Allgemeine musikalische Zeitung* of Leipzig from the year 1798: "Already at the time of *The Magic Flute*, he—to whom day and night were one when he was in the grip of inspiration—would be overcome by spells of exhaustion and brief periods of half-fainting unconsciousness." There are no reports of such incidents in earlier years. Hence, these observations of "half-fainting unconsciousness" which go back to September 1791 can only have been describing the consequences of overwork with normal signs of physical exhaustion. When we recall that in the summer of 1791 Mozart had to complete *La clemenza di Tito* in but a few weeks' time—while he was already working on *The Magic Flute*—and that he was probably also feeling the effects of the influenza infection contracted in Prague, a mention of "spells of exhaustion and brief periods of half-fainting unconsciousness" seems very understandable indeed.

Not only Mozart's psychological state, but also his physical constitution have been the object of speculation. Everyone agrees that he was an enthusiastic and unflagging dancer and had a quick and lively temperament. In this connection, his sister-in-law Sophie Haibel says in her recollections written in 1828:

> He was always good-humored, but even in the best of humors still very pensive, looking you right in the eye, giving a considered answer to everything, whether sad or happy, and yet at the same time he appeared to be deep in thought working on something completely apart. Even as he was washing his hands in the morning, he would go back and forth in the room, never standing still, all the while tapping one heel against the other and being lost in thought. At the table, he often took a corner of his napkin, rolled it tight together, then rubbed it around under his nose and seemed, in his mood of reflection, to be completely unaware of it, and often scowling at the same time....And otherwise his hands and feet were constantly in motion; he was always playing on something as though it was a piano, for example, with his hat, pockets, watch chain, tables, and chairs.

Just how eccentric this motoric need of Mozart and his general disposition for pranks must have seemed to the people around him comes out in a remembrance on Mozart by the aristocratic novelist Karoline Pichler that was published in the *Allgemeine Theaterzeitung* on 15 July 1843 in Vienna:

> Once I was sitting at the piano and playing "Non piu andrai" from Figaro, when Mozart, who happened to be with us, came up behind me, and I must have been doing it right because he hummed along with the melody and tapped the tempo on my shoulder; then he abruptly pulled up a chair, sat down, told me to keep playing the bass, and began to improvise such wonderful variations that everyone there held their breath listening to the melodies of the German Orpheus. But all of a sudden he was fed up with it, he jumped up and, in that crazy way he often had, began to leap over chairs and tables, meowing like a cat and turning somersaults like a boisterous youngster....

Evidently trivial jokes like this provided a balance, a release, that his spirit, which toiled far beyond the limits of a normal person's, needed while he was in the process of composing a great work.

Mozart's brother-in-law Joseph Lange described Mozart this way in his memoirs published in 1808:

> ...From his speech and actions, Mozart was never less to be recognized as a great man than when he was occupied with an important work. Then he not only spoke in distracted, confused ways, but he would also make jokes of a kind one did not expect from him, indeed, he would even deliberately let his behavior go. All the while, he seemed not to be thinking or pondering on anything at all. Either he was deliberately hiding his inner exertions under an external mask of frivolity for reasons not to be divined, or he liked to bring the heavenly ideas of his music into sharp contrast with mundane everyday notions, thus amusing himself with a kind of self-irony. I could understand that such a supreme artist might, out of deep reverence for his art, denigrate and neglect his own person, as if mocking it.

With this eyewitness account, we have a description of the genius whose creative powers went beyond all imagining, yet who could shock the people around him with his unpredictable and, in many respects, eccentric reactions. Some decades ago, an effort was made to combine the volatility of Mozart's nature and his kinetic restlessness (evident even in his childhood) with the evidence of protruding eyes seen in portraits of him from his Vienna days to arrive at a medical diagnosis of hyperthyroidism. It was even proposed that he had died of Morbus Basedow, or exophthalmic goiter. Since then, it has been shown that Mozart inherited a tendency to protruding eyes, one observed in other members of the Mozart family. Moreover, hyperactivity of the thyroid gland would have resulted in a rapid loss of weight. In fact, in his last years Mozart was described as "corpulent," which makes further discussion of this thesis inappropriate.

Another theory was put forward some years ago by Danish writers at an international psychiatric congress in Vienna. According to this notion, Mozart suffered from Gilles de la Tourette's syndrome. This disease is marked by the presence of facial and vocal tics, occasionally leading to coprolalia—that is, the compulsive, stereotyped use of obscene language, particularly words relating to human excrement. Because he often incorporated such expressions in various phrases in his letters to his "Bäsle," the authors made the absurd suggestion that Mozart may have had this rare disease.

The reason Mozart finally sold his horse on 7 October 1791—which he had bought less out of enthusiasm for riding than because his friend Dr. Barisani had prescribed horseback riding as an antidote to his essentially sedentary lifestyle—was not that he was sick but that he was pinched for money. His spirits still were fired with vigor and *joie de vivre* only days before he died, as we can sense from his last completed composition, *The Masonic Cantata* (KV 623), which he wrote for the dedication of his lodge in its new premises and personally conducted in a successful performance on 17 November 1791 just eighteen days before his death. The cantata's jubilant choral ending in the radiant key of C major must convince everyone who hears it that this was not the work of a chronically sick Mozart, ready to yield himself up to death. If we put aside speculations that Mozart suffered some chronic illness, at least in the last months of his life, and instead give our attention to credible accounts that have come down to us, we must be persuaded that he was in good physical and mental health in the autumn of 1791.

It was only on 20 November 1791, three days after he had led the performance of his *Masonic Cantata,* that Mozart became sick. The most detailed account of his last illness is contained in a report written on 7 April 1825 by his sister-in-law Sophie Haibel at the request of Georg von Nissen, while he was working on his biography of Mozart:

> ...Now, when Moz. fell sick, we both made nightgowns for him that he could put on from the front, since he couldn't turn over because of the swelling; and because we didn't know how sick he might be, we made him a quilted robe too...so that when he got up, he would be well taken care of.  And so we often went to see him and he showed how pleased he was with the robe.  I went to town every day to visit him, and once when I came there on a Saturday, M. said to me: now, dear Sophie, you tell Mama that I'm feeling pretty good and that I'm still coming to congratulate her in the week of her name day.  Who could have been happier than I to bring my mother, who could hardly wait to get a report, such good news, so I hurried right home to comfort her, since he himself really seemed very cheerful and to be doing well.

> Then the next day was Sunday:...I said...to Mother: dear Mother, today I'm not going to see Mozart— he was so good yesterday he must be even better today and one day, more or less, won't make any difference.  To that she said:...go to town and come right back with some news of how he is doing. Don't stay long.  So I hurried as fast as I could. Oh God, but wasn't I startled when my sister, half

in despair and trying to control herself, came running toward me, and said: thank God, it's you,
dear Sophie; last night he was so ill I began to
think he wouldn't last till morning. Do stay with
me today, because if he is the same today, he will
surely die tonight, go to him a while, see how he's
doing. I tried to pull myself together and went to
his bed, where he cried out right away: Ah, dear
Sophie, it is good you are here, you must stay
here all night, you must watch me die; I tried to
be brave and talk him out of it but, to all I said, he
only responded: I already have the taste of death
on my tongue, and: who will look after my dearest Constanze then, if you don't stay here. Yes,
dear M., only I have to go to our Mother and tell
her you would like me to remain here today, otherwise she will think an accident has happened.
Yes, do that, but come back soon.—God, how I
was feeling then. My poor sister came behind me
and asked me, in the name of God, to go to the
priests at St. Peter's and ask a priest to come as if
he were just passing by. I did it too, only for a
long time they refused, and it took a lot out of me
to bring such a monster of the clergy to do it—

Now I ran to my anxiously awaiting Mother; it was
already dark…then I ran back to my unhappy sister. There was Süssmayr by M's bed; the famous
Requiem was lying on the covers and M. was explaining to him how he thought he should finish it
after his death. In addition, he instructed his wife
to keep his death a secret until the next morning
after she had told Albrechtsberger about it, because the position [that Mozart had at St. Stephen's
Cathedral] belonged to him before anyone else.
Closset, the doctor, was sought for a long time,
finally found at the theater, only he had to wait till
the piece was over—then he came and ordered

cold compresses be placed on his burning head, which was such a shock to him that he never recovered consciousness before he expired. At the very end, as he tried to sound the drums in his Requiem with his mouth, I can hear it still. Then Müller came from the art gallery and cast his pale, dead face in plaster of paris. I have no words, dear brother, to describe his devoted wife's endless misery as she threw herself on her knees and implored the Almighty's support. As much as I urged her, she could not part from him; if her grief could have grown even greater, then it would surely have done so, for on the day after this dreadful night, crowds of people came by and weeped and wailed for him....

To be able to reach some conclusion about Mozart's last illness, however, we must consider other significant accounts, such as further comments made by Sophie Haibel in 1828, that were also included in Nissen's biography:

My sister-in-law is of the opinion that Mozart did not receive adequate treatment for his sickness, because instead of trying to drive out the skin eruptions even more in some other way, they bled him and put cold compresses on his head, whereupon his strength declined rapidly and he fell unconscious and never came to again. Even when he was most sick, still he did not become impatient and his delicate hearing and sensibility was touched only by the song of his favorite canary, which finally had to be removed from the room next door because it affected him so strongly.

Speaking with Vincent and Mary Novello, who were in Salzburg from 14 to 17 July 1828 during their travels in Mozart's footsteps, Sophie added that her sister Constanze feared the sudden cold of the compresses administered by Dr. Closset had certainly done the sick man harm, "whose arms and legs were very swollen and inflamed." Some not unbiased physicians still choose to ignore

THE 19TH CENTURY'S ROMANTIC VIEW OF MOZART'S DEATH, A PAINTING BY NELSON O'NEIL.

this allusion to inflammatory swellings in order to support their own opinions about the disease. We therefore should note what Mozart's student, Joseph Eybler, had to say in his autobiography. He clearly was referring to the extreme painfulness of the inflammatory swellings when he wrote: "I had the good fortune to keep our friendship intact till the day he died, so that I was even able to help lift him up, lay him down, and nurse him, during his painful final illness."

Other accounts of Mozart's last days are generally less reliable because they do not come from firsthand sources. Still, passages from a letter by Ignaz von Seyfried, a former student of Mozart's and later conductor at the Theater an der Wien, suggest that Mozart probably suffered feverish delirium the night he died. In a letter written in 1840 to Georg Friedrich Treitschke, the revisor of the text to Beethoven's *Fidelio*, he says: "...The evening of the 4th of December, M. was already delirious and imagined that he was attending The Magic Flute at the Wiednertheater; almost the very last words that he whispered to his wife were: 'hush! hush! now [Josepha] Hofer is taking the high F;—now my sister-in-law is singing her second aria, Der Hölle Rache; how strongly she hits the B-flat and holds "Hört! hört! hört! der Mutter Schwur!"'" This obviously acute worsening in Mozart's condition would explain why members of the family suddenly sent for his doctor late in the evening.

The legend of the rehearsal of the *Requiem* that is supposed to have taken place at Mozart's bedside on the last afternoon before he died appears in virtually every biography and is frankly not worthy of belief. It came out of Munich from an unsigned report that appeared in an obituary for the recently deceased friend of Mozart, Benedikt Schack, in the Leipzig newspaper, *Allgemeine musikalische Zeitung*, on 25 July 1827:

> ...[Mozart] wrote most of the Requiem sitting in the Trattner Garden in the Laimgrube. As soon as he had finished a number, he would have it sung, while he played the orchestra part on the piano. Even on the afternoon before he died, he had them bring the score of the Requiem to his bed and (it was two in the afternoon) himself sang the alto

part; Schack, an old friend of the family, sang the soprano part, as he had been used to doing, [Franz] Hofer, Mozart's brother-in-law, the tenor part, [Franz Xaver] Gerl, later bass singer at the Mannheimtheater, the bass part. They had reached the first measures of the Lacrimosa when Mozart began to weep bitterly, laid the score down, and passed away eleven hours later, at one in the morning.

From the account by Sophie Haibel, it seems completely out of the question that Mozart took part in a rehearsal on the last day of his life. We must assume, rather, that this rehearsal of the *Requiem* had been set for some time around the beginning of his last illness, especially since Sophie's account describes a brief, passing improvement in Mozart's condition. However, we must cast some doubt on something Sophie is supposed to have told the Novello couple: "The same day he died, he wrote part of the Requiem and gave instructions to a friend on how he wanted certain passages completed." In the entry in her diary, Mary Novello recorded Sophie Haibel's statement somewhat differently and gave it what was probably the proper interpretation: "On the same day, he called for the Requiem and dictated to Süssmayr what should be done." These instructions, which Mozart could discuss *viva voce* with Süssmayr, almost certainly pertained to questions of instrumentation and some fleshing out of the already completed sketches of the work. Because of the painful inflammatory swellings of his arms, Mozart could not have written the notes of a score while on his sickbed. Studies of Mozart's notation of the *Requiem* have concluded, moreover, that the last entries in his hand, up to the passage "homo reus" in the "Lacrimosa," were made at his desk, on 19 November 1791 at the latest.

## The Fatal Illness

In his biography, Nissen summed up Mozart's last sickness in these words: "Mozart's fatal illness, where he was confined to his bed, lasted 15 days. The onset was marked by swelling of the arms and legs and he was virtually unable to move; this was later followed by sudden vomiting, a sickness called "hitziges Frieselfieber" [acute miliary fever, or 'sweating sickness']. He remained fully conscious until two hours before he passed away." Nissen could hardly imagine how many Romantic legends, irrational speculations, and technical medical discussions he would set in motion with these words.

"Hitziges Frieselfieber" is not a precise medical diagnosis. Rather it reflects a symptom or—as the old Viennese school of medicine used to express it—a "coincidental" side effect that appears with many types of feverish states. The "Frieselfieber" probably corresponds to epidemic occurrences of influenza or viral infections in which poor hygienic conditions and profuse sweating accompanying the fever frequently resulted in vesicular eruptions of the skin that could fester and form pus. The papules and pustules (the "Friesel") appeared primarily on the covered parts of the body, that is, on the trunk, buttocks, and thighs, while the arms and face largely remained free of them. It is therefore easy to understand why members of Mozart's family did not notice these skin eruptions mentioned by Dr. Closset.

From the article on putrid fever published by Dr. Closset in Leipzig in 1783, and from the description in Dr. Mathias von Sallaba's work, *Historia Naturalis Morborum*, which appeared in Vienna in 1791 and was dedicated to Dr. Closset, it is clear that both doctors knew exactly the diagnostic value of the term "hitziges Frieselfieber." Dr. Sallaba was called for consultation on 28 November 1791 because of Mozart's alarming condition. Mozart's personal doctor, Dr. Closset, used the term "Frieselfieber" for the entry in the coroner's report and in the register of deaths in the chancellery of St. Stephen's Cathedral on 5 December 1791. He obviously did so because, according to an imperial ordinance of 24 February 1784, a medically certified coroner was required to provide the authorities with a generally understood "brief notation of the manner of death" in the German language (that is, not in Latin). In keeping with the custom of the time, the two attending physicians, Dr. Closset and Dr. Sallaba, did not issue a medical certificate as to Mozart's actual illness.

When Mozart died, at five minutes before one o'clock in the morning of 5 December 1791, Constanze was apparently beside herself with grief over the loss of her husband. She is said to have lain in Mozart's bed during the night from the 5th to the 6th of December, driven by the desire to die from the same infectious disease. Dr. Closset gave her a sedative and she was taken, probably with her two young sons, to stay at the home of friends.

The citizens of Vienna formally learned of the death of Wolfgang Mozart from a notice in the *Wiener Zeitung*:

> In the night from the 4th to the 5th of this month, the k. k. Hofkammerkompositor Wolfgang Mozart died here. Known throughout Europe from his childhood on for his unique musical talent, he had ascended to the level of the greatest composers through the most fortunate development and steadfast application of the marvelous gifts Nature gave him; his widely loved and admired works are proof of this, and they in turn provide the measure of the irreplaceable loss that the noble art of music has suffered with his death.

The fact that his death was lamented in many newspapers in the larger cities of Europe refutes the often-heard allegation that, by the time he died, Mozart had been largely forgotten.

In this connection, however, a report in the *Musikalisches Wochenblatt* of Berlin on 12 December 1791 was destined to have a malignant influence. A correspondent from Prague added the following postscript to the report:

> Mozart is—dead. He was feeling sick as he arrived home from Prague, and since then he had continued to languish; they say he had dropsy, and he died in Vienna the end of last week. Because his body became swollen after his death, they even believe he had been poisoned.

Ignoring the fact that almost all the details in the report are wrong, the postscript does contain the first mention of a rumor that was soon to contribute to the thesis of Mozart's death by poisoning. This thesis led to the wildest speculations, which in their absurdity reached a seldom achieved level of bad taste and ignorance in a so-called judicial proceeding reported in an English newspaper on 18 May 1983 (discussed subsequently).

The words used by the Prague correspondent suggest that he did not believe the rumor that Mozart had died an unnatural death. However, the matter continued to smolder—almost certainly because the Romantic mentality of the times included a special fondness for bizarre and mysterious happenings. In the 18th century, people normally attributed every unexpected death of a prominent personality to some unnatural cause. And so the legend of Mozart's death by poison began to excite the interest of posterity. Once alight, the rumor could not be extinguished.

Constanze herself added tinder to the fire with her account of the utterance—"I'm sure of it, someone has poisoned me!"—that Mozart supposedly made during a walk in the Prater in Vienna in October 1791. Both Niemetschek and Nissen were aware that Constanze did not believe it and had tried at the time "to show him how groundless his morbid thoughts were." Nevertheless, they both included the statement attributed to Mozart in their biographies, thus lending substance to the rumor. Even as early as 1799—one year after the first edition of Niemetschek's Mozart biography appeared in Prague—a poem on the death of Mozart by Johann Isaak von Gerning in the *Neuer deutscher Merkur*, published by Wieland, said in part: "For the sake of Mankind and Music, we must hope that this Orpheus may indeed have died a natural death!"

The first suggestion as to what poison allegedly was used is found in a diary entry of Supliz Boisserée from November 1815 on the occasion of a visit from the Kapellmeister Franz Seraph von Destouches, who was briefly a student of Joseph Haydn's in Vienna and who had details of Mozart's life to tell: "...he is said to have been given aqua toffana..." This is a reference to a poison made from a mixture of antimony, lead, and white arsenic, which was named for the Sicilian lady Theophania di Adamo. It is reputed to have been used to commit murder for the first time by her daughter, Julia Tofana.

At first, people in Vienna did not seem to take the stories of poisoning very seriously. It was only in 1819, some thirty years after Mozart died, that interest was directed to this lurid topic by an article in the Leipzig *Allgemeine musikalische Zeitung*. Taking a statement by a musician named Sievers as its point of departure, the article openly conjectured that Mozart could have been the victim of a plot by the Italian faction in Vienna. No names were mentioned until 1823, when the Hofkapellmeister Antonio Salieri was singled out by name in connection with the rumor of murder by poison. A newspaper report out of Vienna to the *Allgemeine musikalische Zeitung* of 25 May 1825, only eighteen days after the death of Salieri on the 7th of May, said in a delayed comment from April:

> Our worthy Salieri just cannot seem to die, as the people here say. His body suffers all the pains of old age and his mind is gone. In moments of hallucination and confusion, they say, he even accuses himself of complicity in the early death of Mozart: a delusion that no one believes except the poor, bewildered old man himself.

In fact, many people apparently looked on this delusion as reality. When Salieri attempted to cut his throat with a razor in a moment of mental derangement in the autumn of 1823, rumors ran through Vienna that the old man had confessed to poisoning Mozart. A report in November 1823 by the Viennese editor Johann Schickh said in this connection: "Salieri cut his throat, is still alive though. The odds are one hundred to one that his declaration of conscience is true! The way Mozart died confirms this declaration!" Even Anton Schindler, later a biographer of Beethoven, wrote at the time: "Salieri is having a very bad time of it again, he is totally deranged. In his delusion, he believes that he is guilty of Mozart's death and he poisoned him. It must be the truth—for he wants to confess it as such—and so it is that everyone gets what they deserve." At the beginning of 1824, Beethoven's nephew Karl wrote something similar in one of the conversation books used to communicate with the deaf composer: "Salieri maintains that he poisoned Mozart...."

Some eighteen places in the collected letters of the Mozart family indicate that relations between Mozart and Salieri were often tense. The reason for Mozart's generally negative remarks about Salieri had to do with the favored position Salieri enjoyed at the court of Joseph II, a position that gave him considerable influence over musical life of Vienna. Mozart's letter to Michael Puchberg in December 1789 promising to tell him all about "Salieri's cabals" could well have been referring to one of Salieri's intrigues against Mozart. That Salieri succeeded in keeping the works of other musicians away from the emperor is attested to by documents indicating, for example, that together with other court musicians he prevented the performance of Haydn's string quartets as well as Mozart's chamber music. Given all that, the logical conclusion would be that it was Mozart who must have wanted to get rid of Salieri and not the other way around. It was Mozart who was fighting the losing battle for recognition at court and it was the less gifted Salieri who was standing in his way. All the threads of Vienna's musical life ran through the fingers of the court's musical conductor and president of the musicians' society, Antonio Salieri. Even as an opera composer, he had gauged the public's taste much better than Mozart.

Actually, the relationship between Salieri and Mozart cannot have been as troubled as it usually is portrayed. The representatives of the Italian faction at court had high regard for Mozart's music and even occasionally performed it. In fact, at a concert on 17 April 1791, Salieri chose to conduct Mozart's great G-minor Symphony (KV 550) himself. Salieri also held Mozart's operas in high esteem. Mozart personally went in his carriage to take the alleged antagonist Salieri, with his ladyfriend Caterina Cavalieri, to a performance of *The Magic Flute*. As he reported in a letter of 14 October 1791 to Constanze:

> Yesterday Thursday the 13th…at 6 o'clock I picked up Salieri and Caterina Cavalieri with the wagon and took them to the loge.…You can't believe how friendly they were—and how much they liked not only my music, but the libretto and everything put together. They both said it is a master work— worthy of being performed at the grandest celebrations before the greatest monarch—and they would surely go to see it very often, for they have never seen a prettier or more enjoyable show—

He watched and listened with complete attention
and from the overture to the last chorus, there
wasn't a number which didn't bring forth a bravo
from him, and they could hardly find words enough
to thank me for the favor....After the theater I had
them taken home....

Even these few comments suffice to show how totally absurd
it is to suspect Antonio Salieri of murdering Mozart by poison.
Many of Salieri's contemporaries spoke out vigorously against the
rumor. Johann Nepomuk Hummel, who had been Mozart's student, gave his view in his biography of Mozart: "Similarly I would
take outright issue with the legend that Mozart was poisoned by
Salieri; even if the latter had been jealous of the former's greater
talents, which must have detracted from the Italian taste reigning
at the time, still Salieri was much too honest and generally well-
regarded a man to accuse him in the least way of something like
that." Ignaz Franz von Mosel took a similar stand in the brief
biography of Salieri published shortly thereafter in 1827. But the
most important witness for the exoneration of Salieri, whose students had included Mozart's second son Franz Xaver Wolfgang as
well as Beethoven, Schubert, and Liszt, is the prominent musician
Ignaz Moscheles in a report he made about his last visit to Salieri,
then fatally ill, in the autumn of 1823. In his 1873 biography,
Moscheles wrote:

Our reunion...was sad, for I found his appearance appalling and he talked to me in broken sentences about his death which was surely soon to
come; and then finally these words: "In spite of
this being my last illness, I can declare in good
faith that there is absolutely nothing to that absurd
rumor; you know what I mean—Mozart, they say
I poisoned him. But I didn't! It's malice, sheer
malice, tell everyone for me, dear Moscheles; old
Salieri, who is about to die, has told you himself."

This avowal by Salieri refutes the suggestion, mentioned as
part of the rumor, that he had made a formal confession of guilt
before a priest. Moreover, Salieri's two attendants testified that

no one was allowed access to him except his doctor. This testimony tends to be confirmed in the travel diary of the Polish composer Karol Kurpinsky, published for the first time in 1957. An entry dated 27 November 1823 states: "I wanted to meet Salieri, but they told me at Artaria [music publishers in Vienna] that he would admit no one, not even his best friends, in to see him. The word is that he cut his throat."

The wave of allegations that Salieri was guilty of Mozart's murder reached its peak on 23 May 1824. On that day, Beethoven's Ninth Symphony and parts of the Missa solemnis were being performed at the Redoutensaal in the Hofburg. Suddenly leaflets fluttered down from the balcony with a poem on Beethoven written by the son of the Viennese opera singer Luigi Bassi. It contained unambiguous allusions to Salieri's guilt. This disgraceful defamation of Salieri before a prominent audience led his friend, Giuseppi Carpani, an author living in Vienna, to publish his famous defense in a Milan monthly in August 1824. In his clarion call for justice, Carpani's indignation overflowed: "Silence, you slanderers!...tell us, if you can, where your knowledge of such a terrible misdeed comes from....And even though the story is not true, at least it has been cleverly made up. First it originates in a small circle, then a larger circle throws the echo back and, to the vast majority, the crime is fact—Salieri poisoned Mozart."

The defense Carpani wrote was based primarily on a document which, from a medical point of view, should eliminate all suspicion that Mozart died by poison. The document is particularly valuable today because it is the only expert medical opinion on Mozart's last illness written by a doctor of unimpeachable authority and one who had seen Mozart's body after he died—Dr. Guldener von Lobes, a public health official for Vienna and Lower Austria.

In translation from Carpani's original Italian, the testimonial reads:

> I am pleased to tell Your Grace everything I know about the illness and death of Mozart. In late autumn he had fallen ill with inflammatory rheumatic fever which was going around generally at the time and affected many persons. I only learned of it some days later when his condition had already

turned for the worse. For various reasons, I did not visit him but I did ask Dr. Closset, whom I ran into virtually every day, about him. The doctor regarded Mozart's illness as serious and feared from the beginning it would have an unhappy outcome, in particular, a deposit in the head ("deposito alla testa"). One day he encountered Dr. Sallaba and told him in no uncertain terms: "Mozart is lost, it is no longer possible to stop the deposit." Sallaba passed this remark on to me right away, and Mozart did in fact die some days later with the usual symptoms of a deposit in the head. His death gave rise to sympathy and concern on the part of people generally, but it occurred to no one even in the slightest to entertain suspicion of a case of poisoning. While he was ill, he was seen by many persons, many others asked after him, his family looked after him with care and solicitude, and his highly regarded physician, the gifted and experienced Closset, treated him with all the attention of a conscientious doctor and the personal concern of a friend of many years, so that surely nothing would have escaped his notice, even if there had been the slightest trace of poison to discover. The illness took its normal course and lasted the usual length of time. Closset had recognized and followed it so closely that he had predicted its fatal outcome practically to the hour. The same illness struck numerous inhabitants of Vienna in the same period and, with many of them, had the same fatal result and the same symptoms as with Mozart. Close inspection of the body revealed nothing out of the ordinary. That is all I am in the position to say about Mozart's death. It would please me very much if I could contribute thereby to rebutting the terrible slander of the worthy Salieri.... Döbling, 10 June 1824

Your faithful servant, Guldener.

Dr. Guldener von Lobes sent virtually the same testimonial to Sigismund Neukomm, Joseph Haydn's former student then living in Paris. Neukomm obviously wanted to have it as material to use in connection with an article exonerating Salieri that he was publishing in the *Journal des débats*. Of the few additions or changes in the testimonial at variance with what was sent to Carpani, one sentence appears significant in connection with the rumor of poisoning: "...I viewed the body following [Mozart's] death and it showed no signs other than those customary in such cases." These words make it clear that Dr. Guldener personally saw Mozart's body after his death, perhaps in the capacity of official coroner.

An examination of a corpse was mandatory under the sanitary laws then in force. The relevant passages state:

> Each lifeless body shall be viewed prior to burial to verify that death by violence has not occurred...whether the person died of natural causes or ended life by violence should be established by a formal examination to be undertaken immediately by the authorities since, in the event of murder, suicide, or the commitment of crime, a judicial proceeding must take place.

Dr. Guldener's statement that after Mozart's death "close inspection of the body revealed nothing out of the ordinary" could only mean that the swellings referred to in the *Musikalisches Wochenblatt* in December 1791 were simply the swellings of Mozart's arms and legs already observed before he died. The wording in the newspaper that gave rise to the rumors of poisoning—"because his body became swollen after his death"—is obviously a layman's subjective description, one that the Prague correspondent may have heard in a roundabout way from the medically untrained Weber daughters, Constanze and Sophie.

Even leaving Dr. Guldener's testimony completely aside, however, it is simply unthinkable that Mozart's attending doctors would not have recognized mercurial poisoning if it had been present, as many authors today contend. From the time when Gerhard van Swieten first began to treat syphilis with mercury chloride, the various clinical manifestations of mercury poisoning resulting from an accidental overdose were much better known than they are now. Dr. Closset wrote about the use of mercury for treatment in his dissertation on putrid fever: "...the prolonged use of it [mercury] dissolves our bodily fluids and makes them liable to putrify. One can recognize this by the stinking breath and sweat of those persons who have taken mercury over a long period; their urine is cloudy and similar...to so-called drayhorse urine." Moreover, there was a doctor in Vienna at that time who had devoted himself with particular zeal to the study of different poisons and prompted the establishment of a chair for forensic medicine at the University of Vienna. This doctor was none other than Dr. Closset's friend and consultant at Mozart's bedside, Dr. Mathias von Sallaba.

In short, the thesis of Mozart's murder by poisoning cannot be proved, and the suspicion cast on Salieri does not stand up under examination. Even Mozart's relatives and friends were convinced of Salieri's innocence. Neither Constanze nor her two sons ever suggested otherwise. The note made by the two Novellos to the effect that Mozart's son Wolfgang denied that his father had felt threatened or indeed poisoned by Salieri is confirmation of this. Johann Nepomuk Hummel, who lived with the Mozart family for a long time when he was a young student, also took a clear stand on this matter in his Mozart biography written in 1825.

But legend, as we all know, is more persistent than historical fact, and the myth of Mozart's being poisoned would not die. A sterling example is found in Alexander Pushkin's two-scene dramatic work, *Mozart and Salieri,* written in 1830, in which Salieri is put down as Mozart's murderer. With its emergence as an opera through the music of Nikolay Rimsky-Korsakov in 1897, it became even better known and was widely distributed once records became available. Pushkin's drama with its historical inaccuracies founded on rumors that had reached the German ambassador in St. Petersburg from Vienna can, of course, be excused on the grounds of poetic license. The lack of fact in the Mozart biography published in 1845 by Edward Holmes, with its report of Salieri's alleged confession of murder, is much less excusable.

For a long time, the rumors and myths about Mozart's being poisoned (which have been set forth chronologically in the work of O. E. Deutsch) were not taken very seriously, but in 1861 the nature of the argumentation suddenly changed with the invention of malicious insinuations. In the magazine *Aus der Mansarde*, published in Mainz, an article by Georg Friedrich Daumer (who wrote many poems later set to music by Johannes Brahms) appeared with the title "Lodge and Genius," in which, for the first time, the Masons were held to be responsible for the alleged poisonings of both Mozart and the German dramatist Gotthold Ephraim Lessing. In addition, the article was the first to draw a connection between the question of Mozart's burial and a ritual murder supposedly ordained by the Masons. Even less tenable factually are the charges brought years later against the "murderous machinations" of the Masons, the Jesuits, and the Jews by the Berlin pedagogue Hermann Ahlwardt. In his book *Mehr Licht*, published in 1910, he named as victims not only Mozart and Lessing, but also the German poet Johann Christoph von Schiller, and even hinted darkly at a "Schiller-Lessing-Mozart consumption."

Certainly the most tendentious portrayal of Mozart's death comes from the German neurologist Mathilde Ludendorff, the wife of General Erich Friedrich Ludendorff. First in her book *The Unatoned Crime Against Luther, Lessing, Mozart and Schiller*, published in 1928, and then even more forcibly in the chapter on Mozart that appeared in expanded form as a book, *Mozart's Life and Violent Death*, in 1936, Dr. Ludendorff spoke of a gruesome death by a Jewish ritual that simultaneously showed signs of a typical Masonic lodge execution. In her opinion, the Masons deliberately directed suspicion of the murder to Salieri to avoid appearing guilty themselves. We do not need to go any further into this unsubstantiated portrayal of Mozart's death. Mozart had many friends and acquaintances among Jews in Vienna and we know it did not bother him at all that his friendship with Jews might have been socially harmful—we need think only of his relationship with Nathan Adam Arnstein and especially Arnstein's wife Fanny, for example. He was fully aware, of course, of the anti-Semitic views of Empress Maria Theresa, who shortly before her death in 1780 declared, "I know of no worse plague for a country than this tribe of people."

Mozart showed a similar loyalty to the Masons, and his commitment to the renewal of Masonic concepts can be seen in the ideas and symbolism of *The Magic Flute* and the little *Masonic Cantata*. From these works, it is obvious that Mozart had given neither the Jews nor the Masons any cause for offense. The ceremonial speech on the occasion of Mozart's death delivered at a meeting of the venerable St. Johann lodge "Zur gekrönten Hoffnung" speaks for itself:

> It has pleased the Master Builder of the World to break one of our most beloved and most worthy links from our brotherly chain. Who did not know him? Who did not esteem him? Who did not love him?—our worthy Brother Mozart—It was only some weeks ago that he was still standing here in our midst, still glorifying the consecration of our Masonic temple with his magical music.
>
> Who among us, my Brothers, would then have apportioned him so short a thread of life?—Who among us would have thought that only three weeks hence we would mourn for him?...For Art is Mozart's death an irreplaceable loss—his gifts which he exhibited from his earliest years had long made him the rarest phenomenon of his age—all Europe knew and admired him, exalted persons called him their favorite, and we called him— Brother....Love for his Brothers, agreeableness, readiness to take part in good works, charitability, a true, inmost feeling of pleasure when he could bring some profit to one of his Brothers through the use of his talents, these were the outstanding traits of his character—he was husband—father— friend to his friends—Brother to his Brothers—he lacked only treasure, with which he would gladly have made hundreds happy—.

More than all the rational arguments one could make, words like these show the absurdity of the suspicions that the Masons used poison to dispatch Mozart into the next world for revealing the secrets of the Masonic rites in his opera *The Magic Flute*.

Salieri was once again implicated in Mozart's death in 1953, when Igor Belza published a book discussing Pushkin's dramatic piece *Mozart and Salieri* and Mozart's supposed poisoning by Salieri. Belza quoted an alleged written confession by Salieri that the musicologist Guido Adler supposedly found in the archives of a church in Vienna, complete with all the details of Mozart's murder by poison and the release of the priest who heard the confession from his oath of silence. Adler was said to have disclosed this sensational discovery only to the Russian Boris Assafiev who was visiting Vienna in 1928 and had refrained from telling his fellow scholars about it. Belza's grotesque story has since been refuted by Dr. Boris Steinpress in the official music magazine in Moscow, which should make any further discussion of this unbelievable hypothesis unnecessary.

As it turned out, two German physicians, Dr. Günther Duda and Dr. Dieter Kerner, accepted these revelations without question, obviously because they saw in them support for their frequently expressed view that Mozart had been poisoned. In the Mozart chapter of his book *Krankheiten großer Musiker* (*The Illnesses of Great Composers*) that appeared in 1963—a chapter replete with historical inaccuracies—Dr. Kerner writes concerning the outcome of "scientific studies": "Modern medical research has proved beyond doubt that W. A. Mozart was the victim of mercurial intoxication caused by mercury chloride." Despite the fact that the clinical picture of Mozart's last illness that has come down to us does not conform in the slightest with that of mercury poisoning, the two authors go on to mention a growing number of possible murderers in connection with various hypotheses. At first it was Salieri—perhaps under contract from some obscure secret society such as the Masons—who was the key suspect. Then, however, the circle of possible perpetrators began to expand. To back up the theory of a long, drawn-out poisoning with mercury, suspicion was cast on the Mozart family's longtime friend and patron, Gottfried van Swieten, who was the son of Empress

Maria Theresa's personal physician, Gerhard van Swieten. Duda and Kerner point out that Gottfried van Swieten must have been fully informed of the characteristics of mercury because his father had started to use mercury chloride dissolved in brandy or wine for the treatment of syphilis. Thus the poison could have been administered to Mozart in the course of the musical concerts that took place at van Swieten's home every Sunday. These concerts had already ceased more than a year before Mozart died, one fact among many that apparently was not known to the authors. Their ultimate speculation is that perhaps Mozart happened to poison himself with mercury, unintentionally of course, while trying to treat himself for syphilis incurred through the "bad company of the theater director Schikaneder."

The utter lack of substance in these bizarre, ostensibly scientific inquiries is even more obvious in Dr. Kerner's interpretation of symbols and his cabalistic numerological acrobatics in the book by Duda, Kerner, and Johannes Dalchow, *W. A. Mozart: Documentation of his Death*, published in 1966. The following example is one of many in Kerner's chapter on Mozart:

> With respect to our knowledge of the events surrounding his death, it is interesting that the frontispiece engraving to the original libretto of The Magic Flute shows eight allegorical symbols relating to Mercury (8 is the sacred number of Hermes = Mercury!) on a herm, that is, a square stone pillar at the left of the page, symbols which have their origins in the alchemy of medieval times and others as well (the ibis, snakes, a ram's head, a lyre). Even the Mozart commemorative stamp issued in Austria in 1956 exhibits 8 allegorical symbols of Mercury around the edges, terminating in a sunburst at the corners: to be precise, four times two lyres and caducei....Of particular note in this connection is the fact that, according to the concepts of medieval alchemy, both the number 8 and the color gray are attributed to the planet Mercury, something that brings vividly to mind the "Gray Messenger" who repeatedly terrified Mozart

at the end in Vienna and who commissioned a
requiem mass from him....

Just how the symbols on the commemorative stamp in fact
came to be chosen is something O. E. Deutsch learned from Professor Chmielowski, its designer: "The signs which are said to
have symbolic character actually originate partly from an Empire
clock and partly from a chair out of the same period, both of
which are owned by my cousin, Count Csaky; in case there is any
doubt about this, they may both be seen at any time." In short,
like the misinterpretation of the stamp, all the other propositions
in support of the thesis that Mozart was murdered by poison put
forward by the group around Dr. Kerner collapse in the presence
of more factual and, in particular, more medically based examination (as discussed below in considering the "mercury kidney").

In 1983, two British Mozart scholars, Francis Carr and Horace
Fitzpatrick, made big news with their presentation of a new theory
for the death of Mozart in the context of a make-believe "judicial
inquiry" with the title *The Last Year in Mozart's Life* at a music
festival in Brighton, the English seaside resort. In addition to
Mozart's envious rival Antonio Salieri and his student Franz Xaver
Süssmayr, who just incidentally was suspected of having an affair
with Constanze, a chancery clerk by the name of Franz Hofdemel
was also suggested as the possible poisoner of Mozart. As it
turned out, fully half the "jurors" in this peculiar trial ended up
finding Hofdemel guilty.

This incredible accusation is founded solely on a supposition
by the two Mozart scholars that Hofdemel's young wife Maria
Magdalena, who may have been a pupil of Mozart's, had admitted to having a love affair with him. Hofdemel was one of Mozart's
lodge brothers and had even loaned him some money in April
1789. Mozart took part in the frequent playing of chamber music
at Hofdemel's elegant home in the Grünangergasse in Vienna.
On 6 December 1791, the day after Mozart died, Hofdemel perpe-
trated a horrible bloodbath, first attacking his five-months-preg-
nant wife with a razor and cutting her grievously around the neck,
and then committing suicide with the same weapon. Thanks to
the timely care of the surgeon Dr. Rossmann, Maria Magdalena
survived the assault. Hofdemel's body was sown in a cowhide

and buried in an unmarked grave, as was customary with suicides at the time.

The first report of this attempted murder and the subsequent suicide appeared in the Pressburg newspaper on 7 December without any names being mentioned. Then a week later, the same newspaper mentioned an alleged incident growing out of a jealous scene between Herr and Frau Hofdemel. The edition of 21 December said: "The widow of the suicide, who as we now know killed himself more out of despondency than jealousy, is still alive and not only many ladies but Her Majesty the Empress herself have pledged their support to this woman, whose conduct is known to be irreproachable." We can read from these lines that Frau Hofdemel evidently led an exemplary life and that an unbalanced mental condition, and not jealousy, had caused her husband to commit his frightful deed. Still, gossipmongers in Vienna, noting the coincidence in time between Mozart's death and the murderous attack, soon made a supposed love affair between Mozart and Maria Magdelena Hofdemel into the motive for the attempted murder.

The event of 6 December 1791 had a great impact on people then and later. Not only did Beethoven become aware of the tragic affair, but the people of Vienna would be reminded of it several times—for example, in the operetta *Wolfgang and Constanze* by Franz von Suppé and in the novel *Franz Hofdemel* published in 1932 by Wolfgang Götz. But the ultimate in bad taste was shown by Carr and Fitzpatrick, the initiators of the musical festival in Brighton in 1983 who, with presumptions made up out of thin air in a ridiculous judicial farce, posthumously accused the unfortunate Hofdemel of Mozart's murder by poison.

Today, belief in the absurd legend of Mozart's being murdered with poison can be sustained only through a total lack of knowledge of the clinical picture of mercury poisoning or by the manipulation, deliberate or not, of the biographical and historical facts related to Mozart's death. It is high time that we finally put an end to the constantly recurring discussions of this hypothesis, which has been disproved medically, and to the whole idea of looking further for potential "murderers" of Wolfgang Mozart.

Among the other theories about the cause Mozart's death, the hypothesis of kidney (renal) disease is particularly important because it is advanced by a profound student of Mozart, the dermatologist Professor Dr. Aloys Greither. The first person to hold the view that Mozart had begun to suffer with renal disease in his childhood was the French clinician Dr. J. Barraud. He wrote in the *Chronique Médicale* in Bordeaux in 1905 that in his opinion, the disease gradually developed into a chronic condition and led ultimately to Mozart's death in uremic coma. Even then, the swellings of Mozart's arms and legs were attributed to inflammation of the kidneys subsequent to an earlier attack of scarlet fever. It is now believed that the "scarlet fever rash" that Mozart had in October 1762 was not scarlet fever at all, but another inflammatory rash, known as erythema nodosum.* They appear to be an immunologic response to bacteria such as tuberculosis or to sarcoidosis. In his 1939 dissertation, H. Holz emphasized the anginas and tooth abscesses as the causes, in line with the theory of focal infections prevalent at the time.

Undoubtedly, the most fervent advocate of the kidney thesis is Dr. Greither. He places the start of this fateful kidney disease in the period of the first Italian journey, that is, in the years 1769 to 1771. In so doing, he relies on the passage in Nannerl's letter of 2 July 1819 that says: "...this [portrait] that was painted just when he returned from Italy is the oldest [of three portraits], he was only 16 years old but because he had just recovered from a very serious illness, so his picture looks sickly and very yellow...." But this report refers—as previously mentioned—to the time after Mozart's return in December 1771 from the second of the travels through Italy; he would turn 16 some weeks later. It was only then, shortly after he had finished his Symphony in A (KV 114) at the end of December 1771, that he acquired the "yellow Italian color" which supposedly made him unrecognizable and which, as also mentioned before, almost certainly resulted from jaundice caused by a viral infection of the liver he contracted in Italy. Because we are able to date this occurrence with some precision, Greither must be mistaken when he asserts in his 1971 medical study of Mozart:

> The key to Mozart's fatal illness appears to lie in this first Italian journey...during which he was sick without knowing it for a long time and following which he had to endure an even longer convalescence in Salzburg. Evidence will be provided later that this long illness represented an acute glomerulonephritis which would not heal and which, 25 years later, would lead to Mozart's early death.

Although nephritis is associated with pallor (anemia) and an olive-colored skin, hardly any nephritis leads to such a yellowing of the complexion that the patient becomes almost unrecognizable. In the acute phase of nephritis, the facial complexion is rather pale. Even in advanced stages of a chronic nephritis, we observe only a kind of sallow coloration of the skin. Greither's later argumentation shows how, once the mind is made up, all subsequent developments serve to underpin the initial hypothesis, even when the evidence would point the impartial person in a completely different direction. In his study, Greither continues:

> Should one...cast doubt on the later acute, protracted illness [meaning the one after the first Italian journey] as being glomerulonephritis, then these kidney symptoms were certainly manifest in September 1784 at the latest. From a detailed letter of Mozart's father to his daughter on 14 September 1784, we know that Mozart went through a serious illness with cystopyelitis [inflammation of the urinary bladder and renal pelvis] as its focus, putting him in danger of urosepsis [bacterial infection of the urinary tract].

In the letter cited, Leopold Mozart was reporting on Wolfgang's acute feverish illness, one then prevalent in Vienna, which involved four days of painful colic and vomiting. The word "colic" was used in those days chiefly as a term for gallbladder and abdominal pain—as Daniel Langhans stressed, for example, in his description of dangerous diseases written in 1762. Because the illness clearly was epidemic, it could have been acute epidemic gastroenteritis, with accompanying fever and vomiting.* In their clinical manifestations, viral infections correspond for the most part to the description given by Leopold Mozart. A diagnosis of this illness as febrile cystopyelitis, given our knowledge today, can be excluded, especially in view of its epidemic character.

But Greither's line of argument becomes totally incomprehensible when it addresses the end of Mozart's short span of life. Greither's suggestion that Mozart "was demonstrably seriously ill" during the last months of his life is entirely incompatible with Mozart's enormous activity and productivity in this period. He not only worked on the *Requiem*, but also completed *The Magic Flute*, *Titus*, the Clarinet Concerto, the *Masonic Cantata*, and numerous smaller compositions. Nor is Greither's view consistent with Mozart's last letters to Constanze, letters bubbling over with mirth and exuberance, confidence and the joy of living, letters that tell of an excellent appetite completely at odds with the terminal stages of chronic renal disease.

Greither's preconceived notions are most evident, however, in his interpretation of the swellings of Mozart's arms and legs as described in the extant reports. To support a diagnosis of chronic kidney disease and of uremia as the cause of death, an interpretation of "Nierenwassersucht" (renal hydrops) is introduced. This line of argument for a generalized hydrops, that is, an abnormal accumulation of serous fluid in the tissues, implies that Mozart's attending physicians were incapable of distinguishing the painless swellings of legs and arms from the painful swelling and acute inflammation of the joints. With such an inference, proponents of the kidney disease thesis make a serious mistake, as the relevant chapter from Dr. Sallaba's 1791 *Historia Naturalis Morborum* demonstrates. Under the title "Hydrops," that is, dropsy resulting from heart or kidney disease, Dr. Sallaba gives the following description:

> The illness is exceptionally frequent....Whoever is
> struck by hydrops, however, will persistently com-
> plain of dryness of the throat and the tongue in
> particular, with or without unquenchable thirst, and
> of dryness of the skin and diminution of urinary
> output....The sickness can affect the entire body,

but often as well only part of it. There is a soft swelling of the body, especially in the lowermost parts, in the lower limbs and the feet. When you press in on the swelling with your finger, an indentation remains which afterwards fills up again. The eyelids swell up in the same way....Fever is slight....

Dr. Sallaba had a special interest in acute rheumatic fever. He regarded it as being the consequence of the deposit of an abnormal substance, causing pain and swelling of the joints:

> Rheumatic fever seldom appears as a simple fever, but instead usually strikes a particular part of the body, either inside or out. It favors the membranous, sinewy parts, such as the ligaments and the joints, and is particularly dangerous for the knee joints and the wrists. Once inflammatory rheumatism has established itself in a particular place, exceptionally sharp pains occur which then spread farther; they seem almost more than a person can stand and are cruelly aggravated by the slightest movement of the body or by touching of the stricken part. The sickness is associated with swellings which are usually greater in extent (although with less hyperthermia and a stronger redness) than a true phlegmon. Moreover, the inflammation tends to migrate and leave the place it first occupied, either of its own accord following the application of cold compresses or through the use of other counter-inflammatory measures. It will very often migrate to the inner parts of the body, especially to the head or into the chest, cutting the threads of life and being the most frequent cause of death that comes from this illness.

Given that Dr. Sallaba explicitly noted in the foreword to his book that he and his friend Dr. Closset were in agreement on all important medical questions, we can be sure that both doctors were fully capable of differentiating very precisely between the inflammatory swelling of elbows and knees described above and edema caused by the presence of kidney hydrops. Hence, when they made the diagnosis of acute rheumatic fever and not hydrops due to kidney disease, they surely did so because they had not observed generalized overall swelling of Mozart's body, but rather—as Sophie Haibel recounted to the Novellos—highly inflamed and swollen limbs which—as Eybler noted in his autobiography—caused such pain that Mozart had to be "lifted up, laid down, and nursed" because of the "almost total immobility" of his swollen arms and legs.

This clinical picture is not characteristic of a chronic kidney disease that has reached the stage of uremia, in which we almost never find pronounced edema, but is typical of acute rheumatic fever. Further, Mozart exhibited "hitziges Frieselfieber," a feverish condition with profuse sweating and a consequent skin rash, at the same time as the painful swelling of his arms and legs. Such symptoms are never seen with a chronic kidney disease in the uremic stage, where the skin is noticeably dry because of a lack of tissue fluid. Finally, Dr. Guldener von Lobes stated that there was an epidemic outbreak of similar sicknesses in Vienna in the autumn of 1791. With such evidence, it is really difficult to understand why so many doctors still cling to the thesis of kidney disease as the cause of Mozart's death.

To justify their view, these doctors ignore the inflamed and painful character of the swellings. They argue that the description "much inflamed and swollen" written by the English couple, Vincent and Mary Novello, was a misinterpretation of Sophie Haibel's words caused by the Novellos' lack of familiarity with the German language. But after reading the Novellos' diaries, we cannot give this contention much credence; such simple adjectives as "swollen" and "inflamed" simply cannot be incorrectly translated! Similarly, Joseph Eybler is accused of having insufficient mastery of his mother tongue. Greither contends that, in describing Mozart's "painful" fatal illness which required that he be "lifted up, laid down, and nursed," Eybler really meant the word "painful" to be understood only in a psychological or emotional sense. Such an interpretation can also be rejected, for allusions to Mozart's physical pains are found in other primary sources.

In his biography of Mozart, Nissen writes about an "almost total immobility" of the swollen arms and legs. When Sophie Haibel reports that "due to the swelling," Mozart could not move or turn over and was therefore given "nightgowns he could put on from the front," surely she is not referring to a painful emotional disorder.

Advocates of the notion that Mozart's death was caused by mercury poisoning leading to damage of the kidneys and ending in uremia have put forth even less understandable arguments. They not only ignore the symptoms evident during Mozart's fatal illness that are cited in the primary sources, but also demonstrate ignorance of the clinical picture of mercury poisoning and attendant kidney damage. In common with atrophic kidney resulting from other causes, edema is virtually never present either at the stage of uremia or with mercury poisoning. Nevertheless, the presence of edema is constantly advanced in connection with this line of reasoning. As proof of the "massive swelling of the body," attention is called to a death mask that surfaced in Vienna in 1947 and is alleged to be that of Mozart. From two sources, we know such a death mask once existed. In a letter of 17 February 1802, Constanze informed the publishers Breitkopf & Hartle:

> ...Let me advise you therefore that the k. k. Kammerherr Count [Joseph] von Deym—who used to call himself Müller some years ago and who set up his own art gallery—cast Mozart's face in plaster of paris right after he died and, furthermore, that the actor [Joseph] Lange, who is a good painter, made a large portrait of him, but in profile, and, particularly since he knew M. well, he can probably make a very similar full-face portrait with the help of Deym's molding.

Sophie Haibel's letter, too, says that Count Joseph Deym arrived shortly after Mozart died and "cast his pale, dead face in plaster of paris." The original mask has unfortunately not been preserved and a copy that was made for Constanze was inadvertently broken, which—so the story goes—she dismissed with the disparaging remark that now, thank goodness, "that ugly thing is finally broken in two." The sensational discovery of a bronze casting alleged to be the death mask of Mozart has since turned out to be in error and two scientific commissions have concluded that the casting was made in the 20th century.

Seldom does chronic mercury poisoning result in kidney damage. Instead we find, in addition to a heightened flow of saliva and urine, pathological symptoms of the nervous system. The first to appear is a characteristic slight tremor, a trembling of the hands, which can be recognized in handwriting samples. Evidence of such a tremor cannot be adduced for Mozart. Researchers have not discovered—either in his handwriting or in the flow of his musical scores, including the last notes he ever wrote, in the "Lacrimosa" of the *Requiem*—even the hint of a finger tremor.

From a medical point of view, the utter lack of competence of the advocates of the poisoning theory is demonstrated by the hypothesis put forward by Dr. Kerner that Mozart's fatal illness must have involved the so-called "calomel sickness." What apparently is meant is an allergic hypersensitive reaction to mercurous chloride (calomel), once used as an intestinal purgative. Such reactions are encountered today in connection with many medications. The course of such hypersensitive reactions, which characteristically begin with fever and allergic rashes after about ten days, is usually benign. For this reason, contrary to Dr. Kerner's view, calomel sickness is not related even theoretically to fatal mercury poisoning of the kidneys.

In the last few years, two more hypotheses about Mozart's death have been advanced. In 1983, Dr. Peter J. Davies proposed that Mozart's illness in the late summer of 1784 was a case of a so-called Schönlein-Henoch purpura, with further attacks in 1787 and 1790, which led to chronic glomerulonephritis, that is, an inflammatory injury to all of the functional elements of the kidneys, and terminated in chronic renal failure. According to this theory, Mozart contracted a streptococcal infection while attending the meeting of his lodge on 17 November 1791 during a flu epidemic in Vienna. A few days later, the infection led to a hypersensitive reaction with a skin rash and purpura, that is, bruises and small red patches on the skin, and to acute inflammation of the joints. Because neither Constanze nor Sophie Haibel noticed minute, pinpoint red spots on the skin, the author simply assumes that the rash was limited to the lower half of the body. In Davies' view, however, chronic inflammation of the kidneys was only indirectly the cause of Mozart's death, for he does not allude subsequently to a terminal uremic coma. Rather, he holds that Schönlein-Henoch purpura caused a worsening of Mozart's high blood pressure—which he posits for no explainable reason—and consequently death from a massive cerebral hemorrhage.

Davies interprets various passages from the primary sources to substantiate his hypothesis. For example, he takes Nissen's description of the "almost total immobility" of Mozart's swollen arms and legs and Eybler's statement that, because of his painful sickness, Mozart had to be "lifted up, laid down, and nursed" as indicating paralysis of one side of the body. In addition, he invokes a statement from Sophie Haibel's letter of 7 April 1825 to her brother-in-law Georg Nissen:

> Closset, the doctor, was sought for a long time, finally found at the theater, only he had to wait till the piece was over—then he came and ordered cold compresses be placed on his burning head, which was such a shock to him that he never recovered consciousness before he expired. At the very end, as he tried to sound the drums in his Requiem with his mouth, I can hear it still.

Even this puffing out of the cheeks while breathing in a state of deep unconsciousness, which had been Mozart's condition since the last time he had been bled two hours before he died, is placed in the context of a cerebral hemorrhage; Davies here diagnoses paralysis of the seventh cranial nerve, whose motor fibers supply the muscles of facial expression. Even laymen with no medical training can see through this line of argument. The immobility of a person paralyzed by a stroke can under no circumstances be equated with "swelling of the arms and legs and an almost total immobility." Furthermore, an observer would not say that a paralyzed person "couldn't turn over because of the swelling" or had to be "lifted up, laid down, and nursed" because of "his painful sickness."

The primary sources provide still more indications that the thesis of cerebral hemorrhage with consequent paralysis is unfounded. Sophie Haibel says in her April 1825 letter: "...Now, when Moz. fell sick, we both made nightgowns for him that he could put on from the front...and because we didn't know how sick he might be, we made him a quilted robe too...so that when he got up, he would be well taken care of...." Even these few sentences make it apparent that Mozart could not have been paralyzed. The letter goes on to say: "...once when I came there on a Saturday [scarcely two days before his death!], M said to me: now, dear Sophie, you tell Mama that I'm feeling pretty good and that I'm still coming to congratulate her in the week of her name day...." A patient who is paralyzed could hardly assume that, in a few days, he would be ready to get out of bed and go visit his mother-in-law. Finally, Sophie Haibel's statements in connection with the last two hours of Mozart's life can hardly be construed to suggest paralysis of the seventh cranial nerve. Her statement that Dr. Closset's cold compresses so convulsed Mozart "that he never regained consciousness before he expired" means that shortly before he died he slipped into a state of deep unconsciousness, one probably triggered by the preceding bloodletting and in which the cheeks, flaccid and lacking tonicity, filled up like sails with the coma's labored breathing. Sophie Haibel described this too: "At the very end, as he tried to sound the drums in his Requiem with his mouth...."

The clinical picture discernible in documentary sources shows that we need not examine further the highly original and conjectural diagnosis of Schönlein-Henoch purpura. Such a diagnosis is certainly not founded in either Mozart's previous medical history or by analysis of the clinical picture of his final illness.

Finally, we must examine a recent theory attributing Mozart's death to a genetic, that is, a hereditary, pathologic anatomic condition. Professor A. E. Rappoport of Florida, a prominent pathologist and unabashed admirer of Mozart, proceeds from reports of Swiss and American scientists that numerous abnormalities of the kidneys and urinary tract accompany abnormalities of the ear. In such occurrences the spectrum of kidney anomalies can range from polycystic kidneys to the downward displacement of a kidney.

The Italian urologists Professor Cacchi and Professor Marini had concluded in 1957 that Mozart was afflicted by a hereditary anomaly in the form of a polycystic kidney and had died in a uremic coma as the result of renal failure. The possibility therefore occurred to Professor Rappoport that in Mozart's case there might be concurrent hereditary anomalies of the kidneys and the outer ear. He based this notion on a passage found on page 586 of Nissen's biography: "The facial traits and ears of the son Wolfgang are very similar to those of his father. What seems to be exceptionally noteworthy is the shape of Mozart's ears, which were completely different from what is normal and which, by the way, only his younger son inherited from him." Note, however, that the most profound student of the Mozart literature, O. E. Deutsch, had already pointed out in 1965 that such a characterization of Mozart's ears is not found in any other source and that the 19th century sketch in Salzburg showing such an ear was recognized long ago as being a picture of Mozart's younger son. An English group headed by the author Alex Paton arrived at the same conclusion. Thus, one of the two premises for Rappoport's theory collapses. The second premise, that Mozart died in a uremic coma following renal failure, does not stand up either under serious critical consideration of the relevant biographical and medical factors, as shown in the preceding discussion.

It is striking how the proponents of the different theories of Mozart's last illness seem to agree that his death resulted from kidney failure. For the uncommitted observer, this unanimity is all the more remarkable because a uremic coma presents a clinical picture completely at odds with that described by persons who were witnesses to Mozart's last illness and reported by word of mouth from Mozart's doctors to Dr. Guldener von Lobes. His testimonial in the letter to Giuseppe Carpani is the sole medical certificate relating to Mozart's last sickness, and its significance cannot be overstated. Dr. Guldener, who was kept up to date on the course of Mozart's illness by his colleagues and whose information agrees with the eyewitness reports of laymen, came to a diagnosis of acute rheumatic fever, as we have seen in the full text quoted previously.

This diagnosis based on Dr. Closset's statements has been repeatedly subjected to critical examination, most recently by Professor F. H. Franken. In particular, the point has been made that in Mozart's time, people had a quite different understanding than we do today of the term "inflammatory rheumatic fever." It was used as a lay expression in association with diseases of the heart or lungs, as well as the intestines, the ears, and even the teeth. Medical doctors such as Dr. Closset or Dr. Sallaba, however, certainly understood this expression to mean a well-defined clinical condition, as we can conclude from the relevant passage in Dr. Sallaba's 1791 medical textbook, *Historia Naturalis Morborum*. His picture of "inflammatio rheumatica," which in Dr. Sallaba's opinion has as its focus the deposit of matter causing sickness in the joints, is practically identical in content to the description of rheumatic fever found in modern textbooks on rheumatology and demonstrates that the diagnosis by Mozart's physicians was indeed based on an informed understanding of this clinical picture.

Admittedly, in the context of present-day medical terminology, Dr. Guldener's diagnosis gives a definition that is rather too general. Nevertheless, when we consider Mozart's previous medical history and the symptoms described by his relatives and friends, and then factor in our knowledge of the old Vienna school of medicine, we are able to form a more precise picture. Dr. Carl Bär did so in a particularly systematic way. In his monograph published in 1972, comprehensively analyzing all available sources and taking contemporary conditions, especially the medical-historical aspects, into consideration, Dr. Bär arrived at a diagnosis for Wolfgang Mozart's final illness which, in light of medical understanding today, can justifiably claim the highest degree of probability: acute rheumatic fever.

## Mozart's Medical History: An Analysis

A short recapitulation of Mozart's case history bears out the validity of Dr. Bär's diagnosis of his final illness. Documentary evidence confirms that Mozart suffered three episodes of acute rheumatic fever in his youth, along with frequent and sometimes severe bouts of pain and cramps, as well as tooth abscesses. He had repeated upper respiratory infections, probably with hemolytic streptococci, the bacteria whose metabolic products precipitate the onset of acute rheumatic illnesses. Finally, in 1791, a sickness occurred which, on the basis of the extant descriptions, strongly supports the diagnosis of a new attack of acute rheumatic fever with acute inflammatory arthritis.

The detailed statements of Mozart's relatives and friends cited previously support this view: "...The illness began with swelling of the arms and legs and his almost total immobility...." Apparently they tried hard to avoid any movement of his swollen arms and legs, for even getting dressed caused difficulties "...because he couldn't turn over due to the swelling...." The impossibility of confusing the symptoms of untreated acute rheumatic fever, well known to doctors then, with the painless swelling that accompanies chronic kidney disease is underscored by extracts from the clinical description of acute rheumatic fever contained in the well-known *Textbook of Applied Medicine for Internal Diseases* by Dr. H. Eichhorst. This text was written in 1899 after treatment with salicylic preparations had begun in 1876. For example:

> ...The most constant symptom is pain which is spontaneously present even at rest and can become extremely severe with the slightest movement....Thus, when many joints are afflicted, the patient gives the impression of being completely helpless....Necessary changes in his position, for example, when changing his bed or when defecating, cause the most agonizing pains.

This account clearly illustrates what Eybler meant when he spoke of Mozart's "painful final illness."

The textbook describes still other symptoms that were seen in Mozart. For example: "...A marked characteristic of the disease is the tendency for profuse sweating. There is a constant flow of a peculiar, sour-smelling...sweat, without it having anything to do with the patient's temperature as it does with other infectious diseases...." The heavy sweating undoubtedly was the reason why Constanze and her sister Sophie promptly began to make

several nightshirts for Mozart as soon as he fell ill. Eichhorst
continues:

> ...Normally, the disease in the joints comes to rest
> at first in one or more of the joints of the
> extremities...most often, the knee and ankle joints
> are affected, followed by the wrists, the shoulder
> and hip joints, and finally the finger joints in de-
> scending order of frequency....The affected joint
> is usually swollen, the skin around it is reddish
> and warm to the touch.

The redness and heightened temperature of the swollen joints
can be recognized by anyone, medically trained or not. It is
therefore all the more curious that Mary Novello's account of Sophie
Haibel's fear—that the cold compresses prescribed by Dr. Closset
"...had been harmful to the sick man whose arms and legs were
very inflamed and swollen...."—has been dismissed by Greither
and others of his persuasion as an incorrect assessment of the
swellings, caused by difficulties in translating from German to
English.

Eichhorst continues with his description of acute rheumatic
fever:

> Fever always accompanies disease of the joints.
> The temperature is seldom extreme and normally
> does not rise above 39.5°C. [103°F.]....Even in se-
> vere cases, the mind remains clear. At times, peri-
> ods of agitation may occur. In untreated cases we
> can sometimes observe a dry, even blackened
> tongue.

Such a coating of the tongue could explain the oft-cited statement
Mozart supposedly made to Sophie Haibel the night before he
died: "I already have the taste of death on my tongue...." The
fever must have been rather high, at least toward the end, for
Sophie says that "cold compresses for his burning head" were
ordered by the doctor. We can confidently assume Mozart remained coherent and conscious despite the high fever, for Nissen
says in this regard: "...He remained fully conscious until two
hours before he passed away."

Eichhorst also comments on the various skin disorders that arise in the context of acute rheumatic fever: "...The strong tendency of sweating to occur with acute rheumatic fever has already been mentioned; miliaria (prickly heat) often appears in association with it...." This vesicular skin rash of small blisters, which is present with various sicknesses involving fever, was regarded even then as a nonspecific symptom and given the term "Frieselausschläge"—miliary eruptions. The medical expression "hitziges Frieselfieber," acute miliary fever, was generally used for a sickness that evidently was observed in many people in Vienna in late autumn of 1791. In his deposition, Dr. Guldener said explicitly: "...The same illness struck numerous inhabitants of Vienna in the same period and, with many of them, had the same fatal result and the same symptoms as with Mozart."

Of course, Dr. Guldener was not saying that a large part of Vienna's population was sick with acute rheumatic fever at this time; rather, he was drawing attention to a situation which today we would call an epidemic of febrile illnesses. This is the only interpretation we can give to the similar sentence in the copy of Dr. Guldener's letter to Carpani that was sent to Neukomm in Paris: "...an inflammatory fever which was so widespread at the time that relatively few persons escaped it completely..." Because of the unhygienic conditions common at the time, such nonspecific symptoms were much more frequently responsible for setting off a wave of rheumatic sicknesses than they are today. It is therefore not surprising that, according to Dr. Guldener's testimony, the death rate due to inflammatory rheumatic fever had increased in the years 1786 and 1791.

The vomiting said by Nissen to have occurred toward the end of Mozart's final illness is a symptom the opponents of the rheumatic fever theory like to incorporate into a clinical picture of uremic coma as the last stage of an acute or chronic kidney disease. Nissen's biography of Mozart says: "His fatal illness...began with swellings of the arms and legs...which were later followed by sudden vomiting...." To classify this symptom properly, we need to know something of the customary method of treating rheumatic fevers at the time, as it would have been applied by Dr. Closset and Dr. Sallaba, the two best known students of the celebrated medical pedagogue Maximilian Stoll. Writing in April 1777, Stoll had recommended the following measures: "My method of treatment was: following venesection [bloodletting], I administered potions of saline solutions, using, if necessary, an emetic which I repeated from time to time. After the vomiting, I sought to keep the bowels open...." Maximilian Stoll was the leading advocate of the theory of the humors—the so-called "humoral pathology"—and held firmly to the fundamental principles of the four basic temperaments laid down by the Greek physician Galen. The most essential measure, as Stoll saw it, was the removal of the disease-causing matter—the *materia peccans*—from the stomach by administering an emetic. To do this, Stoll recommended "...four grains of antimoniated tartar dissolved in a half liter of water, with the patient drinking a fourth of it every quarter hour. Following vomiting, I give lukewarm water to drink to alleviate the throwing up...." As Stoll's student and successor, Dr. Closset could well have treated his renowned patient, Wolfgang Mozart, in this way. In short, the vomiting mentioned by Nissen was probably not a symptom of Mozart's illness, but, rather, a consequence of its course of treatment.

By integrating all these pertinent comments, we can make a diagnosis of the cause of Mozart's last sickness, a diagnosis seen from the standpoint of medicine today. It is the same diagnosis that Carl Bär made after his thorough scientific examination of the clinical history and physical findings, and one in accord with that of the doctors who treated Mozart—namely, rheumatic fever.

Critics of this diagnosis counter by contending that such an acute rheumatic fever must have been the first occurrence of the disease, which—as Franken commented—happens relatively seldom in adults and which, if left untreated, can lead to death in only a few weeks even today. However, we now know that the appearance of acute rheumatic fever in middle adulthood does not signify an initial occurrence of this illness, but rather that relapses or recurrences of rheumatic fever can show up at that age. The streptococci that cause the disease take so many forms that successful recovery from one infection confers no immunity against other species in this bacterial group, which is why children who have rheumatic fever with acute inflammation of the

joints caused by such streptococci, as Mozart did, often suffer
severe exacerbations to renewed infection in adulthood. Today,
thanks to effective treatment with antibiotics, cortisone preparations, and medicines that inhibit the inflammation associated with
rheumatism, latter-day recurrence in adults is rare. But to understand the course of this disease in Mozart's time, we must turn
again to Eichhorst for guidance. We learn that the frequency of
recurrence must have been considerably higher in previous centuries than it is today:

> ...Even more frequent is the tendency of the pa-
> tient who once has had rheumatic fever to get all
> the symptoms of a recurrence. Once sick with
> polyarthritis [rheumatic inflammation of multiple
> joints], an inclination for repeated attacks is ac-
> quired, so that such persons can be ill with rheu-
> matic fever three, four, even eight times.

Because Mozart had at least three attacks of acute rheumatic fever
in his childhood, we may assume that his final illness was another
episode of acute rheumatic fever in his mid-adult years.

To understand the progress of this illness, which culminated
in death in the brief span of only fifteen days, we need a knowledge of pathomorphogenesis, that is, the developmental changes
in the clinical picture presented by this sickness during the past
two centuries, and a knowledge of what was seen as an effective
method of treatment given the state of medicine in Mozart's time.
Today we know that, under the social and hygienic circumstances
in those days, acute rheumatic fever not only appeared thirty
times more frequently than it does now, but was much more
severe. Comparable conditions are found today in the so-called
underdeveloped countries, where rheumatic fever is not only a
very common disorder, but one with an appallingly high mortal-
ity rate. In his study published in 1836, J. B. Bouillaud was the
first to point out that all his cases of rheumatic fever that ended in
death were accompanied by inflammation of the heart (inflammation of the heart muscle, the cardiac valve, or the heart sac)
and that this was one of the most frequent complications of acute
rheumatic fever. For this reason, Dr. Carl Bär considered the

possibility that Mozart could have acquired heart damage in child-hood in the course of his three bouts of rheumatism. If a valvular defect of the heart is already present, a new attack of acute rheu-matic fever can cause recurrence of inflammation in the region surrounding the affected cardiac valve or cardiac muscle. The description of the symptoms accompanying Mozart's last illness, however, contains no hint at all that this complication was present. Arguing against such a possibility is the fact that Mozart's physical fitness does not appear to have been impaired or reduced in any way. He was able to indulge his passion for dancing with no difficulties at all and, until shortly before his death, often went horseback riding in the morning.

The rapidity with which Mozart died, after an illness lasting only slightly more than two weeks, could have been due to other factors. One indication of another possible cause is found in Dr. Guldener's testimonial: "...[Dr. Closset] regarded Mozart's ill-ness as serious and feared, from the beginning, that it would have an unhappy outcome, in particular, a deposit in the head. One day he encountered Dr. Sallaba and told him in no uncertain terms: 'Mozart is lost, it is no longer possible to stop the de-posit'..." In other words, a "deposito alla testa," a deposit in the head, was held to be directly responsible for Mozart's death.* In this connection, we must keep in mind the then prevailing hu-moral pathology, which taught that the many symptoms present with rheumatic diseases were due to disease-producing (patho-genic) substances deposited in the bodily tissues. The accumula-tion of such matter primarily in the joints was believed to produce the usual picture of acute rheumatic fever. Matter was thought to accumulate in other parts of the body as well, the thoracic cavity being favored. According to medical teachings toward the end of the 19th century, pleural effusions were relatively common with acute rheumatic fevers as a masked form of the sickness, whereas inflammations in the region of the peritoneum (the serous mem-brane lining the walls of the abdominal and pelvic cavities and covering the abdominal organs) and especially the meninges (the membranes covering the brain and spinal cord) were an infre-quent complication. At the end of the 18th century, if the disease took a threatening course or culminated in death, it was often diagnosed as the dreaded "deposito alla testa." This medical term should not be translated as meningitis but rather, in accordance with Stoll's theory of the humors, as referring to an accompanying inflammation of the brain, something that can occur with every inflammatory process involving elevated fever and which Stoll termed "incidental encephalitis."

For an explanation of the surprising suddenness of Mozart's death, we have to reach back to the experience of doctors in the 19th century who, even after the introduction of salicylates, still had cases which took such a dramatic turn. As late as 1911, Jochmann was writing about the involvement of the brain in connection with acute rheumatic fever:

> ...The first thing to mention concerning manifestations of the central nervous system are the states of excitement which occur in sensitive persons resulting from severe pain and the sleeplessness that goes with it, influenced perhaps by pathogenic effects as well....Particularly noteworthy are those unusual and, fortunately, rather seldom cases of rheumatic fever which we call either cerebral rheumatism because of their serious brain symptoms, or hyperpyretic rheumatic fever because of abnormally elevated fever. In this stage of the disease, regardless whether the case is serious or light, the fearsome situation can ensue whereby the fever inexorably climbs to 40°C. [104°F.], 41° [105.8°], or 42° [107.6°] and even higher. When that happens, it leads to heightened levels of psychomotor activity and to delirium, often to motoric signs of irritation leading to cramps or to irritation of the meninges as well. The pulse races and becomes weak, and death occurs amid signs of collapse. The duration of this stage often amounts to only a few hours, although it can stretch out over days. Because we can learn nothing by anatomically examining the brain, we can only assume an uncommonly virulent toxic effect of the pathogen causing rheumatic fever on the

central nervous system and the centers controlling the body's temperature.

This detailed presentation is instructive in several ways. It accords in essence with the experience of doctors in the late 18th century and their ideas about how a "deposito alla testa" materialized, only here the toxic effect is ascribed to the postulated pathogen causing rheumatic fever rather than to the disease-producing matter. In today's view, rheumatic fever is in fact a delayed symptom of an upper respiratory infection caused by Group A hemolytic streptococcus. The excerpt also coincides remarkably well with the statements about the progression of Mozart's illness shortly before his death. From the extensive comments of Sophie Haibel already cited, we can assume that Mozart must have had a very high fever immediately before he died, for she emphatically mentions "cold compresses on his burning head." Mozart apparently fell into a kind of fever delirium at the end, for Seyfried's account states: "The evening of the 4th of December, M. was already delirious...." But still another source is available to us that reports a sudden worsening in the course of the illness. This source is known as the "Deiner report," which has not been mentioned until now because of the uncertain validity of its testimony. It contains the reminiscences of Joseph Deiner, the man Mozart jokingly called "Joseph the First" in his letters to Constanze, who had worked in a nearby tavern that Mozart apparently visited frequently in the last part of his life. Deiner died in 1823 and his personal remembrances were published in 1856 by an anonymous author in the *Wiener Morgenpost* on the occasion of the 100th anniversary of Mozart's birth. The account says, among other things:

> On 28 November, the doctors held a consultation regarding Mozart's condition. The then well-known Dr. Elossek [Dr. Closset] and Dr. Sallaba, chief physician at the General Hospital, were present.... Because Mozart's illness was becoming more critical by the minute, his wife had Dr. Sallaba come again on 5 December 1791. He arrived and soon after him the Kapellmeister Süssmayr besides, to

whom Sallaba quietly confided that Mozart would
not survive the night....

We can be reasonably certain, then, that at the very end, just
before Mozart died, an extremely high body temperature and finally delirium appeared along with the rheumatic pains in his
joints. This constellation of symptoms fits well with the clinical
picture of "cerebral rheumatism" or "hyperpyretic rheumatic fever" given in Jochmann's 1911 description and could quickly have
led to Mozart's death. With this in mind, we can easily imagine
how meaningful the diagnosis of a "deposito alla testa," a deposit
in the head, was for the physicians of the 18th century in judging
the likely future course of a case of rheumatic fever* and we can
better understand why they often could tell that the outcome was
likely to be fatal. In short, we find a certain vindication of Mozart's
attending physicians that offsets the blame heaped on them by
Sophie Haibel, as mirrored in Nissen's biography: "My sister-in-
law is of the opinion that Mozart did not receive adequate treatment for his sickness, because instead of trying to drive out the
skin eruptions even more in some other way, they...put cold
compresses on his head...," a postscript that relates to Sophie's
previous statement that Dr. Closset "ordered cold compresses be
placed on his burning head, which was such a shock to him that
he never recovered consciousness before he expired...."

Although doctors at the end of the 18th century might well
have seen nothing exceptional in death after only a few weeks in
grave cases of rheumatic fever complicated by cardiac valve inflammation or so-called cerebral rheumatism, one other factor
must be considered that probably contributed decisively to Mozart's
unexpectedly sudden death. A common method of treatment in
those times was the purposeful withdrawal of substantial quantities of blood from the body. Bókay was the first to call attention
to its harmful effects in 1906. The writings of Dr. Closset
and Dr. Sallaba suggest that venesection must have been the treatment they chose for their patient Mozart. In his *Historia Naturalis
Morborum* of 1791, Dr. Sallaba wrote about the importance of
vigorous withdrawals of blood in connection with rheumatic inflammations: "Here the necessity for withdrawing blood is at its
greatest, greater in fact than with a real inflammation, and there is

no other disease known that so easily tolerates the large withdrawal of blood." Accordingly, he would prescribe at least six to
eight venesections or more, a fourth of a liter of blood at a time,
in the first week of an inflammatory illness. Such a loss of blood
could only have had a catastrophic effect on Mozart's slight body,
weakened as it was by fever and outbreaks of miliaria.

That Mozart was in fact subject to this bloodletting therapy
can be derived from two different sources. First, Sophie Haibel
said that "...the family doctor, Dr. Closset, arrived that last night
and undertook the letting of blood...." Second, a doctor later
alluded to this method of treatment. An entry in the diary of
Dr. Carl von Bursy written in 1816 says: "The most famous doctor
in the city diagnosed Mozart's disease as inflammatory and bled
his veins...." The account in the Deiner report that a consultation
between Dr. Closset and his friend Dr. Sallaba took place in Mozart's
apartment in the Rauhensteingasse on 28 November 1791, a week
before he died, might suggest indirectly that they were considering intensifying the venesection therapy. We are aware that the
two friends and colleagues discussed difficult decisions with one
another. Moreover, from remarks made in Niemetschek's biography of Mozart, we can infer that this consultation was called not
because of a lack of certainty about the diagnosis but for the
purpose of considering therapeutic measures. In any event, the
reason behind it was the dangerous rise in Mozart's body temperature. From both Dr. Sallaba's writings and the teachings of
his mentor, Maximilian Stoll, we learn that when fever failed to
abate or, especially, when there was a further rise in temperature,
even more frequent venesections were recommended. Stoll's 1794
textbook comments on this therapeutic approach: "...[those] inflammation fevers which...do not perceptibly lessen after three
bloodlettings are dangerous. For after the third bloodletting, the
illness [that is, the temperature] should at least not rise, if there is
to be any hope [for recovery]."

For Mozart, the venesections apparently did not bring the
hoped-for improvement. Their lack of success must be another
reason for Dr. Closset's prediction of a fatal outcome. Indeed,
Dr. Guldener's testimonial says: "...One day he encountered Dr. Sallaba and told him in no uncertain terms: 'Mozart is

lost, it is no longer possible to stop the deposit.' Sallaba passed this remark on to me right away, and Mozart did in fact die some days later with the usual symptoms of a deposit in the head."

It is beyond question today that for many patients, the treatment of withdrawing substantial quantities of blood brought on death through hypovolemic shock. In view of the indications, both direct and indirect, that bloodletting was used on Mozart, this therapy could well have contributed significantly to his death. Nissen's biography of Mozart contains a striking suggestion of this possibility: "...Accordingly the family doctor, Dr. Closset, arrived that last night and undertook the letting of blood...whereupon his strength visibly ebbed and he fell unconscious and never came to again."

In sum, if we consider all sources available to us, as well as contemporary medical-historical factors and the level of medical understanding at the time, Mozart's fever-ridden illness accompanied by profuse sweating and miliaria-induced skin eruptions, with inflamed and swollen extremities and limited movement as the result of extreme painfulness, was almost certainly an acute polyarthritis with the clinical picture of recurrent acute rheumatic fever. This diagnosis is substantiated by the several previous episodes of acute rheumatic fever in Mozart's youth. The development of "cerebral rheumatism" with impairment of important brain centers, a disease accompanied by extremely high body temperature and often quickly fatal in the absence of the necessary therapy, could well have been critical for the ultimate course of Mozart's illness, one that was much more dangerous then than now, and his death after just over two weeks. But the immediate cause of his death undoubtedly was the withdrawal of blood two hours before he died. All the reported details of Mozart's final illness fit with this diagnostic conclusion and allow no other interpretation. An end to the controversy over Mozart's fatal sickness therefore seems to be in order.

## The Funeral and Burial

Although we are moderately well informed about the last days and hours of Mozart's life, exactly what happened in the time between his death and his burial remains somewhat obscure. Even the exact day of his funeral—the date of 6 December 1791 is entered in the death register of St. Stephen's Cathedral—is not certain. Recent research suggests that Mozart's corpse was consecrated only on the 7th of December, not the 6th, with burial in the cemetery of St. Mark following thereafter. An earlier date for the funeral would be out of the question because Mozart died on the 5th of December and, in accordance with the strict sanitary regulations then in effect, which had been promulgated by Joseph II and remained unchanged under his successor Leopold II, a waiting period of forty-eight hours after death was observed without exception. Various memoirs also point to the 7th of December as the proper date, for they are all in agreement in deploring the miserable and stormy weather that prevailed on the day of the funeral. We find a description in the Deiner report:

> ...The night Mozart died was dark and stormy, and even at the time of the consecration, the weather began to rage and worsen. It both rained and snowed, as though Nature herself was offended with the composer's fellow citizens, who had found their way to his funeral in such meager numbers. Only some friends and three women accompanied the body. Mozart's wife was not present. With their umbrellas up, these few friends stood around the coffin, which afterward was carried through the wide Schullerstrasse to St. Mark's cemetery. Because the storm was getting worse and worse, even these few friends decided to turn back at the Stubentor [a gate in the city walls]... Hausmeister Deiner was also among those present at the consecration.

Karl Friedrich Hirsch, the grandson of Mozart's friend, the composer Johann Georg Albrechtsberger, wrote: "And finally, it is true that at the time of Mozart's funeral services, the weather was very unfavorable, which is why no one except the Albrechtsberger family accompanied the body." And a last report comes from Johann Dolezalek, a musician who came to Vienna in 1799, who said that two of Mozart's students—Franz Jakob Freystädtler and Otto Hatwig—maintained that "...due to the stormy weather, [they] could not accompany the body any farther than the Stubentor because they could not keep up with the wagon which was going so fast."

From records held by the meteorological service in Vienna, we know that the inclement weather recounted by Mozart's contemporaries was the result of a storm out of the southwest in the late afternoon of 7 December. The 6th of December, in contrast, was calm and hazy, a typical late-autumn day. Hence, the date of Mozart's funeral service must have been the 7th of December. The incorrect entry of the 6th of December in the register of the chancellory at St. Stephen's Cathedral probably resulted from the date for the funeral service having been scheduled in advance for the 6th of December when Mozart's death was reported on the 5th of December.

The consecration may have taken place in the Cross Chapel to the left of the main entrance, with the coffin thereafter being "laid to rest"—as they put it then—until evening in the Crucifix Chapel, which served as a mortuary, because conveyance of bodies was permitted only at night. In other words, for the relatives, the actual funeral ceremonies were over once the consecration in the cathedral was finished. The actual movement of the body and its burial took place, in accordance with the official burial regulations, without ceremony and without a priest being present. A court decree by Joseph II dated 23 August 1784 prescribed that all deceased persons "...after being consecrated with the singing of the customary church prayers and laid to rest, will thereafter...be conveyed to the established cemeteries outside the city limits for burial without pomp or ceremony." On 17 July 1790, a special order was issued about the conveyance of bodies to the graveyards on the outskirts of Vienna, which said in part: "...His Majesty decrees that the wagons conveying bodies shall never be driven to the graveyards before 9 o'clock in the evening during the summer period and never before 6 o'clock in the evening during the winter period...." The order was subsequently amended on 28 October 1790 to remedy certain deplorable circumstances that had arisen in connection with conveying bodies to the cemeteries: under threat of penalty, "...drivers of the wagons are not to indulge in drink, while the wagons stand around in front of saloons, so that they are no longer in condition to lead the horses the rest of the way without a torch."

These last two instructions, issued in the reign of Leopold II, make it obvious that a funeral procession was not customary in Mozart's time. St. Mark's Cemetery is more than four kilometers (2.5 miles) from St. Stephen's Cathedral and the people in mourning for Mozart would have had to travel a long way over bad roads and in December's total darkness, a particularly disagreeable prospect given the miserable weather. It is certainly understandable, therefore, that even his closest friends turned back at the Stubentor in the city walls, especially since the wagon driver apparently was driving his horses as fast as they could go because of the stormy weather. It was not from lack of reverence for the departed that only a wagon driver accompanied Mozart's body as it was taken to St. Mark's Cemetery on a black, stormy night, aboard a hearse rented by his family for three gulden; it was simply the custom at the time.

Mozart's body probably was held overnight in the "death shed"—whose doors, by the way, were never locked because of the then prevalent fear of a "false" or apparent death—and the gravedigger Simon Preuschl would have accomplished the actual burial the next morning. Conditions for interment had been laid down by Joseph II that today seem lacking in both respect and good sense and can be understood only when seen against the background of Joseph II's concept of enlightened despotism. His extensive program of reforms encompassed burial practices and, because his whole outlook was rooted in the intellectual attitudes of the Enlightenment, many of his burial regulations were based on quite realistic sanitary public health considerations. When we read these instructions today, however, we are able to appreciate why they met with resistance from the people and why Joseph II ultimately felt compelled to revoke or at least relax some of them. Typical of the way the emperor did things, for example, is the rationale for regulating interments from the year 1784:

> Because burial foresees nothing other than hastening decomposition as soon as possible, and

A Frenchman's portrayal of a pauper's funeral in the time of Mozart (engraving by Pierre Roch Vigneron).

because that would not be impeded when, for the
burial, the corpse is sewn naked and unclothed in
a linen sack, then placed in the burial chest, and
carried in that to the graveyard...once the corpse
has arrived, it should be taken out of the chest
and placed as it is in the linen sack in the trench,
sprinkled over with quicklime, and immediately
covered with dirt."

On 20 January 1785, this sack burial was revoked under pressure
from public opinion and the use of coffins was again authorized,
although sack burial remained in effect for people dying in hospitals until the beginning of the 19th century. The other regulations
were expressly retained, however, among them the prohibition of
"all excessive displays, banquets, the 'Leichenschmaus' [where
the mourners meet to eat and drink after the funeral], and all
eulogies and burning of candles." Moreover, the order "that the
corpse is not to be accompanied by priests to the gravesite...and
is to be placed in the grave with neither ceremony nor the accompaniment of the parish priest" remained in force. Given these
strict regulations, it is obvious that there were no funeral processions at all. Moreover, participation in a funeral procession would
have been unreasonable given the great distance of most of the
cemeteries outside the city, the poor condition of the roads, the
dark of night, and the fact that no graveside ceremonies were
permitted in the unlighted cemeteries. In short, the reason for
Mozart's burial without the presence of either family or friends
was not that they wanted it that way or that the weather prevented them from accompanying the wagon bearing his body,
but that such burials were typical of Vienna at the time.

Under Emperor Leopold II, most of the decrees of Joseph II
were not only confirmed but in part made more strict. To understand the absurdity of the legends that Mozart was buried in a
potter's field or was buried in a mass grave, which originated in
ignorance of contemporary circumstances, we must be aware of
the conditions applying to actual interment. In the days of the
enlightened despotism of Joseph II, putting multiple bodies into a
trench grave was taken as a matter of course and was the most
common form of burial. The order covering the "Burial of Dead

Persons in Vienna" issued by the then sanitary magistrate Dr. Guldener von Lobes on 4 June 1796 says:

> It is prescribed that only four adults and two chil-
> dren, or if there are no children, five adults may
> be placed in the graves of bodies buried in cas-
> kets, and there is therefore no reason why two
> graves with bodies should be open at the same
> time....According to regulations, a grave must be
> 6 feet long, 4 feet wide, and 6 feet deep."

From this decree it is clear that the requirement of placing five to
six bodies in a single grave was stringently applied and compli-
ance was closely monitored.  A gravedigger who did something
contrary to the rules was "to be reported immediately to the high
commissioner of the police, who was to take the guilty person
forthwith to prison, where following admission of his guilt he
was to be punished."

Against this historical background, it hardly seems appropriate to infer a "shameful pauper's grave" or a "burial in a mass
grave" from the remarks made by Nissen: "Mozart's remains were
buried in the graveyard in the St. Mark's district of Vienna.  Because van Swieten took the greatest possible economy for the
family into consideration, the coffin was lowered into a joint grave
and all other expenses were avoided."  The "joint (or communal)
grave" mentioned in this account is entirely consistent with the
usual burial given citizens of Vienna in this period.

Why this simple, middle-class burial was chosen for Mozart
rather than a more elaborate funeral is quite another matter.  We
know that funeral processions and separate graves outside the
city walls were occasionally authorized for exceptionally prominent persons even in Josephinian times.  When the composer
Christoph Willibald Gluck died in 1787 at the age of 73, for example, he was interred in a separate grave in the cemetery in
Matzleinsdorf with people from Vienna present.  Just how seldom
such exceptions occurred in Mozart's day, however, is clear from
a decree first issued in October 1807, apparently as the result of
public pressure, that said the erection of separate graves would,
in individual cases, be authorized "for persons of high rank and

distinguished service," for which a charge of 10 to thirty gulden was to be paid, depending on how the grave was furnished.

Several possibilities have been suggested to explain why such an exception was not instituted from on high for Mozart. The line of argument pursued by even so conscientious a person as Carl Bär—that at the time of his death, Mozart had already slipped into oblivion and been largely forgotten—is not only incomprehensible but totally invalid. It was precisely in the last weeks of Mozart's life that the promise of substantial sums of money came from outside the country, where his operas were being performed in all the major cities of Europe with increasing frequency. Even in the empire, his artistic reputation was acknowledged by all in his last year, as documented not only by the extraordinary success of *The Magic Flute*, but also by the fact that he received the contract from the Bohemian Estates to compose a festive opera in celebration of Leopold II's coronation as King of Bohemia. In short, it is false to say his star had long since faded away in Vienna.

A more plausible explanation may be that this incomparable genius so towered over all his fellow composers that their envy and jealousy were aroused, a point made in Niemetschek's biography: "...And Mozart had enemies, numerous, implacable enemies. But then, how could he fail to have them, for he was such a great artist and such an honest man?" Mozart's remarks, such as "it is the heart that makes nobles of men," did not exactly endear him to the influential aristocratic crowd. Nor was he accorded much appreciation by the court in Vienna, with the exception of Joseph II himself, who endowed him with the title of k. k. Kammerkompositeur and a yearly salary of eight hundred gulden in 1787. The disdain and disinterest that Empress Maria Theresa felt for the youthful Mozart, then known and admired throughout Europe, is evident in the letter she wrote to Archduke Ferdinand when he was considering offering Wolfgang a position. In reply to the archduke's question, Her Majesty deigned to give the following response on 12 December 1771:

> You ask of me whether you may take the young
> Salzburger into your service. I do not know what
> as, for I do not believe you have need of a

> composer or other such useless people....What I
> would say is this, you should not burden yourself
> with useless persons, and certainly never give them
> a title as though they were part of your attendance!
> That would only invite contempt for your court
> when such people then travel around like beggars.

And the wife of Leopold II, Maria Louise, certainly had little regard for Mozart's artistry, or little understanding, for otherwise
she would not have spoken of *Titus* as "German junk" after a
performance of the opera in Prague during the coronation festivities in September 1791.

As such quotations imply, neither Mozart's influential friends
nor prominent circles at court would have been moved to initiate
an out-of-the-ordinary funeral and burial for the composer who
had come out of middle-class circumstances and who—in comparison with Gluck when he died—was still relatively young.
However, the behavior of van Swieten, who had been Mozart's
friend and admirer through the years, seems odd. It might be
explained by the unfortunate coincidence of Mozart's death with
a fateful day in van Swieten's life. Baron Gottfried Bernhard van
Swieten had been appointed by Joseph II to the important position of president of the court's commission on education and
censorship, which made him responsible for the entire field of
education and the implementation of many reform measures.
When Leopold II became emperor, he began to turn away from
Joseph II's program of reforms and planned a wholly new approach to education, along with the restitution of former privileges for the aristocracy and the church. Hence, it was only a
matter of time before van Swieten, who was regarded as a devoted apostle of the Josephinian reforms, would be relieved of
his position. As fate would have it, his ouster was officially announced on the day after Mozart died—a circumstance that would
explain why van Swieten, who had problems of his own at the
time, merely ordered the usual middle-class burial for Mozart.

Penny-pinching on the part of van Swieten has been suggested by many biographers, but that was definitely not a factor.
We know, for example, that it was van Swieten who provided
funds for the education of Mozart's two sons for many years and

he may well have helped Constanze in liquidating the debts which amounted to some one thousand gulden after Mozart's death. Mozart's outstanding debt to Michael Puchberg had also mounted up to about one thousand gulden by that time. Puchberg, who was later repaid in full, agreed to postpone repayment, thus providing some help to the new widow at the outset. We can therefore understand why, among Mozart's friends, even Puchberg probably saw no reason for exerting himself to mount a more elaborate funeral and why Mozart's family could not have considered such a possibility in light of the outstanding debts.

One question remains to be clarified: Where in St. Mark's Cemetery is Mozart's gravesite? The question was passionately debated for a long time and can now be answered with a degree of certainty. First, though, we must remember that, in Mozart's time, family members were not at liberty to mark the grave of the deceased with an appropriate monument, unless it was a separate grave or a walled-in family vault containing several bodies. Because the graveyards were surrounded by walls and thus limited in the number of gravesites they could hold, the authorities were understandably opposed to monuments and markers that took up space. Moreover, the graves were cleared after eight years at the most, so they could be reoccupied, and any gravestone or wooden cross (the only marker normally used by most Viennese to commemorate someone in a trench grave) was also removed at that time. Probably in response to people's desire to erect more permanent monuments to the departed, a concession was decreed whereby "the relatives or friends who wish to set forth an individual lasting monument of their love, reverence, or gratitude for the deceased person are hereby authorized to do so, and this is to be mounted on the walls only, not in the courtyards proper, in order not to use up space."

Because the rows of graves were for the most part unmarked and memorial stones were usually mounted only in the cemetery wall, and because the trench graves were cleared and reoccupied after eight years or so, the result was that particular gravesites could no longer be located accurately after even a few years' time. Mozart's grave too remained as it was with nothing giving his name, nor did Constanze have a wooden cross placed at the gravesite. In time its exact location was lost from memory. Christoph Martin Wieland first called attention to this thoughtless negligence in the *Neuer Teutscher Merkur* in 1799, and even Joseph Haydn is said to have complained bitterly in 1805 that Mozart's grave still had not been marked. Despite efforts in recent times to rehabilitate Constanze's place in history, it nevertheless counts as a black mark against her that she did not voice the wish to visit Mozart's grave until some seventeen years after he died.

The question of just where Mozart was buried came up in connection with the 50th anniversary of his death. When Johann Ritter von Lucam, pursuing his investigations of the matter, asked the Widow Mozart for any information she might have, she responded with a letter of 14 October 1841 about her experience when she first visited St. Mark's Cemetery in 1808 in the company of the diplomat and future biographer of Joseph Haydn, Georg August Griesinger. This was the last known letter by Constanze before she died on 6 March 1842, and the complete text has been lost. A partial synopsis of it records that she wrote von Lucam saying she regretted

> ...being unable to pursue completely the questions raised, for, as is readily understandable, being consumed with pain and falling ill, and especially because of the hard winter at the time, she had been unable to follow after the precious remains of her beloved husband, but when later on it was possible [she] did not hesitate to go to St. Mark's cemetery, with several friends, to visit the grave of this unforgettable man.

> Then, in her own words—"But alas! All our efforts were in vain. The gravedigger told me that his predecessor had died shortly before, and whoever was buried here before he came, he had no way of knowing."

This statement stands in contrast to an account by Franz Gräffer in his *Kleine Wiener Memoires* published in 1845, to which Professor Komorzynski has recently called attention:

> I recently received the following lines from a repu-
> table person: Your essay on Mozart prompts me
> to inform you that the gravedigger at St. Mark's
> knows exactly the location where Mozart was bur-
> ied and where for many years the elderly widow
> of a musician came every year to pray. Because
> so much had been written about it, he made this
> known, and still not one person has come to him,
> and this makes him very mad.

Today we know that the musician's widow was the wife of Johann Georg Albrechtsberger, Mozart's friend and Beethoven's
teacher, who was the first person that Mozart wanted to be informed of his death, according to Sophie Haibel's account. The
accuracy of the gravedigger's statement was confirmed by
Albrechtsberger's grandson, Karl Hirsch, in connection with new
investigations into the question of Mozart's burial place in 1856.
Hirsch was able to report that, until he was fifteen years old, he
was regularly taken by his mother to visit not only the grave of his
grandfather who had died in 1809, but also the gravesite of Mozart.
Because he still continued later to make these visits, he could
locate Mozart's grave quite precisely.

It is moving to learn that the willow tree which then marked
the location of the grave had been planted by a common citizen,
a tailor, at his own initiative and, as Hermine Cloeter writes, even
against the wishes of the gravedigger, who alluded to a decree
that "...no tree shall be planted on a common grave." From that
point on, the Vienna authorities took care of this "oblong rect-
angle, which is marked with a willow" and erected a monument
by the sculptor Hanns Gasser there in 1859. This monument,
unfortunately, was transferred to Vienna's main municipal cemetery in 1891 on the occasion of the 100th anniversary of Mozart's
death, and the gravesite whose location had been the object of so
much effort was threatened yet again with oblivion. And again it
was a simple man of the people, a cemetery caretaker by the
name of Alexander Kugler working at St. Mark's at the end of the
19th century, who preserved the site. He took sculptures left
over from older graves—an angel and a broken column—and

217

THE MEMORIAL TO MOZART AT THE ST. MARK'S CEMETERY IN VIENNA AS IT APPEARED ON 30 OCTOBER 1945.

affectionately put together a small but touching monument to Wolfgang Mozart.

As for Mozart's mortal remains, the mystery seems to go on and on. Ever since an anatomy professor, Dr. Jakob Hyrtl, bequeathed a skull alleged to be that of Mozart to the Mozarteum in Salzburg in 1902, the controversy over the authenticity of this relic has never ceased. It flared up again not long ago when Dr. Gottfried Tichy published the results of recent anthropological studies supporting the skull's authenticity. He claimed that the skull could be shown to be that of a rather small man of slight build whose age, to judge by studying the cranial sutures, the formation of the wisdom teeth, and the degree of erosion of the tooth surfaces, corresponded to Mozart's. Attention was drawn to a premature fusion of both frontal bones, which must have resulted in the formation of small orbital cavities with a consequent protrusion of the person's eyes. This feature would indeed apply to Mozart, and the skull's general profile corresponded to that seen in authentic portraits of Mozart's head.

From an objective point of view, however, two arguments militate conclusively against this skull being Mozart's. First, carious decay is clearly visible in the first upper-left molar, a location completely at odds with Leopold's habitual, pedantically precise accounts of the frequent appearances of swellings following the "usual tooth abscesses" on the right side of the mouth. Second, the most striking argument against the skull's authenticity is that traces of an epidural hematoma are present on the internal surface of the left temporal bone, in other words, evidence that substantial bleeding took place between the dura mater and the skull. Aside from the fact that such hematomas are typically caused by a severe blow to the head and are usually fatal, Mozart's medical history gives no indication or even a suspicion that such a thing ever happened to him.

There are also grounds for doubt in the history of the alleged discovery of the skull. It is said to have been found in the course of the prescribed clearing of the graves every eight years by a gravedigger named Johann Radschopf, who then passed it on to his successor, Joseph Rothmayer. Even if robbing a grave to secure the skull of some prominent person was fairly common in those days, as we have seen with Joseph Haydn, in this case we know of no one who contracted to have it done. Nor is there any apparent reason for two common gravediggers to keep the skull of Wolfgang Mozart for some forty years, only to make a present of it in 1842 to the younger brother of the famous anatomist Prof. Jakob Hyrtl simply because he used to come to the cemetery every day after his mother died. And so the case of the supposed "Mozart skull" to this day remains shrouded in a veil of mystery, one that future generations will find even more difficult to penetrate.

Meanwhile, the magic emanating from that site in the lonely quiet of the graveyard at St. Mark's somehow makes the mystery of Mozart's unfathomable spirit real to us. It is like the aura lingering in the larghetto of Mozart's last piano concerto, suffused with its feeling of Franciscan serenity—music marked by an artistry of subtle suggestion, unique to Mozart, exalted and yet free of self-pity and tears, carrying us to spheres where pain lies beyond perception. And as Edwin Fischer once said, in these realms of ultimate spiritual perfection, Mozart has, "by living, transcended life itself and, like Shakespeare, elevated its tragic to the spacious perspective of the gods."

## Mozart's Doctors

### *Dr. Johann Baptist Anton von Bernhard (1726-1796)*

After receiving his doctor's degree in 1750, Dr. Bernhard joined the medical faculty of the University of Vienna. At the time he was called to attend the illness of six-year-old Wolfgang Mozart on 24 October 1762, he already carried the title of councillor conferred by a Polish king and a prince of Saxony. From 1768 to 1770 Dr. Bernhard was Dean of the medical faculty of the University of Vienna and from 1772 to 1773 was Rector Magnificus.

Dr. Bernhard appears to have been one of the music-loving doctors of Vienna who performed chamber music at home. After young Mozart's recovery, Dr. Bernhard held a concert evening in his home on 5 November 1762 at which members of Vienna's lesser nobility and probably untitled academicians from the city as well may have had their first opportunity to make Mozart's acquaintance.

### *Dr. Thomas Schwenke (1693-1767)*

Dr. Schwenke was director of the school of anatomy at The Hague and personal doctor to Prince William V of the principality of Orange. He treated Nannerl and Wolfgang Mozart for typhoid when they fell ill in The Hague in 1765.

## Dr. Sigmund Barisani (1758-1787)

Dr. Barisani was born in Salzburg and was Mozart's childhood friend. His father was personal physician to the Salzburg Archbishop Sigismund von Schrattenbach. He was only twenty-nine when, despite his relative youth, he was named by Emperor Joseph II to be the fourth chief physician at the Vienna General Hospital. We know from something Dr. Barisani wrote in Mozart's guest book on 14 April 1787 that he had at least twice taken care of his friend Wolfgang when he was ill in Vienna. Dr. Barisani died not long thereafter, on 2 September 1787, of a disease contracted in the course of his medical duties, a fate that obviously befell doctors frequently in those days because of the horrendous hygienic conditions in the hospitals. With his passing, Mozart lost not only his doctor but a dear friend from the days of his youth.

## Dr. Thomas Franz Closset (1754-1813)

In 1777, Dr. Closset came to Vienna to complete his medical studies under the then world-famous clinician Maximilian Stoll, the successor to Professor de Haens at the medical clinic. In 1783, Dr. Closset published his paper on putrid fever and soon thereafter began to assist his mentor, Dr. Stoll, not only in his academic presentations but also in his medical practice, through which he "earned the approbation of all the learned doctors and the general respect of the public." After Maximilian Stoll died in May 1787, Dr. Closset was one of Vienna's best known and most sought-after doctors, who was called repeatedly as a consultant by members of the imperial family. In 1797, he became a senior member of the medical faculty of the University of Vienna.

From Mozart's correspondence, we know that Dr. Closset was asked to treat the Mozart family for the first time in July 1789. Constanze was suffering from a leg infection that had appeared during her fifth pregnancy and apparently involved phlebitis. Because of his fine reputation, Dr. Closset also took over treatment of Mozart in November 1791 during his last, ultimately fatal illness. Evidently Dr. Closset had been personally acquainted with the Mozarts long before, because he was characterized as Mozart's "friend of many years" in Dr. Guldener's medical testimonial of 10 June 1824.

## Dr. Johann Nepomuk Hunczovsky (1752-1798)

As professor at the Josephinum, Dr. Hunczovsky first lectured on general theoretical medical matters and later specialized in the fundamentals of surgery and especially gynecology. As gynecologist, he probably assisted at the birth of Constanze Mozart's baby girl on 16 November 1789. The newborn daughter Anna did not survive even her first day and Mozart apparently put the blame on Dr. Hunczovsky, for in one of his letters Mozart intimates that he had turned down Dr. Hunczovsky "(for certain reasons) in a rather unfriendly way" as the family doctor in the future. Dr. Hunczovsky, like Dr. Barisani, was a victim of a disease contracted in the course of his professional duties.

## Dr. Mathias von Sallaba (1764-1797)

Dr. Sallaba was also a student of Maximilian Stoll and was named to be the fifth chief physician at the General Hospital in Vienna in 1797. He published a series of scientific essays and his magnum opus, the often cited *Historia Naturalis Morborum,* was dedicated to his friend Dr. Closset. Soon after assuming his position as chief physician at the General Hospital, he died from an illness contracted in the performance of his duties there.

Dr. Sallaba was called by Dr. Closset as consultant on 28 November 1791, when Mozart's illness took a turn for the worse. Thus, two of the most distinguished and renowned doctors in Vienna—representatives of the most advanced school of medicine in all of Europe at the time—were looking after Mozart during his last illness.

## Dr. Edmund Vincenz Guldener von Lobes (1763-1827)

Dr. Guldener von Lobes arrived in Vienna from Prague shortly before 1790 and soon became one of its most prominent practitioners. In 1800 he became a senior city public health official for Vienna, and in 1814 medical superintendent for the province of Lower Austria. In these capacities, he was responsible for general public health matters, including public coroner duties and everything related to burial and interment of the dead. As a public health official in Vienna, he was also responsible for all medical aspects of criminal cases.

Dr. Guldener was personally acquainted with both doctors treating Mozart, Dr. Closset and Dr. Sallaba, and had a friendly relationship with the Mozart family that continued with Constanze after Mozart's death. Dr. Guldener is the author of the well-known medical testimonial on Mozart's final illness, which he wrote in the Döbling suburb of Vienna on 10 June 1824 at the request of Giuseppe Carpani. It is the unique report of a medical doctor who, as public health official and medical superintendent, can be regarded as particularly precise and reliable in his testimony. He had been kept regularly informed of the progress of the disease by his friends Drs. Closset and Sallaba during Mozart's fatal illnesses and viewed the body after Mozart died. The testimonial prepared by Dr. Guldener von Lobes is therefore especially significant.

### Dr. Alexandre-Louis Laugier (1719-1774)

Dr. Laugier was the emperor's personal physician and an enthusiastic music-lover. His home was a meeting place for the music world of Vienna.

# Ludwig van Beethoven
## (1770 - 1827)

Ludwig van Beethoven counts as one of those extraordinary personalities in Western cultural history whose artistic perfection "…we only begin to understand when they have passed beyond, when their personal eccentricities no longer distract us and the far reach of their influence becomes more evident to us every hour and every day," as Goethe said. His immortal works have such an aura of inviolability that, to the present day, not the slightest hint of disparaging criticism has been cast in their direction. Beethoven's music fills us with the reverence we feel on entering a holy shrine, whether we consider ourselves religious or not. And because our intellect does not enable us to fully understand his language, which came as if from another, more exalted world, we sense the divine character of his music all the more, music that has probed to the farthest reaches of art. His late works especially have an unrivaled intensity of expression, brought to a perfect cohesive unity through concentrated mastery of the musical ideas. The peak is reached in the final choral movement of Beethoven's Ninth Symphony, where his love of mankind is expressed in every sense of the word. The essence of Beethoven's music was aptly characterized by Albert Apponyi with these closing lines from a talk in 1927 on the centennial of Beethoven's death:

> He who has been seized by Beethoven's inspiration has gained a clear view of the highest elevations, of the mountain chain connecting the summits of religion, ethics, philosophy, and the arts; he inhales the essential unity of their atmosphere and, in that unity, enjoys the most

complete harmony and the greatest dignity of man's existence.

The illnesses that beset Beethoven have long been of particular interest. Knowing that he became deaf touches us deeply because we can hardly imagine how, in such a creative musician, any other of the senses could compensate for lost hearing. We find it incredible that his conception of musical sound remained perfectly intact and that emotionally he withstood the inability to hear and pass review on his most mature works. The burning passion with which he "grabbed fate by the throat" and the artistic commitment that enabled him, in this terrible affliction, to summon forth even deeper shades of emotion are the most impressive evidence of sheer human willpower. But Beethoven's loss of hearing has overshadowed his other chronic illnesses, which for decades repeatedly affected him physically and emotionally even more than his deafness and interfered substantially with his creative labors. In particular, he had hepatic disorders in his latter years and obstinate, recurring abdominal problems. These illnesses have generally been the subject of vague speculation in most biographies and have been given closer scrutiny, often with contradictory conclusions, in more recent medical articles.

## Beethoven's Ancestry

To come to some understanding of Beethoven's psychic development, a glance back into the history of his family is helpful. Meticulous research has shown that the name Beethoven—spelled in a variety of ways, ranging from Piethoffen to Bethof—surfaced as early as the 13th century in the chronicles of cities in Flanders. The "van" is simply an indication of Flemish ancestry and not a title of nobility. Aside from the tragic story of the wife of one "van Beethoven" who was burned at the stake as a witch in 1595, we find nothing in the family history of any particular note until the 18th century. Evidence of musical leanings comes clearly into view only with Ludwig's grandfather, Louis van Beethoven (1712-1773). The first member of his family to have musical talent, he is regarded as the most stable and affirmative personality among Beethoven's ancestors. He became a member of the court orchestra of Elector Clemens August in Bonn in March 1733 and was promoted to official Kapellmeister in 1761. He is described by his contemporaries as being a man of integrity, who was proper and just, who was greatly respected at court. He owned a comfortably furnished apartment in the home of a baker's family named Fischer, as learned from remembrances published later by the youngest son, Gottfried Fischer.

This grandfather, with his strong sense of fairness and justice, may well have been a shining example for Ludwig van Beethoven, even though the two could hardly have had much of a personal relationship before the grandfather died on 24 December 1773. The influence could have come more from vivid personal memories preserved in the family, for—as his lifelong friend from Bonn, Franz Gerhard Wegeler, tells it—"his gentle and pious mother, whom he loved far more than his father, who was only strict, must have told him much about his grandfather. His portrait done by the court painter Radoux is the only one he had sent from Bonn to Vienna and it gave him pleasure till he died." The grandfather sought to supplement his income by dealing in wines, a grievous decision, for unfortunately his wife Josepha subsequently took to drink. She is described as a neurotic woman afflicted with an inherited disease,* "who devoted herself all too well to the pleasure of wine and, as a result, caused her husband many hidden sorrows until he finally came to the idea of placing his wife in the keeping of a family in Cologne." At the time her husband died, she apparently had long been sequestered in a cloister.

The third and sole surviving child of this couple, Johann (c. 1740-1792), was the father of Ludwig van Beethoven. Johann has always been characterized as an excessively demanding, even cruel father, who was interested only in exploiting the precocious talent of his son Ludwig. Even Wegeler spoke of him as a "father little distinguished by intellect or ethics." His fondness for the bottle has frequently been mentioned; in fact, Fischer wrote in his remembrances: "Johann van Beethoven was accustomed early on to sampling the wines." When he died, the elector is supposed to have commented, "The taxes collected on alcoholic drinks are bound to drop now that Beethoven's dead." But these charges surely apply only to Johann's last years. Until his wife died in 1787, he was "appropriately behaved" in the performance of his duties as court musician, as noted in an official report in 1784. Moreover, the nobility and upper class would hardly have entrusted a drunkard with the musical education of their children, to whom Johann gave lessons as a way of helping his financial situation. Finally, Fischer also reports that, despite the numerous presents of wine he received constantly as a music teacher, Johann was noted for his "moderation." He ends by saying: "Herr Johann van Beethoven was, in any event, a serious man." However, when Johann's wife, Maria Magdalena, died of tuberculosis in her early forties, life appeared to lose its meaning for him and he began to yield to drink, a weakness he may have inherited from his mother.

A person's emotional and psychological makeup is not determined solely by hereditary factors, but by family and social environmental influences as well. Ludwig van Beethoven's coarse and aggressive behavior and his tendency to introspection and melancholy were present in his ancestors, as was overindulgence in alcohol. Today we know that many genetic factors are involved in the hereditary transmission of depression and that the risk of the occurrence of depression in another member of a genetically afflicted family runs somewhere between 15 and 20 percent. Recent studies, particularly research on twins, have shown that genetic factors are also implicated in chronic alcoholism, either enhancing addiction or suppressing it. There is a firm scientific foundation for the observation that alcoholism tends to occur in families. Although environmental conditions, especially the social drinking habits of one's closest company, undoubtedly have a decisive role in the origin of chronic alcoholism, a genetic predisposition often determines the degree to which a person can or cannot resist alcohol addiction. A Danish-American study in recent years shed light on the importance of these genetic factors by showing that the sons of alcoholics who were separated from their parents shortly after birth and adopted into nonalcoholic families later developed as many problems with alcohol as sons who grew up with their alcoholic parents. These considerations are relevant to Ludwig van Beethoven because both his grandmother and his father must be considered to have become overtly addicted to drink.

Of the seven children born to Johann and Maria Magdalena van Beethoven, only three survived infancy: the second of the children, Ludwig, and his two younger brothers, Caspar Anton Carl, who was born in 1774, and Nikolaus Johann, who was born two years later. The exact date on which Ludwig was born is uncertain, but his baptismal certificate is dated 17 December 1770. Because church rites required children to be baptized not later than twenty-four hours after their birth, we can reasonably assume Ludwig van Beethoven first saw the light of day on 16 December 1770. Little is known of his childhood, and in what is known there are many contradictory details. The Fischer manuscript says young Ludwig suffered for a long time from a "problem" that his mother attempted to treat with simple home remedies. Whether this was an infectious illness that led later to inflammation of the auditory nerve and thus gradually to his deafness, as F. Zobeley is wont to believe, seems highly questionable. However, there is no doubt at all that Beethoven had smallpox at some time in his childhood. In the 18th century that infectious disease struck its victims without regard for social status, the emperor's family as well as the poorest classes. Like Gluck, Haydn, and Mozart, Beethoven survived this scourge. Only a few pockmarks remained as evidence of the infection.

## Childhood and Adolescence

In his early years, young Ludwig, like many children, was left largely to look after himself. Not to be constantly in the way of his parents, he frequently whiled away his time playing in the stone-paved courtyard of the house, even when it was rain-drenched and cold. His consequent repeated colds and chills are alleged to have been the basis for his later loss of hearing—a thesis that must be rejected as false, however. For the most part, young Ludwig was a lively child, ready for pranks of all kinds, but obviously an unusually serious and reflective youngster. He would stand, head in hand, gazing from the window, so lost in thought that he would not react at all when someone spoke to him, for which he would then immediately excuse himself. This behavior led people to call him "withdrawn," "shy and taciturn," or "morose."

Ludwig's interest in music became evident at an early age, encouraged, no doubt, by his father for whom the example of Mozart the Wunderkind could have suggested tempting money-making possibilities. "Music started to become the first of my youthful activities from the time I was four," Beethoven said later. Even if his father Johann did not have anything like the pedagogical talents of a Leopold Mozart, in the last analysis it was he who guided the child's first musical steps, putting the lad on his knee and giving him his first lessons, however irregular and unnecessarily strict they may have been. Whether or not the tales told after Beethoven's death are true—"the drunken father dragged the sleeping boy out of bed over to the piano and tortured him with having to do finger-exercises until the early hours of dawn"— is hard to say. Ludwig's feelings for his father are unknown, for he never spoke of them, but he always remembered his mother with the greatest fondness. His formal education was limited to the elementary schooling normal for those days and ended when he was eleven years old. It included, in addition to the usual reading, writing, and arithmetic, lessons in religion and singing and a little Latin. For the rest of his life, Beethoven's spelling and punctuation were poor and simple mathematics remained for- ever an impenetrable mystery.

Young Beethoven profited most from the instruction of his teacher, Christian Gottlob Neefe. He was indebted to Neefe not only for his exceptional virtuosity as a pianist, but also for a sub- stantial part of his schooling in music theory. Very soon Neefe was offering to let his young student substitute for him as organist at the early services in the elector's chapel, and in 1782 he named the twelve-year-old lad "orchestra cembalist [harpsichordist]," a key position for all rehearsals and performances. Ultimately, it was Neefe who, after the thirteen-year-old Beethoven had dedi- cated three piano sonatas to the prince-elector, first recommended he be sent abroad to study, writing in Cramer's *Magazin der Musik*: "This young genius deserves support so he can travel. He would surely become a second Wolfgang Amadeus Mozart if he were to continue as he has begun."

Ludwig van Beethoven was thirteen years old when his name appeared for the first time as a paid member of the elector's *Hofkapelle und Musik* in one of the lists from the year 1784. In Fischer's remembrances we find a hint as to how the budding musician, with his "sturdy, almost pudgy physique," may have struck his colleagues: "...short and stocky, broad in the shoul- ders, short neck, massive head, round nose, dark brown com- plexion; he always walks somewhat bent forward. Even in his youth, people at home called him 'the Spaniard.'" Already in those times, his contemporaries noted his unusually prominent, broad-domed forehead, a personal characteristic that will figure in the discussion of the medical diagnosis related to his deafness.

When the brother of Emperor Joseph II, Archduke Maximilian Franz, was chosen as successor in the Electorate of Cologne, he brought new life and a new forward-looking spirit to Bonn. He was a liberal-minded ruler who soon established a university there. In particular, he had a genuine love of music. Musical events multiplied at his court and he often took his musicians with him when he made state visits. From one such occasion, we hear of the impression the young pianist Beethoven made on an enthusiastic listener:

> As I see it, one can surely estimate the magnitude of this engaging, soft-spoken young man's virtuosity by the inexhaustible wealth of his ideas, the completely individual style of expression of his playing, and his skill....His playing differs so much from the usual way of treating the piano that it would appear he intended to blaze a totally personal trail to reach the goal of perfection where he now stands.

Stimulated perhaps by Neefe's recommendation, Elector Maximilian Franz, who was deeply involved in reorganizing the musical affairs at his court, gave Beethoven permission in 1787 to go to Vienna to study. Unfortunately, the circumstances of the trip were not favorable. Emperor Joseph II was leaving for Russia to pay a visit to Catherine the Great, so Beethoven's letter of recommendation for an audience with the emperor was of no avail. Even the long hoped-for meeting with Mozart, who had just returned from Prague and was fully engaged in composing *Don Giovanni*, was disappointing for Beethoven. In his biography of Mozart, Otto Jahn provided this account:

> Beethoven, who had come to Vienna in the spring of 1787 as a young man of great promise but then had to return home after only a short stay, was taken to Mozart and at his request played something for him, to which he, taking it to be a showpiece learned for the occasion, gave rather cool praise. Whereupon Beethoven, noting this, asked him for a theme to extemporize on and, as he always used to play best when he was stimulated and now moreover was fired up by the presence of the master he venerated so, held forth at the piano in such a way that Mozart, with interest and excitement growing, finally stole softly in to his

friends sitting in the next room and told them point-
edly, "Keep him in mind, some day he will make
people talk about him."

Beethoven may have taken some lessons from Mozart, but
there is no positive evidence that he did.  His stay in Vienna
lasted only two weeks—from 7 to 20 April 1787.  He received an
urgent plea from his father to return quickly to Bonn because his
mother's health was rapidly deteriorating.  A letter dated 15 September 1787 to the lawyer Dr. Schaden in Augsburg, whom
Beethoven had visited briefly in April on his return trip, provides
some details and gives, incidentally, the first indication of an illness Beethoven himself had:

> I must confess that from the time I left Augsburg,
> my pleasure began to run down and my health
> along with it; the nearer I came to home, the more
> letters I got from my father to travel even faster
> than usual for my mother was no longer well; so I
> hurried on as fast as I could, because I was not
> feeling well either: but the yearning to be able to
> see my sick mother once more cleared all obstacles
> before me and helped me overcome the greatest
> difficulties.  I found my mother still alive but in
> the most desperate state of health; she had tuber-
> culosis and finally passed on about seven weeks
> ago, after much pain and suffering....Since I've
> been here there have been few pleasant hours for
> me to enjoy; the whole time I've been affected by
> asthma ["Engbrustigkeit"] and I'm afraid it could
> lead to tuberculosis; then, in addition, there is
> melancholy, which is almost as great a calamity
> for me as my illness.

The illness that Beethoven called "Engbrustigkeit" has been given
a variety of interpretations—from asthma to tuberculosis—by his
biographers.  His concern that it might turn into tuberculosis was
undoubtedly due to the impression made on him by his mother's
fatal pulmonary tuberculosis; besides, Beethoven was inclined to
hypochondria in his later years.  However, in the autopsy report
after his death, his lungs and pleura (the membrane investing the
lungs and lining the walls of the thoracic cavity) are described as
unexceptional—"The rib cage and the organs inside showed no

significant abnormalities"—verifying that Beethoven never had pulmonary tuberculosis. As there is no further talk of asthma-like circumstances in Beethoven's medical history, the "Engbrustigkeit" must have been a persistent bronchitis such as we find with respiratory tract infections of various kinds, particularly with so-called parainfluenza, but with other viral infections as well. Beethoven later mentioned repeated "colds and chills" and "rheumatic pains" to his friends, and in July 1816 he said he suffered from a "sickly chest condition," which must also have been a reference to bronchitis. Only once, in 1817, are his troubles supposed to have been diagnosed "now finally as pulmonary disease" by his doctor.

The fact that Beethoven wrote that his illness was joined by "melancholy" after his return to Bonn is not surprising given the tragic death of his mother on 17 July, at the age of forty years. Beethoven had to face the death of his one-and-a-half-year-old sister Maria Margarethe on 25 November of the same year. Moreover, the family had fallen into severe financial difficulties, as emerges from a petition to the prince-elector made by Johann before his wife died:

> Court musician van Beethoven most respectfully declares that he has come into very unfortunate circumstances resulting from the protracted and unrelenting illness of his wife and has already been forced to sell some effects and pawn others and that he no longer knows what to do to help his sick wife and many children.

Battered by the blows of fate, Johann took increasingly to drink, with the result that the seventeen-year-old Ludwig not only had to provide for the care and upkeep of the family but once even had to prevent his constantly tipsy father from being placed under arrest. Given these circumstances, it is more than understandable that he would have been unhappy and dejected, as he wrote in the previously mentioned letter of 15 September 1787: "Imagine yourself in my place....Fate is not promising to me in Bonn."

The only source of relief and comfort for Ludwig in Bonn was his circle of friends, who had a healing influence on his stricken emotional condition and also stimulated his intellectual growth and the development of his personality. The counterweight to the depressing situation at home was his intimate relationship with the Breuning family, whose handsome house served as meeting place for the most important people of Bonn. Franz Gerhard Wegeler, who would later become professor of medicine at the university in Bonn, had introduced Beethoven into this family and wrote in this connection: "Here he felt at ease, here he had no worries. Everything worked together to cheer him up and brighten his spirits." Almost from the beginning, Ludwig was treated as though he were a member of the family. The climate of a happy, untroubled family life created by the lady of the house gave him a sense of love and security that was lacking in his own home.

In addition to the Breuning family circle, other intellectual centers in Bonn contributed to developing young Beethoven's personality. Bonn ranked with Mainz as a citadel of the Enlightenment on the Rhine River. In 1787, a "Lesegesellschaft" or literary society had been founded with the approval of the liberal Elector Maximilian Franz. Its participants were largely members of the rationalistic German society called the Order of Illuminati. Harry Goldschmidt, one of today's most prominent musicologists, is surely correct when he points out that Beethoven's contacts with this "vanguard of the Enlightenment"—which included such members of the court orchestra in Bonn as Nikolaus Simrock, Franz Ries, and Christian Gottlob Neefe—could well have been decisive in shaping his intellectual outlook. In the nine years that it was tolerated, the Order of Illuminati even briefly transcended in importance the Masonic societies, which it had infiltrated. However, contrary to charges by its enemies, it had no revolutionary plans for political change. The group's aims were summed up in the documentation of van Dülmen: "However much freedom and equality may have been part of their creed, the Illuminati in no way desired democracy, but rather an aristocracy of the intellect, a view which went along essentially with the program of enlightened despotism."

Beethoven frequently met with his friends from among this group of Illuminati at the tavern Zur Zehrgarten, which served as a kind of drinking and literary club. As an expression of his personal attachment to these gatherings at the Zehrgarten, he decided to set all the verses of Friedrich Schiller's ode (written in 1785), *Freude, schöner Götterfunken (Joy, Thou Purest Spark Divine)*, to music—a goal he clung to into the last years of his life and which he finally achieved with stirring programmatic effect in his Ninth Symphony. The conception of freedom united with humanity and an unyielding love of truth, as expressed in the *Ode an die Freude*, had its roots deep in the company of the Illuminati from the days of his youth in Bonn.

During his last four years in Bonn, Beethoven was already composing a considerable number of piano and chamber music works as well as variations and songs, albeit still very much in the traditional 18th century style. Undoubtedly the most significant compositions from these years are the two cantatas, *On the Death of Joseph II* (WoO 87; "WoO" stands for "Werk ohne Opuszahl" or work without opus number) and *On the Elevation of Leopold II to the Imperial Dignity* (WoO 88), which Beethoven showed Joseph Haydn in June 1792 during Haydn's brief stay in Bonn on his way back to Vienna from London. Haydn probably was impressed by them, for it was certainly through Haydn's personal intervention that the prince-elector approved the plan to have Beethoven go to Vienna to study with him. The stay in Vienna, to which the elector contributed five hundred gulden over and above the regular salary, may originally have been set for just one year.

In farewell, Beethoven's friends gave him a friendship album filled with more or less lighthearted good wishes. Interestingly, it contained not a single line from his father. But the entry written by Count Ferdinand Ernst Gabriel Waldstein, a close friend of the elector and an early supporter of Beethoven, is proof of the high regard the count had for his protégé: "Dear Beethoven! Now you are going to Vienna to fulfill your long-frustrated desires....By working hard, you will receive: the spirit of Mozart from the hands of Haydn."

Beethoven left his friends and his home on the Rhine on the 2d or 3d of November 1792, carrying numerous musical sketches in his luggage, and arrived in Vienna in the second week of November. From his travel diary, we learn that at first he had to put up with an attic room for quarters. But only a short time later, people were talking about him as one of the most interesting and original personalities in the musical capital of Vienna. The new technical dimensions of his piano playing and the novel modes of expression excited attention. Soon he gained access, as a friend and teacher, to the highest circles of nobility. Prince Carl Lichnowsky, who become his most important patron in the early Vienna years, offered him a room at his city palais. His prolonged residence in the prince's palais, from the end of 1794 to the middle of 1796, brought him the maternal solicitude of Princess Christiane and a feeling of family care and attention. It also gave him welcome opportunities to become personally acquainted with important members of the nobility and of Vienna's music circles, with all that meant for his future career. Beethoven expressed his thanks to the prince for the many favors by dedicating his Opus 1, a set of three piano trios, to him.

In early 1793, Beethoven started his lessons with Haydn. He became dissatisfied, however, with the alleged superficiality of Haydn's corrections of his work. So when Haydn left on his second journey to London in 1794, after first having briefly received some gratis lessons from Johann Schenk, composer of the opera *Der Dorfbarbier*, Beethoven went to Johann Georg Albrechtsberger, a friend of Mozart and author of a book on composition. But he was not satisfied with Albrechtsberger either, calling him a "musical pedant" (and who in return called him "an eccentric musical agnostic who won't ever create anything proper"). Beethoven ultimately studied with Antonio Salieri and remained on friendly terms with him until 1809. He dedicated his op. 12, a set of three violin sonatas published in 1799, to Salieri. At the same time, he was composing chamber music, such as the famous Septet in E-flat, op. 20, as well as numerous sets of variations and arrangements. Particularly noteworthy among the latter is the 1796 Quintet in E-flat for piano, oboe, clarinet, horn, and bassoon, op. 16, modeled after Mozart's E-flat Quintet (KV 452) and subsequently rearranged as a quintet for piano and strings.

Overall, Beethoven's first years in Vienna were ones of satisfaction and high spirits. Beethoven kept a horse, just as Mozart had, and he largely adopted the dress and lifestyle of his aristocratic surroundings. From a witty little duet written in this period, we glean the information that Beethoven must occasionally have worn glasses during these first Vienna years. After he had composed a duet for viola and cello (WoO 32) for his friend Nikolaus Zmeskall von Domanovecz, who was an object of Beethoven's jokes and funny names, he gave it the inscription, "Duet for Two Obbligato Eyeglasses," which in its pun on the word "obbligato" (from Italian, meaning both "a part that may not be left out in the performance of a piece" and "mandatory") suggests the two of them needed glasses to play the piece. This assumption is confirmed by a statement from Karl Friedrich Hirsch, who as a child took lessons from Beethoven: "Now and then the maestro used glasses to read the notes, but he did not wear them all the time."

## The First Signs of Illness

In 1795, we first hear mention of an illness—intestinal disease—that would be with Beethoven throughout his life. Franz Gerhard Wegeler, his best friend from youthful days in Bonn and who lived several years in Vienna, reports that Beethoven was almost not able to finish his early Piano Concerto in B-flat, op. 19, on time for his first public appearance as a composer in Vienna in a concert at the Burgtheater on 29 March 1795. "It was only two days before the concert…that he composed the rondo, and that moreover while gripped with the rather severe abdominal pains which he frequently suffered." Wegeler's comment suggests that Beethoven could well have suffered repeatedly from similar abdominal colics in previous years, at least since 1790 (while he was still in Bonn). This early date for the beginning of his intestinal problems is significant for the diagnosis to be discussed subsequently.

Beethoven's second chronic affliction, his hearing disorder, could also have begun in the middle 1790s, although the instigating cause still cannot be finally determined. Beethoven may have presumed that this calamity originated in a case of typhoid fever, as suggested in a report by Alois Weissenbach. After spending 1814 in Vienna, Weissenbach, the chief surgeon at the St. Johannis Hospital in Salzburg, wrote in his booklet, *My Trip to the Congress of Vienna*: "At one time, [Beethoven] had survived a terrible case of typhoid fever; the decline in his nervous system and probably in his hearing as well, which he found so embarrassing, dates from this time. I spoke about it with him often and at length." This doctor was a passionate admirer of Beethoven and provided the text for the cantata *Der glorreiche Augenblick* (*The Glorious Moment*), op. 136. We are obliged to take his words at face value, even though Beethoven does not mention typhoid fever in any of his letters. The sole, rather vague hint of such a severe sickness is found in the Fischhoff manuscript, a collection of some sixty pages of miscellaneous matter relating to Beethoven:

> On a hot summer day in 1796, Beethoven returned
> home hot and perspiring, tore open the doors and
> windows, took off everything but his trousers, and

cooled himself in the breeze at the open window. The result was a dangerous illness whose effects settled in the mechanism of the ear during his convalescence, after which his deafness progressively increased.

Although it seems quite clear from this account that Beethoven was seriously ill in the summer of 1796, the ailment can hardly have been typhoid fever as we understand it today. That term was often used at the time for a variety of sicknesses with high fever and disorientation or mental confusion, such as epidemic typhus or other bacterial and viral infectious diseases involved in inflammation of the meninges or the brain. The autopsy report on Beethoven suggests the latter, as it describes a swelling of the soft meninges at the base of the brain. Unfortunately, on the basis of this report, unqualified persons later postulated that Beethoven's deafness had been caused by syphilis,* a factually erroneous view that is clearly refuted by both the clinical progression of the deafness and the autopsy findings of the other organs. It therefore should be banished once and for all from serious medical discussions of Beethoven's illnesses.

We begin to learn about Beethoven's early hearing difficulties from letters written in 1801. They contain chronological implications that he had already noticed the earliest signs of his hearing disease in 1796. It is striking that his first awareness of this affliction, one doubly bitter for a musician, seems not to have been reflected in his composing. It was in this period, for example, that he wrote the light and pleasant set of piano sonatas, op. 10, and the downright rollicking Piano Trio in B-flat, op. 11. The catchy theme in the last movement of this chamber music work earned it the name *Gassenhauer-Trio* (roughly, *The Hit Song Trio*). Actually, however, Beethoven's psyche could already have been burdened by feelings of depression in these times. Anton Schindler (who became a kind of private secretary and general factotum to Beethoven in his last decade or so) later pointed out that with the largo movement in the otherwise cheerful D-Major Piano Sonata from the set in op. 10, Beethoven intended to reflect somber forebodings of approaching inescapable fate. Tradition has it that Beethoven described this movement, unquestionably the slowest of all his slow movements apart from the lente movement of his last string quartet, as "the state of the soul of one lost in sadness." The icy monotone of the first sixteen treble notes, sounding in the starless night of this largo movement, is the expression of incomparable solitude and symbol of life's dark melancholy—a meditation "on the anguished heart of man," as Vladimir Horowitz once said!

Fearing that his hearing infirmity, if known, could damage the so far successful development and promotion of his career in Vienna and hoping that there could still be a change for the better, Beethoven entrusted no one, not even his best friends, with this secret for several years. Only in 1801, as the specter of threatening deafness took on substance, did he reveal the secret to two of his closest friends. One was Karl Amenda, an excellent violinist from the Duchy of Courland on the Baltic Sea (now a part of Estonia). Beethoven had come to know him in 1798 when Amenda was a tutor at Prince Lobkowitz's. Amenda had returned to Riga in 1799 to resume his theological studies. It was to this friend that Beethoven had dedicated his String Quartet in F, op. 18, as a "small tribute to our friendship" on Amenda's departure from Vienna. Beethoven's special attachment for Amenda has led some modern psychoanalysts, in a total misreading of the European letter-writing style customary in the Romantic era, to suggest that Beethoven manifested "unconscious homosexual tendencies." Beethoven first confided his fate in a letter written on 1 June 1801:

> ...how often I've wished you were here, for your Beethoven is living an unhappy life, out of sorts with nature and its Creator; how often I have cursed the latter for abandoning his creatures to the merest chance of fate....You should know that the noblest part of me, my hearing, has greatly deteriorated; even when you were still here with me I felt signs of this and I said nothing, but now it has grown steadily worse; whether it will still be able to be cured remains to be seen, perhaps it is attributable to my stomach troubles; so far as they are concerned, I am about all recovered now, whether the hearing too will be better now is something I hope for, of course, but I'm doubtful, for such diseases are the most incurable....Please keep this matter of my hearing a deep secret and don't tell anyone, no matter who.

Four weeks later, on 29 June 1801, Beethoven wrote to his friend in Bonn, Franz Gerhard Wegeler, with further details about the state of his health:

> You would like to know something about my situation; well, it's not too bad…my compositions bring in a lot.…And I have six, seven publishers for every piece and could have still more if I wanted to make a point of it:  they don't bargain with me anymore, I ask and they pay.…But that green-eyed monster, my dreadful health, has played a rotten trick on me, specifically:  for the last three years, my hearing has become steadily worse, and this was probably caused in the first place by my belly—which was miserable even then, as you know, and since being here has only gotten worse, being bothered constantly with diarrhea and terribly weak as a result.  [Dr. Johann Peter] Frank tried to restore some vigor to my body using fortifying medicines and to fix my hearing with oil of sweet almonds, but wouldn't you know, nothing came of it, my hearing only got worse and my stomach stayed as it was; that went on into autumn of the past year, and often drove me crazy. Then came a medical ass who prescribed cold baths for my condition; then someone more clever, the usual lukewarm Danube bath; that worked like a charm; my stomach was better, but my hearing was unchanged, or even worse.  This past winter I really felt dreadful; I had truly terrible colics and I sank back into my previous condition, and so it remained until about four weeks ago when I went to see [Dr. Gerhard] Vering, thinking maybe this condition might even require a surgeon and anyway I've always had confidence in him.  He succeeded in almost completely stopping the bad diarrhea; he prescribed lukewarm Danube baths, into which I had to pour a little bottle of some stimulants each time, he gave me no medicine whatsoever until about four days ago and then pills for the stomach and a tea for my ears, and now I can tell I'm feeling stronger and better;

except that my ears continue to buzz and ring night and day.

It's a miserable life, I tell you; for almost two years now, I've avoided society completely for I can't bring myself to tell people: I am deaf. If I had some other profession, then it wouldn't be so bad, but for my profession, it's a terrible thing; and besides, what would my enemies, and I have a few, say to that! —To give you an idea of this marvelous deafness, I will tell you, for example, that at the theater I must lean right on the orchestra to be able to understand the actors. When I'm some distance away, I can't hear the higher tones of the instruments and singers; it is amazing that there are people who never notice it at all when we're talking together; because I've always been somewhat absentminded, people attribute it to that. Often I can hardly hear people who are speaking softly, their voices, of course, but not their words; and the minute someone shouts, I find it unbearable. Dear heaven knows what will come of all this. Vering says it will surely get better, even if not completely. I've certainly cursed the Creator and my existence often enough; Plutarch has brought me to a state of resignation. If nothing else is possible, I mean to resist and defy my fate, although there will be times in my life when I shall be God's most miserable creature. Please tell no one of my situation, not even Lorchen [Wegeler's wife], yours is the secret alone; I would appreciate it if you would sometime exchange letters with Vering about it....Resignation! what a wretched means of refuge, and yet it seems to be the only one left to me.

On 16 November 1801, he again addressed a detailed letter to his friend Wegeler:

You would like to know how I am and what I need; as little as I enjoy talking about the subject at all, still I would most prefer to do it with you. For some months now, Vering has been putting vesicants [an agent that induces blistering] on both arms, which come from a certain bark, as you know. —It is a most unpleasant treatment, for it robs me of the free use of my arms (until the bark has drawn out enough), to say nothing of the pain; it's true, I cannot deny it, the buzzing and ringing are a bit less than before, especially in the left ear where my hearing difficulties actually began, but my hearing is certainly not a whit better; I might even say it had become somewhat worse. —Things are going better with my stomach; especially when I use the lukewarm bath for a few days, then I feel pretty good for eight, even ten days; very seldom take anything strong for the stomach; I'm also starting now with herbs on the stomach as you advised. —Vering won't have anything to do with shower-baths; all in all, I'm not very satisfied with him; he really has too little interest and patience for such a disease; and if I didn't go to him, and that takes a lot of effort, then I would never see him. —What do you think of [Dr. Johann Adam] Schmidt? I don't like to change, but it does seem to me Vering is too much the practical type to come by many new ideas by study. —In this regard, Schmidt appears to me wholly different and perhaps wouldn't be so neglectful either. —People here are saying wondrous things about galvanism; what do you think about it? A doctor told me he saw a deaf-and-dumb child (in Berlin) recover his hearing, and a man who had also been deaf for seven years and has regained his hearing. I hear your Schmidt is even experimenting with it.

In light of his condition, we can well imagine the despondency Beethoven fell into time and again in these years, but he sought to hide it. It can be seen how little the beginnings of his deafness were noticed by the people around him, as documented in an account by Carl Czerny, who first met Beethoven in this period. Czerny, as a ten-year-old boy, had the following rather unsettling impression:

I was about ten years old when...I was taken to
meet Beethoven....Beethoven was wearing a
morning coat of some shaggy, dark-gray cloth and
trousers to match....His bushy jet-black hair stood
out from his head. His beard had not been shaved
for days and made the lower part of his already
swarthy face look even darker. And I noticed too,
with that quick glance children have, that in both
ears he had cotton cloth which seemed to have
been dipped in a yellow liquid. At the time, however, he did not give the least sign of being hard
of hearing.

Beethoven's inner struggle with the fate of his health unquestionably left its mark on his personality, contributing especially to
his growing suspiciousness, his morbid sensitivity, and his quar-
relsomeness. Nevertheless, it would be wrong to try to explain
these negative aspects of Beethoven's behavior solely in terms in
his increasing deafness, for many idiosyncrasies in his character
were already apparent in his youth. The essential source of his
exaggerated irritability, combativeness, and dominating attitude
that bordered on arrogance was almost certainly the inconceivable intensity with which he worked. He sought, by sheerest
concentration, to control the ideas teeming within him and strived
heroically to give the greatest possible condensation to his creative inspirations. Such an excruciating, all-consuming way of
working must inevitably have brought his brain and nervous system to their very limits, in a constant state of tension. In this
unceasing compulsion to improve the unimprovable, he often
held onto commissioned works long after it was necessary, with
Olympian disregard for agreed-upon completion dates.

In spite of his frequent abdominal complaints and his increasing deafness, Beethoven was by no means a loner or a moody
recluse. The writings of his friends tell us he could be extremely
animated and was fond of jokes. Beethoven, like Mozart before
him, was a lover of puns and wordplays, turning syllables around
and the like. Moreover, we find no evidence in his compositions
that his early hearing defect materially affected his creative activities. And it is true especially of Beethoven that the span of time
between his first inspirations, the intellectual preoccupation and
work, and the final writing down of a piece could extend over
years. Therefore, a correlation in time between a biographical

event and one of his compositions can hardly ever be traced exactly. An example of how futile such speculations are can be found in the history of the often cited *Moonlight Sonata*, op. 27, with its song of lament in the moonlit darkness of C-sharp minor. People have tried repeatedly to associate it with the beautiful Giulietta Guicciardi because in the years when it was being composed, 1800—1801, Beethoven had hoped to win Giulietta's love. Actually, the first movement of this sonata may be connected with the death of a poet Beethoven admired. It could also be related somehow to the deep shadows beginning to be cast at this time over his spirits by his hearing disorder. Remarkably, Beethoven noted in his sketches for this work (discovered by Georges de Saint-Foix) the despairing eighth-note triplets from the death music for the commendatore in Mozart's *Don Giovanni*. We hear them, transposed, in the *Moonlight Sonata*.

## Years of Crisis: 1802 and 1812

Just how depressed Beethoven's fading hearing could make him at times is evident his letter of 16 November 1801 to Wegeler: "...You can hardly imagine how sad and empty a life I've led these last two years; my loss of hearing followed me everywhere like a ghost, and I fled from people, had to pretend I hate mankind when I don't at all." And yet, in the midst of his despair, his burning enthusiasm for his calling as an artist suddenly breaks through:

> There is no greater joy for me than to apply and display my art....The time of my youth, yes, I can feel it, it is only just beginning; haven't I always been a little bit sick? For some time now, my physical strength has been growing more than ever and my mental vigor too. Every day I'm getting nearer to the goal I can sense but not describe. And this is the only way your Beethoven can live. Let's hear nothing about taking it easy!...I want to grab fate by the throat; and this is certain, it shall never bring me down. —O life, it is so beautiful, O to live a thousand lives! But a quiet life, no, I can tell I'm not made for that.

Despite such high-spirited and defiant declarations, Beethoven must have been gripped again and again by deep despair. His depression, with thoughts of suicide, reached its nadir in what has become known as the Heiligenstadt testament written following the summer of 1802. This heart-moving statement, conceived as a kind of farewell letter to his two brothers (only Carl's name is written out; where Johann's name is implied, Beethoven left a blank), was found among his papers after his death. It shows the full extent of his spiritual anguish and allows an unparalleled glimpse into his innermost being. The document, originating in the pastoral solitude of the little village of Heiligenstadt, also gives a picture of the state of his health.

> For my brothers Carl and ———— Beethoven
> Heiligenstadt, 6 Oct 1802
>
> Oh, you mortals, you who think or call me antagonistic, stubborn, and a people-hater, how unjust you are, for you do not know the secret he has who seems like that to you. From the time I was a child, my heart and mind were inclined to tender feelings of friendliness, ready even to do great things. But now reflect, it has been six years since I was struck by an incurable condition, one made worse by stupid doctors, deceived in the hope of being cured from year to year, driven finally to see it as a lasting calamity (whose cure may take years or even be completely impossible); born with an ardent and lively temperament and susceptible to society's diversions, I soon had to hold myself aside and live my life alone; if sometimes I wanted to change all that, oh, how roughly I would be set back by the doubly miserable experience of my bad hearing, and yet still it was not possible to say to people: speak louder, shout, for I am deaf; oh, how could I possibly confess imperfection in the one sense which should be more perfect in me than in others, a sense I once possessed to the greatest perfection, certainly to a perfection few others in my profession have or have ever had. Oh, that I cannot do, and so forgive me if you should see me draw back when I

would gladly be in your midst, my misfortune makes me doubly sorry for its being misunderstood; for me, there can be no amusing social life, no polite conversations, no stimulating give-and-take; I may sometimes permit myself the pleasure of society, but only to the extent absolutely necessary; otherwise I must live all alone, like one who has been banned; if I approach a group of people, a sudden anxiety grips me and I fear running the danger of having my condition noticed. And it has been the same this last half year spent in the country; in ordering me to protect my hearing as much as possible, my eminently sensible doctor was going along with my own natural inclination, even though the yen for company has often led me astray. But how humiliating it has been, when someone stood by me and heard a flute playing in the distance and I heard nothing, or someone heard the shepherd singing and again I heard nothing; incidents like this have brought me to the brink of despair; only a little more and I would have ended my life. It is art and art alone that held me back, yes, for it seemed impossible to me to leave the world before I had brought forth all I feel capable of, and so I continued to eke out this miserable existence—it is truly miserable to have a body so sensitive that a sudden change can take me from the best of shape to the worst. Patience—as they say, I must choose patience to lead me, and I have. —I firmly hope my determination will persevere until it pleases the inexorable Fates to break the thread; perhaps things will be better, perhaps not; I am ready.

It is no easy thing to be forced to become a philosopher when one is only 28 years old; and for an artist, harder than for others. Oh, God Divine! You look down on my inner being, you know what is there, you know the love for my fellow man and the urge to do good that dwell therein. Oh my fellow men, when you finally read this, so

LAST PAGE OF THE HEILIGENSTADT TESTAMENT, WRITTEN BY BEETHOVEN AT A TIME OF DEEP DEPRESSION IN OCTOBER 1802.

remember that you treated me unjustly, and whoever is unhappy may be comforted to learn of another just like him, who despite all nature's difficulties nevertheless did all in his power to be accepted into the ranks of worthy artists and men. —And you, my brothers Carl and ——————, if Dr. Schmidt is still alive when I die, please ask him in my name to describe my illness and to attach this page to the story of my sickness so that as far as possible the world will become reconciled to me after my death at least. —At the same time, I hereby declare you both to be the heirs to the small fortune (if one can call it that) I have. Divide it honestly among you, and support and help one another. You know I have long ago forgiven you for anything you did against me. And you, brother Carl, I thank you especially for the acts of devotion you have shown me in recent times. May you both have a better, less troubled life than I have had; teach your children virtue, for it alone brings happiness, and not money, I speak from experience; it was virtue that raised me from my misery. Thanks to it, and to my art, I did not take my own life....Now it is done: —With joy, I hasten toward death. If it comes before I have had the chance to develop all my artistic abilities, then in spite of my harsh fate it will still have come too soon and I would still want it to come later— yet even so I would be satisfied, for would it not then free me from a state of eternal suffering? Come then when you will, I shall meet you bravely— adieu and do not wholly forget me when I am dead, I deserve that from you, for in my lifetime I thought of you often and how to make you happy, so be happy then!

Ludwig van Beethoven

This Heiligenstadt testament is, in the last analysis, a kind of farewell to the world. Curiously enough, it had been only a few months before that Beethoven had professed a strong will to live and a confident view of the future in his 16 November 1801 letter to Wegeler, the letter ending with the cry, "O life, it is so beautiful, O to live a thousand lives!" In the same letter, he had also indicated to Wegeler that his deep feelings for Giulietta Guicciardi, to whom he had dedicated the *Moonlight Sonata*, may have contributed to an improvement in his distrust of people: "...a dear, bewitching girl who loves me and whom I love; over the past two years we have had some blissful moments together, and now for the first time I have the feeling that marrying could make me happy; unfortunately she is not from my social class—and now—

of course I could not marry at the moment; now I must push bravely on." All these comments to his friend Wegeler not long before he wrote the Heiligenstadt testament strongly suggest that, with this cry from his soul and by repeatedly reliving the loss of his hearing (so calamitous for a musician!), Beethoven wanted to get the worst of it off his chest, and thus surmount and subdue the trauma. It is striking indeed that once he had written this document, he hardly ever mentioned his hearing disorder again until the year 1810.

From the fall of 1802 on, Beethoven was totally caught up in his artistic activities once more. At practically the same time that he was putting his wounded heart's cries of pain on paper in Heiligenstadt, his pleasant, lighthearted Second Symphony (in D major, op. 36) was being born, a symphony that does not betray the slightest hint of depression. This work is evidence that the Heiligenstadt testament fundamentally reflected a fleeting moment when Beethoven's depression had reached its lowest point, and that the act of writing out his thoughts was essentially a conscious acknowledgment, an act of self-therapy by which he sought to free himself from the depression racking his soul. The sunlit, joyous nature of the Second Symphony shows that he attained his therapeutic goals of being able to work steadily again, unencumbered by the course of his hearing difficulties, and of being governed by patience.

Dramatic proof that Beethoven's creative powers remained intact is revealed by the fact that he now found time to compose a group of important sonatas—the Violin Sonata in A Minor ( the *Kreutzer*, op. 47) in 1803 and the Piano Sonata in C Major (the *Waldstein*, op. 53) and the *Appassionata* (in F minor, op. 57) in 1804—in the same period when he was working on the Third Symphony (the *Eroica*, in E-flat, op. 55) and his opera, *Fidelio*. The mental resilience that enabled him to overcome his depression also freed enormous impulses that led to the development of a new style in his compositional art. Not surprisingly, the audience was somewhat perplexed after the first public performance of the *Eroica* symphony on 7 April 1805 at the Theater an der Wien with the composer conducting. The *Allgemeine musikalische Zeitung* reported: "...a completely new symphony of Beethoven...is written in a totally different style. This long, technically very difficult symphony is actually an extremely broadly conceived, daring, and stormy fantasy." Just how strongly

Beethoven's self-confidence had returned can be seen in his reply to this newspaper: "If you think you can do me harm with
something like that, you are mistaken; you are far more likely to
bring your own newspaper into disrepute."

It can now be taken as fact that Napoleon Bonaparte served
as an ideological ideal in Beethoven's "heroic" years. If the story
is true that the French ambassador (and later King of Sweden)
Jean Baptiste Bernadotte gave Beethoven the first impetus for
composing this heroic symphony at a meeting with him in 1798
in Vienna, it is astonishing that Beethoven took fully six years to
bring it to completion. A more likely possibility, according to
recent investigations, is that its completion was related to
Beethoven's plans to travel to Paris. We learn from various passages in letters of his pupil Ferdinand Ries that Beethoven had
planned to move to Paris and therefore wanted to have a symphony dedicated to Bonaparte ready in reserve. But Beethoven
became outraged when Napoleon was proclaimed emperor in
May 1804. Ries tells us:

> ...I was the first to bring him the news that
> Bonaparte had himself proclaimed emperor, where-
> upon he flew into a rage and cried out, "Then he
> too is nothing but an ordinary man after all! Now
> he will crush everyone underfoot merely to gratify
> his ambition."...Then Beethoven went to the desk,
> grabbed the title page at the top, tore it away and
> threw it on the floor. The first page was newly
> written and only then did it receive the title,
> "sinfonia eroica."

With that act, not only was the subject of the dedication wiped
out, but also the whole project of a move to Paris, with all it could
have meant for Beethoven's artistic development. Beethoven's
outburst of rage at the news of Bonaparte's elevation to emperor
clearly was due to both political considerations and artistic concerns of a most personal nature.

Although Beethoven did not complain about his hearing loss
for a while after writing the Heiligenstadt testament, we know
from the Fischhoff manuscript that he visited a nature healer, Father Weiss of St. Stephen's in Vienna, on the recommendation of
his friend Zmeskall. Schindler says the clergyman had "brought
about many fortunate cures," both with prayers and with the help

A LIFE MASK OF BEETHOVEN MADE BY FRANZ KLEIN.

of various medicinal herbs. According to the Fischhoff manuscript:

> After considerable effort, Herr von Zmeskall finally prevailed on Beethoven to go there with him. And in the beginning, he would follow the advice of the doctor; but because he had to go to see him every day just to have some liquid dropped into his ears, this became even more irritating when, in his impatience, he thought he detected little or no improvement, so he stopped going. The aforementioned doctor informed Herr von Zmeskall, who asked him to place himself at the disposal of the difficult patient and meet with him at his convenience. The clergyman, well disposed to helping Beethoven, went to his apartment, but after a few days his efforts were in vain for Beethoven gave instructions to say he was not at home, thus frustrating any possible help or improvement in his condition.

The oil and medicine injections that Father Weiss employed to try to improve Beethoven's hearing, especially in the better left ear especially, had no positive effect, which was only to be expected.

What we do hear about more frequently in this period are illnesses accompanied by fever and a worsening of Beethoven's intestinal troubles.  For example, we read in the work by Alexander Wheelock Thayer, Beethoven's most important biographer, that no sooner had he moved into an apartment with his friend Stephan von Breuning in May 1804 than he "had a severe, almost critical illness" followed by a persistent "intermittent" fever that smoldered on long after his recovery.  In a letter of 13 November 1804 to Wegeler, Breuning reported on his friend's illness:  "He had scarcely moved in with me before he had a severe, almost critical illness which eventually turned into an obstinate intermittent fever."  From 1805 on, similar reports show up constantly in letters. In November 1805, Beethoven wrote to the singer Friedrich Sebastian Mayer, the first Pizarro in *Fidelio* and a posthumous brother-in-law of Mozart (being, since 1797, the second husband of Mozart's sister-in-law, Josepha Weber): "I can't come because I've had colic pains—my usual disease—since yesterday."  In May 1806, he was making a similar complaint to Baron Peter von Braun, the impresario who staged *Fidelio*.

From 1807 on, Beethoven would also speak of "terrible headaches," as seen for example in a letter to Baron von Gleichenstein written in June 1807.  Such headaches could have had a considerable effect on Beethoven's composing at times.  After mentioning his "head troubles" in a letter to Prince Nikolaus Esterhazy on 26 June 1807, he went on to add that "in the beginning [they] did not allow [him] to work at all, and later and even now only a little."  In the meantime, the poet Heinrich von Collin, author of the tragedy *Coriolan* for which Beethoven wrote an overture, heard from him about a "severe fingernail operation" that had to be performed on one of his fingers, probably as the result of an inflammation of the tissues surrounding the fingernail, i.e., perionychium.  Such infections, usually caused by staphylococci, are accompanied by painful purple swelling of the affected finger and can lead to sepsis (blood poisoning) if the pus is not drained by a surgical incision.  From what Beethoven wrote, the finger must have looked very ominous indeed some days before.

Beethoven's intestinal troubles evidently came and went constantly, with temporary improvements followed by recurring attacks.  The symptoms flared up again and again.  Beethoven had told Heinrich von Collin that "his colic was better now" in March 1808, but at the end of 1809 he informed the publishers Breitkopf and Härtel that he had been considerably shaken up by a fever caused by "having caught a cold," and in 1810 he complained repeatedly that he did not feel well and was suffering again from acute abdominal pains. After 1811, these constant, virtually identical complaints of a general feeling of being ill, of headaches or fever or "inflammation in the gut," took a great amount of space in the many letters he wrote to his most prominent pupil, Archduke Rudolph. Evidently he expected particular understanding for his health problems from the Archduke, who himself was the victim of a hereditary Habsburg defect, epilepsy.

With such a general state of poor health, it is no wonder Beethoven often felt depressed. Even in the autumn of 1806 when he was in an ecstasy of composing, his friend Breuning wrote: "Most of the time he is in a very dejected frame of mind." Beethoven's incredible output from 1804 to 1812 is therefore all the more astonishing. In 1806 he finished the Fourth Symphony (in B-flat, op. 60), as well as the *Razumovsky Quartets*, op. 59, the marvelous Fourth Piano Concerto in G Major, op. 58, and the Violin Concerto in D Major, op. 61. In 1807 and 1808 he completed the Fifth Symphony (in C minor, op. 67) and the Sixth (the *Pastoral*, in F major, op. 68), both performed for the first time on 22 December 1808. With the Fifth Piano Concerto (the *Emperor*, in E-flat, op. 73), Beethoven reached a new zenith in his composing. The exalted nature of the work reflects Beethoven's reactions to events in 1809 when the French besieged and occupied Vienna. After a temporary lull in his creative efforts over the next two years, marked only by the Piano Trio in B-flat (the *Archduke*, op. 97), Beethoven brought the year 1812 to a close with the composition of his Seventh Symphony (in A major, op. 92) and his Eighth (in F major, op. 93).

Because Beethoven himself said little about his hearing problem after he wrote the Heiligenstadt testament, we can only refer to statements from people around him to assess his hearing up to the year 1812. Perhaps until 1806 Beethoven could still hear relatively well, even if he apparently had difficulties now and then when he was conducting. The cellist Dolezalek, for example, says that, during rehearsals for the *Eroica* in 1804, Beethoven was never able to hear the wind instruments distinctly enough. Later, in 1808, the horn player Johann Friedrich Nisle said that once when he was visiting Beethoven, the servants had to ask him to speak louder because the master did not hear well.

On this occasion, however, Beethoven had his back to his visitor at first and was unable to follow the spoken words from his visitor's lips. When he sat directly facing the person to whom he was talking, he was able to carry on a conversation, as the playwright Franz Grillparzer reported from the same year. Because Beethoven always made every effort to avoid calling attention to his difficulties when he was around strangers, it is quite understandable that "his loss of hearing made him unsociable," as the author Karl August von Varnhagen noted in 1811. The persons he saw frequently obviously had a different impression of Beethoven's powers of hearing than did those less familiar with him. In fact, Beethoven's well-known student Carl Czerny and the esteemed Kapellmeister Ignaz von Seyfried both believed that "until approximately the year 1812 [Beethoven] could hear perfectly well."

An event that took place during the cannonading of the metropolis on the Danube by Napoleon's soldiers on 31 May 1809 is interesting in this connection. Because Beethoven's lodgings on the street called the Walfischgasse were directly in the artillery's line of fire, he took refuge in the cellar of the house of the poet Ignaz Franz Castelli. Ries recounted later that Beethoven "even covered his head with a pillow" to protect his ears from the booming noise of the exploding shells—a piece of evidence that is significant for a diagnosis of his hearing troubles.

Since 1802, Beethoven's personal physician had been Dr. Johann Adam Schmidt, whose treatments with galvanic current Beethoven hoped would lead to an improvement in his hearing and to whom he dedicated a piano trio arrangement (op. 38) of his popular Septet in E-flat, op. 20, in gratitude for his efforts. After Schmidt died in 1809, Beethoven turned to Dr. Johann Malfatti and soon developed a close relationship with the family. He became especially infatuated with the doctor's cousin, the young Therese, to whom he dedicated the well-known bagatelle *Für Elise* (WoO 59). In the spring of 1810, he ventured to offer her a proposal of marriage through the good offices of his friend Ignaz von Gleichenstein. When it was refused, he was deeply hurt, as we can gather from a letter to Gleichenstein in April 1810: "Your news threw me from the heights of happiness into the depths once again." Beethoven had already made several efforts to found a family and nothing had come of any of them. After his attempt to win the love of Giulietta Guicciardi in 1801, he particularly courted Josephine Brunsvik, the widow of Count Joseph Deym, through the years when the two were close from 1804 until the fall of 1807. As we can deduce from thirteen recently rediscovered letters, she evidently returned Beethoven's love, and yet as a widow she could not bring herself to marry again because of her children. How full Beethoven's heart was with love for her is revealed in his letters. For example, he wrote in the spring of 1805: "...O you give me hope that your heart will long beat for me—mine will only stop beating for you when it beats no more—beloved." The thirteen letters cast light for the first time on biographical aspects of the character of Leonore in his opera *Fidelio*. From Josephine's mutual love, Beethoven had hoped to find the strength to bring his opera to a conclusion and, as Goldschmidt expressed it, "in Florestan and Leonore, the counterparts to the unfulfilled reality were found." His disappointment was so great after the break in their relationship that he apparently had no firm hopes of marrying until his suit for the hand of Therese Malfatti in 1810.

Beethoven's famous letter to the unnamed "Immortal Beloved" ("Unsterbliche Geliebte") is, aside from the Heiligenstadt testament, undoubtedly the most important biographic document in Beethoven's hand. Recent studies have suggested that Josephine Brunsvik could have been the person to whom the letter was addressed. Of all the other female personages around Beethoven who might be considered, the most likely is Antonia Brentano. This letter must have been of singular significance to Beethoven, because he preserved it to the end of his life. His experience with the "Immortal Beloved" made it clear to him once and for all that leading a normal domestic family life was not compatible with a life dedicated to art. A journal entry from 1812 shows how painfully he felt this final renunciation: "You [meaning Beethoven himself] are not allowed to be a normal person, it is not for you, only for others; for you there is no longer happiness except in yourself, in your art. —O God! give me the strength to conquer myself, nothing must chain me to everyday life!"

On the advice of his doctor, Beethoven spent the summer months of 1812 at health resorts in Teplitz, Franzensbad (Franzensbrunn), and Karlsbad to alleviate his severe and persistent headaches. During the stay in Teplitz, two of art's greatest figures—Goethe and Beethoven—met for the first time. The composer's long wished-for encounter with the poet he so admired must also have impressed Goethe, who previously had shown relatively little enthusiasm for the overwhelming and titanic music of Beethoven. On 13 July he wrote to his wife in Karlsbad: "Another artist more intense, dynamic and dedicated, I have never seen. I can easily understand how peculiar the world must seem to him." Goethe's impression of him corresponds to something Beethoven once said, according to Bettina Brentano who had arranged the meeting of the two artists: "Music must strike fire from the heart of man." It may have been not only Beethoven's music that startled Goethe, however, but also his rough, uncouth conduct, for on 2 September 1812, he wrote to his good friend and director of the Berlin Singakademie, Karl Friedrich Zelter:

> I got to know Beethoven in Teplitz. His talent amazed me; only, unfortunately, he is a completely raw personality who may not be wrong in finding the world a detestable place but certainly does not make it any more enjoyable either for himself or for others thereby. On the other hand, he is very much to be forgiven and pitied because his hearing is leaving him, something that hurts the musical side of his being more than the social side. He is a taciturn type in any event and will become doubly so because of this defect.

Despite his admiration for Goethe, Beethoven was disappointed in certain of Goethe's traits, as came out in a letter to the Breitkopf and Härtel music publishers on 9 August 1812: "The court atmosphere is too seductive to Goethe, much more than is seemly in a poet. There is really little more to say about how foolish music virtuosos are if poets, who should be esteemed as the nation's leading teachers, can forget everything else for the sake of this glitter." Beethoven saw through Goethe's vanity and his rather cold self-importance, and many years later his impression was confirmed in a personal matter. On 8 February 1823, the composer—now alone and ill and completely deaf—wrote to Goethe with a request that he use his influence with the Duke of Saxe-Weimar to secure a subscription for Beethoven's *Missa solemnis:*

> ...I know you will not fail to intercede for an artist, who feels only too keenly how remote the business of having to earn one's living is from art itself, where need compels him, for the sake of

others, to toil and act for others. —The good is always clear to us, and so I know that your Excellency will not refuse my request. A few words from you would bring me happiness. I remain, your Excellency, with most sincere and unbounded respect, Beethoven.

The prince of poets simply left the letter unanswered—proof of a regrettable disinterest and lack of feeling on the part of a pampered, comfortable artist with no cares for the future.

The year 1812 was a year of crisis for Beethoven just as 1802 had been. The earlier crisis had led to the Heiligenstadt document; the one in 1812 led to the letter to his "Immortal Beloved." This final rejection of love's happiness had a far-reaching effect on his private life and his creative activities. The enormous emotional tensions provoked by the events of the summer months were considerably increased by his conflict with his brother Johann, who lived in Linz with Therese Obermayer in what, to Beethoven's way of thinking, was an intolerable extramarital relationship. Only after his brother had finally married her did Beethoven feel the full force of his dammed-up emotional tensions. He slipped into a muddled, depressed state which may even have included thoughts of suicide. This condition obviously persisted into the summer of 1813, for it was only on 4 July that Beethoven wrote Joseph von Varena, one of the founders of the musical society in Graz, that his health was better. The ragged state of his emotions was reflected too in neglect of his appearance, whereas before he had usually paid scrupulous attention to how he looked.

In this period, Beethoven probably did not always stick to his chaste moral principles. We learn from letters to his friend Zmeskall that he began to turn to the company of prostitutes—whom he called "morsche Festungen" (literally translated as "broken-down or dilapidated fortresses") in their correspondence—to relieve his sexual needs. Dr. Andreas Bertolini, who was his doctor from 1806 to 1816 and a personal friend, later wrote that Beethoven was almost constantly embroiled in one love affair or another with the society ladies he knew, and Wegeler also said: "The truth, as my brother-in-law Stephan von Breuning, as Ferdinand Ries, as Bernhard Romberg [a musician from Beethoven's time in Bonn], and as I myself came to know it, is this: Beethoven was never without a love and most of the time extremely taken with her." We know furthermore that in wooing these high-born ladies, his approach was always one of special tenderness. How conflicting it must have seemed to Beethoven, then, to give himself over to sex for hire. The Fischhoff manuscript contains a diary entry that relates to this situation: "Carnal pleasure without communion of the souls is always brutish: afterward, one enjoys no trace of noble feeling, but only of regret." Speaking in a similar vein to Karl Holz, a friend during his last years, Beethoven said he most deplored the fact that his body's "need" would seduce him into doing that which contravened his better nature.

The crisis of 1812, with its attendant inner turmoil and distress, inevitably had an effect on Beethoven's creativity. Moreover, his old troubles flared up again and must have continued until the middle of 1814, for it was in this time that he was informing Archduke Rudolph of the latest details: "I was sick and suffering the whole time, particularly in my head, and I still am....Since yesterday evening, I have had to apply vesicants, with which the doctor hopes to cure me in a few days not only for a little while but for all time." His condition must have been rather serious, because he noted in his diary: "Deciding by the doctors about my life. If no recovery is possible, then what *** do I need??? Only it still ought to end more quickly, something impossible before. Consultation with ***." These words have been interpreted by many biographers as an indication that Beethoven was considering taking poison to put an end to an incurable disease, a disease presumed to be syphilis. They base their views on an alleged statement by Beethoven biographer Alexander Wheelock Thayer that Beethoven's "venereal disease was known to many people." However, the original of this statement has disappeared, just as has another "proof" about which Jacobsohn reports: "In a private collection there is a note not publicly known which is written in Beethoven's own hand and which in all probability alludes to a venereal disease." Similarly, a prescription for an ointment of mercury allegedly written for Beethoven is supposed to be held privately somewhere, but has never been brought to light.

The thorough analysis contained in the report of Beethoven's autopsy provides no indications whatsoever that he suffered from syphilis. Efforts to prove otherwise can only be explained by the fact that it seems to have become fashionable to try to establish connections between genius and certain diseases—particularly insanity and syphilis. The serious illness that Beethoven mentions in his 1814 diary was probably his abdominal trouble once more, for in one of his letters he speaks of "inflammation of the gut" that brought him almost to death's door. These abdominal miseries could well have gotten worse from one year to the next, with "colic pains," his "usual disease," reappearing particularly when he had eaten "something indigestible." For this reason, his doctors prescribed a strict diet for him, such as panadel (an Austrian soup made with stale bread), noodles, veal, fish, and softboiled eggs. Because he had to depend on his house servants, however, he seldom could keep to this diet. And besides, Beethoven was looked on as a willful and difficult patient who frequently disregarded instructions and who would drink wine and strong coffee whenever he wanted to.

Starting in 1815, complaints about increasing hearing problems surfaced once more in Beethoven's letters. From about 1813, the right ear had become largely deaf, while the left one probably still retained some hearing. Beethoven attempted to use various mechanical hearing aids, primarily with the left ear. As early as 1812, Johann Nepomuk Mälzel, the inventor of the metronome, had constructed four different ear trumpets for the composer, only one of which Beethoven found acceptable. In his frustration, he finally made himself a long wooden stick, one end of which he would take between his teeth while placing the other end in contact with the sounding board of his piano. None of these devices materially improved his ability to hear. Because he was no longer able to hear the sound of his piano even when he played it fortissimo, he asked the piano manufacturer Johann Andreas Streicher to install an apparatus to amplify its sound. It was a soundwave-reflecting attachment looking something like the prompter's box in a theater. Beethoven would sit under it when he played.

In 1814, the first signs of difficulties in playing the piano appeared. As a result of his deafness, Beethoven was slowly losing his mastery of the piano. In this year, he gave his last public concert as a pianist, playing the *Archduke* Piano Trio in B-flat, op. 97. The composer Ludwig Spohr heard him in rehearsal in 1814 and had this to say about his piano playing:

> It was no pleasure, first, because the piano was
> badly out of tune, which did not bother Beethoven
> very much for he could not hear it anyway, and
> secondly, on account of his deafness, there was

> very little of the artist's skill left we all once so
> admired. Playing forte, the poor deaf soul ham-
> mered on the strings till they rattled, and in piano
> passages, he played so softly whole chords went
> unheard.

From this time on, Beethoven would improvise on the piano only
when surrounded by his circle of friends, and then only when he
was in the mood.

## His Nephew Karl

A new personal crisis arose in October 1815 when the health
of Beethoven's brother unexpectedly began to deteriorate. Carl
had been suffering from tuberculosis for some time when it suddenly turned into galloping pulmonary tuberculosis and led to his
death on 15 November. His end came so quickly that Beethoven
suspected his brother's wife of poisoning him, a suspicion that
could only be erased by an autopsy carried out by Dr. Bertolini.
With the death of his brother, the "tragedy of a tyrannical love"
began, that is, the difficulties involved in trying to create a father-
son relationship with his nine-year-old nephew Karl by becoming
his sole guardian.

Because his brother's will had assigned guardianship of Karl
concurrently to Ludwig van Beethoven and the child's mother,
Johanna, Beethoven began litigation to secure sole custody of the
boy, working himself more and more into his self-styled role as
the boy's real father. After the court had finally decided on
9 January 1816 in favor of Beethoven as the sole guardian, he
wrote the lawyer Johann Nepomuk Kanka in Prague in September 1816: "I am really the natural father of my dead brother's
child." He revealed a similar fondness for this fantasy to Wegeler
at the end of September: "You are a husband and a father—I am
too, but without a wife." Beethoven sought to build a moral
foundation for his actions with the argument that he was trying
"to wrest a poor, unhappy child from an unworthy mother." To
be able to demonstrate his role as saviour of the child, he accused
his sister-in-law of poisoning her husband and even of engaging
in prostitution.

In addressing Beethoven's extremely complicated relationship
with his sister-in-law, psychoanalysts have suggested that
Beethoven's degrading of Johanna to the status of a prostitute

may have been an expression of his sexual yearning for this woman and that the alleged rescue of the boy, as well as the fantasy of his "fatherhood," came about primarily to protect himself against his unconscious desire to possess the wife of his deceased brother. In 1954, Richard and Editha Sterba published their book, *Beethoven and His Nephew: A Psychoanalytic Study of Their Relationship*, which attempts to explain the psychological origins and consequences of these critical events and relationships in Beethoven's life. In his book *Beethoven Essays*, Maynard Solomon summarized the Sterbas' conclusions (with brief quotations from their book) as follows:

> The basic conflict in Beethoven's character arose from "the polarity between the male and female principle, which he vainly sought to reconcile in his behavior." This polarity was partially manifested in unconscious homosexual tendencies which had earlier found their outlet in his devotion to his brother Caspar Carl, whom he tried to control in the manner of a jealous and overprotective mother [he had attempted something similar with his other brother Johann in Linz in 1812]. With the death of Caspar Carl, Beethoven grasped the opportunity of appropriating his child "as a suitable substitute...as an object of maternal love." In order to accomplish this, it became necessary to supplant the boy's real mother, whom Beethoven persecuted as a rival and as the embodiment of feminine evil. He was therefore acting out a rescue fantasy, attempting to save a "close male relative...from woman's fatal claws"; in the process his apparently innate aggressive and sadistic tendencies overwhelmed his ego, causing a "regression in his erotic development," disturbing his psychic equilibrium, "to such a degree that composition became almost impossible" for several years, and, ultimately, following Karl's suicide attempt, leading to his death.

This representation of the situation cannot be accepted entirely without reservation. First, Beethoven's alleged homosexuality must definitely be called into question. Second, such a picture of Beethoven disregards the fact that the father role, one that first fell to him when he was still quite young, was deeply rooted in the Beethoven family history, not least in the dominating figure of his grandfather. Beethoven's exaggerated stress on "really" being a father could have had its psychological origins in an oedipal relationship with his parents and his grandfather. After his shattered efforts to enter into a lasting union with his "Immortal Beloved" and found a family, and the deep emotional crisis with thoughts of suicide that his disappointment set in motion, he now had an opportunity to transfer his aggression—which at first he had directed against himself—to an appropriate object, his sister-in-law. In keeping with Freud's theory of ambivalence, Beethoven's hatred for Johanna could have been accompanied by an unconscious erotic need. Johanna's claim during a court proceeding that her brother-in-law was in love with her, as well as the name "Ludovica" given to a child she bore out of wedlock in 1820, conforms with such a possibility.

In this psychoanalytical view, the focus of Beethoven's conflict was not his nephew but his sister-in-law Johanna. Of course, as Goldschmidt has properly observed, in the context of Beethoven's ambivalent behavior toward his sister-in-law, his repeated willingness to find some reconciliation and his frequent offers of financial help need not have been solely the reflection of an unconscious erotic attraction. Strong feelings of guilt would explain his behavior equally well. To suggest that Beethoven's attitude toward the eternal feminine is symbolized by his mystical creation of fatherhood with no help from a woman would be overly simplistic. The fact that his innermost desires for marriage and family remained unfulfilled was not due to excessive inhibitions on his part or a lack of manhood, but because prospects were utterly lacking from the outset, through his choice of women who were either aristocrats, married, or already had children of their own. Beethoven apparently had a need for these emotionally taxing situations in order to place his life completely at the service of his artistic calling. From this point of view, "all his unhappiness provoked and unprovoked, all the wrongs experienced or caused, all his identification with Odysseus, that 'most unhappy of mortals,' [can] never be understood except as a spur to his creativity...to reach and maintain his artistic best."

## A Low Point in Beethoven's Health

Beethoven spent the summer of 1815 in Baden and in the autumn new symptoms of ill health appeared. In a letter of November 1815 to Archduke Rudolph, he said: "From the beginning of last month in Baden, I had started to feel ill but I only kept to my room and bed from the 5th of October on and then for about eight days. I had a rather dangerous inflammatory catarrh ["Entzündungskatarrh"]; I am still only able to go out a little." Exactly which illness this "Enzündungskatarrh" may have involved is not known, but it might certainly have been his intestinal troubles once again. In letters written in 1816, Beethoven again spoke of a colic attack, acute paroxysmal abdominal pains, in connection with a worsening of his condition that drove him to take to his bed in the months of February, May, July, and November. Just how upsetting he found these colics is clear from a note made by Fanny Giannatasio del Rio, the daughter of the director of the school that Beethoven's nephew Karl attended. On 11 April 1816, she wrote that Beethoven had talked to her about this indisposition and had told her that "these attacks of colic will be the end of him." Beethoven raised new complaints in February 1817, as we see in a letter to his friend Franz von Brentano: "As for me, for some time I have been in parlous health." Presumably, this is a reference to a prolonged period of sickness that could already have started in October 1816, for a letter from this time to the publisher Simrock says: "Since 15 October I have been very sick with an inflammatory catarrh, and I still suffer from its effects and it will probably take the whole spring or summer before I am well again." We learn more details of this illness from a letter to Countess Erdödy on 19 June 1817:

> I have been too pressed for time, too burdened with cares, and constantly in poor health since 6 October 1816, afflicted with a severe inflammatory catarrh since 15 October so that I had to stay in bed a long time and it took months before I could go out again even briefly; up to now I haven't been able to shake the effects of all this. I changed doctors because mine, a sly Italian [Dr. Malfatti], was just after my money and lacked both honesty and judgment; that happened in April 1817. Then, every day from 15 April to 4 May, I had to take six

doses of powder, six cups of tea, that lasted until
4 May; from then on, I received another kind of
powder, of which I had to take six a day again,
and had to rub myself three times a day with a
vaporizing ointment. Then I journeyed here where
I take the waters. Yesterday I again received a
medicine, a tincture, that I must take twelve spoon-
fuls of each day. Every day I pray for an end to
this depressing state; although things have improved somewhat, nevertheless it appears it will
still take a long time before I am completely well.
You can imagine what all this must do to my existence! My hearing has gotten worse, and is no
more capable now than it was before of taking
care of me and my needs..., and my worries have
become all the greater because of my brother's
child.

Just what kind of "inflammatory catarrh" it was can be drawn
from a letter written four days earlier, on 15 July 1817, to the poet
Wilhelm Gerhard, who had asked Beethoven to set some of his
Anacreontic verses to music and to whom Beethoven excused
himself with the words:

In part, my constant state of ill health for almost
four years now is to blame if I am able to answer
so many only with silence. Since October 1816,
my tendency to get sick has only increased, I had
a severe inflammatory catarrh and thus lung trouble
as well; I tell you all this so that you will not think
me discourteous or otherwise misjudge me, as so
many others do.

He expressed himself in a similar vein to Nanette Streicher, who
often helped him master the disorder of his household, in a letter
of 7 July 1817 from the village of Nussdorf just outside Vienna:

My dear friend!...the nasty weather two days ago
kept me from visiting you when I was in the city;
I hurried back here yesterday in the morning only
to find my servant was not at home, and he had
even taken the key to the lodgings with him. It
was very cool and I had nothing on from the city
except a thin pair of trousers, so I had to wander

around for three long hours, this did me no good
and made me feel rotten all day....In addition there
is the fearful prospect that perhaps I will never be
better, besides I even have doubts about my present
doctor, and now at long last he has diagnosed my
condition as lung trouble ["Lungenkrankheit"].

This "Lungenkrankheit" was probably persistent bronchitis
brought about repeatedly by Beethoven's odd living habits. He
would jump up suddenly after concentrated work at his desk and
set off—scantily dressed—for hour-long strolls in the cold or the
rain. After returning from hiking, flushed and hot, he would
open the doors and windows and pour pitchers of cold water
over himself to cool down. He would stand up suddenly in the
middle of strenuous work on a composition and douse his heated
head with water—a personal habit that brought him repeatedly
into conflict with the neighbors below because the water frequently ran through the floor into their rooms. The aforemen-
tioned "inflammatory catarrh" may also have been caused by his
habit of drinking excessive quantities of cold water or by his
staying in quarters that were insufficiently heated. He certainly
complained often enough about ovens that went unheated because of his servants' negligence. He expressed his opinion of
servants to his friend Zmeskall: "By the way, it drives me crazy
that because of the state of my hearing, I am condemned to spend
most of my life with this most ignominious class of human beings
and even to depend on the same."

Beethoven's "lung troubles" were probably a source of great
concern to him, for both his mother and his brother had died of
pulmonary tuberculosis. Writing in 1816 in her diary, Fanny
Giannatasio noted: "Then it happened that he sat with us at the
round table all evening long, seemingly lost in thought...all the
while spitting into his handkerchief...and each time inspecting it,
so that I often thought he feared finding traces of blood."

Time and again during the fall of 1817, Beethoven's health
left much to be desired, as we see in excerpts from a series of
letters written to Nanette Streicher from Nussdorf: "Some days
after your visit with Winter I had such a terrible case of rheumatism that it will be tomorrow or the day after before I can go out
again"; a few days later he wrote: "I don't feel very well and
therefore cannot visit you—I have just received the medicine and
think it will surely be all better in a few days. My thanks to you,

dear Frau von Streicher, for your good wishes." He also wrote to his friend Zmeskall on 9 September 1817: "In my situation with a cold, I feel even worse now, couldn't get a carriage here and, as much as I normally like to walk, going by foot is not possible, given my condition." Finally, he repeatedly had to cancel music lessons with his high-born student Archduke Rudolph for health reasons. For example, in December 1817 he wrote: "Your Imperial Highness! I had to take some medicine again today but still I thought I would be able to have the pleasure of waiting on Y. I. H.; but unfortunately I am feeling weaker than I did yesterday. I tried going out but after a few minutes I had to come back; the bad weather is surely to blame." Some weeks later he wrote: "You will please most generously forgive me today if I do not attend Y. I. H., for with this weather and my coughing, I cannot leave the house." This illness must have been particularly bad at the turn of the year, for on 28 December 1817 he wrote Nanette Streicher:

> Yesterday I had a visit from your dear, sweet daughter, but I was so sick I hardly remember it;…this bitter cold, especially here in my place, has made me so stiff, and yesterday I couldn't move a bone for practically the whole day. Coughing and the worst headaches I've ever had were with me all day long; I even had to put myself to bed at 6 in the evening. I'm still lying there, but in the meantime I'm feeling better.

On this occasion his sinuses may have been affected by a severe headcold, leading to the bad headaches. Just how susceptible Beethoven was to respiratory infections is shown by reports to Nanette Streicher at the beginning of 1818: "Again I have a cold with terrible sniffles and coughing" and "When I came home last night, the pain was such that all I could do was lie down on the sofa."

Beethoven was at his lowest ebb from 1816 until the first half of 1818. His recurring intestinal difficulties and his fear that he might have tuberculosis made him irritable and disinclined to work. His fevers and frequent attacks of bronchitis, which would hang on for months at a time and were usually associated with a worsening of his abdominal troubles, often led to such feelings of infirmity and weakness that he could not leave his bed. To make matters worse, his increasing deafness made him suspicious and inclined to be hard on people around him.

Psychologically, however, the conflict over the guardianship of his nephew Karl was undoubtedly what weighed on Beethoven most. When the young man was finally separated from his mother after the court judgment and had been entered in the private boarding school run by Cajetan Giannatasio del Rio on 2 February 1816, Beethoven tried to achieve a better understanding with his sister-in-law Johanna, while keeping this effort a secret from his group of friends. Beethoven's constant criticism and nagging, however, along with the unceasing pressure to perform well at school, led the lad finally to run away and go back to his mother on 3 December 1818. When Karl testified before the court that he feared maltreatment at the hands of his uncle, who once had threatened to throttle him, Beethoven lost the guardianship of his nephew. He finally regained guardianship in April 1820 after much effort.

All these factors explain why Beethoven's creative productivity fell off noticeably after 1815 and may even have ceased altogether for a time in the crisis years of 1817 and 1818. A general impression arose that no more major compositions were to be expected from Beethoven, that he had already "written himself out." Yet at the same time, his reputation as a composer continued to grow, as we can see in a review in the *Wiener Allgemeine musikalische Zeitung* of January 1819: "We call him the greatest of our, of Europe's composers and Vienna gratefully acknowledges what it possesses in having him." In fact, the public would soon be set straight, just as Beethoven himself had prophesied after hearing the rumors that his inventive powers now sufficed for trifles at best: "Just wait, you will soon learn differently." Beethoven appeared to gather new strength once again as though from a subterranean stream eternally inaudible to ordinary mortals. A new and powerful period of creativity was about to start and would reach its culmination in his *Missa solemnis* and the Ninth Symphony.

Beethoven's work on these vast compositions was certainly made more difficult by his personal concerns, those associated with the guardianship of his nephew in particular, but also by illnesses of various kinds. It is remarkable that the new surge of creativity would be born in the years of sickness and suffering, 1817 and 1818, in a time when Beethoven did not have enough confidence in himself even to accept an invitation to go to England.  In his despair, he wrote to Zmeskall on 21 August 1817:

> God have mercy on me, I am as good as lost....My
> health means I should eat at home and in greater
> leisure, what do you think about that?  If the situation does not come to an end, then I won't be in
> London next year but maybe in the grave—thank
> God, the role is about played out.

In this period of depression, Beethoven broke with Dr. Johann Malfatti.  He replaced him with the energetic Dr. Jakob Staudenheim, who even then tried to forbid Beethoven from indulging in wine and beer.  It is incredible to realize that in these unhappy times Beethoven began work on his *Hammerklavier* Sonata (in B-flat, op. 106).  "The sonata was written under oppressive circumstances, for it is hard to write just to be earning your daily bread, so to speak, and that was how far I'd come," as Beethoven wrote about this monumental work, which was dedicated to Archduke Rudolph and published in 1819.  The German musicologist and composer Hugo Riemann regarded the adagio of this sonata, perhaps the greatest sonata of them all, as its crowning touch:

> It is surely the most moving song of lamentation
> ever written for the piano....All the deep sorrow
> which the master's heart had taken unto itself in
> these years is gathered here and strains to make
> itself heard....The fashion in which the surrender
> to the inevitable slowly takes place and comes to
> an end full of forebodings in that F-sharp major
> chord—that cannot be described in words.  A more
> beautiful adagio for the piano has never been written, and we have no reason to hope anything like
> it will ever occur again.

But we could just as well call the closing fugue, possibly the boldest and greatest ever composed for the piano, the climax of this enormous work.  In this fugue, the soul soars into those extraterrestrial regions where pain is absent and incarnates the victory of the divine over the misery of human existence—a victory Beethoven achieved over himself.

At the time Beethoven was finishing the *Hammerklavier* Sonata, in 1818, he was losing the ability to hold verbal conversations, even with the help of ear trumpets.  From then on, communication with the outside world was feasible only by means of exchanges written in the famous conversation books. They record almost all the talks up to his death. The last fifteen books forcefully describe his last days, the scene of his final illness, and the measures taken by the doctors. These books are documents of incalculable worth.

The books provide details about the continuing efforts to cure Beethoven's hearing defect. For example, toward the end of November 1819, he was informed in one of the conversation books:

> Dr. H. Graff has something to cure your hearing. He wants you to know about it....The man opposite, a count somebody, told about the experience he had with his wife who had lost her hearing and got it back using a simple remedy; he asked me to write it down for you;—Specifically, you take fresh horseradish, just as it's pulled out of the ground, and grate it onto cotton cloth, which is quickly rolled up and stuck in the ear;—this must be repeated as often as possible, always using fresh horseradish; he saw himself that with this simple remedy his wife had her hearing back in 4 weeks. At least it couldn't hurt anything says his neighbor, a doctor.

We can assume that Beethoven actually gave this suggestion a try, because it struck visitors repeatedly that the master had cloth stuck in his ears. He said himself once: "Cloth in the ears at the piano relieves my hearing of the noise that's so unpleasant."

In 1816, Beethoven's nephew Karl was operated on for hernia by Dr. Carl von Smetana, who was said to have earned a reputation for the treatment of hearing diseases as well. For a time, Beethoven placed himself under his care. He commented later, however, that this doctor with his various medicines "only wanted to busy himself with relieving his supplicant's hearing with something or other, without having the least hope of curing the disease." Beethoven soon turned anew to the nature healer Father Weiss to have him administer his recommended applications of oil in the ears. The excellent psychological attention that the good father showed the patient could have given Beethoven confidence, for Schindler says: "The sympathy that the worthy man showed him was touching, and while promising nothing, still Beethoven felt himself so pleasantly invigorated thereby that he himself had hopes for some success."

In addition, Beethoven's attention was caught by dubious announcements of machines of various types promising to help the hard of hearing. In 1819, for example, he got involved with a so-called electro-vibration machine that a certain Dr. Carl Josef Mayer advertised in a Viennese newspaper as suited for the successful treatment of roaring in the ears, hearing difficulties, and deafness. In a conversation book from 29 February 1820, we read about another technical innovation by a Viennese craftsman named Wolffsohn: "The head-machine for the hard of hearing. An ingenious device in the form of a flat-pressed diadem, which, with a front of hair, can be worn without being noticed. Wolffsohn guarantees it will bring decisive advantages to our immortal Beethoven."

## New Symptoms Appear

At the beginning of the second half of 1818, Beethoven's health seems to have been better, as indicated by a comment in a letter to his friend Vinzenz Hauschka: "By the way, my health is much improved." And his spirits had improved along with it, for in this same letter a renewed sense of humor (albeit, somewhat on the scatological side) breaks through: "Now farewell, Hauschka-boy, I wish you open bowels and the most lovely crapper." This improvement obviously lasted into 1820, for in the intervening years he made only occasional reports of such indispositions as the sniffles, coughing spells, or spasms of pain in connection with his intestinal troubles. For the most part, these complaints were directed at Archduke Rudolph. In 1819, for example, Beethoven spoke of "severe catarrh" and in a letter of 15 July 1819 he said: "Since the last time I was to attend Your Imperial Highness in the city, I have not been feeling well at all." In August of 1819 his "catarrhal condition" and his stomach troubles may have hung on somewhat longer, for on 31 August he wrote the Archduke from the Vienna suburb of Mödling:

> I hope I will soon be feeling better again. So much misery has had an adverse effect on my health and I don't feel well, having to dose myself again for some time now, with the result that I can hardly give myself to that dearest gift of heaven,

my art and the muses, for even a few hours of the day.

Just how susceptible he was comes out in his next letter to Archduke Rudolph: "Yesterday for the first time I was able to go out and felt rather well; only, as a patient still in recovery, I had forgotten or it slipped my mind to head for home again in time and as a result I had to put up with another attack." Finally, Beethoven reported a further indisposition in a letter to the Archduke from Mödling written on 2 September 1820:

> Since Tuesday evening I have not been well, but I thought surely by Friday I would again have the pleasure of appearing before Y. I. H. That was a mistake, however, and only today am I able to tell Y. I. H. that I certainly hope to be able to attend Y. I. H. again either on next Monday or Tuesday....My indisposition can be ascribed to the fact that I took an open post carriage.

Apart from such passing spells of weakness, Beethoven apparently was spared serious illness through all of 1820. But the next year, the problems started again with various "rheumatic incidents" whose true nature is not known for lack of specific information. In a letter of 7 March 1821 to the publisher Schlesinger in Berlin, Beethoven reported having been bedridden for a considerable time because of a "bout of rheumatism": "You are probably thinking unfavorably of me, but you may well change your mind when I tell you that I was laid low by a serious bout of rheumatism for the last six weeks, but now it is better. You can well imagine that lots of things had to be put aside." In addition, 1821 brought a new illness, one that would turn out to have fateful implications—jaundice. Beethoven wrote Archduke Rudolph about it on 18 July 1821:

> I heard yesterday of Your Highness's arrival here, which as much as it delights me is a rather sad occasion for me too, for it may be some time before I can have the pleasure of waiting on Y. I. H. After feeling very ill for a long time, I finally broke out completely with jaundice, which I find a most atrocious sickness. I hope at least that I will be sufficiently recovered to be able to see Y. I. H. here before your departure. In the past winter,

> too, I had the worst bouts of rheumatism....How
> sad it makes me that the jaundice I am suffering
> from prevents me from hurrying immediately to
> Y. I. H.

From this letter, we can conclude that the jaundice showed up at the start of summer and lasted two or three months, as Beethoven wrote his friend Franz von Brentano on 12 November 1821:

> I have been constantly ill from last year to this,
> and the whole summer long too I have been seized
> with jaundice. That went on until the end of Au-
> gust. Following Staudenheim's orders, I had to go
> to Baden in September. But because it was cold
> in that neighborhood, I came down with such a
> bad case of diarrhea I couldn't continue the cure
> and had to flee back here again. Now, thank God,
> things are better and finally it seems my health
> wants to liven me up again in order to put new
> life in my art too, which certainly hasn't been the
> case for the last two years, both because my health
> has been poor and because of so many other hu-
> man tribulations.

From Beethoven's account, we can speculate that in the summer of 1821 he probably suffered from viral hepatitis, inflammation of the liver caused by a virus. In uncomplicated cases, this disease normally wanes after three to four months. Frequently it is preceded even weeks before the outbreak by a series of general symptoms such as loss of appetite, fatigue, headaches, and occasionally pains in the muscles and joints, which even today can be misdiagnosed as signs of "rheumatic" inflammation until the cause of the complaints becomes more clear with the emergence of jaundice.* These symptoms and diagnoses are certainly consistent with Beethoven's complaints of "bouts of rheumatism" in the spring of 1821, as well as his report to Archduke Rudolph on 18 July—"after feeling ill for a long time, I finally broke out completely with jaundice."

Pathological studies of Beethoven have raised the speculation that this jaundice was the first indication that he had cirrhosis of the liver. However, medical knowledge today shows that this view cannot be sustained. Persons suffering from cirrhosis with increasing damage to the liver first have an accumulation of fluid in the legs and abdomen as well as an elevation of pressure that causes bleeding in the veins of the esophagus. Jaundice is a late symptom as a rule. Moreover, once jaundice has appeared in a person with cirrhosis of the liver, it generally persists to some degree. Beethoven's jaundice, in contrast, had fully receded after a few weeks.

Beethoven's dream of finally becoming completely healthy never came true. As early as 6 April 1822, he wrote Ferdinand Ries: "Dear, good Ries! Having been in ill health over half a year now, I couldn't answer your letters....I continue to mull over the idea that I shall indeed go to London if only my health will permit it, perhaps next spring?" He made similar remarks during the next months, such as this one from a letter of 19 May 1822 to Franz von Brentano: "...I have been constantly afflicted with gouty arthritis of the chest again for the last four months...." Understandably, this tendency to be sick inhibited Beethoven's creativity, as he mentioned in a letter of 20 June to Georg August Griesinger, the biographer of Joseph Haydn: "Having been sickly for the last 5 months, I can only be very sparing with the results of my art." His doctor had prescribed mineral water and baths for him, in addition to various medicines, as he wrote the publisher Peters in August 1822. We learn something about his treatment in taking the waters, which was all the rage in Vienna at the time, from his account to his brother Johann in late July 1822:

> Concerning my health, it's coming along; for some days, I've had to drink Johannes mineral water, take the medicine of the day four times daily, and now I'm supposed to go to Baden to take 30 baths there...in the meantime, the Josephstadt has put me to work here [a reference to his commission to compose music for the opening of the Josephstadt theater], which really complicates matters what with my mineral water and bath treatments, the more so since Staudenheim advised me to bathe only 1 1/2 hours.

This treatment with mineral water and baths was obviously prescribed because of his abdominal troubles and may have given him some relief. He wrote his brother Johann again on 8 September: "Although I cannot say with certainty that there has been a real improvement in the state of my health, still I think the difficulties have been, if not cured, then certainly suppressed with the help of the waters."

In 1823, Beethoven was plagued not only with his intestinal difficulties, including repeated attacks of diarrhea, but also a protracted, painful inflammation of the eyes that began in April, continued into August, and recurred in the following year.  The first mention of this condition is in a letter to Ferdinand Ries on 25 April 1823: "At present, the perpetual misery of my situation makes it necessary that I write whatever brings me as much money as I have need for at the moment.  And now, what a sorry development for you to discover!!  I'm not feeling well because of having to put up with lots of annoyances, because, yes, even my eyes hurt!  But don't worry about it; you'll soon receive the symphony." Beethoven said something similar to Anton Schindler in this period:

> Nights I have to cover my eyes and am supposed to take good care of them, otherwise, Smetana writes me, I shall not write many notes more....Here is the previous work for Diabelli and a part of the new. My eyes, which are still rather worse than better, only allow matters to go ahead slowly.

These eye troubles—almost certainly a case of iridocyclitis, inflammation of the iris and the conjunctiva (the delicate membrane lining the eyelids and covering the eyeball)—were a particular hindrance to Beethoven in completing his Mass in D (*Missa solemnis*, op. 123), which had originally been intended for the elevation of Archduke Rudolph to the office of Archbishop of Olmütz in Moravia.  Because of the delay, Beethoven addressed himself to the Archduke several times during the summer.  On 1 July 1823 he wrote: "Since the departure of Y. I. H., I have been feeling poorly, and indeed lately have been stricken with severe eye trouble, which has improved only to the extent that for the last eight days I have been able to use my eyes again, but with care."  He referred to his eye troubles again when writing the Archduke on 3 July 1823:  "Word has reached me here that Y. I. H. will arrive here tomorrow.  If I am not yet able to follow the wishes of my heart, so I would ask you to blame it on my eyes. They are much better, but I must not expose them to the air in the city, which could still affect my eyes badly." His eyes probably could not stand the clouds of dust kicked up by the numerous horse-drawn carriages and wagons in the city streets. Two weeks later he reported: "As far as my eyes are concerned, things are going better, but very slowly....If I did not need eyeglasses, it would get better more quickly."

Beethoven's perennial stomach problems and the new difficulties with his eyes hampered his creative endeavors considerably. To his brother, Beethoven wrote with resignation:

> Per Staudenheim's instructions, I have to continue taking medicine, and should not even exercise too much. Let me ask you, instead of going to the Prater today, come to me with your wife and daughter....Let there be peace between us, God forbid that that most natural fraternal bond should again be unnaturally severed; and in any case, my life may not last much longer. I tell you again that I have nothing against your wife....Anyway, as a result of my poor state of health these last three and a half months, I am very, indeed extremely sensitive and irritable.

Although his eye troubles slowly got better, his abdominal sufferings got worse again. He sent Anton Schindler the following lines from the village of Hetzendorf where he was staying in July 1823: "I'm not feeling well at all, had terrible diarrhea today. Among these living Hottentots, anything can happen. Am taking medicine for my poor, ruined stomach. In the meantime, expecting to see you tomorrow as early as possible."

On 13 August 1823, Beethoven moved from Hetzendorf to Baden. Writing from there on 16 August, he informed his nephew about his various physical ailments in the course of passing along some well-intended advice:

> At first I didn't want to tell you anything until I was feeling better here, which is not yet entirely the case; I arrived here with catarrh and a cold, both of them hard on me because my general state of health is catarrhal in any case, and I'm afraid of these two cutting the thread of life or, even worse, gnawing it away bit by bit. Then too my wrecked belly still has to be cured with medicine and diet,

and for that, one has the ever-faithful servants to thank!

Just how persuaded Beethoven was that his abdominal problems were due primarily to lack of attention and care from his servants emerges even more clearly from a letter he wrote his brother Johann on 19 August 1823:

> As for my situation, my eyes are not yet completely well, and when I got here, I had an upset stomach and a dreadful catarrh, the first from that arch-sow of a housekeeper and the second from an animal of a kitchen-maid whom I have already driven away once only to take her back again.

Some days later, he also told Archduke Rudolph about his stomach miseries:

> I arrived here on the 13th feeling very poorly; now, however, things are better. I was taken ill all over again with my somewhat improved catarrhal disease, and along with that my abdomen was still in the worst shape, together with my eye trouble, in short, my whole system was totally shattered....Praise God, the eyes have improved so much that I can use them quite a bit during the day now. And my other problems are also doing better.

This improvement seems to have continued, for only a few days later Beethoven wrote the Archduke: "Yesterday my doctor assured me my illness was getting better, but I still must pour down a whole portion of medicine within 24 hours, which, because it purges the bowels, leaves me feeling extremely weak."

The conversation books mention obviously severe bouts of diarrhea throughout 1823. In January, Beethoven's brother Johann made the following entry: "Haven't you gotten over your irregularity [euphemism for diarrhea] yet? You're supposed to take some powdered rhubarb and at the same time keep your diet, and especially not eat fish. It's all the result of too much eating and drinking too much water." And in fact, Beethoven liked fish and was particularly fond of oysters. In the conversation books, we read time and again about oysters having freshly arrived: "The oysters arrived today by special mail. —Tomorrow and every Wednesday fresh oysters arrive from Venice. —We are definitely going to eat fresh oysters and fried oysters and drink champagne, etc. etc." It could have been his fondness for fresh oysters that gave him viral hepatitis with jaundice. According to present-day scientific understanding, oysters are a common source of infection for Hepatitis A virus; the virus, present in seawater contaminated with the feces of infected patients, reach a thousandfold concentration in oysters.

Beethoven had a great fondness for fat-rich foods as well, particular favorites being blood sausage with potatoes and head-cheese. His personal physician, Dr. Smetana, wrote in a conversation book in 1823: "For your catarrh, you may not eat anything else during the day except barley gruel a couple of times; the irregularity will get better when you don't eat anything greasy or heavy for some days and put water in the red wine you take with your meals." From this entry, we can conclude that Beethoven's repeated "catarrh" was only occasionally an illness of the upper respiratory tract and was probably more frequently a so-called catarrh or inflammation of the gut.

Just how Beethoven was able to work purposefully on his *Missa solemnis* all these years and at the same time compose his three last great piano sonatas on the side, so to speak, is hard to imagine. In these sonatas, we hardly think of compositional technique, but simply purest expression—outbreaks of passion at its most fierce and the most intimate metamorphosis of the soul. In the Sonata in A-flat, op. 110, the slow movement in particular (marked "*Klagender Gesang,*" "Song of Mourning") reveals to us a world of pain that surely can be taken as an expression of Beethoven's personal suffering. The depth of his resignation seems literally to speak to us from the recitative-like passage of this movement. As though in dialogue with God, Beethoven seems with this passage marked "*Passionsrezitativ*" to utter the words "*Eli, Eli, lama sabachthani?*" ("My God, my God, why hast thou forsaken me?") from Bach's *St. Matthew Passion*, all the while subsequently striking the twice-accented "A" louder and faster, as if in desperation, until—for all about is silence—he begins in wearying resignation to intone, with lamenting vocal arioso, the viola da gamba solo to the alto aria, "*Es ist vollbracht*" ("It is finished") from Bach's *St. John Passion*. The way the fugue in three voices develops out of this dirge and ascends to a triumphant transfiguration is a masterpiece of the art of counterpoint found elsewhere only in the last movement of Mozart's *Jupiter Symphony* and in the finale of Anton Bruckner's Fifth Symphony. The last piano sonata Beethoven wrote—in C Minor, op. 111—is, with the heavenly set of variations of its second movement, the creation of a man "who breaks all bounds and plunges his work deeper than a probe has ever sounded." After such a movement—just as following the slow movement of Schubert's *Unfinished Symphony* or the ecstatic adagio of Bruckner's Ninth Symphony—there is nothing left to say.

The *Missa solemnis* was finally handed to Archduke Rudolph on 19 March 1823 with the words "From the heart—may it go to the heart again" written over the Kyrie. Thus was the creation completed by which Beethoven meant, in his own words, "to awaken religious feelings in the singers as well as the audience and make them perpetual." He had dedicated himself to the work on this mass with such fervor that people became seriously concerned for his health. If in composing this enormous work Beethoven was in essence involving himself in metaphysics, in religion, then surely he was doing so as an individual seeking to come to grips with a personal God. For him, it was not a matter of the institutionalized power of the Church. Rather, he was grappling with his own view of faith, with his own beliefs in immortality, and making a prayer for peace, not only in a life to come, but among all mankind. The *Missa solemnis* is not simply another musical accompaniment for the text of the mass, but a transcendent work of art that happens to have been written for religious performance.

In the Ninth Symphony in D Minor, op. 125, by setting to music Friedrich Schiller's *Ode to Joy*, Beethoven wanted to underscore the programmatic nature of the work as a kind of counterstatement to the politics of the so-called French (or Bourbon) Restoration after 1814. The first performance of the Ninth Symphony took place in the Kärntnertortheater on 7 May 1824, along with the Overture in C (*The Consecration of the House*, op. 124) and excerpts from the *Missa solemnis*. The occasion also provided final, heart-wrenching proof that the master had become completely deaf. Although the concert announcement said, "Herr Ludwig van Beethoven will personally take part in the direction of the entire ensemble," in fact all the singers and musicians had been instructed not to pay any attention to Beethoven and to follow instead the tempo indications given by Kapellmeister Michael Umlauf, standing at his right side. Even after the timpani

passage in the scherzo, but especially at the end of the symphony, the audience broke out into such wild applause that Anton Schindler later noted in one of the conversation books, "In
my whole life, I have never heard such stormy and yet such warm
applause as today!" The people clapped with their hands and
drummed with their feet until the hall vibrated with the noise—
and Beethoven heard nothing. In his personal world of impenetrable silence, he remained fixed in touching helplessness, his
back to the audience, still looking at the score before him, until
the soprano Caroline Unger softly tugged at his sleeve and turned
him to the people. Then the storm of applause and enthusiasm
doubled and redoubled, and Beethoven had to take one bow
after another.

Musically, the concert was an overwhelming success; financially, it was very disappointing—the sum taken in barely covered the costs. The composer, whose deafness had made him
increasingly suspicious anyway, believed he had been swindled
and wrongly fixed on Anton Schindler as the culprit. At the end
of August, Beethoven was again complaining to his nephew Karl
about abdominal pains: "My stomach is terribly upset and there's
no doctor!...Since yesterday, I've eaten nothing except soup and
a couple of eggs and plain water; my tongue is completely coated,
and without purgatives and tonics my stomach will never, despite
this fool of a doctor, never get well." In November, he advised
his publisher Nägeli that he was "swamped and not having taken
good enough care of [himself] in this late time of the year [he was]
feeling poorly." Archduke Rudolph heard from him on 18 November 1824: "Being sick when I came here from Baden, I was prevented from attending Y. I. H. as I had wished because I was
forbidden to go out; yesterday was the first day I was allowed to
indulge myself in some fresh air."

## Liver Disease: The First Signs

In 1825, for the first time, symptoms appeared that were attributable to severe chronic liver disease and that suggested a
shortened life expectancy. Having lost faith in Dr. Staudenheim,
Beethoven now turned to a professor of natural history and general practitioner, Dr. Anton Braunhofer, writing him on 18 April
1825: "I am not feeling well and hope you will not refuse me
your help, for I am suffering great pain. If it is possible for you to

pay me a visit today still, I would sincerely ask you to do so." In May 1825, Beethoven experienced the first bleeding from the esophagus, probably coming from dilated and congested veins, a symptom commonly observed in advanced stages of cirrhosis of the liver. Even before the end of 1824, this esophageal bleeding evidently had been preceded by bleeding from the nose. The blood would have been swallowed or coughed out, giving Beethoven reason to regularly examine the sputum in his hand-kerchief without regard for the presence of others because of his fear of tuberculosis. The seriousness of his situation must have become clear to Beethoven at least from the time of the first vomiting of blood. He graphically described his symptoms in the form of an imaginary dialogue between himself and Dr. Braun-hofer, which he sent to his doctor from Baden in a still optimistic letter written on 13 May 1825:

> Doctor: How are you doing, patient?
>
> Patient: Not very well, am still very weak, belch-ing, etc. I think some strong medicine is really needed, but something that doesn't plug you up, and I should be able to drink some white wine with water too! because this devilish beer is noth-ing but revolting. The situation with my catarrh goes like this: specifically, I am spewing out quite a bit of blood, probably only from the windpipe; even more often it pours out of my nose, which has happened frequently this winter. No doubt about it, my stomach is terribly weak, indeed my general physical condition. And from what I know of my situation, it will be hard to get my strength back on my own.
>
> Doctor: I shall help you, with a little bit of Brown and a little bit of Stoll [a reference to rival schools of medical thought: the Scottish doctor John Brown saw the source of sickness in the sensitivity of the organs and the Viennese doctor Maximilian Stoll, a pathologist, regarded illness as caused by the presence of disease-producing matter in the body].

Patient:   I would indeed appreciate having the strength to be able to sit at my desk again.  Give it some thought!

The end.

P. S.   As soon as I am back in the city, I'll see you,—just tell Karl when I should meet with you. It would help if you could yourself pass on to Karl what should happen next (I took the last medicine only once and have lost it since).

With respect and thanks, your friend, Beethoven

Beethoven rounded off this letter by including with it a canon on the text, *"Doktor sperrt das Tor dem Tod, Note hilft auch aus der Not"* ("Doctor, close the door on death, notes [i. e., music] will also help in need"), a pun on the double meaning of *Not(e)* in German.  There is a further reference to the canon in a comment in one of the conversation books from 1825: "My doctor helped me, for I couldn't write any more notes, but now I'm writing music ['Noten'] that will help me out of my difficulties ['Nöten']."

Beethoven had previously dedicated a song, *Abendlied unterm gestirnten Himmel* (*Evening Song Under Starry Skies*, WoO 150), to Dr. Braunhofer in 1820 and always felt obliged to him even though the good doctor, as one who would not put up with nonsense and failure to follow orders, was rather brusque and strict with him.  Beethoven was, of course, anything but a submissive or obedient patient. (In his biography of the composer, Anton Schindler wrote:  "There it was written down:  'Take one teaspoonful every hour.'  Ah, but what good could only one teaspoonful do?  That means it might as well be a tablespoonful. And that is how medicine was taken.") But because of the commanding tone in which Dr. Braunhofer's orders were given, Beethoven was rather subdued and appeared to obey.  In conversation books from the period we find directions from Braunhofer such as:

—No wine, no coffee, no spices of any kind.

—I won't trouble you very much longer with taking medicines but definitely will with the prescribed diet, which won't starve you to death.

—Every fever lasts a little while, yours is already
  going away.

—If you want to be completely well and still live a
  long time, then you must live according to
  nature's rules.  You have a strong tendency to
  inflammations, and it wouldn't have taken much
  before you would have gotten a right good intestinal inflammation.  The inclination is still
  there in your body.

—I'll give you a powder.

—I'll bet if you take something alcoholic, in a few
  hours you'll be lying there weak and worn-out.

Here too we see that Beethoven's abdominal pains and diarrhea
were accompanied by fever.

Of course, when Beethoven started feeling bad again, his confidence in Dr. Braunhofer was quickly shaken.  On 18 May 1825,
not a week after he had written his witty doctor-patient dialogue,
he wrote the following lines to his nephew:

> Tomorrow I really must have some coffee; who
> knows if it isn't better for me than the chocolate,
> for the instructions of this Braunhofer have already
> gone wrong several times, and anyhow he seems
> pretty limited to me and a crazy man besides; he
> surely knew about the asparagus.  —After eating
> at the inn today, I had considerable diarrhea—and
> we have no white wine.

These lines are further evidence of how little attention Beethoven
paid to his doctor's dietary restrictions prohibiting coffee and
alcoholic beverages.

His discouragement over his physical condition since April is
clear in a letter Beethoven sent to his nephew Karl on 9 June:
"You know how I'm living here, particularly given the cold weather.
Constantly being alone only makes me that much weaker, for my
weakness often comes really to the edge of fainting.  Oh don't be
offended any more, the grim reaper won't be a long time in coming anyway."  His illness naturally affected his psyche too, and his
irritable and quick-tempered nature became increasingly apparent, often in embarrassing ways.  Once, for example, when his
copyist Ferdinand Wolanek ventured to call his attention to a

A CANON BEETHOVEN SENT TO HIS DOCTOR, DR. BRAUNHOFER, WITH A LETTER OF 13 MAY 1825.

possible mistake, Beethoven responded: "You miserable scribbler! Stupid oaf! Correct the mistakes you've yourself made through your ignorance, presumptuousness, self-conceit, and sheer stupidity. That would be far more fitting than your presuming to instruct me, for that is exactly as if the sow intended to teach Minerva." Sudden outbursts could also lead him to throw a chair at his housekeeper. And once at an inn the waiter brought him the wrong bowl; when he gave Beethoven a rather flippant response, Beethoven promptly turned the bowl over on the waiter's head so the soup ran down his face.

In spite of his poor physical and emotional condition in 1825, Beethoven composed such masterworks as the two string quartets, in B-flat, op. 130, and in A minor, op. 132. And we should not overlook the fact that he occasionally exaggerated his sickly disposition simply to evoke understanding from the Archduke for his frequent absences from the scheduled lessons or to wring higher fees from his publishers. A comment along these lines in a letter of 17 July 1825 to his nephew is revealing: "By the way, you should always remember that my sickliness etc. and circumstances force me to focus on what is to my advantage more than I might otherwise; bargaining is hard for me, but there's no other choice."

We know that Beethoven went to Baden in the autumn of 1825 and was in rather good spirits. How cheerful and boisterous he could be when he was with friends is reflected in a letter of 2 September 1825 to the Danish composer Friedrich Kuhlau written on the day after the night before:

> I have to confess the champagne went very much to my head too, and once again I had to learn the lesson that something like that tends to stifle my working powers more than it helps them out; for as easy as it is for me otherwise to respond with something on the spot [he had written a canon for Kuhlau in the course of the party], today I can no longer tell what it was I wrote yesterday.

In short, we should not picture the ill-stricken Beethoven of 1825 solely as a depressed, ill-tempered, and irritable man. Moritz Schlesinger, the publisher who had traveled from Paris to negotiate a prospective edition of Beethoven's complete works, said later that he found himself confronted with a relaxed composer who captivated him with his "charming friendliness." The events of the year are reflected artistically in the A-minor String Quartet. Both sections of the slow movement carry inscriptions in Beethoven's hand: the first theme is inscribed "A convalescent's sacred hymn of thanksgiving, in the Lydian mode," and is immediately followed by a hopeful-sounding andante with the inscription "Feeling new strength" as an expression of his new-found optimism. The other string quartet from 1825, the one in B-flat, could be called a kind of "diary of the spirit" in which all shades of emotion pass before us, from defiant vexation with fate to a dance full of humor to a cavatina lustrous with the tears of the composer's sufferings and pains.

When October came, Beethoven returned to Vienna and moved into what would be his last dwelling, the Schwarzspanierhaus (so called because it had been built by the black-garbed Benedictines of Spain). His childhood friend from Bonn, Stephan von Breuning, happened to live close by and the two were in frequent contact. Beethoven's state of health seems to have been rather stable this autumn, even though he complained occasionally about his "bad stomach" to his friend Breuning. But then, as the calamitous year of 1826 began, troubles that he called "gout pains" began to affect him again toward the end of January. In February 1826, he wrote to Dr. Braunhofer: "Please pay me a visit, have been suffering for a while with a rheumatic or gouty condition." Dr. Braunhofer's influence seemed to induce Beethoven to follow his directions fairly strictly at this point, or so it appears from a letter of 23 February 1826:

> I am very much obliged to you for the care you have taken of me. As far as I was able, I have followed your orders; wine, coffee, everything as you directed. At the same time, it is difficult to say just how far the effect of these has been felt in these last couple days; the pain in my back is not great, but it shows the trouble is still there...

All the events in these months were overshadowed, however, by growing tensions in his relationship with his nephew Karl. Beethoven's behavior toward his nephew—treating Karl, then almost twenty years old, as though he were a child, telling him what he could and could not do, and spying on him—finally led the young man to try to free himself from the shackles of this "tyrannical love." Bitter arguments, even violence, between the two of them became more frequent. Moreover, Karl began seeing his mother on the sly again, perhaps assisted by Beethoven's brother Johann. Beethoven had already found occasion in May the year before (1825) to write an angry letter to his nephew:

> As God is my witness, my only dream is of being totally separated from you and from my wretched brother and this detestable family that's been wished on me. May God hear my prayers, for I can't trust you anymore. Unfortunately your father, or, better yet still, not your father.

Such outbursts caused increasing antagonism in their relationship until finally, in June 1826, the tension reached a dramatic peak with Karl about to commit a deed with far-reaching consequences.

In an effort to calm the situation, Beethoven wrote him: "Don't take any step that will make you unhappy and cut my life short. I couldn't get to sleep until 3 o'clock because I was coughing all night....Don't make me worry and be anxious any more. For the time being, farewell. Your real and true father."

But the distrust that now existed between the two of them could no longer be removed by such letters. The confused, unhappy young man could not tolerate his "imprisonment by Beethoven," as he put it later, and fled to Baden on 30 July after having purchased two pistols. He then wrote two letters—one to a friend and the other to his uncle—and climbed up to the ruins at Rauhenstein. There he shot himself in the left temple, or rather he shot at himself, for the bullet from the first pistol missed altogether and the bullet from the second penetrated the flesh but only grazed his skull. A passing wagon driver found him and Karl was taken to his mother. Having been notified, Beethoven hurriedly sent the following message to Dr. Carl Smetana, who had known Karl since the hernia operation: "A great calamity has happened which Karl accidentally brought on himself; still possible to save him, I hope, especially by you if you only get there quickly. Karl has a bullet in his head, how it happened you will soon learn. Only quickly, for God's sake, quickly." In fact, Karl's recovery at the Vienna General Hospital was relatively quick. But for Beethoven, all illusions that he might be able to create a kind of family life with the nephew who would be a son to him, these illusions were finally dead. A conversation book from this time contains the entry: "Here's to death. From the late Beethoven." To his friend Karl Holz, he wrote on 9 September 1826: "I am weary and for me there will long be no more joy." However, the atmosphere relaxed somewhat when, after Stephan von Breuning's intercession, Beethoven finally acquiesced to Karl's desire to enter military service.

We cannot but feel compassion when we read that even in these times of adversity Beethoven still had not given up all hope of some improvement in his hearing. In August 1826, we find conversation book entries such as: "The man on the left knows about a newly discovered remedy for the hearing which works very well for one of his friends. Green walnut-shells steeped in warm milk; and some drops of it in the ear every day." A few days later, Beethoven noted: "Wednesday, 16 Aug. + new ear trumpet." The last piece of information in connection with treatment for his deafness was recorded in a conversation book in early September 1826: "2 hearing machines." After Karl's recovery from his suicide attempt, Beethoven decided that he and his nephew should spend some time relaxing at his brother Johann's estate in Gneixendorf, a village not far from Krems in the Danube valley. They arrived in Gneixendorf on 29 September and there Beethoven found the tranquillity he needed to calm his nerves and regain his emotional balance. The thoughts that were ever with him, his pining for family and friendship as well as his nostalgia for the days of his youth in Bonn, come forth most eloquently in his letter of 7 October 1826 to his friend Wegeler:

> Memories of the past hold me in their grip and it is not without many tears that you receive this letter....I still have the silhouette of your [wife] Lorchen, which shows you how dear to me still is all that was good and precious in my youth....I can't write you as much today as I would like, unfortunately, because I'm confined to my bed....You wrote that somewhere I am put forward as being the illegitimate son of the dead king of Prussia; someone else also mentioned this to me once a long time ago. I have made it a rule nevermore to write anything about myself, nor to comment on anything written about me. Therefore, I am happy to leave it to you to acquaint the world with the probity of my parents and of my mother in particular....As I always say, Nulla dies sine linea [no day without a line], and if I'm letting the muse sleep at the moment, it is only so she will waken more powerfully later. I still hope to give birth to a few more major works and then, like an old boy, bring my earthly career to an end somewhere in the company of pleasant people.

In fact, in Gneixendorf, Beethoven soon felt in the mood to resume composing. The first piece to be finished was the String Quartet in F Major, op. 135, whose conception goes back to the beginning of July. It is infinitely more simple and artless than the C-minor quartet that preceded it and its very artlessness has caused many musicologists to see it as Beethoven's "instinctive presentiment of death." Perhaps the inscription over the last movement—

"A difficult decision. Must it be? It must."—led to false interpretations. The truth is that the background to this inscription is anything but serious. When a wealthy music connoisseur in Vienna, who happened to miss the first performance of Beethoven's B-flat string quartet, boasted that he could hear the piece performed privately at home with parts lent to him by the composer any time he wished, Beethoven sent him word that first he would have to pay fifty gulden for the privilege. The startled gentleman is supposed to have replied, "Well, if it must be." Whereupon Beethoven had to laugh out loud and subsequently wrote a facetious canon to the text, *"Es muss seyn, ja, ja, heraus mit dem Beutel"* ("It must be, yes, yes, out with your purse.") The motive from this canon later became the humorous basis for the finale of the last string quartet. This little story reminds us of how careful we should be in trying in retrospect to relate events in an artist's life to his psychological condition or creative activities.

The first weeks in Gneixendorf passed pleasantly enough for all concerned. But little by little, Beethoven's crankiness, his dislike of his brother's wife, and tensions with his brother Johann who, after the third week there, asked for some payment for room and board, led to conflict and quarreling. But in addition, a rapid worsening of Beethoven's health since the beginning of autumn had caused an obvious and sudden physical decline. In this connection, his brother Johann said: "Because of poorly prepared food, he would eat nothing but a few softboiled eggs at noon but then would drink wine all the more, so that he often suffered from diarrhea; as a result, his belly had gotten bigger and bigger at the end, which led him to wear something to bind it for a long time." His legs were also increasingly swollen and he must have been bedridden from time to time. In spite of his condition, toward the end of 1826 Beethoven started work on a string quintet in C major, of which only the slow introduction ultimately was completed.

## Beethoven's Last Days

At the end of November, after a quarrel with Beethoven, Johann finally made it clear in writing that he would be glad to see his brother go, taking the nephew with him. The composer decided he would leave for Vienna immediately. The trip home began on 1 December 1826 under the worst imaginable circumstances and, because of the advanced state of Beethoven's illness, turned into a catastrophe. No public transportation was available and Beethoven and nephew Karl had to travel in an open horse-drawn wagon, "the devil's own vilest wagon, a milk-wagon," as Beethoven wrote later. Details of this appalling homeward journey are given in the history of Beethoven's final illness written by his last doctor, Dr. Andreas Wawruch:

> The month of December was raw, cold, damp, and freezing, Beethoven's clothing could not have been less suited for this unfriendly time of the year, yet still he was driven on by an inner anxiety, a gloomy foreboding of disaster. He was compelled to spend the night in a village inn where, other than a roof over his head, he found only an unheated room with single-paned windows. Toward midnight he had his first attack of feverish chills and a dry hacking cough accompanied by terrible thirst and pains in his side. When the fever began, he drank two quarts of ice-cold water and, in his helplessness, longed for the first light of day. He was laid, sick and feeble, in the wagon and finally arrived, exhausted and spent, in Vienna. I was not called until the third day.

His two previous doctors, Dr. Braunhofer and Dr. Staudenheim, who had been summoned as soon as Beethoven arrived in Vienna, had in fact refused to come to the Schwarzspanierhaus where he lay ill. In Ludwig Nohl's opinion, Dr. Braunhofer, realizing the illness was fatal, could not bring himself to take responsibility for Beethoven's death, which was sure to come shortly. Consequently, the director of the Viennese medical clinic, Professor Dr. Wawruch—who was mentioned by Karl Holz in one of the conversation books as being "known here as one of the most capable doctors"—was asked to attend the deathly ill composer. Dr. Wawruch had not met the patient before and introduced himself by means of the ubiquitous conversation books with the following words: "A great admirer of yours who will do everything possible to give you relief soon. Prof. Wawruch." The doctor's account of Beethoven's last illness was written in May 1827. It was found among his effects after he died and published for the

first time by the *Wiener Allgemeine musikalische Zeitung* in 1842.
In it, we learn details about the course of Beethoven's illness:

> I found Beethoven afflicted with the most serious
> symptoms of pneumonia; his face was burning,
> he was spitting blood, suffocation threatened his
> breathing, and the pains in his side made it ago-
> nizing for him to lie on his back. Strong treatment
> directed against the inflammation soon produced
> the desired relief; his natural strength asserted it-
> self and a timely crisis freed him from the appar-
> ent danger of dying, so that he was able to sit up
> on the fifth day and tell me with much animation
> about the difficulties he had endured up to then.
> On the seventh day, he felt so much better he was
> able to get up and walk around, and read and
> write. On the eighth day, however, I was no little
> alarmed. At the morning visit, I found him stricken
> and suffering from jaundice over his entire body;
> the most dreadful vomiting and diarrhea had threat-
> ened to kill him the night before....Shivering and
> shaking, he was doubled up with pains raging in
> his liver and intestines, and his legs, which up to
> then were only moderately bloated, were terribly
> swollen. From now on, dropsy began to develop;
> the amount of urine voided was sparser, the liver
> showed clear signs of hard nodules, the jaundice
> increased....By the third week, nightly attacks of
> suffocation appeared; the enormous amount of
> accumulated water required quick treatment, and
> I felt it necessary to recommend an abdominal in-
> cision, a tapping, to prevent the danger of sudden
> rupture.

After a few moments of serious reflection,
Beethoven gave his consent to the operation, all
the more readily because Dr. Staudenheim, who
had been asked to offer his medical advice, also
strongly urged the same course as being absolutely
mandatory. The chief surgeon of the General
Hospital, Dr. Johann Seibert, made the tapping*
with his usual skill, so that Beethoven, happy to

see the water pouring out, called out that the surgeon reminded him of Moses who struck the rock
with his staff and brought forth the water. Relief
came quickly. The amount of liquid weighed
25 pounds, and the afterflow was surely five times
as much. The rash act of loosening the bandage
covering the incision in the night, presumably to
bring about the rapid expulsion of remaining water,
came close to spoiling Beethoven's pleasure in
feeling better. A fierce red erysipelas-like inflammation appeared, displaying the first round patches
on the skin, but careful drying of the incision's
borders held the trouble in check.

Erysipelas is caused by Group A hemolytic streptococci as the
result of insufficient surgical asepsis or sterility after abdominal
paracentesis (puncture) to remove ascitic fluids (serous or edematous fluids that have accumulated in the peritoneal cavity). We
must assume that Beethoven would not consent to enter a hospital, for otherwise this operation would almost certainly not have
been undertaken in his bedroom where conditions were anything but hygienic. Of course, in those times, erysipelas occurred
in hospitals too, especially since the ascitic fluid provides a favorable medium for the growth of streptococcal bacteria. Given the
absence of an effective analgesic agent to relieve pain, the incision or puncture in the wall of Beethoven's abdomen and the
subsequent insertion of a glass tube must have been extremely
painful. Beethoven must have conducted himself well under the
circumstances, as indicated by Dr. Wawruch's conversation book
entry, "Nobly done." This first abdominal puncture was performed
on 20 December 1826, leaving the patient hoping for a rapid
recovery.

When his nephew Karl (who had selflessly helped to care for
his uncle) left on 2 January 1827 to join his regiment in Iglau,
Beethoven, freed at last from the burden of having to worry about
him, seemed to have felt a kind of deliverance. On the very next
day, he took steps to prepare his last will and testament and
designate Karl as his heir. He also began to busy himself with
plans for future compositions, such as a tenth symphony. The
people around him sought to provide diversion for the patient
with reports about performances of his works and to cheer him
up with daily news of all kinds. Beethoven himself, always a

great reader, looked for solace in his situation by reading the poets, surrounding himself, according to Schindler, especially "with his oldest friends and teachers from Greece, with Plutarch, Homer, Plato, Aristotle and other such worthies." Among the many people who came to see him, undoubtedly Gerhard von Breuning, the thirteen-year-old son of his friend Stephan, was the most entertaining. With the directness and candor of youth, he knew how to cheer up the sick old man. The delightful exchanges between child and composer give us some insight into the discouraging situation in which Beethoven now found himself. Here are some of Gerhard's entries in the conversation books:

—Has your stomach gotten smaller?

—Do you still need these notes? If you don't need them anymore, then give them to me, I save them.

—But I would argue that the noodles and ham couldn't have been any good because if you buy so little ham, you only get a bad piece.

—That must be this year's wine, it is so sour it leaves your mouth completely puckered up.

—I really do have lots of hope you'll be better by summer.

—I won't wear you out today with too much talking.

Another entry by Gerhard that is particularly touching in its childish frankness gives us a picture of Beethoven's unhappy circumstances: "I heard today bedbugs make you miserable and bother you so much they constantly wake you out of your sleep, whereas sleep is very good for you; therefore I'm going to bring you something to get rid of them."

In the first weeks of January, so much fluid had again accumulated in Beethoven's abdominal cavity that Dr. Wawruch considered a second tapping necessary, and it was carried out on 8 January. Dr. Seibert told Beethoven that this time the ascitic fluid was much clearer and flowed out in a far greater amount than the first time, but such calming words could no longer blind the stricken man to the seriousness of his situation.  With his condition steadily worsening, Beethoven rapidly lost confidence in his physician; whenever he heard Dr. Wawruch's name mentioned, he reportedly would turn his face to the wall and groan, "O that ass."  For this reason, his friends undertook to persuade his former friend, Dr. Johann Malfatti, to make a sick call on Beethoven.  Although the two had fallen out some years before, Beethoven had always had the greatest confidence in Malfatti as a doctor.  At first, Malfatti did not want to interfere in the treatment being given by Dr. Wawruch and he wrote: "Tell Beethoven that, as a master of harmony, he will understand I must also live in harmony with my colleagues."  But finally he consented to come.

Apparently in view of Beethoven's hopeless situation, Dr. Malfatti concentrated essentially on bringing him some inner relief and restoring his spirits.  This would explain why he permitted Beethoven to have drinks with alcohol once more, as a kind of sedation.  Johann Baptist Jenger commented in a letter to Maria Pachler-Koschak, a pianist married to a lawyer in Graz and an "autumnal love" of Beethoven's from the year 1817, that Dr. Malfatti had said Professor Wawruch's treatment of Beethoven up to that point had been entirely wrong.  Malfatti can only have meant that it was wrong from a psychological point of view.  His prescription of alcoholic drinks did indeed give the patient a tremendous lift.  In great good spirits, Beethoven wrote Schindler: "Miracle of miracles!  The erudite gentlemen are both confounded. Only through the science of Malfatti shall I be saved."  In Dr. Wawruch's account, we read:

> Then Dr. Malfatti, who supported me with his advice from now on and who, being a friend of many years, understood how to take Beethoven's prevailing fondness for spirits into consideration, had the idea of prescribing frozen punch [a mixture of rum, tea, and sugar].  I am bound to say that this approach had a wondrous effect at least for a couple days.  Beethoven felt himself so immensely invigorated by the alcoholic contents of the frozen punch that he slept peacefully through the first night and at the same time began to sweat enormously....But, as could be foreseen, his joy did not last long.  He started to abuse the prescription and addressed himself to the punch with

vigor. The alcohol soon caused the blood to rush to his head; he became drowsy and he rattled when he breathed like one completely drunk, began to rave in his speech and this was sometimes coupled with an inflammatory sore throat along with hoarseness, even complete loss of voice. He became more difficult, and because the cooling of his bowels led to colic and diarrhea, it was high time to take this delicious refreshment away from him.

The famous Dr. Malfatti was not infallible in other matters either. On 24 January he was still attributing the growing size of Beethoven's abdomen to gases and flatulence, whereas Dr. Wawruch believed that the abdominal cavity was filling with fluid again. The third tapping, performed on 2 February 1827, confirmed Dr. Wawruch's opinion. As before, Beethoven endured the operation quietly, when "only seldom did a sound of complaint issue from the lips of the sorely suffering patient," as Gerhard von Breuning later wrote in his memoirs. Beethoven's forbearance with all that was going on is evident in a letter to his friend Wegeler in Bonn written on 17 February 1827: "My recovery, if I can call it that, is still going very slowly. Presumably, a fourth operation is to be expected, although the doctors still don't talk about it. So I just remain patient and think: all evil leads occasionally to some good." He expressed himself in a similar vein in a letter of 18 February to his friend Nikolaus von Zmeskall who, like himself, was laid up in bed at the time: "I haven't given up hope; most painful, however, is my utter inability to work."

Beethoven must have expected favorable results indeed from the permission to indulge in drinks with alcohol, as is clear in letters he wrote in the last weeks of his life. For example, he said in a letter to Schott Söhne publishers in Mainz on 22 February: "My doctor has ordered me to drink very good, old Rheine wine. But to get that here in unadulterated form is not possible at any price. So if I were to receive a few bottles of it, I would be glad to express my appreciation with something for the 'Cäcilia' [a musical journal put out by the publishers]." In response, Beethoven received word that twelve bottles of "fine Rudesheim Bergwein vintage 1806" were being shipped, with the lines: "But in order that some enjoyment might be offered you even earlier, we have today forwarded to you a little case [with four bottles of wine] as well as a little package [which contained herbs supposed to be helpful with abdominal dropsy] by post-wagon to your address." The "little case" unfortunately arrived too late for Beethoven to enjoy it.

He also wrote to Baron Pasqualati, the owner of the house on the Mölkerbastei where he once had lived, that his doctors permitted him to drink champagne, of course, but with wines he had to take heed of certain sorts: "Now as regard wine: Malfatti first wanted me to have Moselle wine; but since you can't get the genuine thing here, he says, he himself gave me several bottles of wine from Gumpoldskirchen [a wine-producing region just outside Vienna] and asserted they were the best for my health because there is no genuine Moselle wine to be had here." He came back to the subject of the Gumpoldskirchen wine again in another letter to Pasqualati on 16 March: "Regarding the wine, they [meaning his doctors] find the Grinzing wine good for me, but they prefer the mature Gumpoldskirchen wine before all others."

At the end of February, Dr. Malfatti ceased calling on Beethoven, sending his assistant, Dr. Röhrich, instead. Whether Malfatti did this because he was really ill, as he claimed, or because he feared rebuke from Beethoven over the progression of his illness, remains an open question.

On 27 February, only twenty-five days after the third operation, a fourth was necessary, with "7 quarts 1 pint" of fluid being removed. After each of these operations, an even greater amount of fluid would subsequently be secreted through the open wound for several days, although it was always covered with a bandage. In the conversation book of 27 February, Dr. Seibert told Beethoven: "We have always wrapped up your stomach after the operation; the water will certainly flow out if you will only remain lying on the right side and with your head not too high. In the morning we will take the bandage off." This massive outflow of fluid meant that Beethoven was becoming increasingly sore from lying on sheets and mattresses that were thoroughly soaked. From entries made in the conversation books by Schindler on the last days of February, we can form an idea of the pitiable state of the patient and how much fluid was running from the incision:

—The maid will put a wooden pail under the bed
so the water won't run in the room.

> —Just stay in this bed now and let them add some
> more to it. There is still no straw in the house
> to fill the other bed up. The straw was com-
> pletely rotten. The other will be all filled up by
> evening and you can still have it tonight.

> —Today someone recommended that I advise you
> to lie on a deerskin which is the only thing that
> will protect you from bedsores.

Another note from Schindler to Beethoven in a conversation book
suggests that bleeding from the mucous membranes lining the
nose and upper throat (the nasopharyngeal cavity) must have
begun again: "Malfatti suspects the nose-bleeding comes from
your head and asked me whether you ever complain about headache."

Beethoven's hopes of recovery were gradually dwindling, as
we can read behind the words of encouragement and determination that Schindler and Stephan von Breuning were writing in the
conversation books as February came to a close:

> —It is absolutely necessary that you drive these
> concerns out of your mind as much as you can,
> for nothing can be done about it, and it doesn't
> help to get you well.

> —Who will yield to despair? You must be of good
> cheer, because unhappiness only hinders your
> recovery.

Beethoven recognized that these attempts to cheer him up
were nothing but well-intended words. The massive loss of serous fluid in the course of four abdominal punctures, and the
concomitant heavy loss of protein, had emaciated him and made
him ever weaker. Added to his physical deterioration were worries about his precarious financial situation. He had barely enough
money on hand to pay the rent that was due. It was a last great
joy to Beethoven, therefore, that the Philharmonic Society of London, after being made aware of Beethoven's dire financial situation by the harp manufacturer Johann Andreas Stumpff via Ignaz
Moscheles and Sir George Smart, straightaway sent one hundred
pounds sterling to the fatally ill composer, with an indication that
further help would be forthcoming if needed. Deeply touched by

this gift, Beethoven dictated a moving letter of thanks to the Society with the promise "that, when God has granted me my health once more, I shall endeavor to express my feelings of gratitude with compositions....Only let heaven give me my strength back soon, and I shall show the magnanimous gentlemen of England how deeply I appreciate their concern for my unhappy fate."

But the truth is that, weeks before, he had given up all hope of ever being able to realize his plans, as we can read in Gerhard von Breuning's memoirs. Beethoven said to him: "I wanted to write so many things more. First the tenth symphony, then I wanted to compose a requiem too and the music to Faust....But now I'll never do it." Inwardly filled with impatience, discouragement, and despair, outwardly racked by bedsores from lying constantly in soaked sheets on wet, rotting straw and tortured by vermin, the slowly dying composer gradually gave up every thought of being saved. Even his faith in Dr. Malfatti was shaken by the order that he should have steam baths with birch leaves, a procedure Beethoven found so intolerable that it had to be discontinued immediately, as Gerhard von Breuning reported:

> ...A kind of steam bath obviously so worsened the condition of the eternally hopeful patient that it had to be dropped after the first application. Pails filled with hot water were arranged in a tub and covered thickly with birch leaves, with the patient perched on top, while the tub and the body—except for the head—were enclosed in a sheet. Malfatti intended thereby to do the skin some good and to cause copious sweating of the organism; but the direct effect was just the opposite; instead, the tapping that had been done shortly before had so drained the body of water that, like a block of salt, it sucked in the steam from the pails of water and swelled so perceptibly that a new insertion of the cannula into the still unhealed incision was required.

If we go by the conversation books, this steam bath probably took place on the 27th or 28th of January. But there, contrary to Breuning's report, we read that it was not a steam bath with birch leaves, but rather one with hayseed, with which Malfatti hoped to achieve a sweating and dehydrating effect:

—The bath with dry hayseed is supposed to make you sweat; Malfatti says we have to try it since the internal medicine is not having the desired effect.

—It is nothing but two layers of hayseed with warm pitchers [of water] added; but the first time [you should] not stay longer than half an hour in the tub.

—When you've had your bath tomorrow morning...you should be sure to go right to bed after getting out of the bath so you'll really sweat.

Dr. Wawruch portrayed the resignation of the sick man in these words:

Following the fourth paracentesis, Beethoven himself foresaw his approaching death in his dark hours of reflection and in this he was not mistaken. My consoling words were no longer able to raise his spirits, and when I promised him hope of relief from his suffering with the approach of revivifying spring weather, he countered with a smile, saying: "My day's work is done. If a doctor were able to help me now, his name shall be called wonderful." This touching allusion to Handel's Messiah affected me so powerfully that, in my heart, I had to agree with the truth of his words.

The composer and pianist Johann Nepomuk Hummel and his student, Ferdinand Hiller, were among Beethoven's last visitors. In Hiller's diary, we can read some final impressions of the dying Beethoven. When Beethoven was informed that Hummel had come to visit on 8 March 1827, he is supposed to have said, "I must not receive him in bed." He got out of bed, put on his robe, and seated himself by the window. The sixteen-year-old Hiller, who had keenly looked forward to the moment of this first personal meeting with Beethoven, wrote in his diary:

We were no little amazed to find the master sitting by the window, to all appearances quite at ease....Emaciated from his serious illness, he

BEETHOVEN ON HIS DEATHBED (DRAWING BY JOSEPH EDUARD TELTSCHER).

seemed quite tall to me when he stood up, he was unshaved, his thick, greying hair fell in disorder around his temples....Beethoven complained very much about the state of his health. "I've been lying there now for four months," he exclaimed, "You finally lose patience!"

Five days later, on 13 March, the two visitors found Beethoven in much worse condition:

He was lying in bed, seemed to be in great pain, occasionally gave a deep groan, but still he talked a lot and with animation. It seemed to be very much on his mind that he had never married. He had even joked with Hummel about that at our first visit...."You," he said to him this time with a smile, "You are a lucky man; you have a wife who looks after you, who loves you—but poor me!"— and heaved a great sigh.

When the two visited him again on 20 March, they found him extremely weak, able to speak only in faint and broken sentences and to raise himself from time to time only with effort. On greeting them, he whispered, "I shall certainly soon be on my way up there."

Their last visit took place on 23 March:

Weak and exhausted, he lay there groaning deeply now and then. Not a word escaped his lips any longer—sweat stood out on his brow. When it happened that he could not immediately find his handkerchief, Hummel's wife took her handkerchief of finest batiste and dried his face with it several times. I shall never forget the look of gratitude his illness-dimmed eyes bestowed on her.

Beethoven's death was imminent. In his medical review, Dr. Wawruch wrote about Beethoven's last days:

Now the fatal day was drawing ever nearer. My proper and so often heavy professional duties as physician told me it was time to direct the friendly patient's attention to this fateful day so he might fulfill his civic and religious duties. With the gentlest of care, I wrote my words of counsel on a

piece of paper (for this was the only way we had
ever communicated with one another). With complete composure, Beethoven read slowly and
thoughtfully what I had written, his countenance
like one transfigured; then he solemnly and warmly
reached his hand to me, and said, "Have someone
call the priest." Then he was quiet and reflective,
and nodded a friendly "I'll see you again soon" in
my direction. A short time later, Beethoven said
his prayers in a spirit of devout submission which
contemplates eternity with confidence and said to
the friends around him, "Plaudite, amici, comoedia
finita est" ("Applaud, friends, the play is over").

Because spells of disorientation and confusion were becoming more frequent, Beethoven's friends feared that his mind would
not be clear much longer. They presented the dying man with
the short last will and testament drafted by Stephan von Breuning
along lines previously discussed. With pillows pushed under him
and supported in a half-upright position by his friends, Beethoven
laboriously copied it out with a trembling hand:

Mein Neffffe Karll Soll alleini—Erbe sejn, daβ
Kapital meines Nachlalaβes soll jedoch Seinen
natürlichen oder testamentarischschen Erben
zufallen.
Wien am 23 Marz 1827        Luwig van Beethoven

Translated without Beethoven's spelling difficulties:

My nephew Karl shall be the sole heir; the capital
of my estate shall, however, devolve upon his natural or testamentary heirs.
Vienna, 23 March 1827        Ludwig van Beethoven

Around noon on the 24th of March, the special shipment of
four bottles of wine arrived from Mainz. Seeing them, Beethoven
could only murmur, "Pity, pity, too late." These were his last
words. Toward evening he fell into a deep coma that lasted until
life took its leave of him late in the afternoon of Monday, the 26th
of March 1827. In his memoirs, Gerhard von Breuning has given
a vivid picture of the drawn-out death struggle:

On the day after the 24th and the next day, the
powerful man lay gripped by the process of

disintegration, unconscious, his rattling breathing
heard from afar.   His strong body, his un-
weakened...lungs fought mightily with the death
setting in.  It was an awful sight....Already on the
25th, it was expected his death could come that
night; and yet we found him still alive on the 26th—
breathing perhaps even more noisily than the day
before.  In the end, it was reserved for the 26th of
March, in the afternoon, to earn the dubious fame
of being the date of Beethoven's death....We could
already see how the rattle of the breathing was
gradually getting weaker....On this afternoon, enormous masses of clouds were looming up in the
sky.  In the meantime, my father and Schindler...
decided to find a suitable gravesite and left the
sad scene in Beethoven's room.  I had remained
there with the dying man and his brother Johann
and Sali, the housekeeper; between 4 and 5 o'clock,
the thick, gathering mass of clouds obscured the
light of day more and more, and all of a sudden a
violent thunderstorm, with snow flurries and hail,
broke out....At 5:15, I was called home to my
teacher....I had been home hardly a half an hour
when the housekeeper came to report that death
had occurred at 5:45.

Anselm Hüttenbrenner, from the city of Graz, happened to be
present for this last day, and thirty years later he wrote down his
indelible memories of the last moments in the life of this giant in
the world of music:

After Beethoven had lain there, unconscious,
breathing heavily in his death struggle, from 3 in
the afternoon when I arrived until 5, a flash of
lightning accompanied by a violent clap of thunder fell from the heavens and bathed the dying
man's room in a sharp light (outside there was
snow in front of Beethoven's house).  After this
unexpected stroke of nature which greatly startled
me, Beethoven opened his eyes, raised his right
hand, and stared up to heaven several seconds
long with his fist clenched and a grim and

BEETHOVEN'S LAST WILL AND TESTAMENT, WRITTEN ON 23 MARCH 1827, THREE DAYS BEFORE HE DIED.

threatening look on his face....As he let his raised hand sink back to the bed again, his eyes became half-closed. My right hand lay under his head; my left one rested on his chest. There was no breathing, no heartbeat more! The genius of the great composer fled this world of deceit into the realm of truth.

Preparations for the burial began in all haste. The notice of Beethoven's death was written by Stephan von Breuning and handed out at the music store of Tobias Haslinger. It read:

Invitation
to the funeral service for Ludwig van Beethoven,

which will take place at 3 o'clock in the afternoon of 29 March. The funeral party will gather in the apartment of the deceased in the Schwarz-spanierhaus No. 200 on the glacis in front of the Schottentor. The procession will set out from there for the Trinity Church of the Minorites in the Alsergasse.

The musical world suffered the irreparable loss of the famous composer on 26 March 1827, toward 6 o'clock in the evening. Beethoven died in his 56th year as a result of abdominal dropsy, after

> receiving the holy sacraments.  The day when the
> exequies will be held will be announced later by
> Ludwig van Beethoven's
> Friends and Admirers

At the suggestion of the tenor Ludwig Cramolini, the young painter Josef Danhauser made a death mask of the composer on 28 March.  However, according to a comment by Gerhard von Breuning, the mask bears relatively little resemblance to the facial features of the living Beethoven because of the things done to the skull in the autopsy performed by Dr. Johann Wagner on the evening before.  Nor do the features of the dead composer depicted in a drawing by Danhauser really look much like him because they have been idealized.

The funeral ceremony took place on the afternoon of 29 March.  The crowd of people gathered before the Schwarzspanierhaus was so large that military reinforcements were needed to clear a path for the procession to make its way to the Trinity Church.  After the mass had been said, the casket, accompanied by hundreds of persons, was carried to the graveyard in the village of Währing.  There, before the gate to the cemetery—for in those times, no ceremonies were permitted inside the graveyard—the famous Burgtheater actor Heinrich Anschütz delivered the funeral oration written by Franz Grillparzer.  It ended with these words:

> If he shunned the world, it was because in the
> depths of his feelings of love he found no reason
> to struggle against it; if he withdrew from people,
> it happened because they could not rise to him
> and he could not go down to them.  He was one
> alone because he found no equal.  And yet to the
> day he died, he retained a human heart for all
> humanity, a paternal heart for his loved ones and
> theirs in all the world.  As he was then, so was he
> when he died, and so will he live for all time.

## The Autopsy and the Disinterments

The full text of the report of the postmortem examination carried out privately in Beethoven's apartment on 27 March 1827 is a record fundamental to a medical assessment of Beethoven's illnesses.  Until recently, the Latin-language original of the

A PAINTING BY FRANZ STÖBER OF THE THRONG ATTENDING BEETHOVEN'S FUNERAL SERVICE ON 29 MARCH 1927.

autopsy record was regarded as lost, and all pathological studies of Beethoven were based only on the copy made by Ignaz von Seyfried in 1832 in a German translation. However, the original of the autopsy record was discovered among various documents removed from the Pathological-Anatomical Institute of the University of Vienna, which were taken over by the Pathological-Anatomical National Museum in Vienna, and was reproduced for the first time in the Beethoven pathological study published in 1987 by Messrs. Bankl and Jesserer.

The particular significance of this discovery is that now we know with certainty that Dr. Johann Wagner, who performed the autopsy and dictated his report to a secretary (the only part in his own hand being his signature), did not provide any synoptic diagnosis at the conclusion of his dictated report. Instead, the autopsy report ends merely with the words:

> Sectio privata die 27 Martii MCCMXXVII
> Doktor Joh. Wagner
> Assistent beym pathologischen Musäum

> Private autopsy, the 27th of March 1827
> Doctor Johann Wagner
> Assistant in the Pathological Museum

This is a final rebuff to all the writers and biographers who thought there must have been a concluding diagnostic statement and looked on its absence as evidence of possible deception and cover-up and thus grounds for suspecting that Beethoven might have had a venereal disease.

In translation, the text of the autopsy report reads:

> Autopsy report concerning the body of Ludwig van Beethoven, which was examined in his apartment in the presence of Dr. Wawruch and is the subject of the following findings.

> The body was very emaciated, especially the arms and legs, and covered with petechiae [minute red spots of blood just under the skin]; the lower abdominal region was inflated and tense, with an abnormal accumulation of serous fluid. The outer ear was large and regularly shaped, the auricle of the external ear, and especially the hollow of the

same, was very spacious and half again as deep as usual; the form of the various angles and turns was pronounced. The external acoustic canal appeared covered with shiny flakes of skin, especially toward the hidden eardrum.

The Eustachian tube was very thick, its mucous lining was swollen and somewhat constricted toward the bony portion of the tube. Some pitted scars could be seen at the opening of the tube and by the tonsils. The air spaces of the mastoid process, which was large and not marked by any indentation, were covered with a bloody mucous lining. The entire petrosal bone [the hard, dense portion of the temporal bone] was permeated by a system of large vessels and displayed a similar blood-filled character, especially in the vicinity of the cochlea, whose posterior wall membrane appeared to be slightly reddened.

The facial nerves were unusually thick; the auditory nerves, on the other hand, were shriveled and unmedullated [lacked the layer of myelin or white matter that normally surrounds the cranial nerves], and the arteries that ran alongside were extended to the width of a raven's quill and made up a mass of tissue. The left auditory nerve was much thinner and emerged in three extremely thin gray furrows, the right one in a thicker clear white furrow, out of the fourth ventricle of the brain, whose substance here was firmer and more vascular. The convolutions of the brain, which was otherwise spongy and much softer, appeared to be much deeper and more numerous than normal.

The bone of the skullcap was uniformly dense and had a thickness of about half an inch.

The rib cage and the organs inside showed no significant abnormalities.

There were four quarts of a cloudy greyish-brown liquid spread throughout the abdominal cavity. The liver appeared shrunk to half its volume, hard as leather, greenish-blue in color, and infested with pea-sized nodules on its bumpy surface as well as inside the organ itself; all of its vessels were very narrow, thickened, and devoid of blood. The gall-bladder contained a dark-brown liquid together with numerous gritty gallstones. The spleen appeared twice the normal size, was black and rough; in the same way, the pancreas also seemed larger and harder, and its excretory duct was the width of a goose feather quill. The stomach, including the intestines, was very inflated with air. Both kidneys were encased in an inch-thick capsule completely soaked by a cloudy, brown liquid; their tissues, pale red and breaking up; each individual kidney recess was filled up with a wart-shaped chalky stone about the size of a split pea.

Private autopsy, the 27th of March 1827
Doctor Johann Wagner
Assistant in the Pathological Museum

The remembrances published by Gerhard von Breuning in 1874 under the title, *Aus dem Schwarzspanierhause*, add to the autopsy report:

To facilitate making a more precise examination of the long-atrophied organs of hearing of this titan in the realm of music, the petrous portions of the temporal bone were sawn out on both sides and taken away. As Dr. Hyrtl told me recently, when he was a student, he had seen these hearing organs over a considerable length of time standing in a covered glass jar kept by the long-serving departmental assistant Anton Dotter; later they were said to be missing.

The credibility of Breuning's statement is underscored by the autopsy report, which indicates that the petrosal bones had in fact been sawn away during the autopsy. Because no mention of such a specimen has been found in the meticulous records of the

Pathological-Anatomical Museum, the petrosal bones may indeed have been kept in a preservative in that "covered jar" of the former departmental assistant. The autobiography of Carl von Rokitansky, who was both professor at the Pathological-Anatomical Institute of the University of Vienna and custodian of the Pathological-Anatomical Museum at the same time, suggests the correctness of the name "Anton Dotter," for it mentions an anatomy assistant with the initials "A. T." (Anton Totter?) who was a rather disreputable person. A rumor circulated in Vienna that he had turned over the invaluable preserved relics of Beethoven to a foreign doctor for a certain sum of money.

In 1863, a plan to place the mortal remains of Beethoven and Schubert "in metal caskets and bricked-in vaults with a view to helping preserve the same" led to the first disinterment. In keeping with Franz Joseph Gall's science of craniology (previously mentioned in connection with Joseph Haydn and still of interest at the time of Beethoven's death), it was thought that a person's natural talents and abilities could be discerned from externally perceptible forms of the brain and the skull. Therefore, interest was concentrated primarily on Beethoven's skull after the exhumation. However, because the petrosal bones around the auditory canal had been sawn away during the autopsy and could no longer be found in the Anatomical Institute, no new knowledge was obtained. Accordingly, the examination was limited to making anatomical measurements of the remainder of the skull (which, incidentally, was reverently safeguarded by Gerhard von Breuning in his bedroom during the nine days needed to prepare the reburial).

Beethoven's eternal rest was disturbed once more on 21 June 1888 when his remains were transferred, along with those of Franz Schubert, to a memorial tomb in Vienna's Zentralfriedhof (main cemetery). Because on this occasion a period of only twenty minutes was available for inspection of the remains, the persons involved limited their efforts to examining and measuring the skull, which in the meantime had decayed so much that a cast of the inner surfaces could not be made, nor was there "any other basis [for determining] the capacity of the cranial vault." Thus the scientific yield of the second disinterment was even less than that of the first, from which we still have at least a photograph of the skull and of a plaster of paris cast of it by the sculptor A. Wittman. The two photographs were taken by J. B. Rottmayer. From the second exhumation, only a simple pencil sketch of the skull by Dr. Choulant was accomplished. It sounds rather blasphemous when we read in the official report of the 1888 exhumation "that the skull of Beethoven did not correspond in the least to our ideas of beauty and harmonious proportions."

To provide a sound interpretation of Beethoven's illnesses and the cause of his death, the following discussion takes fully into account the current state of medical science and is based on the comprehensive picture of Beethoven's medical history derived from all currently available sources, including the reports of the autopsy and the two disinterments. Because physicians of the most diverse branches of medicine have repeatedly addressed these questions in this century alone, some of their lines of argument and conclusions are examined, particularly those that cannot be substantiated.

## Beethoven's Deafness

The single most heartrending aspect of Beethoven's life, the impairment of his hearing, began in his youth and gradually became worse, until it left him totally deaf eight years before he died. The cause of this auditory dysfunction, whose inception may go back to the year 1795 (Beethoven would have been twenty-five years old at the time), has been the subject of innumerable efforts to provide a tenable explanation. It would weary the reader to recount them all; for details, interested readers are referred to the comprehensive medical-historical dissertation on *Beethoven's Illnesses and their Assessment (Beethovens Krankheiten und ihre Beurteilung),* written by Walther Forster and published in 1955. Just what exotic blossoms have been cultivated in this garden of speculation, not only by the medically untrained but also occasionally by physicians of considerable repute, is illustrated by three curious examples.

First, the doctor and noted Beethoven scholar Theodor von Frimmel maintained around 1880 that Beethoven's deafness was the result of atrophy of the auditory nerves. He based his view on a story that Beethoven supposedly told the English pianist Charles Neate about once having thrown himself on the floor in a rage: "When I got back up, I found I was deaf and have remained so ever since; the doctors say the nerve is damaged." Frimmel contended that the physical impact of the composer's

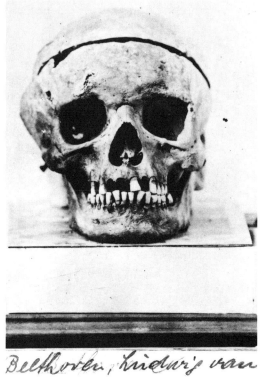

BEETHOVEN'S SKULL, PHOTOGRAPHED BY J. B. ROTTMAYER AT THE TIME OF THE FIRST DISINTERMENT IN OCTOBER 1863.

action caused minute vascular bleedings in the brain's auditory center for both acoustic nerves. However, apart from the fact that this event is said to have taken place in 1810, whereas the hearing defect had already been noticed in 1795, such a symmetrical appearance of bleedings, especially in the auditory center of the brain, is so improbable that we need not discuss this contention further.

A second totally absurd theory, one devoid of any objective basis, including the autopsy report, was propagated by I. Niemack-Charles, who tried to establish a relationship between the cause of Beethoven's ear troubles and arteriosclerosis (vascular calcification) and, in this connection, attributed heart trouble to Beethoven too, just to make things simpler. He then used this theory to elucidate, with a breathtaking flight of fancy, the particular genius of Beethoven's musical creativity:

> The standing excess of pressure in the labyrinth
> caused by sclerotic inflammation of the middle ear
> has the effect of a continuous stimulus on the fine
> nerve ends; moreover, the pulsebeat of the larger

> neighboring arteries is heard directly....Among
> other things, the frequent contrasts [in Beethoven's
> musical compositions] between the higher descant
> passages in opposition to the deep rolling basses
> is most readily explained as being an unconscious
> attempt to rid himself of these insistent sounds by
> expressing them in musical form....The second
> kind of sound of a rhythmic character and which
> corresponds to the heartbeat is particularly impor-
> tant to us....This also explains Beethoven's inabil-
> ity, as testified to by Schindler, to keep to a strict
> tempo in his own compositions. He was con-
> stantly taking his cue from his heartbeat at the
> moment....He was subject to such daily fluctua-
> tions because the master suffered from hardening
> of the arteries (arteriosclerosis) and a defective
> heart.

It takes a certain amount of cheek for someone to presume to
enlighten us as to the incomprehensible reaches of Beethoven's
music with such absurd medical notions made up out of thin air.

The third example of unfounded speculation is seen in the
many efforts to place Beethoven among the imposing number of
famous syphilitics. What renowned artist has not been the subject of such a charge, whether true or not! In a book called *The
Brilliant Syphilitics (Die genialen Syphilitiker)*, Brunold Springer—
a lawyer—wrote:

> Once he had overcome the frugal years of his youth
> and had trod the streets of Vienna and felt the first
> firm ground under his feet, his lust for life in every
> meaning of the word broke out, fiercely and unre-
> strained; nor did he scorn the fleshly pleasures.
> His innocent, carefree devotion to life's joys in the
> mecca of free spirits came to a bitter end. His
> disease must have been acquired early on.

Countless times in the last hundred years, even doctors and
other medically trained persons have considered the possibility
that syphilis was the cause of Beethoven's hearing defect. This
notion is especially hard to understand when we consider how
well screened the source materials have been and the current

level of medical science. Proponents of the syphilis theory essentially base their position on several groundless arguments.

First, they attempt to interpret various cryptic notes found in Beethoven's effects as indicating the presence of a venereal disease. One is the entry in his diary mentioned previously, reproduced in incomplete form in the Fischhoff manuscript, where for unknown reasons two words were deleted and replaced with three asterisks by the copyist of the manuscript. The entry reads: "Deciding by the doctors about my life. If no recovery is possible, then what *** do I need??? Only it still ought to end more quickly, something impossible before. Consultation with ***." A careful reconstruction of Beethoven's medical history shows, however, that this notation was made in his diary at the beginning of 1814 and was written in a time of deep depression when Beethoven had repeatedly mentioned the idea of suicide. Even in the letter of 2 May 1810 to his friend Dr. Wegeler in Bonn, asking him to obtain his birth certificate because he planned to ask Therese Malfatti to marry him, Beethoven said: "I would be happy...if the Devil had not made his home in my ears. If I hadn't read somewhere that man must not leave this life voluntarily as long as he is still capable of doing a good deed, I would have long ceased to exist and that from my own hand." These references to thoughts of suicide, which had appeared earlier in the Heiligenstadt testament, show they were triggered by fits of depression brought on by his steadily worsening hearing problems and probably too by the unceasing attacks of stomach pains.

A second argument used to support the syphilis theory is based on a note by Beethoven from the year 1819 indicating that he planned to buy a book, *L'art de connaitre et de guerir toutes les contagions veneriennes (The Art of Recognizing and Curing all Venereal Diseases)*, by L. V. Legunan. So far, it has not been possible to find this note in German sources and it may be the one mentioned by Jacobsohn as "a note not publicly known written in Beethoven's own hand." We do not know whether Beethoven ever owned the book or what his interest in it would have been. Perhaps he intended to use the book as a source of information in raising his ward Karl, who would have been thirteen years old at the time and whose "immoral mother" Beethoven had accused of being a known streetwalker. In the same year, he had informed the Vienna city officials in detail about the plan of education he had in mind for Karl: "In any case, I have had his salvation constantly in mind, that is, removing him from the influence of his mother. Riches may be earned but virtue must be...inculcated early." This comment suggests his intent may have been to enlighten his nephew Karl, who was just entering puberty, as to the perils of venereal diseases.

A third argument of the syphilis theorists is based on a comment by Dr. Andreas Bertolini, the assistant to Dr. Malfatti, who became a friend of Beethoven in 1806 and was his personal physician beginning in 1808. The relationship between the two must have been a very confidential one and they could have discussed matters of the most personal nature. Among the papers left by the famous Mozart biographer Otto Jahn after he died was one containing a statement Dr. Bertolini supposedly made about Beethoven's love affairs: "Beethoven generally had flames, the [Countess] Guicciardi, for example, Frau von Frank, Bettina Brentano; in addition, he was accustomed to having little love affairs, which didn't always work out." Beethoven's courtship of the ladies was not exactly crowned with success where physical love was concerned, which is probably why, in response to his normal masculine needs, he occasionally turned to women of easy virtue. However, to conclude on the basis of Bertolini's comment that Beethoven was infected by a venereal disease is absurd.

A weightier argument, in the minds of the syphilis theorists, is the fact that Dr. Bertolini, at a time when he had contracted cholera and was expecting to die, directed that all his notes about Beethoven and the letters the composer had written him be burned "because some of them were such that he did not want to let them fall into irresponsible hands," as Ernest Newman wrote. Undoubtedly there were numerous communications among them that Bertolini, as a close friend and great admirer of Beethoven, viewed as confidential and intended only for a physician. And certainly there were medically related statements in these documents that were meant only for the attending doctor and whose possible publication, in view of Beethoven's fame, Bertolini could only have regarded as a gross breach of his professional oath of confidentiality. But just as important to Bertolini would have been the entirely private matters discussed in the letters. To speak of a systematic destruction of the letters and notes directly for the purpose of suppressing references to a syphilitic disease, as Kerner has done, is a bald insinuation.

The "demon" of Beethoven as syphilitic appears to have been "unleashed" by Alexander Wheelock Thayer, who as author of the first comprehensive Beethoven biography was directly in touch with many contemporaries of the great composer in preparing his work. The demon has turned out to be particularly long-lived. Writing to the Beethoven scholar Theodor von Frimmel on 29 October 1880, Thayer is supposed to have spoken of Beethoven's having a venereal disease, which, according to Thayer, many people knew about. To this day, however, no proof of this assertion has been found, nor has the privately owned (and allegedly incriminating) notation in Beethoven's hand that is said to allude to a venereal disease, or of a prescription that is supposed to have been written for Beethoven and is said to be in some American museum. This prescription, which Adam Politzer, the author of the first *History of Otology*, is said to have found, purportedly left no doubt about Beethoven's syphilis. These ostensibly incriminating "proofs" serve no purpose if they cannot be subjected to a critical examination—which would mean, of course, first establishing that they are in fact genuine. Moreover, persons who possess such documents would be disregarding Beethoven's testamentary admonition "to report everything strictly according to the truth, even when it affects [his] very person."

Still another spurious argument for the syphilis theory shows what confused, incompetent results are obtained when amateurs attempt to draw inferences about a venereal disease from methods of treatment and medical prescriptions. The lawyer Brunold Springer, in a woefully misguided effort to make medical practice in Beethoven's time responsible for the composer's fate, wrote: "Beethoven seems even more to have fallen victim to his treatment: criticism is finally beginning to expose those doctors who destroyed the poor, great composer with their excessive prescriptions of mercury (volatile ointment)." But in fact, the salve he speaks of was an ointment made of poppy-seed oil and an ammonium liniment, generally used in those days for rubbing into the skin in connection with rheumatic and other pains. If this "volatile [meaning vaporizing] ointment" had in fact been a medicine for syphilis, Beethoven would hardly have chosen to mention it in his letter of 19 June 1817 to the Countess Erdödy, an aristocratic friend for whom he had a high personal regard.

As one last argument, Dr. Jacobsohn, a fanatic advocate of the syphilis thesis, points to a rise or swelling on the right temple of

Beethoven's skull "which could well have been caused by syphilis." He maintains, moreover, that this localized thickening of the right parietal bone can be detected not only in the photograph of the plaster cast of the skull taken at the time of the first disinterment, but also in the mask made by Franz Klein during Beethoven's lifetime. We have long known that Rottmayer's photograph showing the supposed swelling simply documents a fault that occurred in making the plaster cast. Because the petrosal bones and the hinges of the jaw had been sawn out of the skull during the autopsy in 1827 and because there was "a piece missing out of the middle of the cranium," as noted in the official report of the first exhumation, Gerhard von Breuning took it upon himself to rejoin the parts of the skull and hold them together with clay. The bulge on the plaster cast is simply an artifact made of clay. The rise noted on the living mask is caused by the "small sideburns in front of his ear," which affected the molding of the mask to the side of Beethoven's head. No specific change in the right half of Beethoven's skull was mentioned either in the meticulous description of the skull at the time of the autopsy or by the pathologists who examined the skull when Beethoven's corpse was disinterred.

There were no organic changes in Beethoven that were in any way indicative of his having had syphilis. Neither soft spots in the brain, nor syphilitic changes in the membranes covering the brain, nor—particularly important—soft, gummy tumors of the sort especially characteristic of syphilis are described in the autopsy report. An association of Beethoven's auditory dysfunction with a venereal disease must be firmly rejected on clinical grounds as well. As the prominent director of the nose-ears-throat clinic in Vienna, Dr. Heinrich Neumann, has emphasized in a comprehensive paper, when the auditory nerve is diseased with syphilis, the vestibulocochlear nerve that involves the organ of equilibrium is almost invariably affected also. The characteristic clinical picture includes dizziness, loss of balance, and vomiting, symptoms never reported by the otherwise rather sensitive patient Beethoven. Moreover, the course of Beethoven's hearing loss, with its insidious beginning and its slow but steady progression leading gradually to complete deafness, tells clinicians it could not have been due to syphilis of the auditory nerve, which progresses in sporadically occurring episodes. From the preceding detailed rebuttal of the arguments of the claim that the cause of Beethoven's deafness was a syphilitic infection, even persons who are not medically trained can recognize that this grave assertion is totally unfounded.

A review of the important relevant aspects of Beethoven's medical history is helpful in finding the most likely explanation for his hearing disorder. From statements in his letters, the beginning of his deafness can probably be fixed at about 1795, apparently as the result of a serious attack of typhoid fever. At first, only his left ear was affected, but soon thereafter the hearing in his right ear also began to deteriorate. From the beginning, he could no longer hear the higher tones of voice or instruments and he found loud tones or noises, such as the cannon shots during the French siege of Vienna, especially painful. In 1802, the hearing loss led to episodes of severe depression and thoughts of suicide. Up to a few years before he became completely deaf, he could hear vibrations transmitted through the external ear canal to the bones of the middle ear, as demonstrated by his use of a piece of wood between his teeth and the sounding board of his piano to transmit the sound. The frequently reported fluctuations in his ability to hear could have been associated with headcolds, which in turn could have led to an accompanying inflammation of the Eustachian tube. Research has turned up no medical history of defective hearing among his ancestors or his siblings.

These aspects of Beethoven's medical history cast doubt on the diagnosis advanced by numerous authors as the cause of his deafness—namely, otosclerosis (the formation of spongy bone in the capsule of the labyrinth, causing the auditory ossicles, especially the stirrup, to become fixed and less able to pass on vibrations when sound enters the ear). The absence of a similar disease among his blood relatives, especially on the female side, its beginning with an infectious sickness, the initial disappearance of high tones, and the unbearable effect of loud noises (which are often a relief for patients with otosclerosis) are all factors that argue against a diagnosis of otosclerosis for Beethoven. Furthermore, recall that the autopsy report did not mention any stiffening or hardening of the auditory ossicles—the hammer, anvil, and stirrup—in the middle ear, which is a characteristic of that disease. A pathologist as precise as Dr. Wagner, who described the posterior wall membrane in the vicinity of the cochlea, would certainly have inspected the middle ear and the space around the stirrup. He would definitely have noticed a fixation of the stirrup, which is required to establish otosclerosis. Moreover, the thickening of the Eustachian tube, with the swelling of its mucous lining and its narrowing toward the bony portion as described in Wagner's autopsy report, also tends to argue against a diagnosis of otosclerosis, for with that disease we usually find a rather wide Eustachian tube with a filmy, mucous lining.

Although the classical form of otosclerosis hardly qualifies as the cause of Beethoven's deafness, his known symptoms tend to fit the progressive form of the inner-ear type of otosclerosis: the insidious beginning in his younger years, the gradual progression of the affliction, albeit with occasional sharp attacks, the loss of the higher tones, especially notable with consonants, the rushing sound in the ears, and finally the so-called positive recruitment, that is, the heightened sensitivity to loud sounds about which Beethoven complained repeatedly when his hearing defect was in its early stages. This abnormal sensitivity is characteristic of a disorder of the labyrinth or inner ear, but is not present in primary inflammatory diseases of the auditory nerves. Later in his life Beethoven reported nothing more about this abnormal sensitivity to loud sounds, probably because the auditory nerves had degenerated, as confirmed in the autopsy report.

In recent times, an effort has been made to associate Beethoven's hearing defect with one of the three diseases named after Sir James Paget, specifically, Paget's disease of bone. This disease disturbs the growth of new bone tissue in the skull and elsewhere in the skeleton, with the result that the bones often thicken, become soft, and coarsen in texture. Even Dr. Heinrich Neumann drew attention to the greatly thickened frontal bone of Beethoven's skull, which would fit a clinical picture of Paget's disease of bone. Dr. V. S. Naiken of Philadelphia considered this diagnosis substantiated on the basis of a study of sketches of Beethoven made by Johann Peter Lyser in 1823 and by Joseph Böhm in 1820 that are in the Beethoven-Haus in Bonn. But this conclusion overlooks the fact that, even as a youth, Beethoven had a noticeably prominent "Olympian" forehead and tended to walk with his upper body bent slightly forward. According to Breuning, Beethoven always wore his hat on the back of his head, with the brim resting on his collar, to leave his brow free. We certainly ought not to look on this peculiar habit as indicative of the existence of Paget's disease in a person whose hat has become too small because the bones of the skull have thickened.

Nor is it appropriate to interpret the broadening and coarsening of the facial section of the skull, which occurs in everyone, as a sign of Paget's disease.

A diagnosis of Paget's disease of bone for Beethoven would enable its proponents to put forward yet another hypothesis for the cause of his deafness. Studies have shown that impairment of hearing to the point of total deafness is found in about one-fourth of the cases of this rather uncommon disease, although in almost all cases the auditory dysfunction does not begin until after the fortieth year. In these cases, thickening of the petrosal bone causes constriction of the internal acoustic canal, creating increased pressure that leads to degeneration or atrophy of the auditory nerves, which in turn results in sensorineural (inner ear) hearing loss. Apart from the fact that the presence of Paget's disease is an unproved hypothesis, two factors clearly suggest that Beethoven did not have an atypical otosclerosis caused by Paget's disease: the early onset of the hearing defect in his twenty-fifth year and the medical statements of Dr. Wegeler and Dr. Weissenbach that the first hearing difficulties followed a severe case of typhoid fever.

But there is more evidence. Recently pieces of bone from Beethoven's skull have been rediscovered and their examination by Messrs. Bankl and Jesserer provides final proof that Beethoven did not suffer from Paget's disease. The story of the rediscovery is interesting. From the written reports of the two disinterments, it was obvious that, in addition to the petrosal bones removed at the time of the autopsy, pieces of the occipital bone at the back of the skull and of the parietal bone forming the sides and roof of the cranium had been missing since the time of the first disinterment, a fact long known in professional circles that Theodor von Frimmel noted when he wrote on a copy of C. Langer von Edenberg's 1887 scientific study, *The Craniums of Three Musical Masters*:

> Beethoven's skull, back part of cranium,
> a piece missing near the lambdoid suture
> the left parietal bone is missing
> at the base in back, both mastoid processes
> are missing

Thus, it was clear that, during the first exhumation, some pieces from Beethoven's fragile skull had been surreptitiously removed and hidden away as valuable relics of the composer. Through fortunate circumstances, Bankl and Jesserer succeeded discovering that Albert Seligmann, the grandnephew of Adalbert Franz Seligmann, possessed these bone fragments. He had received the preserved skull fragments of unquestioned authenticity in a labeled metal box from his father, Franz Romeo Seligmann, who had taken part in the examination of the skull during the first disinterment and hidden away some of the bone fragments.

These pieces of bone from Beethoven's skull were made available to Bankl and Jesserer for examination after Albert Seligmann's death. The two experts were able to conclude that although the bone fragments are somewhat thicker than normal, they are completely normal in structure and show no evidence of pathological change, particularly none suggestive of the presence of Paget's disease of bone, which characteristically shows increased new bone formation in the skull. Therefore, the theory that Beethoven's deafness was a consequence of Paget's disease of bone is refuted once and for all.

The most probable explanation of Beethoven's deafness is that it was a disorder of the auditory nerves of the labyrinth or inner ear. A review of all the symptoms associated with Beethoven shows that this diagnosis is supported by such factors as the multiple indications of the specific loss of the higher tones from the beginning of the hearing problem, the persistent noises in the ear described as ringing and buzzing, the painful sensitivity to loud sounds and noises, the fact that bone conduction (the transmission of sound through the external ear canal to the bones in the middle ear) persisted intact for a long time. Furthermore, the course of the disease reconstructed from Beethoven's detailed history is typical of this disorder. The insidious, almost imperceptible start was characteristic of a hearing loss associated with pathological change in structures within the inner ear or in the auditory nerve. Once the disease had reached a certain stage, the progression could hardly be detected for years and seemed even to have stopped. Only later did the process resume and continue inexorably to a state of total deafness. This slowly advancing course with yearlong pauses corresponds perfectly to the typical picture of a chronic inflammation of the auditory nerves.

An inquiry into the source of this inflammatory occurrence leads to the typhoid fever mentioned by Dr. Weissenbach. Of course, we still are not certain whether this illness was truly

TWO DRAWINGS BY CONTEM-
PORARIES OF BEETHOVEN:
FROM THE SIDE, BY JOHANN
PETER LYSER IN 1823; FROM
BEHIND, BY JOSEPH BÖHM IN
1820.

typhoid fever and just when it occurred. It could have been epidemic or louse-borne typhus which, like typhoid fever, frequently affects the auditory nerves. In his textbook on historical-geographical pathology, August Hirsch wrote more than a hundred years ago: "The most severe period of typhus in the 18th century occurred in its last decade [the decade in which Beethoven is said to have been ill with the disease]; it began in France at the time of the revolution and came to an end only in the second decade of the following century." He added that "the epidemics caused by war, and particularly typhus...spread across all Europe." According to Hirsch, typhoid fever and epidemic typhus occurred in equal measure. Unfortunately, we do not know which disease is meant in the Fischhoff manuscript's mention, dated to 1796, of "a dangerous illness whose effects settled in the mechanism of the ear during his convalescence, after which his deafness progressively increased," nor do we know whether that "terrible case of typhoid fever," which Beethoven told his friend Dr. Weissenbach about later, had preceded it. An account from the year 1845 enables us to speculate that this event could have occurred during 1787, when Beethoven was seventeen years old. Writing in the *Wiener Zeitschrift* of 16 September 1845, the author and illustrator who went by the pen name of Johann Peter Lyser (his actual name was Ludwig Peter August Burmeister) told of the following curious incident in Beethoven's life:

> Beethoven was visiting his mother in Bonn before she died [in 1787], when his deafness became apparent. One evening he was at the home of the Simrock family, where a young relative of the children was telling fairy tales. Beethoven sat with his head cocked forward, his hands on his knees and listening intently. He interrupted her frequently, however, asking how was that?, what?, what did he say?, what did he do?, and then would often say the oddest things, leading the children to laugh out loud at his mistakes. Finally the singer Haberkorn, now deceased, called out: "Lad, are you crazy or deaf?," whereupon Beethoven said not another word.

Whether there is a causal relationship between the hearing defect that had evidently already begun then and the hint of an early case of typhoid fever from which Beethoven had recovered is something we do not know. If this typhoid fever occurred at some time prior to the fairy tale incident—and in 1922, Schweisheimer had already attributed Beethoven's typhoid fever to 1787 from his study of documentary sources—then a disorder of the inner ear resulting from typhoid fever would be the most likely interpretation of his hearing defect, a view expressed by Dr. Neumann as early as 1927. Such a conclusion is completely consistent with Beethoven's written remarks to Dr. Wegeler, from which we can conclude that his hearing ability must have deteriorated appreciably even before 1796, and that the 1796 illness mentioned in the Fischhoff manuscript was merely a later episode. Recent research indicates that in children and adolescents infected by the pathogenic agent *Hæmophilus influenzæ*, which can cause meningitis, hearing loss is observed with particular frequency, especially when treatment is started late or—as in Beethoven's time—no effective treatment is possible. The description of the changes to the soft meninges near the auditory center of Beethoven's brain noted in the autopsy supports such an interpretation, for "the shriveled and unmedullated auditory nerves," as described in the autopsy report, could have resulted from pressure caused by some swelling in the localized inflammation of the meninges.

Generally, such a post-infectious pathological process in the auditory nerves comes to an end after a certain period of time but may progress when new infections occur. As Neumann stressed: "Once such a disease of the auditory nerves exists, then it becomes more and more severe with every insult that strikes the organism. And many such insults are found in the life of Beethoven." Along with numerous cases of otitis media (inflammation of the middle ear) in connection with his many headcolds, the traces of which were noted in the autopsy report, and his frequent intestinal diseases that could have had a harmful effect on his diseased center of hearing, it is especially the diminishment of hearing as he grew older that suggests a progressive inner-ear hearing loss that culminated in total deafness.

## Beethoven's Abdominal Troubles

In biographies of Beethoven, we are continually confronted with the puzzling abdominal complaints that began in his youth and stayed with him to the end of his life.  Despite many more or less medically plausible attempts to explain these chronic difficulties, there has been no convincing demonstration of their true nature.  We first hear of an illness involving severe diarrhea in the year 1789.  Because of it Beethoven had to stay in bed and be attended by his friend Wegeler, who was some five years older and had just finished his medical studies.  Wegeler reported that Beethoven fell ill again with intestinal complaints in 1795 and 1796 and that, in his opinion, "as early as 1796, the source of his misfortune, his loss of hearing and his last, fatal dropsy...[lay] in his diseased abdomen."  Recall that on 29 March 1795 Beethoven was almost not able to complete the composition of one of his early piano concertos in time for his first grand public appearance in Vienna.  He was seized by intense abdominal colic, that is, acute paroxysmal abdominal pains, and had to be treated by Dr. Wegeler, who used simple medications to try to relieve the accompanying diarrhea.  In his medical report on Beethoven, Dr. Wawruch flatly termed Beethoven's chronic intestinal difficulties "a problem with hemorrhoids," from which we can tentatively conclude that Beethoven experienced minor bleeding with defecation.

From 1795 on, Beethoven grumbled repeatedly about bouts of sickness with fever that accompanied a worsening of his intestinal complaints.  As he told Wegeler in the letter of 29 July 1801: "...and my belly—which was miserable even then, as you know, and since being here has only gotten worse, being bothered constantly with diarrhea and terribly weak as a result—...stayed as it was; that went on into autumn of the past year, and often drove me crazy....This past winter I really felt dreadful; I had truly terrible colics and I sank back into my previous condition, and so it remained until about four weeks ago."

Stephan von Breuning, who had shared an apartment with Beethoven at one time, told Wegeler in his letter of 13 November 1804 about one such event that had been particularly serious: "He had scarcely moved in with me before he had a severe, almost critical illness which eventually turned into an obstinate intermittent fever."  And in the following years up to 1812, musically Beethoven's most creative period, the composer referred time and again in his letters to the dubious state of his health.  His constantly recurring abdominal colic, which he called his "usual sickness" and which were very often accompanied by fever, frequently forced him to take to his bed and to undergo various treatments with baths and mineral waters. Because he came to think that his colic was triggered chiefly by ill-prepared meals, he decided in 1809 to hire a married couple as servants. He wrote a friend at the time: "I have to have someone to cook; as long as the food continues to be so poor, I'll always be sick."

Beethoven must have had an especially serious illness in the fall of 1816, as we can deduce from his letter of 19 June 1817 to Countess Erdödy: "...constantly in poor health since 6 October 1816, afflicted with a severe inflammatory catarrh since 15 October so that I had to stay in bed a long time and it took months before I could go out again even briefly..." And in this period too, Beethoven repeatedly mentioned acute attacks of colic. Moreover, in this protracted period of being sick, obviously with episodes of fever, he must also have caught a respiratory disease, for he wrote Nanette Streicher on 7 July 1817: "In addition there is the fearful prospect that perhaps I will never be better, besides I even have doubts about my present doctor, and now at long last he has diagnosed my condition as lung trouble." His letters contain numerous passages along this line, speaking of acute rheumatic pains in his limbs and one headcold after another.

In 1823, attacks of diarrhea flared up again, linked with stomach pains and complicated by a prolonged and painful inflammation of the eyes that began in April and lasted into August. The eye troubles gradually cleared up in the course of the summer, but Beethoven's intestinal malady occurred again in July, this time with increased discomfort, as he told Anton Schindler in a letter: "I'm not feeling well at all, had terrible diarrhea today....Am taking medicine for my poor ruined stomach." And at the end of August, he wrote Archduke Rudolph: "I was taken ill all over again with my somewhat improved catarrhal disease, and along with that my abdomen was still in the worst shape...." We should not assume that Beethoven's term "catarrh" meant a catarrhal inflammation of the throat or the respiratory tract. It probably referred much more often to inflammation of his intestines, as is apparent, for example, in his doctor's entry in a conversation book in the summer of 1823: "For your catarrh, you may not eat anything else during the day except barley gruel a couple of times; the irregularity [diarrhea] will get better...." In the spring of 1824, a new attack of intestinal complaints led once again to an eruption of the eye inflammation, which must have involved sensitivity to light and considerable pain. Beethoven wrote at the time: "Nights I have to cover my eyes and am supposed to take very good care of them."

A year later, in the spring of 1825, there are reports of bleeding from the nose and the esophagus, and symptoms of his intestinal difficulties occurred again. Along with stomach pains and diarrhea, fever was apparent for some time, as is clear from an entry in the conversation books from these weeks made by Dr. Braunhofer: "Every fever lasts a little while, yours is already going away....You have a strong tendency to inflammations, and it wouldn't have taken much before you would have gotten a right good intestinal inflammation. The inclination is still there in your body." Beethoven recovered from this attack, but his susceptibility to colic and diarrhea continued into the years that followed. We hear for the last time of paroxysmal intestinal pains and diarrhea during the final weeks of Beethoven's life when Dr. Malfatti, recognizing his patient's hopeless situation, allowed him to have frozen punch—a cold drink made with rum.

What was the cause of these chronic abdominal troubles? Statements of Dr. Alois Weissenbach, who is supposed to have heard directly from Beethoven that he had been seriously ill with typhoid fever in his childhood, led some people to conclude that the intestinal symptoms resulted from that disease. Aside from the lack of definite proof that Beethoven had typhoid fever, however, consequences of this nature have never been observed over such an extended period in the aftermath of that particular infectious disease. Consequently, Dr. Horst Scherf suggested that Beethoven could have suffered from Bang's disease (brucellosis, or undulant fever as it is sometimes called), an infection caused by various species of Brucella bacteria and marked by attacks of fever that fluctuate widely at regular intervals. His attempted line of argumentation was intended to banish in advance "all doubt as to the correctness of the Bangs diagnosis" by forcing all of Beethoven's symptoms of illness into the broad clinical picture produced by the Brucella bacteria. But that approach is simply not medically defensible. First, if an infection of this kind did occur when Beethoven was still a youth in Bonn, it is inconceivable that its ill effects would have continued for many decades to come. In addition, important symptoms in Beethoven's clinical history simply do not fit the picture presented by this infectious disease. With chronic Bang's disease, episodes of diarrhea are almost never observed and the patient's general feeling of well-being is seldom adversely affected despite the attacks of high fever. Beethoven, on the contrary, felt greatly weakened and worn out by the long-lasting feverish episodes. Finally, it is medically out of the question that acute hepatitis with jaundice could develop more than thirty years later; we know today that such an event could only occur in the acute stage of Bang's disease. Dr. Scherf made a vain attempt to quash such objections in advance by assuming that Beethoven could have contracted such an infection repeatedly. For example, he regarded Beethoven's severe case of pneumonia after he returned from Gneixendorf in late 1826 as a "recurrence of Bang's disease." These few counterarguments suffice to bring discussion of this thesis to an end.

A more plausible idea put forward by doctors in recent times is that Beethoven suffered from chronic inflammation of the pancreas (chronic pancreatitis) caused by alcoholism, which could have been responsible for his decades-long stomach troubles. Some American authors began to consider this possibility more than twenty years ago, and more recently F. H. Franken has examined the evidence for this thesis. He was helped in this effort by the autopsy report, which says: "The spleen appeared twice the normal size, was black and rough; in the same way, the pancreas also seemed larger and harder, and its excretory duct was the width of a goose feather quill." This passage from the report implies that the pancreas must have been coarser than normal and the pancreatic duct somewhat enlarged (to the extent we can draw conclusions today from approximate diameters expressed in terms of the feathers of geese). It confirms the presence of a chronic inflammatory alteration in the pancreas, but tells us only what we already know from extensive observation: that about half of all patients with alcoholic cirrhosis of the liver have a chronic inflammatory change in the pancreas. By itself, this finding certainly cannot explain Beethoven's intestinal sufferings that went on for many years.

Today we know that before such a chronic inflammation of the pancreas can develop, it must be preceded by the regular consumption of considerable amounts of alcohol over a long period of time. Given that Beethoven was plagued with colic and diarrhea from the age of twenty, he would have had to begin consuming alcohol in considerable quantities at a very tender age indeed. Besides, chronic pancreatitis is marked by attacks of dull, seldom colicky, pains in the stomach. Spells of diarrhea and especially ones coupled with prolonged periods of fever do not fit the clinical picture of this disease at all. Only after chronic pancreatitis has been present a long time—when the gland (or acinar) tissue has already been extensively replaced or supplanted by fibrous tissue—are bulky, fatty, foul-smelling stools produced. They have nothing in common, however, with the "diarrhea" attributed to Beethoven. Moreover, the fact that Beethoven's spells of diarrhea began before he had turned twenty completely excludes the possibility that they were due to a progressive loss of pancreatic function. We can therefore confidently conclude that neither Beethoven's attacks of abdominal colics nor his diarrhea were caused at any time in his life by the alteration in the pancreas noted at the time of the autopsy and common in cases of cirrhosis of the liver.

The American physician Dr. London proposed a diagnosis of so-called spastic colon, which is now called irritable bowel syndrome, a psychosomatic disorder of the large intestine or colon, with episodes of diarrhea or constipation or both alternately, and often violent stomach pain as well, which is usually triggered by situations of psychological stress. From a review of Beethoven's clinical history, it is evident that his intestinal troubles flared up especially often in times of psychological tension. Nevertheless, what contradicts a diagnosis of irritable colon for Beethoven is that this clinical disorder is usually not accompanied by episodes of fever; nor do the paroxysmal stomach pains or attacks of diarrhea reach such proportions that they lead to prolonged spells of weakness and infirmity as were repeatedly observed in Beethoven from 1800 to 1825.

The sole diagnosis that fits all of the symptoms described in connection with Beethoven's intestinal complaints is Crohn's disease, or regional enteritis as it is also known. This chronic, recurring inflammatory disease can in theory affect any segment of the entire intestinal tract, but is usually located in the terminal portion of the ileum (in the small intestine, just before the large intestine). In the vast majority of cases, the disease begins between the twentieth and thirtieth years, although there are isolated instances of its occurrence in teenagers. The early symptoms are mostly nonspecific and marked by a typical combination of diarrhea, abdominal pains, and fever. Normally the diarrhea is mild at first, but in later years can occur in such severe bouts that it leads to extreme infirmity and weakness, with considerable loss of weight resulting from malnutrition and the loss of fluids. Erosions in the anal mucosa and local infections in the anal aperture frequently develop early. They may lead to bleeding and are often misdiagnosed as hemorrhoids. The accompanying pains may be felt as a chronic, nagging discomfort in the lower right side of the abdomen or in the umbilical region, but often they become more cramplike and not localized. Paroxysmal abdominal pains are particularly sharp just before the onset of diarrhea, and they usually abate somewhat in the course of the active diarrhea. Episodes of Crohn's disease are often accompanied by moderately elevated temperatures, which may be the sole symptom of the disease in many of these episodes over a long span of time.

The course of Crohn's disease is highly variable. We know today that many patients with Crohn's disease remain completely free of any symptoms for years at a time until—frequently following episodes of psychological stress—a new attack of the disease occurs. In most cases, however, the disease leads to a lowering of the general state of health and to the appearance of complications, the most dangerous being internal and external colonic fistulas and especially intestinal obstruction. Less dangerous for the patient but still very wearing are accompanying inflammatory attacks in the region of the major joints and the spinal column. These attacks fluctuate widely in intensity and correlate in time with the occurrence of new intestinal complaints. The same is true of the more complicating eye diseases, which most often involve inflammation of the conjunctiva (the membrane lining the eyelids and covering the eyeball) and the iris. These eye afflictions, which can suddenly erupt with an attack of Crohn's disease, are marked particularly by sensitivity to light, discomfort in the eye socket, and headaches, and can last for months at a time. Finally, patients with long-term Crohn's disease can have a greatly increased tendency for the formation of kidney stones as well as stones in the gallbladder. We have become aware of this tendency only in recent years as the result of increasing experience with this common disease.

If we compare Beethoven's medical history with the clinical syndrome of Crohn's disease, we find many of the symptoms typical for the disease: abdominal colic beginning early in his youth, tied in with attacks of diarrhea and fever, which recurred frequently in the decades to follow and more than once led to such a severe impairment of health that Beethoven despaired of ever recovering; the early mention of hemorrhoids; the frequency with which stomach pains and diarrhea were triggered by psychological factors, and later repeated complaints about rheumatic or gouty pains as well; and finally the two occurrences of a prolonged and painful eye affliction. Moreover, another finding in the autopsy report that has attracted relatively little attention until now would fit this diagnosis: specifically, kidney stones were present in almost all the calyces of the kidney pelvis, and chalky, gritty stones were present in the gallbladder.

The obvious conclusion is that Beethoven contracted Crohn's disease, regional enteritis, in his early years, and it was this disease that was with him until the day he died and that he came to call his "usual illness" because of its frequent episodes, often persisting for months. Thanks to the research of C. Hawkins, we now know that in the early 19th century, many cases of a chronic inflammatory intestinal disease that we would diagnose today as Crohn's disease were described and corroborated by autopsies. Thus, the existence of Crohn's disease in Beethoven's time can be substantiated.

One argument against a diagnosis of Crohn's disease in Beethoven is that the doctor who conducted the careful postmortem examination made no report of any abnormalities of the large and small intestines. We know, of course, that Crohn's disease may become completely cured from a clinical point of view, but hardly, if ever, without leaving telltale signs, ascertainable in an autopsy, of definite inflammatory changes in the large and small intestines. A possible explanation in Beethoven's case could be that Dr. Wagner, who conducted the autopsy, elected to concentrate almost exclusively on the organs of the ear and on the organs related to Beethoven's liver disease, and gave relatively little notice to the rest of the digestive tract. Such a clinical approach would be more understandable for a "private autopsy" conducted in Beethoven's apartment.

As early as 1932, Burril B. Crohn, the first doctor to define and describe the disease, pointed out that even the most outstanding pathologists at the beginning of this century had not noticed the changes that usually occurred in highly localized sections of the intestines. As Crohn saw it, the reason such a thoroughly evident clinical picture was overlooked for so long was that this disease does not lead directly to death and therefore the pathologists directed their attention to other interests.

Lacking a morphological foundation confirmed by postmortem examination, we can put forward the likely diagnosis of Crohn's disease on the basis of the clinical syndrome. Because the disease caused no obvious decline in Beethoven's physical condition despite having lasted decades—indeed, Beethoven remained vigorous and alert until shortly before his death—the disease may have been essentially an affliction of the large intestine. The possibility of ulcerative colitis, a recurrent acute and chronic disorder characterized by extensive inflammatory ulceration of the colon, can probably be ruled out. Even though it may run a prolonged course over years with intermittent attacks, it seldom involves fever and is normally marked by bloody, mucoid diarrhea. Similarly, assigning Beethoven's intestinal ills to the category of irritable colon, an intestinal disease with a psychosomatic component, would not be consistent with important symptoms in Beethoven's medical history. Spastic colon is never associated with long periods of fever, nor does it ever lead to bouts of diarrhea extending over weeks or even months of the sort attributed to Beethoven. In all, the symptoms of Beethoven's intestinal troubles are most readily incorporated into the clinical picture presented by Crohn's disease, and hence that diagnosis is the most probable.

## Beethoven's Liver Disease

The final illness that resulted in Beethoven's death has never been in doubt. The careful description of his clinical symptoms by Dr. Wawruch, who was able to determine that along with jaundice and dropsy, "the liver showed clear signs of hard nodules," and in particular the report of the autopsy, in which the liver was described as having "shrunk to half its volume, hard as leather...and infested with pea-sized nodules on its bumpy surface as well as inside the organ itself," enable us to advance the diagnosis of cirrhosis of the liver with absolute certainty. In this disease, the liver cells die and are replaced by coarse, fibrous bands of connective tissue that prevent the normal reconstitution of the liver's microscopic lobes. The regenerating nodules and the extensive buildup of interstitial tissue constrict and distort the organ's blood vessels and obstruct the flow of blood inside the liver. The result is substantial congestion of the blood in the veins of the esophagus and the spleen and "leakage" of serous (edematous) fluid within the abdominal cavity, which was known as abdominal dropsy and is now termed ascites. The autopsy reports says in this connection that "all the vessels [of the liver] were very narrow, swollen, and devoid of blood," that the spleen "appeared twice the normal size, was black and rough," and that "four quarts of a cloudy greyish-brown liquid" were found in the abdominal cavity.

Unfortunately, as no close inspection of the esophagus was made during the autopsy, we lack direct information about its veins. But Beethoven himself provided an indirect indication of greatly distended esophageal veins in the informative letter with the "dialogue" that he sent to his physician, Dr. Braunhofer, on 13 May 1825: "...I am spewing out quite a bit of blood, probably only from the windpipe; but more often it pours out of my nose, which happened frequently this winter." Contrary to what Beethoven thought, this bleeding did not come from the windpipe. Bleeding of the respiratory tract may lead to the coughing up of blood, but it never results in the vomiting of blood, which is always due to bleeding in either the stomach or the esophagus. Without a postmortem examination of the esophagus, we do not know whether the bleeding Beethoven mentioned came in fact from congested esophageal veins. Because Beethoven obviously suffered often from nosebleeds at the time, he could have swallowed blood running back from the nose and vomited it later. His marked disposition to have nosebleeds tells us, incidentally, that by this time his liver disease had already begun to affect the normal clotting of his blood. The clotting disorder would be reflected in the appearance of numerous small points of blood under the skin, a condition confirmed by the autopsy report: "The body was...covered with petechiae...."

The diagnosis of Beethoven's liver disease and its fatal consequences are clear and uncontested; the actual cause of the disease is not. Beethoven's friend Dr. Wegeler was the first person who saw that "as early as 1796, the source of...his last, fatal dropsy...[was] his diseased abdomen," which is undoubtedly why Dr. Schweisheimer later thought the cause of Beethoven's cirrhosis of the liver was typhoid fever suffered in his youth, whereas Dr. Scherf attributed it to a brucellosis infection—Bang's disease—

acquired in that period. Today we are aware that cirrhosis of the liver never develops from typhoid fever, but disorders in the liver ranging from hepatitis to cirrhosis are known to result from Bang's disease, although they are rare. Because Bang's disease can be excluded on clinical grounds, no further discussion of it as a possible cause of Beethoven's cirrhosis of the liver is necessary.

We might suspect Crohn's disease as a cause of Beethoven's liver problems, for Crohn's disease, as well as ulcerative colitis, pathological changes in the liver occur in more than 50 percent of the cases. Mostly, however, these changes involve inflammatory processes of the smallest bile ducts that are usually imperceptible to the patient. Occasionally, they can bring about fever with jaundice and pains in the upper region of the abdomen, but these symptoms normally soon recede and rarely, if ever, progress to cirrhosis of the liver.

Finally, the jaundice that appeared in 1821 must be considered. It was surely due to a viral inflammation of the liver at the time, which could have been caused by contaminated water or by the oysters that Beethoven was so fond of eating. In that case, however, the infection would have been Hepatitis A virus, which never progresses to cirrhosis of the liver. Cirrhosis would be conceivable only with a Hepatitis B virus infection which might indeed be a possibility given the span of some months between the premonitory symptom of rheumatism in the spring of 1821 and the appearance of jaundice in the summer. Actually, we do not know whether at the time Hepatitis B virus existed in a form that was transmitted almost exclusively through contact with blood and blood products, or in a form similar to the 20th century disease that can be transmitted via body fluids such as saliva and semen.* If the latter form did already exist, it would have been transmittable through sexual intercourse, a possibility that obviously cannot be excluded for Beethoven.

Having eliminated the other possibilities, we can conclude that the cause of Beethoven's cirrhosis of the liver was almost certainly liver damage brought about by his regular consumption of alcohol, a habit that can be established from the time he was a young man in Bonn and which must also have been the cause of the chronic inflammatory alteration in the pancreas. As mentioned previously, tolerance for alcohol varies greatly from person to person and is influenced by a number of genetic factors. Only about 20 percent of the population runs the risk of incurring damage to the liver or the pancreas from the regular consumption

of alcohol, for the susceptibility of these organs is highly variable
and depends on numerous hereditary and environmental factors.
For a person who has a low tolerance, the daily consumption of
only two to five ounces of alcohol—the amount in, say, four pints
of beer or one to one and a half pints of wine—can suffice over a
course of years to cause cirrhosis of the liver. In other words, a
person who develops alcoholic cirrhosis is not necessarily a drunkard in any sense of the word. Given the appropriate genetic
predisposition, a relatively small amount of beer or wine each
day over fifteen or more years will bring about cirrhosis. It is
therefore difficult to understand why, in discussing Ludwig van
Beethoven, it should be a sacrilege to attribute to alcohol the
disease described by the autopsy report as a typical nodular liver
cirrhosis, particularly when a review of all available documentary
sources points in that direction. Hereditary factors were present
in Beethoven's case. Beethoven was certainly not a drunkard,
but he was fond of drinking, particular in his days in Bonn, and
because he had the notion that wine was good for his health, he
usually drank a small bottle of wine every day with his meals. We
also have reports from Beethoven's doctors about his drinking
habits. Dr. Wawruch wrote in looking back on the last period in
Beethoven's life:

> Never being accustomed to take medical advice
> seriously, he began to use alcoholic drinks to stimu-
> late his waning pleasure in eating, and to take
> long fatiguing walks to give a little relief to the
> weakness of his stomach brought on by overin-
> dulgence in strong punch and ices. It was just
> such a turn in his way of living that had brought
> him to the edge of the grave some seven years
> before.

Even in the autumn of 1826, when abdominal dropsy developed
during his stay on his brother's estate, Beethoven was still partak-
ing freely of the local wines. His brother Johann recounted that
Ludwig "would eat nothing but a few soft-boiled eggs at noon but
then would drink wine all the more...."

Anton Schindler vigorously criticized the comments in
Dr. Wawruch's medical report, claiming that with such remarks
the doctor had declared Beethoven to be a "drunken sot" while
admitting at the same time "that even before Wawruch's report,

this nasty rumor was widespread." According to all the documentary sources, Beethoven was neither an alcoholic nor a drunken sot, but, like many of his friends, he did enjoy beer and wine and consumed them regularly throughout his life. To deny the role of alcohol in Beethoven's life with a moralizing allusion to "Beethoven's noble character and his unshakable faith in his earthly mission" would not do justice to the human side of this genius. Let us therefore simply stay with the factual medical diagnosis of alcoholic nodular cirrhosis of the liver that was exacerbated by an acute pneumonia early in December 1826 and from then on led inexorably to Beethoven's death in a hepatic coma only a few months later.

That Beethoven died in the midst of a raging winter storm with snow squalls, thunder, and lightning prompted Dr. Wawruch to end his account with the following words: "In ancient Rome, such a coincidental turmoil of the elements would have surely led a soothsayer to foretell his apotheosis!" It will always seem miraculous that Beethoven's total commitment to discipline and his powerful, single-minded striving to reach the most exalted heights of art that man is capable of scaling were possible in a body that was plagued by intestinal disease from the early years of his maturity and until he died, and which, in the last years of his life, was increasingly tormented by the effects of his fatal liver disease. Even more incredible is the fact that, as a relatively young man, Beethoven had been forced to face the specter of progressive deafness, yet was not held back in storming from one creation to the next, ever finding new forms of musical expression, right up to those overwhelming last works whose music he himself could never hear.

# Beethoven's Doctors

## *Dr. Franz Wegeler (1765-1848)*

Dr. Wegeler was Beethoven's first doctor. The close personal friendship formed during their youth together in Bonn was interrupted for a short time when Wegeler went to Vienna to complete his medical education. The two came together again when Wegeler returned to his hometown in October 1789 to assume his medical duties as professor for forensic medicine and obstetrics at the newly founded (1786) university in Bonn. "After I returned...we enjoyed just as warm a bond, until Beethoven himself left for Vienna the end of 1792, where I followed in October 1794." Because he was regarded as an outspoken enemy of the new French Republic, he had been forced to flee temporarily to Vienna when the French army entered Bonn, but was back in Bonn by the middle of 1796. From that time on, the two friends corresponded regularly, with Beethoven repeatedly informing his doctor friend about the state of his health and seeking his medical advice on various matters.

## Dr. Johann Peter Frank (1745-1821)

Born in the Palatinate district of Germany, Dr. Frank studied medicine despite the opposition of his parents and at the age of twenty-one years had already developed plans for his life's work: to found a kind of "medical police force." In a work of several volumes, under the motto "preventing is better than curing," he created the prerequisites for further development in the fields of public health and forensic medicine.

Dr. Frank came to Vienna in 1795 and on 25 November of that same year was named director of the General Hospital and made a professor at the University of Vienna. Under his direction, wide-ranging reforms for the benefit of the patients were set in motion covering all aspects of hospital practice. A victim of intrigues and hostility, he left Vienna in 1805 to accept a professorship in Vilna, Lithuania, but was soon called to St. Petersburg to be personal physician to the Czar. In 1808, he returned to Vienna.

Dr. Frank was the first doctor to delve into the health problems of the thirty-year-old Beethoven in detail. The relationship between the two apparently began on a social basis, for there was much music-making at Frank's home and Beethoven often played the piano accompaniment for the doctor's daughter when she sang.

## Dr. Gerhard von Vering (1755-1823)

Born in Westphalia in northern Germany, Dr. Vering was only twenty when he came to Vienna. He joined the army and soon became a regimental surgeon. He was among the physicians selected by Emperor Joseph II to undertake scientific scouting expeditions to various European countries. Later, Dr. Vering was an executive officer in the medical corps in Lower Austria and, later still, overall director of the hospitals and larger sanitary installations during the Napoleonic wars.

In the summer of 1801, Beethoven, who had been under Dr. Frank's medical care since 1800, placed himself in the hands of Dr. Vering with high expectations. By November 1801, not having seen the hoped-for results, he had lost confidence in this respected doctor.

## Dr. Johann Adam Schmidt (1759-1809)

Dr. Schmidt was from Würzburg and began his career as an army surgeon with the position of professor for general pathology and therapy at the newly established Josephinum in Vienna. His main interest, however, was ophthalmology, the science addressing the functions and diseases of the eye, and in this area he quickly found fame. He was so successful that he soon was able to afford to maintain his own institute, where for several years he treated poverty-stricken patients at his own expense. His publication of innumerable medical articles contributed to his renown as a scientist.

Dr. Schmidt was one of Dr. Wegeler's friends and, as such, had Beethoven's trust right from the start. Moreover, this famous doctor was very fond of music and was himself a good violinist; his daughter played the piano. Beethoven's close ties to Dr. Schmidt are expressed most notably in the explicit, grateful reference to him in the Heiligenstadt testament, in which Beethoven enjoined Dr. Schmidt to describe his illness after he died and to attach the testament to his account "so that as far as possible the world will become reconciled to me after my death at least." A further token of friendship, which perhaps was intended also to be a kind of payment for medical services rendered, is Beethoven's arrangement of his famous Septet in E-flat op. 20 for piano, violin or clarinet, and cello as the new opus number 38. When this trio appeared in Vienna in 1805, it bore this dedication from Beethoven to his doctor friend: *"à Monsieur Jean Adam Schmidt, Conseiller de Sa Majesté l'Empereur et Roi, Chirurgien* [surgeon] *Major de Ses Armés."*

During the winter of 1801—1802, Dr. Schmidt tried to treat Beethoven's hearing disorder with the help of the then novel method of galvanism, based on Franz Anton Mesmer's theories of animal magnetism that were very popular in Vienna at the time and regarded as the latest thing in science. Mesmer had been born in Iznang on Lake Constance in 1734 and had lived in Vienna since 1759, where he was able to amass a great fortune, in part through his magnetism treatments but mostly through his marriage. Mesmer's life was constantly accompanied by music, as is usually pointed out in connection with his fondness for a rococo artifact, the armonica (or glass harmonica). It was at Mesmer's house that the first performance of Mozart's Singspiel, *Bastien und Bastienne* (KV50), took place in 1768. Although Beethoven's galvanic treatments at the hands of Dr. Schmidt were not successful, the two remained friends until Dr. Schmidt died of a stroke in February 1809.

## *Dr. Johann Malfatti von Montereggio (1776-1859)*

Dr. Malfatti was born in Lucca in Italy and studied under the renowned Luigi Galvani ( 1737-1798) in Bologna and Dr. Johann Peter Frank in Pavia. When Dr. Frank later came to Vienna, Dr. Malfatti followed him. After receiving his doctor's degree, he first became a resident physician at the Vienna General Hospital and in that capacity founded the society of general practitioners in 1802. When his teacher Dr. Frank left Vienna in 1805, Malfatti gave up his position at the General Hospital and began a successful private practice. He rose to become the personal physician to Archduke Charles (1771-1847) and Archduchess Beatrix von Este and, because of his outstanding reputation, many of the foreign diplomats present for the Congress of Vienna from September 1814 to June 1815 placed themselves in his care. In 1837, he was made a member of the nobility. Dr. Malfatti was, like Dr. Schmidt, an exponent of galvanic treatments which, incidentally, once involved him in an unpleasant court case.

Dr. Malfatti owned a villa in the Hietzing district of Vienna near the Schönbrunn palace and a country estate in the Währing suburb, where Beethoven presented his little cantata *Un lieto brindisi* (WoO 103) on 24 June 1814, composed for Dr. Malfatti's name-day. Soon after a friend had introduced Beethoven into the Malfatti family, the composer took a great liking to one of the two daughters of Dr. Malfatti's brother, the twenty-one-year-old Therese, and apparently entertained thoughts of marrying her. It was to the young Therese that he dedicated his delightful piano piece, *Für Elise*.

Dr. Malfatti, who advocated the curative value of "taking the waters" and to whom spas such as Bad Ischl owe much of their fame, prescribed a stay at the health resort in Teplitz for Beethoven in 1811. The close relationship between the two lasted until 1817, when Beethoven broke with this "sly Italian," as he called him in a letter. At the very end of the composer's life, however, Dr. Malfatti appeared once more when he responded, at first hesitantly, to Beethoven's urgent plea to come to a consultation at his bedside.

## Dr. Andreas Bertolini

Dr. Bertolini, who at first was an assistant to Dr. Malfatti, became Beethoven's close friend in 1806 and, after 1808, his personal doctor besides. The friendship must have been very close indeed; of all his doctors, apparently none had as personal a relationship with the composer as Bertolini. It is from him that we know how susceptible Beethoven was to the charm of graceful, delicate women and what pleasure he always took in a glass of wine.

The two of them appear to have been very close in musical matters as well. For example, in 1814, Beethoven composed a polonaise for the Empress of Russia at Dr. Bertolini's suggestion, after first allowing his friend to choose the most appropriate theme for it from several that he had improvised at the piano. Unfortunately, it was a matter of music that also led to a rupture in the friendship in 1815. In brief, through Bertolini's intercession, an English music-lover visiting Vienna approached Beethoven with the proposal that he compose a symphony for which he would be paid a substantial amount of money, but with the provision that the symphony be more like his earlier ones, simpler and easier to understand. Beethoven was so incensed by this stipulation that he refused the commission and broke all relations with the well-meaning Bertolini, who had acted with the best of intentions.

In spite of what happened, Dr. Bertolini must have preserved his feelings of friendship for Beethoven for the rest of his life. When he came down with cholera in 1831 and believed he was about to die, he had all the letters he had received from Beethoven destroyed. They unquestionably discussed many highly personal matters that Bertolini did not want to become public. Incidentally, Bertolini subsequently recovered from the attack of cholera.

## Dr. Jakob Staudenheim (1764-1830)

Dr. Staudenheim, who was born in Mainz, initially went to Paris to study chemistry with the famous French chemist Antoine François Fourcroy in preparation for further education with the famous clinician Maximilian Stoll in Vienna. His successful rescue of Count Karl Harrach from a near-fatal disease brought him the fabulous fee of ten thousand gulden and his growing reputation led to his being called to the bedside of Emperor Francis I. Later, he was named personal doctor to the Duke of Reichstadt, the son born to the marriage of Napoleon with the daughter of Francis I.

In 1817, Dr. Staudenheim was Beethoven's personal physician. As a strong proponent of the use of baths in the treatment of disease, he suggested that Beethoven visit Karlsbad and Franzensbad and, both in 1820 and 1822, recommended that

Beethoven take the waters at Baden near Vienna. Dr. Stauden-heim also strongly urged his patient to avoid all forms of alcohol, a recommendation Beethoven did not heed. Beethoven's disinclination to follow his doctor's orders is probably to blame for the sudden end to their relationship in 1824.

### Dr. Carl Smetana (1774-1827)

Beethoven's contacts with this doctor, who was not ranked among the most prominent physicians of Vienna, appeared to be somewhat more formal. Dr. Smetana became personally acquainted with the composer in 1816 when he successfully performed a hernia operation on Beethoven's nephew Karl. When Beethoven took the novel step of turning to Dr. Smetana in 1819 in connection with his hearing difficulties, Karl noted his astonishment at this decision, writing in a conversation book: "But Smetana is just a surgeon!" According to Anton Schindler, however, Smetana had also made a name for himself in the treatment of hearing disorders.

Beethoven went to Dr. Smetana again in the fall of 1822 after the unhappy experience his deafness caused at the presentation of his opera, *Fidelio*. As before, the treatments failed. Still, Beethoven consulted Dr. Smetana for treatment of his severe eye inflammations in 1823 and 1824.

### Dr. Anton Braunhofer

Dr. Braunhofer, professor of natural history and a popular general practitioner, became Beethoven's doctor of preference in the summer of 1824. Anton Schindler tells us that Braunhofer had "a certain Viennese vulgarity," which obviously worked its charm on Beethoven who rigorously complied with his orders for a relatively long time. Writing from Baden, where Dr. Braunhofer had sent him to rest and recover, Beethoven reported in detail on the state of his health.

The relationship with Dr. Braunhofer must have been a warm and friendly one at first, for on 11 May 1825, in response to the doctor's request for some bars of music from him—"only a few insignificant ones, it's just to have something in your own handwriting"—Beethoven sent him the well-known "little canon" on the text, "*Doktor sperrt das Tor dem Tod, Note hilft auch aus der Not*" (WoO 189). And before then, on 28 March 1820, a song that

Beethoven had composed just for Dr. Braunhofer had appeared as a supplement to the *Wiener Zeitschrift für Kunst* with the inscription "*Abendlied unterm gestirnten Himmel*, set to music and dedicated to Dr. Braunhofer by Ludwig van Beethoven."

Unfortunately, this friendship too went on the rocks because of Beethoven's growing lack of confidence. He wrote in a conversation book on May 1825: "...the instructions of this Braunhofer have already gone wrong several times, and anyhow he seems pretty limited to me and a crazy man besides." Despite this loss of confidence, Dr. Braunhofer maintained his relationship with Beethoven and took care of him again in February 1826 when he was having trouble with "a rheumatic or gouty condition." Only at the end of 1826, when Beethoven was sick with his mortal illness, did Dr. Braunhofer, and Dr. Staudenheim too, refuse to provide any further care, which suggests that both of these outstanding doctors felt they had previously been treated harshly by Beethoven.

## Dr. Andreas Ignaz Wawruch (1773-1842)

Dr. Wawruch came from the Moravian part of what was once Czechoslovakia and studied philosophy and theology at the university in Olmütz before going to Prague to study medicine. After receiving his doctorate, he became a resident physician at the medical clinic for doctors in Vienna, directed by Professor Johann Valentin von Hildenbrand. By an imperial decree of 16 June

1811, Dr. Wawruch was granted permission, as docent for medical history and literature, to hold lectures in Latin. With a further imperial decree in May 1812, he was called to Prague as professor of pathology and pharmacology, where he was one of the university's most popular teachers until he left in 1819. In that year, he became director of the medical clinic in Vienna and professor for clinical pathology and internal therapy for advanced surgeons, a position he held until his death on 21 March 1842. Dr. Wawruch was a member of the imperial doctors' society in Vienna and a contributor to an imperial medical journal in which many of his scientific works were published. In addition to writing his *Essay on a Pathological Solution to the Nature of East Indian Cholera*, he devoted himself especially to the study of tapeworm disease (*taeniasis*) and wrote an extensive monograph on the subject.

Dr. Wawruch was an enthusiastic musician as well and a very good cellist, who for this reason took Beethoven's case during the last phase of his final illness very seriously. When he assumed responsibility for Beethoven's treatment, on the third day after the composer had returned to Vienna from Gneixendorf at the beginning of December 1826, he introduced himself to his new patient with the words, "A great admirer of yours who will do everything possible to give you relief soon." Dr. Wawruch was already highly regarded in Vienna at the time and had been asked to come by Beethoven's friend Karl Holz after both Dr. Staudenheim and Dr. Braunhofer had refused.

Seen from today's perspective, Dr. Wawruch's treatment of Beethoven was completely appropriate and correct and, given the contemporary state of knowledge, expertly applied. Therefore one must take strong exception to later, unqualified criticism of this outstanding doctor by Anton Schindler and by Gerhard von Breuning in his memoirs, *Aus dem Schwarzspanierhaus*, published in 1874. We can dismiss Schindler's remarks as those of a layman, but Breuning, who was a doctor, provides a very poor recommendation for himself as a physician with his disparaging remarks about Wawruch's care of Beethoven, without putting forward any alternative solutions of his own.

Soon after Beethoven died, Dr. Wawruch, as his last doctor, wrote a precise account of his illness, which the modest man never published. Only after Dr. Wawruch died did his writings become known to the public through the efforts of his widow.

In Dr. Wawruch's presence, Dr. Johann Seibert, chief surgeon of the General Hospital, made four abdominal punctures to relieve the accumulation of fluid in Beethoven's abdominal cavity.

## Dr. Johannes Wagner (1800-1832)

Dr. Wagner was born in Braunau in Bohemia and became assistant to Professor Dr. Lorenz Biermayer at the pathological museum of the anatomical institute in Vienna. In this capacity, Wagner served as the dissector at Beethoven's autopsy, which was carried out in the composer's apartment in the *Schwarzspanierhaus* on 27 March 1827, the day after he died.

After Dr. Biermayer was dismissed in 1829, Dr. Wagner was named his successor and made an associate professor for pathological anatomy. Dr. Wagner was a very gifted person and contributed significantly to developments in this field. He drew his conclusions about the nature of a disease from typical and distinctive organic changes and ascribed particular importance to the correct interpretation of anatomical findings. His most famous student was Dr. Carl von Rokitansky, who became assistant to Dr. Wagner at the pathological-anatomical institute in 1831.

# Franz Schubert
## (1797 - 1828)

Hardly any other great composer's music has found its way so directly to the hearts of so many people as that of Franz Schubert, and no other great composer has paid a higher price for his art. For years, Schubert—a true favorite of the gods and a born master of melody—was perceived by many people as essentially a shy, modest, and rather simple musical schoolmaster, with funny round glasses and quaint Biedermeier clothes, who created music purely from inspiration and little more. Musical operettas and fictionalized biographies contributed to the trivializing cliché of the composer Schubert in Heinrich Berté's operetta *Das Dreimäderlhaus* (produced in America and England as *Blossom Time*), and of the roly-poly Schubert, who was called "Schwammerl" (literally "little mushroom") by his friends.

This old, trite picture of Schubert began to be corrected in recent years. Publication of the complete edition of his compositions has enabled us to see the incredible riches in his life's work. We have been able to address his biography in both psychoanalytical and sociopolitical terms, and the stereotype of "sweet, lovable Franzl" has fallen by the wayside. Unfortunately, efforts to lay bare the psyche of Schubert the man and Schubert the artist have themselves led to a new form of legend-creation, with Schubert coming to be portrayed as a neurotic. Neurosis is supposed to have lent him a defense mechanism against mental collapse, the strength needed for his intense and profound creative activity. With this shift in emphasis, Schubert's music has been interpreted as an act of self-therapy, a working-out of his grief from traumas suffered in his childhood and adolescence by which he struggled to surmount conflicts arising from his oedipal complex.

Such a psychoanalytical approach obviously overemphasizes the effects of Schubert's family environment on his personality development and gives too little attention to historical events in the period from 1815 to the March 1848 revolution. It underemphasizes the significance of contemporary social and political factors on Schubert's ability to achieve artistic independence through the medium of his musical expression. Today we know that his depressive personality structure and the "death wish" we sense in many of his works were the result not just of decisive childhood experiences but, in addition, of contemporaneous reactions of resignation and weariness with life induced by the repressive social climate of the Metternich era.

The reinterpretation of Schubert's biography in terms of such psychological and sociopolitical factors has contributed materially to a fundamental revision of the age-old prettifying cliches. But the tendency of recent times to glorify Schubert can only end in yet another distortion of the man and his work. By declaring him to be some kind of superman possessed of a demonic creative urge and the quintessential musical genius, we compromise the rational view of Schubert that has only recently been won after so much effort. Moreover, we risk attracting the "deconstructionists," whose only interest is making money through the now-fashionable process of systematically taking great artists apart in books and films.

The key to Schubert, who seems to be so popular and yet so little understood even today and about whom Beethoven on his deathbed said, "Truly, a divine spark lives in this man Schubert," lies in each person's ability to discover for himself the inconceivable wealth of detail and inimitable charm of his music, which is able to sweep us from the sun-flooded heights to the unreachable depths. How difficult this discovery can be for some people is shown by a comment George Bernard Shaw wrote during his early years as a music critic. Discussing Schubert's *"Great C-major Symphony"* (which in the competent view of Robert Schumann was "the greatest piece of instrumental music written since Beethoven"), Shaw wrote: "a more exasperatingly brainless composition was never put on paper." The reason Schubert was so fundamentally misunderstood by the music world for so many years may be that the unprecedented originality and daring of his music could be fully grasped only gradually as music's expressive possibilities developed further in the decades after his death. We are fully justified in including him among the greatest composers, for with the boldness of his music, ranking with that of Beethoven's last string quartets, he proclaimed himself the direct heir to the three great Vienna classical masters: Haydn, Mozart, and Beethoven.

In an effort to explain this rather problematical personality and artist, Schubert research has sought to trace every step of his life. The discussion to follow will highlight the medical aspects, which have often been either misinterpreted or simply neglected for lack of medical knowledge and understanding, and will attempt to place them in the context of relevant biographical, historical, sociological, and artistic circumstances. This may help us to better understand his individual periods of productivity as well as his specific musical compositions.

## At Home and in the Boarding School

At 1:30 in the afternoon of the last day of January 1797, Franz Peter Schubert was born in the Vienna suburb of Himmelpfortgrund. His birth took place in the kitchen of one of the sixteen small apartments in the building known as "Zum roten Krebsen" ("The Red Crab"). He was the son of the schoolteacher Franz Theodor Schubert and his wife Elisabeth, née Vietz. Schubert is the only great Viennese classical master who was born in that city, even though his parents were not originally from Vienna. They came from the Altvatergebirge region in the Moravian district of what is now the Czech Republic. Fourteen Schubert children were born within the confines of the barely 380-square-foot apartment. Only five of them lived past their first year. In a family living so crammed together in such a small space, the deaths of baby brothers and sisters would inevitably leave deep and lasting impressions on the surviving children. Even Franz Schubert, who was the twelfth to be born, consciously experienced the death of his little sister Aloisia Magdalena when he was three years old, or at least he must have felt the sorrow immediately around him from the grief of his parents, especially his mother.

Such early childhood impressions could well have caused Schubert's demonstrably early melancholy disposition and his affinity for themes that turn on the subject of death and dying. H. J. Fröhlich seeks to substantiate this possibility with the text from Schubert's first surviving song, *Hagars Klage in der Wüste* (*Hagar's Lament in the Desert*, D5, where "D" is a reference to Otto Erich Deutsch's catalogue of Schubert's compositions), composed on 30 March 1811 when he was fourteen years old and which begins with the words: "Here I sit on a hill of burning sand and before me lies my dying child." Modern psychoanalysis demonstrates convincingly that early childhood experiences are important and not to be underestimated, and we obviously should not ignore their possible impact on the psyche of Franz Schubert.

The child Franz undoubtedly was confronted directly with poverty, pain, sickness, and death in the family's crowded quarters. But the immediate physical contact with his siblings and especially with his mother, who loved him dearly, gave him strong feelings of comfort and security. These feelings are evident in his exceptionally strong attachment to his brother Ferdinand, his elder by two years, to whom he once wrote in a moment of severe emotional crisis many years later: "You and only you are my closest friend, tied to me with every strand of my heart!" And these feelings would explain the deep pain he felt when his mother died, an emotion that became a permanent part of his music.

In the autumn of 1801, Schubert's father moved the family to a house he had purchased in the Säulengasse. The move must have been a major experience for the young Franz, even though the house was only about three minutes away from the old apartment. It meant not only the loss of old, familiar surroundings, but also the beginning of the first lessons to prepare him for elementary school, as intended by his pedagogically ambitious father. It is certainly conceivable, perhaps even probable, that these changes made a meaningful contribution to the emotional development of the four-year-old lad; but to try to turn the primal experience of "moving" into the explanation for Schubert's later fondness for the theme of "the wanderer," as H. J. Fröhlich is inclined to do, is probably going too far. In its new environment, the family continued to be a closely integrated society, one in which Franz, as the youngest of the brothers, was brought up with affection and indulgence by a father who was otherwise inclined to preside over the household with patriarchal severity.

In 1803, Franz began to attend the school run by his father and apparently stood at the head of his class right from the start. It quickly became evident that his greatest interest was music. Indeed, his gift for music was so pronounced that soon neither his older brother Ignaz, who gave him piano lessons, nor his father, who had begun to instruct him on the violin when he was eight years old, had anything more they could teach him. Franz therefore was passed on to Michael Holzer, choir director and organist at the nearby Lichtental parish church, for instruction. Holzer was supposed to teach him harmony and counterpoint as well as how to play the organ. From his brother Ferdinand, we learn that even then Schubert composed songs and short pieces for the piano and had written a string quartet. Schubert may not have been a Wunderkind like Mozart, but he shared with him a precocious urge to compose music. Still, it was a surprise when, after a short time, Holzer came to the boy's father and, with emotion, told him, "I never had such a pupil before. When I wanted to teach him something new, he already knew it. Finally I no longer gave him any more lessons, but just enjoyed myself with him and silently watched him in wonder." Holzer probably was the first to encourage the budding creative impulses of the exceptionally sensitive child and was the first person outside the Schubert family whom the boy came to trust. The enduring impression left by this simple man on Schubert's soul can be gauged by the fact that, at thirteen, Schubert dedicated his first work for the church, a mass, to Holzer in grateful remembrance. He remained devoted to Holzer until he died.

According to a source held privately in Switzerland and mentioned for the first time by E. Hilmar, at a point prior to applying for Franz's admission to the Kaiserlich-königliches Stadtkonvikt (an imperial boarding school at the high school and university levels for commoners), Schubert's father went to see Antonio Salieri, Vienna's most highly regarded teacher of music composition at the time, probably to ask the famous and influential maestro to take on his son's further musical education. In this connection, it seems likely that Salieri personally interested himself in Franz Schubert's acceptance as a choirboy in the imperial court chapel. Salieri was of special importance to Schubert's further growth as a composer, because for the first time the boy came into contact with a first-class musician who—unlike Holzer—could give him valuable advice and ideas on how to compose.

After passing the entrance examination, Franz Schubert, together with a boy named Franz Müller, was admitted on 1 October 1808 as a choirboy to the imperial boarding school located on the Universitätsplatz in Vienna. The school's announcement soliciting applications for the two vacancies indicated that, in addition to having the relevant scholastic and vocal qualifications, the applicants would have to certify that they had already survived a case of smallpox. Therefore we know that Schubert must have had this disease at some time in his early years. In reading the record of "The Births and Deaths in the Family of the Schoolteacher Franz Schubert," we find that Franz's brother Josef died of smallpox on 18 October 1798 at the age of five. In view of the tight living conditions in the little apartment at The Red Crab, it seems reasonable to assume that young Franz, then not quite two years old, was also infected by this widespread disease and, fortunately, unlike his older brother, was able to survive. The reason details of Schubert's bout with this disease are lacking is that smallpox occurred often among the poorer elements of society, as the result of extremely poor sanitation and crowded living conditions. Smallpox was reported only when it had a fatal outcome.

The boarding school, run by Catholic priests, was regarded as an outstanding educational institution for students who were not members of the aristocracy and acceptance into it was a sign of distinction in and of itself. The solid literary education Schubert was able to acquire there is apparent in the numerous literary texts he adapted for his songs. Schubert had the unanticipated good luck to have as school director Dr. Innocenz Lang, a priest with a personal interest "in making up a full orchestra solely of pupils from the school and training all of us young people of various ages...to the point that we were able to perform a full symphony and, as a finale, the noisiest overture possible every evening." By this time, music came before everything else with Schubert, so it is hardly a surprise that even his first report card, from the year 1809, noted his "special musical talent." A year later, the school authorities ordered that "particular care be given to Schubert's musical education because he has such an outstanding gift for the art of music." Schubert subsequently received instruction in basso continuo as well as in playing the piano, viola, and violincello from the court organist Václav Ruzicka. His reaction was much the same as choir director Holzer's had been. After only a few hours of instruction, Ruzicka shook his head, saying, "I can't teach him anything, he's learned everything from God." Because of his extraordinary musical aptitude, Schubert was entrusted with the post of "assistant director" of the orchestra in 1811 when he was fourteen years old, without turning the older members against him.

In addition to receiving a comprehensive musical education, Schubert made many fast friends at the boarding school who would turn out to be important to both his artistic development and the emergence of his whole personality in later years. Schubert and his circle of friends undoubtedly had one thing in common—a desire for change in the political conditions at the time, which imposed tight restraints on personal freedoms. If these young men were not revolutionaries in the true sense of the word, they certainly made up the advance guard leading to the riots and insurrections of 1830 and 1848.

In the old cliché, Schubert was pictured as a dreamy, unrealistic, naïve musician, interested only in his music and barely aware of what was going on around him. Today we know the social evening gatherings that centered around Schubert at the piano playing his own music (and hence came to be called "Schubertiads") were very much devoted to discussion of current events and political developments. An incident with his friend Johann Senn (to be discussed shortly) shows that Schubert himself ran into trouble with the police. Even if he did not end up being convicted as his friend was, from that time on he was on the police list of suspicious persons. This could be one of the

reasons why many publishers hesitated to accept his compositions or even turned them down. George R. Marek has called
attention for the first time to a recently discovered document (unfortunately damaged by fire) dated 15 September 1829 that relates
to this situation. In this document, Count Sedlnitzky, the chief of
police in Vienna, recommended to the emperor that he suspend
the plan to award Franz Schubert's father a gold medal for long
service in the field of education. Clearly, Schubert once seemed
so politically unreliable to the reactionary authorities that his father's
career was in jeopardy. Schubert had another brush with the
police when a club to which he belonged—the Ludlamshöhle—
was raided and its members were jailed.

Life in the boarding school was strictly regimented, teaching
methods were applied with military discipline, and the students
were allowed out only in groups accompanied by a priest. This
environment naturally took its toll on the young man's emotional
development and could have been decisive in his early total commitment to music. "Always was serious and less friendly...seemed
quiet and indifferent, but reacted to the effects of music in the
most lively way"—so Schubert was portrayed by Josef von Spaun,
a fellow student some nine years older and one of his best friends
in later life. In every free moment granted to the pupils for recre-
ation, Schubert stood at his desk and sought to clothe his feelings
in song. Is it any wonder, then, that the very earliest of his works
to be preserved is a piano fantasy (in G, D1) for four hands composed of "twelve different pieces" completed between 8 April
and 1 May 1810?

Schubert's first years at the boarding school must have been
very hard on him, as shown by the words he spoke to Spaun
when the latter was leaving the school in the fall of 1809: "Now
you, you lucky person, are escaping from prison." Such a mental
outlook perhaps explains why Schubert was such an enthusiastic
fan of the ballads of the contemporary poet Johann Rudolf
Zumsteg and of the youthful Schiller's often rather exalted verse,
and why he chose again and again the themes of death and the
transience of life, even in his later works. For example, after the
first song, *Hagars Klage*, came a series of songs with titles that
seem most unusual for a young man of fourteen years: *Der*

*Vatermörder* (*The Son Who Killed His Father*, D10), *Totengräberlied* (*Song of the Gravedigger*, D44), *Leichenfantasie* (*Fantasy on a Corpse*, D7), and others.

Schubert's intensive preoccupation with music inevitably led to poorer scholastic performance in other school subjects, a matter that drew rising displeasure from his father, who expected more of his son than just becoming a music teacher. As early as 1809, his father must have complained about his composing activities, for Schubert told his friend Spaun that his father must not know he often secretly wrote down his musical ideas and intended to dedicate himself to music. In 1811 a battle over this issue broke out between father and son. Schubert's father told him he would no longer be permitted to come home if he persisted in composing. This quarrel caused severe emotional conflict in the boy, who had been raised to honor his father, and shook the still immature lad to his very core. The hardest blow, however, came on 28 May 1812 when Schubert's beloved mother died of typhoid fever in her fifty-sixth year. Moved to reconciliation by the tragic event, his father, lifted his threat and began to acquiesce somewhat to his son's wish to compose. Spaun wrote in his remembrances: "Now the bars were down; his father acknowledged his son's great talent and let him do as he liked." Salieri even announced that he was prepared to provide instruction to the highly gifted student at no cost, and on 18 June 1812 Schubert made a note: "Began counterpoint."

Despite the reconciliation, the fundamental differences between father and son would never be fully bridged. Now, however, Schubert could go about composing to his heart's content without feeling guilty or being secretive about it. Because his voice was changing, he had not been a soprano soloist in the imperial court chapel for some time. Finally he dropped out of the choir altogether, which gave him even more time to devote to his study of music. His handwritten note of relief is found in the score of one mass: "Schubert, Franz, screeched for the last time, 26 July 1812." One last year at the boarding school remained, and it was a thoroughly happy one for Franz, a period in which he wrote his first opera score as well as the first string quartets and numerous minuets and trios "of exceptional beauty."

Dr. Johann Adam Schmidt, who once had played quartets with Mozart and whom Spaun had shown some of Schubert's early compositions, uttered the prophetic words: "Given that this minuet was written by a not yet grown child, then this child is destined to become a master such as has seldom existed." Life in the Schubert family was not upset when the father brought home a new wife, Anna Kleyenböck, twenty years younger than he, in April 1813. She was a kindly woman, sincerely concerned with being on good terms with Franz. He decided not to remain at the boarding school this year and went home to live. As a kind of homecoming present, he brought with him the score of his first symphony (in D major, D82), dedicated to the school director, Dr. Lang, as an expression of his gratitude and sealed with an inscription signifying his final departure from the school: "Finis et fine [Finished and done]. Vienna, 28 October 1813." He did not stay long at home with his parents, however. After being called three times by military authorities to serve as a conscript, Schubert decided to steer clear of such problems in the future by becoming a schoolmaster's assistant, according to his brother Ferdinand. But even before his final examination at the teachers' training school on 19 August 1814, he had completed an opera, *Der Teufels Lustschloss* (D84), and presented it to his teacher Salieri, who made the enthusiastic comment: "He can do everything—songs, masses, string quartets, and now an opera besides!"

A much more important step in Schubert's life was his Mass no. 1 in F (D105). Its first performance at the Lichtental church was so successful that it was repeated some ten days later, on 26 October 1814, in the court church of St. Augustine, with the seventeen-year-old composer conducting in the same place where he had served as a choirboy for five years.

As exhilarated as he was with this success, Schubert had yet another experience that led to a veritable ecstasy of composing: he fell in love. The object of his emotions was Therese Grob, sixteen years old, for whom he had written the soprano solos in his mass. Only three days after the first performance of the mass, his love for Therese inspired him to write the composition that today is generally looked on as marking the true beginning of the

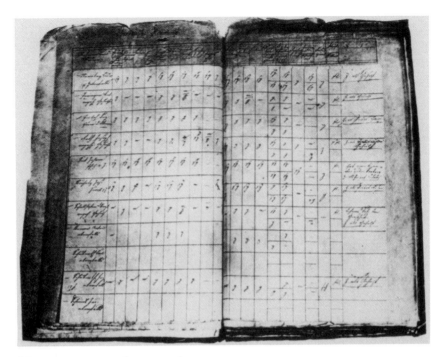

THE RECORD OF SCHUBERT'S GRADES AS A STUDENT AT THE TRAINING
SCHOOL FOR ELEMENTARY TEACHERS IN 1814.

genre of German lieder, *Gretchen am Spinnrade* (*Gretchen at the
Spinning Wheel*, D118).

The outpouring of works that followed can only be likened to
the eruption of a volcano. In 1815 alone, Schubert composed 144
songs, including one of the greatest lieder ever written, *Erlkönig*
(D328), as well as two symphonies, two masses, two sonatas, five
theatrical works, a string quartet, and various choral works. The
next year was almost the same; besides two more symphonies
and many other works, he wrote an incredible one hundred and
six lieder. One of these songs, *Der Wanderer* (D489), has been
called the "incarnation of romantic 'Weltschmerz'" (i. e., a mood
of sentimental sadness) and may have been prompted by his farewell to life at home with his parents and, simultaneously, a final
leave-taking from the schoolteaching he found so burdensome.

A freehand drawing of Franz Schubert by his friend Moritz von Schwind.

Because of strains at home, Schubert moved in with his friend Franz von Schober and Schober's mother. But when Schober's older brother returned home, Schubert was forced to live with his parents again. Having only the usual slim resources of the free-lance artist, he was compelled once more to help his father with the chores of teaching. Relatively few compositions date from this difficult period and although Schubert, like Mozart before him, had a marked dislike of giving music lessons, he was happy enough under the circumstances to accept an invitation of Count Johann Carl Esterhazy von Galántha to give instruction in music to the count's two daughters at their estate in Zseliz on the Hungarian border during the summer months of 1818.

In the first weeks in his new surroundings, Schubert was "delighted to have tossed every worrisome burden aside." In one of his letters from this time, he said, "I live and compose like a god." In fact, however, his output was quite modest apart from the piano pieces for four hands he needed for instructional purposes, a form of chamber music he would later do so much to enrich. The blame for this lapse almost certainly lay in Schubert's lack of stimulating conversation partners, about which he complained in one of his letters: "Surrounded by all these people, actually I'm all alone." And this situation was little helped by a summer love affair with a pretty chambermaid, Pepi Pöckelhofer, who was later accused—wrongly—of having infected Schubert with a venereal disease; chronological grounds alone serve to refute the charge.

## Free at Last

After his return from Zseliz in November 1818, Schubert was determined to turn his back on school teaching once and for all. This decision led to violent quarrels with his father and ended in a rupture in their relationship. From an allegory Schubert wrote some four years later, we get an idea of how shattering he found this break between them. His decision to follow the uncertain career of a composer also resulted in the loss of the love of his young life, Therese Grob. Years later, long after she had married a baker, Schubert would still recall affectionately, "She was sweet and kindhearted...and since then, no one else has succeeded in pleasing me as well or better than she did."

The active support of his friends helped Schubert to cope with these bitter experiences. But most helpful was his trip to the province of Oberösterreich (Upper Austria) west of Vienna in June 1819 with his new friend Johann Michael Vogl, a baritone at the court opera, who would become the finest interpreter of his lieder. Schubert enjoyed getting to know this lovely part of Austria, especially since so many of his closest friends—Spaun, Holzapfel, Stadler, and Johann Mayrhofer—came from there. They sent news of Schubert's arrival ahead to the town of Steyr, Vogl's birthplace. The warm reception, the recognition, and admiration he received there greatly helped him to get over his emotional crisis.

Evidence of the carefree happiness of this summer can be found in the Piano Sonata in A Major (D664), which Schubert composed in Steyr for the daughter of one of his hosts, and especially in the refreshing loveliness of the Piano Quintet in A Major known as *Die Forelle* (*The Trout,* D667), which Schubert began there under commission from Sylvester Paumgartner, general manager of a local mine and an ardent cellist.

The commission was prompted by Paumgartner's wish to have a chamber music version of the song, *Die Forelle* (D550), which Schubert had written in 1816 and Paumgartner never tired of hearing. Latter-day Schubert researchers assume that, in setting to music this particular text written by the German poet Christian Friedrich Daniel Schubart (1739-1791), the composer wanted to express something crucial, something reaching far beyond the fable it tells, and that Schubert must have found the message concealed in the poem an inviting way of doing so. We know, for example, that the "catching of the trout through cunning and deceit by an underhanded thief" was an obvious, if somewhat veiled, allusion to the fate of the poem's author. The poet was abducted under perfidious circumstances by the reactionary, despotic Duke Carl Eugen of Württemberg in 1777 for making critical remarks about the nobility. He was later incarcerated in the fortress Hohenasperg and kept there in solitary confinement for ten years.

F. Reininghaus is certainly correct in assuming that this poem appealed especially to Schubert. He and his circle of friends were confronted by similar arch-conservative political conditions under the Metternich regime in Vienna, and the opportunity to disseminate its encrypted message by means of Schubert's song suited them very much. Although such an interpretation can be challenged, of course, it fits well with the current view that Schubert was not, as previously assumed, indifferent to political developments in the years before the 1830 and 1848 uprisings. An event that shook Schubert's circle of friends in 1819 provides evidence of his political involvement. When Schubert's friend Johann Senn, son of one of the leaders of the uprising in Tyrol in 1809, was arrested during a student assembly, Schubert must also have been taken into custody for a short time by the police. The police report says that "the friend who was with [Senn], the teaching assistant Franz Schubert from the Rossau district...spoke up in similar tones and harangued the arresting officials with taunts and insults."

In many respects, 1820 was a critical year for Schubert. The slender success of his two operas, *Die Zauberharfe* (*The Magic Harp,* D644) and *Die Zwillingsbrüder* (*The Twin Brothers,* D647), disappointed and depressed him. Moreover, his financial situation was increasingly precarious. Finally some of his friends banded together to publish Schubert's compositions at their own expense.

Chief among them were Schubert's "man Friday" Josef Hüttenbrenner and Leopold von Sonnleithner, at whose home evening musical concerts were regularly held in which many of Schubert's works had already been introduced to a broader group of music lovers. Then, after difficult and depressing years, things started unmistakably to improve from an artistic point of view. In the field of lieder particularly, new works were born, such as the first of the so-called *Suleika* songs (D720), which Johannes Brahms regarded as the most beautiful lied ever written. In the first months of 1822, unusually positive reviews of his works and increasing public acclaim gave Schubert the feeling that, in the realm of music, not only had he been called, he had been chosen.

The most important development in that year, however, was Schubert's new reconciliation with his father. It must have occurred before the summer began and it liberated him from a heavy emotional burden. The break with his father must have made his feelings for his deceased mother even more intense. The grief felt by the then fifteen-year-old boy at the death of his mother must have been unbounded, and he may well have never fully gotten over it. His pain is evident in a series of youthful compositions such as the Salve regina (D27) composed four weeks after her death. But the song *Grablied fur die Mutter* (*Dirge for Mother*, D616), which he wrote in June 1818 for Josef Ludwig von Streinsberg, a fellow student from boarding-school days who had just lost his mother, was certainly composed with his own dead mother in mind, too. The reconciliation with his father could suddenly have brought vividly to mind all his memories of happy childhood. It is moving to read Franz Schubert's confession of the soul where, in the form of an allegory, later titled Mein Traum (*My Dream*), he reveals to the world all the emotional pain and suffering he had experienced. This document, which psychoanalysts find extremely informative and could be called a kind of autobiography, was written by Schubert on 3 July 1822 (he was twenty-five years old). Because of its importance in understanding the development of Schubert's personality, it is given here in its entirety.

> I was a brother of many brothers and sisters. Our father and our mother were good to us. I felt a

deep love for all of them. Once upon a time my father took us to a merry feast. My brothers were very happy to be there. But I was sad. Then my father came to me and commanded me to eat the delicious food and enjoy it. But I could not, which made my father angry and he banished me from his sight. I turned away and, with a heart full of endless love for those who rejected it, journeyed to faraway places. For years and years I was divided by feelings of great pain and great love. Then I learned of my mother's death. I hurried to see her, and my father, moved by sorrow, did not keep me from entering. I saw her body there. Tears flowed from my eyes. I saw her lying as she was before in the dear days of old when we did as she would have us do.

And we followed her in grief and the coffin sank from sight. From this time on, I remained at home as before. Then one day my father led me to his favorite garden. He asked me if I liked it. But I found the garden repellent and I was afraid to say anything. Then, in a rage, he asked me a second time if I liked the garden? Trembling, I answered no. Then my father struck me and I fled. And a second time, I turned away, and with a heart full of endless love for those who rejected it, journeyed yet again to faraway places. For years and years, I sang my songs. When I would sing of love, it would be like pain to me. And yet when I would sing only of pain, it was like love to me. Thus was I divided by love and pain.

And one day I learned of a blessed maiden who had just died. And around her tomb a circle turned in which many youths and ancients slowly walked forever as though in bliss. They spoke softly not to awaken the maiden.

Sublime thoughts seemed to flash everlastingly out
of the maiden's sepulcher onto the young men,
like sparks of light sounding softly. Then I felt a
great yearning to walk there too. Only a miracle,
the people said, leads into the circle. But with my
lowered gaze fixed on the tomb, I slowly approached in deep devotion and perfect faith and
before I knew it I was in the circle from which the
most pleasant sound arose; and I experienced bliss
eternal as though crushed into a single moment.
And I saw my father too, reconciled and loving.
He closed me in his arms and wept. And I wept
even more.

Franz Schubert

There is hardly a more stirring indictment from one who has
been expelled from his father's house than this one, and hardly a
more moving testament to a son's inextinguishable longing for
his dead mother. In addition, there was his own longing for
death, his own death wish.

Arnold Schering once sought to demonstrate that this alle-
gorical tale could be seen as the first draft of Schubert's B-minor
Symphony (D759), called the *Unfinished Symphony*, and that the
division in two parts mentioned in the allegory explains why the
symphony finally came to consist of only two movements. The
Mass no. 5 in A-flat Major (D678) that came before the symphony,
as well as the four-movement Piano Sonata in C (D760), known
as the *Wanderer-fantasie* that came just after it, are also said to
have had their origins in this dream allegory, an interpretation
that we are not necessarily obliged to share. Schubert's poetry in
prose, *Mein Traum*, seems rather to indicate the design behind
his entire artistic creative activity: "When I would sing of love, it
would be like pain to me. And yet when I would sing only of
pain, it was like love to me." The whole magic of Schubert's
music lies essentially in this division between joy and pain: "This
singular aura of nostalgia which hovers over even his gayest works
and yet, on the other hand, the powerful affirmation of life with
which the fundamentally tragic tone of so many of his works is
lightened by a warm and restful glow of quiet confidence."

Perhaps the dichotomy also reflects the odd fact that, from the beginning, Schubert's periods of dejection and nostalgia alternated constantly with times of belligerent assurance and vigorous self-assertiveness. Such polarity is found in the *Unfinished Symphony* and the immediately following *Wanderer-fantasie,* as well as in many works from his later years.

## An Ominous Disease

Fate caught up with Schubert in 1823.  Signs that he must have contracted syphilis some time in 1822 appeared in the first days of January.  His friend Franz von Schober, regarded as something of a Casanova, may have enticed him into the sexual affair that would prove to have grave consequences. A possible indication of when it took place comes from the words of warning, taken from one of Goethe's poems, that Schubert had written in a friend's album on 28 November 1822:

> To each his own, nothing fits all,
> What he does, let each beware,
> Where he is, let each take care,
> And he who's upright, that he doesn't fall.

In some brief comments to their friends on New Year's Eve, Schober too appeared to be summoning courage and fortitude for Schubert and himself, in case the coming year should "prove to be dismal and grim or perhaps even ruinous."  In the first weeks after the outbreak of the disease, Schubert understandably sought to keep his illness a secret from his friends. We know only that he moved in with Schober, and thus could more easily stay out of sight and could be cared for by the two physicians who were treating Schober, Dr. August von Schaeffer and Dr. Josef Bernhardt.  His closest friends accounted for his absence from the evening musical gatherings by assuming that he was involved in grand composing projects. Schubert apparently took only his friend Anselm Hüttenbrenner into his confidence, meeting with him in the company of Schubert's brother Ferdinand on the neutral ground of Frau Sanssouci's apartment. Hüttenbrenner's diary, which unfortunately he burned in 1841, probably would have been the sole source from which we might have derived some immediate details as to the nature and extent of Schubert's symptoms.

The first evidence of the disease to come directly from Schubert himself is in a letter of 28 February 1823 to the music publisher Ignaz von Mosel about his plans for the opera *Alfonso und Estrella* (D732): "Dear honorable Hofrat! Please forgive me for bothering you with a letter again, for the state of my health still does not permit me to leave the house. I have the pleasure, your Honor, to forward herewith the 3d and last act of my opera, including the overture to the 1st act." From this comment we can infer that Schubert's illness had already lasted a few weeks at least, apparently without preventing him from composing. On the contrary, he seems to have reacted to this devastating blow of fate with nothing less than a feverish outburst of composing. In the early months of the dramatic year 1823, many of his best songs were written, such as *Du bist die Ruh* (D776) and *Auf dem Wasser zu singen* (D774), and composition of the opera *Alfonso and Estrella* was completed. But his mood of sadness and regret, his longing for bygone happier days, and his desperate efforts to overcome his emotional distress are most clearly reflected in the Piano Sonata in A Minor (D784), composed in February.

Whether this disease that so drastically affected Schubert's future was the final tragic episode in a long, dissolute way of life or was only the chance outcome of one of his few affairs with women cannot be answered with certainty today, for the views of his friends that have come down to us diverge widely. For example, in 1829, a year after Schubert's death, his friend Johann Mayrhofer, with whom he shared an apartment for long periods of time, wrote: "Duplicity and envy were completely alien to him; in his character, he was a mixture, gentle and rough, pleasure-loving and guileless, sociable and solitary." One of his closest friends, Josef Spaun, gave the Schubert of his memories a similarly positive report: "Schubert was always a man of moderation, and if it wouldn't have been so naturally, his financial situation would have driven him to it." In contrast, Josef Kenner, a former fellow student at the boarding school and later the district commissioner for Freistadt, was definitely more critical in his remarks, which reflected the irreproachable way of life associated with his career. He wrote to Ferdinand Luib in connection with a commemorative publication for the Vienna state archives in 1858: "Whoever knew Schubert knows how he was put together from two natures, each utterly alien to the other, how powerfully in any case his craving for pleasure pulled his psyche down to the cesspool."

In 1868, forty years after Schubert died, Franz von Schober, Schubert's fellow sufferer in those first weeks of their venereal disease (and the person Josef Kenner held accountable for having debauched Schubert), wrote in his memoirs: "Schubert grew more and more dissipated, he visited sleazy districts, hung around in bars, also composing some of his loveliest songs in them, of course." This statement gives the irresistible impression that in publish'.g such a portrayal of Schubert, Schober (who also referred elsewhere to Schubert's "inordinately lewd and sensual living and its inevitable consequences") was intent on absolving himself of the suspicion that he had driven Schubert to such a way of life. Reports of this sort, including a similar one from Wilhelm von Chezy, the vain and moralistic son of the author of *Rosamunde, Princess of Cyprus*, repeatedly picture Schubert as a *bon vivant* who loved good food and drink despite being chronically hard up for cash. But these reports hardly mean that he must therefore have been a loose-living note-scribbler with a fondness for the bottle—a view which Anton Schindler, formerly Beethoven's secretary, emphatically had rejected in 1855.

Contrary to widespread views, Schubert was not invariably shy around women. Only with ladies of the upper classes did he feel inhibited; with women of his own class, he showed no shyness at all. For example, he told his brother Ferdinand in a letter of 29 October 1818 from Zseliz that he hoped for deliverance from his emotional isolation through "a pair of really good girls," and in a letter of 15 July 1819 to him from Steyr, his interest in the fair sex is clear: "In the house where I'm living, there are 8 girls, almost all pretty. You see, I've got to get busy." The reason no lasting tie resulted from Schubert's "fervent and deeply committed love" for Therese Grob is that he feared it would constrict the freedom he needed as an artist to fully develop his creative powers. Why some psychoanalysts attribute Schubert's behavior to a homosexual element in his makeup or charge him with having a troubled relationship with women, because of a neurotic fixation on his mother, is hard to understand. To be able to document a fear of the gentle sex as the basis of a neurosis manifested in a total inability to achieve bonding with a woman (as Fröhlich proposes), the alleged fear of women must first be established. Known passages from letters and notes, in which Schubert repeatedly speaks of the bother girls have caused him, contradict such a notion.

As enthusiastic as Schubert may have been about the fairer sex from time to time, he himself probably was not especially attractive to women. A detailed description of Schubert, who was only five feet, two inches (157 cm.) tall, was written by Dr. Georg Franz Eckel, then the director of the Institute for Veterinary Medicine in Vienna:

> Small in stature but sturdy, with firm muscles and well developed bones not sticking out but more rounded; a short, strong neck; broad and full in the shoulders, chest, and hips; round arms and thighs; small hands and feet; an energetic, powerful stride. A head of thick, brown curly hair crowned his fairly large, round, and massive head. His facial features, with the predominating forehead and chin, were less handsome actually and more expressively severe. His gentle eyes were light brown, if I'm not mistaken, and when he was provoked, they would blaze; they were shaded by bushy eyebrows in a rather marked arch and, from the frequent squinting that shortsighted persons tend to do, seemed smaller than they really were. His stub nose was average size, somewhat turned up.

This description generally agrees with what Anselm Hüttenbrenner mentioned in a letter to Franz Liszt about Schubert's appearance in 1854: "Schubert's looks were far from striking or prepossessing. He was small, with a round, full face and rather chubby. He had a high, bulging forehead. Because he was shortsighted, he

always wore glasses which he even kept on while he slept."
Schubert had a tendency to put on weight as he grew older, as
indicated by comments Bauernfeld made in a letter to him in
1825: "How are you doing, my fat friend? Your tummy has surely
gotten bigger." Wilhelm von Chezy, who did not rate as one of
Schubert's closest friends, referred to him as a "tub of lard" in his
memoirs written in 1863.

These descriptions of Schubert's looks could furnish one explanation for why, as a man, he must not have made any particular impression on women, and his rather clumsy manner may
also have contributed to the meager success of his overtures to
them. Writing to Ferdinand Luib in 1858, Anselm Hüttenbrenner
said bluntly: "So far as the fair sex is concerned, he was an
uninspired suitor, and anything but chivalrous. He neglected his
clothes, and especially his teeth, strongly smelled of tobacco, was
in other words not the least suited to go a-courting." Because
Schubert was also a healthy young man with normal sexual needs,
however, it should not be surprising that he probably turned occasionally to the widely available services of prostitutes, especially when he had the experience and élan of Schober to help
him overcome his presumably strong initial inhibitions. The fact
that Schubert never established a lasting, lifelong relationship with
one woman certainly was due to his enormous desire for freedom, something as necessary for his one great love—composing—as the air he breathed. Freedom must have been the essential
reason for the bachelor life he chose to live, not timidity and
shyness toward women as Schubert caricaturists portray, or an
alleged oedipal complex as so many psychologists try to con-
struct in terms of hatred for his father and love for his mother.
And just as farfetched is the oft-repeated view that Schubert had
homosexual tendencies.

Schubert's sexual desires were undoubtedly satisfied in the
way customary among young men in those days when they were
not married and had no fixed tie to a particular woman. They
passed some hours in sexual dalliance with women of easy virtue. According to official statistics, there were some ten thousand
women of that description—professionals and nonprofessionals
alike—in Vienna during the second decade of the 19th century.

The danger of infection then was especially great, for it was only in 1827 that a form of public health supervision was decreed, at least for professional prostitutes. Even these measures were only sporadically carried out. Consequently, the number of persons suffering from venereal diseases was high.

As if the physical consequences of Schubert's syphilis were not bad enough at the start of 1823, the shock to his mental and emotional state led to a genuine crisis. Schubert revealed the full extent of his despair and desperation most openly in a poem he wrote on 8 May 1823. In it, he captured all the feelings and thoughts that assailed him during this terrible period. Schubert's death wish, already apparent in his prose poem *My Dream*, was made even clearer in this poem, *Mein Gebet* (given here in a literal prose translation):

### My Prayer

With deep desiring born of righteous fear, reaching out for
    better worlds,
Wanting to fill darkest space with love's omnipotent dream.
Holy Father, as recompense for terrible pain, grant your son
    at last
Your love's eternal gleaming as a feast of redemption.
See, my life's tortured way lies annihilated in the dust,
Prey to unheard-of grief as it nears eternal doom.
Destroy it and destroy me too, let all fall into oblivion,
And then, O almighty One, let a pure, strong life be born
    again.

8 May 1823                                         Frz. Schubert

Around Easter, the state of Schubert's health must have improved. In the very month in which he wrote *My Prayer* he decided to tackle the project of composing a song cycle. The poems that make up the cycle were written by Wilhelm Müller, who had chosen from "77 poems from the papers left by a traveling horn player" those known as *Die schöne Müllerin (The Fair Maid of the Mill)*. They must have inspired Schubert because their melancholy nature fully matched his mood of the moment.

The first allusion to Schubert's disease to come from his circle of friends appears in a letter Leopold Kupelwieser wrote on 26 July

1823 to Franz von Schober: "At Collin's yesterday I heard that Schubert is sick; Bradesky is supposed to have brought the news." Matthäus von Collin was the son-in-law of Dr. Bernhardt, one of the two doctors taking care of Schubert, who apparently had dropped a comment about the composer's serious illness. In spite of it, Schubert left for Upper Austria, probably on 25 July, to spend some weeks recuperating, again in the company of Johann Michael Vogl. On 14 August, he wrote to Schober: "I have been busily corresponding with Schaeffer and am feeling fairly well. Whether I'll ever be completely healthy again, I'm inclined to doubt." From this letter, it is apparent Schubert was fully aware of the gravity of his disease and, because he had been constantly in touch with Dr. Schaeffer who was handling his case, symptoms must also have continued in evidence during the trip. It is characteristic of Schubert that even in his illness, he sought to draw nearer to Schober, that elegant tempter whom Schubert looked on as a truly "göttlicher Kerl" (roughly "a really great fellow"). Schober, however, decided to play it safe and go to Breslau for two years to try his luck as an actor there and, probably, to distance himself from the unpleasant business with Schubert.

By the time Schubert had returned to Vienna in the autumn of 1823, his disease must have broken out again after seeming to get better. This recurrence is suggested in a letter Baron Karl von Doblhoff wrote to Schober on 12 November 1823, telling about a side trip he had made to Steyr where Schubert was staying in August and September: "I turned off at Amstetten and went to Steyr by way of Seitenstätten to pay a visit on our beloved 'Schwämmelein.' I found him really quite ill at the time, but you certainly know that already." Back in Vienna, Schubert at first went to live with a friend, but soon thereafter had to be admitted to the Vienna General Hospital for treatments that lasted several weeks. He fell into a deep depression and apparently was able to overcome it only by plunging into a hectic period of composition. Incredibly, Schubert was able to complete his cycle of songs, *Die schöne Müllerin* (D795), in the oppressive surroundings of the hospital, probably in the months of October and November. Wilhelm von Chezy commented: "He had composed the beguiling 'Müllerin' lieder to the accompaniment of a completely different set of pains than those coming from the mouth of the miller's helper suffering from unrequited love, which Schubert made immortal with his music." We do not know any details of this period in the hospital, for no medical records about it can be found in the archives. Letters among Schubert's group of friends, however, indicate that his stay there must have lasted until the middle of November, or at least Schubert was bedridden and in need of treatment up to then. A letter from Moritz von Schwind to Schober on 9 November says:

> Kupelwieser left for Rome day before yesterday. The day before, we had a kind of bacchanal at the Crown. Everyone was there to eat except Schubert, who was still in bed that day. Schaeffer and Bernard [Dr. Bernhardt] who had seen him assure us that he is well on the way to recovery and speak of a period of 4 weeks when he will perhaps be all well again.

Kupelwieser's fiancée Johanna Lutz, in a chatty letter of 18 November, made the offhand remark that "Schubert is healthy again" and then on 9 December added "Schubert is feeling pretty well and already showing signs of not wanting to follow his strict diet much longer." However, the true state of his health was probably being presented in overly optimistic terms. Schubert himself was rather more cautious, as we see in a letter to Schober written on 30 November 1823: "I'm hoping, incidentally, to gain my health back again, and this dear possession, once regained, will make me to forget much of the pain." Curiously enough, he had begun this letter with a much more positive comment on the condition of his health: "Except for the matter of my health, which (thank God) seems finally to be completely settling down, everything is dreadful." Whatever the case may be, the fact that Schubert both began and ended the letter with allusions to his disease suggests that worries about his recovery must have been uppermost in his mind.

By the end of December the worst seems to have been over. A letter written by Schwind to Schober on 24 December 1893 (which gives us the first specific clue about the nature of Schubert's

illness) says: "Schubert is better and it won't be long now before
he will have his own hair again, which had to be cut off because
of the rash. He is wearing a very comfortable wig....He is constantly in the company of his crotchety doctor [Bernhardt]." Just
how well Schubert may have been feeling is indicated in a report
on the New Year's celebrations that Schwind sent to Schober on
2 January 1824: "The New Year's Eve party was a merry affair.
We all gathered at Mohn's....Shortly thereafter Schubert and
Dr. Bernhardt announced their arrival with a little target practice.
Schubert scored and the broken window pane caused an uproar."
Schober heard something similar from Doblhoff, who closed his
7 January 1824 account of this party by saying: "Schubert is almost completely well and almost constantly in the company of
Bernhardt." Schubert's condition was improved enough for him
to take part in drinking bouts even though he had been placed on
a diet by his doctors at this time. We learn some details from a
letter sent by Schwind to Schober in February 1824: "This is how
it was on Schubert's birthday [31 January]. We had a brawl at the
Crown, and although we were all completely drunk, still I really
wish you had been there, for the sake of Schubert's joy over your
good fortune. In vino veritas. They all acted more or less silly,
Schubert went to sleep....Now Schubert has to fast for two weeks
and is staying at home. He looks a lot better and is in high spirits,
is very funny about being famished, and writing innumerable
quartets and 'Deutsche' [so-called 'German' dances] and variations."

Among these variations was the one for flute and piano (D802)
on a theme taken from the song *Trockne Blumen (Dry Flowers)* in
the *Schöne Müllerin* cycle and composed for Schubert's flautist
friend Ferdinand Bogner. More important, however, is the Quartet in A Minor (D804). The completely new realms of sound it
opens up reflect Schubert's true feelings: painful grief over the
fate that had befallen him. And yet, because of his seemingly
quick recovery, he bubbled over with joy of living and cheerfulness as expressed in his well-known Octet in F (D803) written in
February 1824. On 22 February, Schwind informed Schober in a
letter that Schubert had put his wig aside and his hair was showing "the first signs of sweet little curls." A cautious optimism on
the part of Schubert, who was still directed to diet, is reported in

a new exchange of letters between his two friends in early March: "Schubert is really doing well. He says he had felt after some days of the new treatment how the disease was finally broken and everything was different now. He continues to live one day on panadel [bread soup], the next day on veal scallops, and drinks tea by the gallon."

Unfortunately, the improvement did not last. Already by the end of March, new symptoms of a worsening of the disease appeared, as evidenced by a note Schubert made on 27 March 1824: "No one knows another's pain, and no one understands another's joy! We always think we are encountering one another, when we are always only passing one another by. O agony for him who sees that!" Schubert's sheer despair over the recurrent outbreak of symptoms of his disease is betrayed in a letter of 31 March to Leopold Kupelwieser. This cry from the heart reveals the seeming hopelessness of his situation and the true extent of his anxiety:

> I've had the urge to write you for a long time, but I never knew how to get started. Now however I have the chance…and finally I can completely unburden my soul to someone once more. You are so good and trustworthy, surely you will forgive me for many things that others would misunderstand. —In a word, I feel I'm the most unhappy, most wretched man in the world. Imagine a man whose health will never be sound again and who in despair only makes it worse and not better; imagine a man, I say, whose most shining hopes have come to naught, for whom the bliss of love and friendship offers nothing but the greatest pain, for whom the passion (at least something stimulating) for beauty threatens to die away, and ask yourself then if that isn't one wretched, unhappy man? —"My peace is gone, heavy is my heart, find it again shall I never, never again," this I can certainly sing now every day, for every night when I go to bed I hope I'll never wake up, and every morning only reminds me of yesterday's grief.

Schubert must have been unusually upset emotionally when he wrote this letter for, as pointed out by Heinrich Werlé, in a subsequent passage he used the verb *komponieren* in three successive sentences and spelled it differently each time: *componiert, komponiert,* and *componirt.*

We do not know exactly in what way Schubert's condition had worsened toward the end of March 1824. Evidently he had diffuse but severe pains in his left arm. An allusion made by Doblhoff in a letter to Schober to the effect that Schubert was complaining about muscle pains can be so construed, and Schwind mentioned them when writing to Schober on 14 April: "Schubert is not completely fit. He has such pains in his left arm that he can't play the piano at all. Otherwise, he's doing fine." From this comment we can infer that these "muscle pains" probably were not a manifestation of the venereal disease, but rather periostitis, inflammation of the connective tissue at the point of attachment of the underarm muscles, brought about by overexertion, which is fairly common with excessive piano playing. However, because Schubert composed for hours at a time during the winter months, wrapped in blankets and sitting in unheated rooms, the pains could just as well have been caused by long exposure to cold. Evidently his condition soon improved, for Schwind wrote to Kupelwieser on 31 May: "Schubert has gone off to Hungary. He has an opera libretto with him written by Dr. Bernhardt on the theme of the enchanted rose, and he is also thinking about writing a symphony."

When Schubert went to Zseliz with the Esterhazy family for the second time in May 1824, he must have been feeling much better and had considerable artistic plans in mind—including working on the libretto prepared by Dr. Bernhardt. Both his father and his brother, who were aware of the nature of his disease, wrote to tell him how glad they were for the continuing improvement in his health. Of course, his father could not resist making some moralizing comments:

> We are all happy over the state of your health and for your reception into the noble household. Do endeavor, therefore, to guard and preserve your health, that foremost of our earthly possessions....

> We may, indeed, we should enjoy the innocent
> pleasures of life happily and in moderation, in a
> feeling of thanks to God; but in unhappy circum-
> stances as well, we must never let our spirits fail;
> for suffering, too, is one of God's blessings.

His brother Ferdinand wrote a much warmer letter on 3 July,
asking with concern how his health was coming along and telling
him that he was unhappy over Schubert's absence from Vienna.
Schubert answered on 18 July:

> Dearest brother! You can take my word for it, I
> was really somewhat put out that I have only now
> heard from home [that is, his father] and from
> you....Was it merely the pain of my absence which
> caused your tears to fall...or were you remember-
> ing all the tears you have seen me shed? Be that
> as it may, in this moment I feel it even more clearly
> that you and only you are my closest friend, tied
> to me with every strand of my heart! To make
> sure these lines won't tempt you to think I'm not
> well or not in a cheerful frame of mind, let me
> hurry to assure you the contrary. Naturally, that
> happy time when every object seems enveloped
> in a halo of youth is gone, replaced by that fatal
> recognition of reality's misery which I attempt to
> beautify with my imagination (thanks be to God)
> as much as possible....A grand sonata and varia-
> tions on an original theme, both for four hands,
> which I have just composed will serve as proof
> thereof.

The two pieces mentioned were the Sonata in C (D812), known
as the *Grand Duo*, virtually symphonic in its structure, and the
A-flat Variations (D813), in which the dark tones of grief and pain
are constantly dissolved into brighter hues through surprising trans-
formations of the theme.

Schubert's physical well-being probably did not suffer during
the prolonged stay in Zseliz, even though he must have been
nervous and uncertain about what might come next. In a letter to

his friend Schwind in August 1824, he said rather carefully: "I am still well, thank God." What oppressed him most was that, as before, he had no one he could talk to. Writing to Schober on 21 September, he was clearly complaining about this situation: "Here I sit now, all alone in farthest Hungary, where I unfortunately allowed myself to be enticed for the 2d time, without having even one single person to exchange a clever word with." His acute awareness, in his solitude, that his lot had been wrenched by disease and his nostalgic memory of the days when his heart was young and gay are revealed in a poem he wrote and sent with the letter to Schober. The tone of resignation pervading this poem, written "in one of those gloomy hours when I was in particular pain over the vacant, meaningless living that marks our days," reflects how depressed he was.

Even if Schubert did not find anyone to talk to in his "gloomy hours," he found something else to make life in Zseliz interesting: Caroline Esterhazy, the nineteen-year-old daughter of the count. Although Schubert was constrained to hide his infatuation with the "very present beckoning star" (as he called her once) and was fully aware from the beginning that, because of the unbridgeable difference in their social standing, his silent adoration would never be requited, he could not prevent "Cupid's arrow from boring ever deeper in his heart," as Eduard Bauernfeld later reported. His mute affection for Caroline was obviously not reciprocated, even though she must have taken note of it. Baron Karl von Schönstein, a friend of the count's with an excellent tenor voice, confirms this situation indirectly in his account of an exchange between the two: "Once when she jokingly accused Schubert of never having dedicated any of his compositions to her, he replied: What do you mean, everything I do is dedicated to you." And indeed, Schubert remained faithful to his love for Caroline— remembered by his friends as "his visible muse, the Leonora of this musical Tasso"—for the rest of his days. For her, he wrote a series of piano works for four hands, including the popular Fantasie in F Minor (D940). Found among her effects after she died was the autograph score for the Piano Trio in E-flat (D929), which Schubert began in November 1827. Caroline had a calming, restoring effect on Schubert and, in the unanimous opinion of his friends, she remained his "exalting spirit" until he died.

## "Carefree as a Cloud and Healthy"

Schubert finally returned to his beloved Vienna and to his brothers and friends on 16 October 1824. Schwind told Schober on 8 November: "Schubert is here, carefree as a cloud and healthy, rejuvenated anew through pleasure and pain and the merry life." On 2 December Schober wrote a long letter to Schubert in which he said significantly: "How glad I am that you are all well again, soon I will be too." Schober's mention of his own illness in this connection is surely an intimation that the two friends had contracted the same venereal disease.

After 1824, a period of uncertain health, we hear of no health problems worthy of mention in the following year. Schubert resumed his creative activity. As Schwind wrote to Schober on 14 February 1825: "Schubert is well and, after stagnating a while, busy again." With stability in the state of his health, Schubert's good humor returned. Even his renewed disappointment over the arrogant, almost hurtful lack of response from the prince of poets, Johann Wolfgang von Goethe, could not disrupt it. Goethe did not even deign to return the collection of songs forwarded with a dedication from Schubert, much less answer Schubert's letter of early June 1825, which said: "Your Excellency! If with the dedication of these settings of your poems I have succeeded in expressing my boundless admiration for Your Excellency and perhaps gained thereby some slight notice of my insignificant being, then I would celebrate my desire's auspicious success as the most beautiful event in my life."

A letter that Anton Ottenwalt wrote from Linz, where Schubert was visiting him, to Josef von Spaun in Lemberg on 19 July 1825 is informative in many respects. It not only confirms that Schubert was feeling well, but testifies to the resurgence in his creative activities:

> Schubert is here, so far all by himself....Schubert looks so healthy and energetic, is in such a cheerful mood, so friendly to talk to, that you have to

> take heartfelt pleasure in it....He tells us that since
> then, some of his lieder have been taken from
> [Sir Walter] Scott's "The Lady of the Lake." By the
> way, in Gmunden, he worked on his symphony
> which is supposed to be performed in Vienna this
> winter....Only today I wished so much you could
> hear the wonderful new songs that Schubert com-
> posed and sang.

We can read into these words that Schubert, at the time, behaved "like the handsome prince in a fairy-tale"; the letter also provides the first written mention of the lost "Gmunden-Gastein" symphony. That it once existed is confirmed by Schwind in a letter of 14 August 1825 as well as the obituaries for Schubert written later by Spaun and Bauernfeld, which state that "in Gastein, [Schubert] composed his grandest and most beautiful symphony," "of which he was particularly fond." This makes its loss to us all the more unfortunate.

Of all the songs from Scott's *Lady of the Lake* composed by Schubert in Gmunden, certainly the most famous and best loved is the one popularly known as *Ave Maria* (D839). In the same period, Schubert wrote three piano sonatas of unusual beauty, including one in C major (D840), profound and full of feeling, that was never finished and is known as the *Reliquie*, and one in A minor (D845) of such mastery that it brooks every comparison with Beethoven's great piano sonatas. Robert Schumann was especially struck by the reverie of the first movement which, he said, "can bring you to tears." As was characteristic of Schubert, after composing these two rather moody, dreamlike sonatas, he wrote an effervescent, optimistic work, the Sonata in D (D850), in which we can hear reflections of his regained strength and confidence. He even wanted to pass some of his self-assurance and inner strength to his friends to help them in their emotional needs. From Linz, for example, he wrote to his friend Spaun, who was visiting in Lemberg: "Don't get gray worrying that you are so far from us, fight the good fight against stupid fate....Sorrow is a mean and miserable thing which steals upon a noble heart, cast it far from you, and crush the vulture before he feeds on your soul." These words express the confidence of a Schubert restored to health. How fit he must have been feeling at the time is evident from his letter of 25 July 1825 to his parents in Vienna: "Am glad about everyone's good health, to which I—the Almighty be exalted—can add my own." In this same letter, he also urges his brother Ferdinand not to yield to his depression caused by imaginary physical ailments:

> Ferdinand...will surely have been sick again 77 times and have imagined he was about to die 9 times, as though dying were the worst thing that could happen to us humans. If only he could once see these heavenly mountains and lakes...he would not love his speck of human existence so much that he wouldn't take it as a great piece of luck to be endowed with new life again through nature's incomprehensible power.

This clear profession of his attitude toward death reveals Schubert's intimate ties to nature and hardly comports with the "I believe" of the clergy. In fact, it is well known that he deliberately struck the dogmatic words *"Credo in unam, sanctam, catholicam et apostolicam Ecclesiam"* ("I believe in one holy, catholic and apostolic church") from the Credo of each of his Latin masses. No doubt life in the boarding school under the discipline and coercion of the clergy had led the young man to look critically on the role of the priesthood. Many statements from his own hand show how much he resented the priestly control that was manifested in those days in so many ways. For example, he was only twenty-one when, in October 1818, he wrote from Zseliz to his brother Ignaz, with whom he shared the same general outlook about many things:

> You, Ignaz, you are still the same man of steel. Your implacable hatred of this tribe of the high and mighty does you honor. But you really have no conception what the clerics here are like, bigoted as an old crone, dumb as the dumbest donkey and crude as the crudest lout, you hear sermons here compared with which those of the venerated Father Nepomucene are nothing at all. They go

> on from the pulpit about sluts and scoundrels and
> so forth until it would be a pleasure to bring a
> skull to the pulpit and say to them: Now look
> here, you mottled humpbacked good-for-nothings,
> this is how you will look one day too.

Schubert's upbringing by a sanctimonious father and his experiences with the priests at the boarding school must have led ultimately to his feeling of being repelled by this kind of religiosity. The piety he disclosed in his sacred works is not one intended to satisfy strict dogmatic dictates, but only to persuade through the ethereal purity of music that lightly goes to the farthest corner of doubt in a believing heart. His brother Ferdinand had a proper appreciation of this, saying in a letter of 4 August 1825:

> That a hymn to the Holy Virgin which you com-
> posed causes thoughts of devotion in all who hear
> it will not be surprising to such people if they
> have heard your mass in F, your first "Tantum ergo"
> and your "Salve regina." For through these sacred
> compositions, every person, if there be but a spark
> of feeling in him, must be roused to religious medi-
> tation.

At the beginning of October 1925, Schubert was back in Vienna. There is only a single remark about the state of his health from this autumn and it is in a letter from Anton Ottenwalt to Spaun on 27 November: "I wouldn't know anything new to tell you and ourselves about Schubert; in his works is revealed his genius for creating the divine...he is in good humor and, I hope, health too." Schubert fell ill for a short time at the turn of the year, but it has not been possible to learn anything about this brief—and therefore probably harmless—illness. In Bauernfeld's diary entry for 2 January 1826, we find merely the succinct comment: "New Year's Eve at Schober's but without Schubert who was sick." On 16 January, however, Bauernfeld noted: "Day before yesterday a dance at Schober's place, Schubert had to play waltzes."

Although Schubert was becoming better known and steadily gaining recognition as a composer, 1826 turned out to be a distinct disappointment for him. His financial situation worsened

CLOSING LINES FROM ONE OF SCHUBERT'S LAST LETTERS TO HIS FRIEND
ANSELM HÜTTENBRENNER.

appreciably, to the point that he thought of giving up his career
as a free-lance composer. On 7 April 1826, he applied unsuccess-
fully for the position of vice director of the imperial court chapel.
He was no more successful later in applying to be Vizekapellmeister
at the Kärntnertortheater. His opinion about how his living as an
independent artist might be assured comes out in a remark he
once made to his good friend Josef Hüttenbrenner: "The government should take care of me for I was really born for only one
thing, composing."

In February 1826, Schubert finally completed the somber, passionate String Quartet in D Minor (D810), *Der Tod und das*

*Mädchen (Death and the Maiden)*, which he had largely already accomplished in the difficult days at the beginning of 1824 and which mirrored the mood of desperation reflected in the previously mentioned letter to Leopold Kupelwieser of 31 March 1824. The music of this string quartet powerfully expresses a despair beyond all hope. In these lacerating sounds between revolt and defeat, between consolation and despondency, one literally feels how Schubert wanted this music to be understood as a vision of death. What drove Schubert to compose such music in 1824 was mainly the renewed outbreak of his disease, whereas now in 1826 it was surely the complete lack of prospects in his situation just as he was finishing this work. In the summer of 1826, he was so down on his luck that he could not even afford to rent a piano and was driven to cancel his plans for a summer trip through the lakes and mountains of the Salzkammergut near Salzburg. On 10 July, he wrote to Bauernfeld: "It is absolutely impossible for me to come to Gmunden or anywhere else, I don't have any money and I'm not doing well at all."

Then, in October 1826, Schubert showed, in composing the wonderful Piano Sonata in G Major (D894), that his bedraggled circumstances could not perpetually dominate his emotional outlook. "But I don't care and I enjoy myself," he had added to his report to Bauernfeld, and the bravura passages of the sonata, with its defiant motifs, could be interpreted in just this sense, even though the gentle, heartfelt melodies at the beginning are melancholy. Franz von Hartmann, for whom Schubert played this sonata on 8 December, must have sensed this, for he wrote to Spaun: "Then Schubert came and played a splendid but very sad piece he had composed."

Schubert may have been ill again in late summer. An entry in Bauernfeld's diary from August 1826 provides the first specific indication of the nature of the venereal disease, even if only euphemistically: "Schubert half sick, he ought to have 'young peacocks' just like Benvenuto Cellini." The famous goldsmith and sculptor Benvenuto Cellini (1500-1571), who is said to have suffered from syphilis, was fond of eating young peacocks, which later came to be used as a discreet roundabout way of referring to this socially disreputable disease. The diary entry also tells us that the true nature of Schubert's disease did not remain hidden from his friends and that they were inclined to view every short-lived illness as in some way associated with his affliction.

In the spring of 1827, Schubert and his friends were deeply affected by the death of Ludwig van Beethoven. Schubert was one of the torchbearers accompanying the casket and stood before the gate to the cemetery in Währing during the funeral oration, written by Grillparzer, in which Beethoven was lauded as "resounding song's most profound master." What happened after the funeral was reported later by Beethoven's youthful friend Gerhard von Breuning. Knowing as we do what would come all too soon, this account touches everyone who reads it:

> Franz Schubert, Benedikt Randhartinger and Franz Lachner went together to the inn Zur Mehlgrube in the Neuer Markt [in Vienna's inner city]. They ordered wine to drink, and Schubert lifted his glass with the cry, "To the memory of our immortal Beethoven!," and when the glasses had been emptied, he filled his a second time, proclaiming: "And now, this is to that one of us three who is the first to follow after our Beethoven."

However much Beethoven's death may have shaken him, Schubert may have experienced a certain liberation in feeling that his artistic endeavors would no longer be overshadowed by those of the towering musical genius. Even during his boarding-school days, Schubert had spoken to his friend Spaun of his enormous admiration for this titan: "Of course, I often secretly believe I have it in me to accomplish something—but who will be able to do anything after Beethoven?" Now, as bearer of a blazing torch at Beethoven's funeral rites, he had symbolically taken this heroic artistic figure's burning flame unto himself as his heritage.

Despite tending to fall sick time and again and being in financial difficulties, Schubert was urged on by one desire: to compose. He produced the cheerful, vivacious Piano Trio in B-flat (D898) with its captivating second movement and, ignoring the censor's prohibition of the text written by his friend Bauernfeld, persisted in working on the opera *Der Graf von Gleichen*. As a public sign of his growing reputation, the Vienna Gesellschaft der Musikfreunde named him as a representative. And yet, his depressing living circumstances often left him feeling discouraged, as is evident in a remark he once made to Bauernfeld: "What will become of me, a poor music-maker? In my old age, I will end up creeping from door to door like Goethe's harp-player and having to beg for my bread!"

Concern for his later years, however, is a clear sign that, whatever his adversities, Schubert was not thinking about dying and that the darkness appearing from time to time in his compositions by no means represents forebodings of early death. The torment expressed in his music is surely only in part a consequence of his dreadful, ominous affliction; the greater part must originate in the emotional traumas of his youth and disappointments in his later life. His setting of the poem *Der Jüngling und der Tod* (*The Youth and Death*, D545), written for him by Spaun, is eloquent testimony to a mood of dejection and depression that could extend to thoughts of self-destruction. His prose poem, *My Dream*, and the *Unfinished Symphony* that followed it, as well as the particularly distinguished *Quartettsatz* in C minor (D703), also reflect Schubert's deeply melancholy nature. Finally, many of the lyrics of his songs exhibit an apathy and weariness with the world, a longing for an end to it all, that obviously attracted Schubert and was characteristic of the general emotional climate then prevalent in artistic circles and among young intellectuals. Nikolaus Lenau described it as a mood of "death at dusk." He believed the essential cause of the contemporary social malaise was the political helplessness felt by people generally in the years before the revolutions of 1830 and 1848.

With this context in mind, we can easily understand the particular force with which the catastrophe of his venereal disease must have struck the sensitive and emotionally vulnerable artist. Just how critical it was for Schubert is shown by the poem *My Prayer*, written in May 1823 at a time of deepest despair and betraying the presuicidal phase of a man on the verge of taking his life. In the D-minor string quartet, *Death and the Maiden*, with its characteristic "rhythm of the dead," Schubert's pain was virtually palpable.

FIRST PAGE OF THE AUTOGRAPH SCORE OF SCHUBERT'S *QUARTETTSATZ* IN
C MINOR FOR STRING QUARTET (D703), COMPOSED IN DECEMBER 1829.

The full extent of his despair and death wish is most vividly
mirrored, however, in his most important song cycle, *Die
Winterreise* (*The Winter Journey,* D911). He began to set the
lyrics of the twenty-four poems, which he took from the same
"poems from the papers left by a traveling horn player" used for
*Die schöne Müllerin,* in February 1827. In October he was applying himself to finishing the cycle with such all-consuming intensity and fervor that signs of exhaustion were evident to his friends,
the more so because Schubert appeared to be in an unusually
dejected frame of mind and visibly worn out during this time.
Like no other work of his, this one shows the depths of despondency his soul had already reached and how saddened he was by
the realization that people were fundamentally indifferent to his
pitiful fate. In these verses of Wilhelm Müller, he saw "the uncertain steps to the invitingly opened grave captured with

bittersweet realism," and in them he recognized his own yearning for death in the shape of the wanderer on his wintry way who, in the cycle, "flees from people through the impenetrable winter landscape, his steps sinking silently in the snow, with his eyes still fixed on one road, a road of no return." Many people regard *Die Winterreise* as a further presuicidal expression by Schubert in which he movingly delineates the hopelessness of his fate through his identification with the wanderer. Thus the "winter journey" appeared to him, as H. J. Fröhlich has put it somewhat poetically, "to be a journey through the realm of death, the wanderer as Schubert's self-portrait, each word an expression of his pain and at the same time its symbol—a passion's way with 24 stations, a work of the most profound pessimism which knows no redemption, but ends in complete resignation."

From an account by his friend Spaun, we learn of the enormous strain Schubert was under as he was bringing this song cycle to an end:

> For some time, Schubert was in a gloomy mood and looked worn out. When I would ask him what was going on with him, he would only say: "You will hear it soon and then you'll understand." Then one day, he said to me: "Come to Schober's today, I'll sing you a cycle of ghastly songs. I'm curious to see what you'll say. They have shaken me more than it ever was with other lieder." And he was right, for soon we were all enamored of these mournful songs...more beautiful German lieder than these do not exist.

Then, in keeping with his enigmatic creativity principle, as a contrast to this gloomy, nostalgic song cycle, Schubert composed his "bustling" Piano Trio in E-flat (D929), although even in that work the singular "rhythm of the dead" can be found.

An indication that he previously had suffered from headaches is found in a notation appended to the score of a simple piano piece for four hands, a child's march (*Kindermarsch*, D928), that Schubert wrote in the summer of 1827 for young Faust, the son of Dr. Pachler and his wife, during his stay in Graz. On 12 October 1827, to gratify the wish of Frau Pachler, who was an excellent

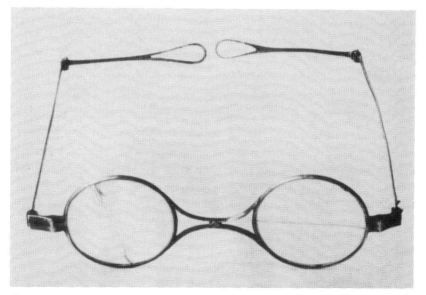

SCHUBERT'S GLASSES.

pianist and had become a good friend of Beethoven in 1817, he sent her the score he had promised her, with the note: "I hereby forward to Your Grace the piece for four hands for little Faust....I hope Your Grace is feeling better than I am, for my usual headaches are plaguing me all over again." These headaches need not have been associated with Schubert's venereal disease, as many people have assumed. The fact that they appeared intermittently with varying degrees of intensity prompts the judgment that they stemmed rather from the pronounced myopia he had developed in childhood. The real reason for his frequent headaches may well have been the long hours he spent every day writing the notes of his scores under poor lighting conditions, as well as the likelihood that his glasses did not properly correct for his nearsightedness.

In a recent book on Schubert, George R. Marek addresses the question of Schubert's myopia. He took the glasses held in the Schubert Museum in Vienna, which have a correction of -3.75 diopters sphere (the minus sign indicates the correction is for nearsightedness; "sphere" means there is no correction for astigmatism), and asked a prominent ophthalmologist in New York for her diagnosis without disclosing the name of the glasses' owner. The ophthalmologist offered the opinion that the person who wore them could have had only a slight myopia. This assessment is of relatively little use, however, in judging how well Schubert could see. We have no idea when these particular glasses were made. Moreover, simply examining the lenses affords no information as to the actual visual acuity of the person using them. For example, people often continue to wear glasses of a certain prescription for years even though their eyes may have gotten worse in the meantime.

Schubert must have been sick again briefly in October. In a letter of 15 October addressed to Nanette von Hönig and long regarded as lost, he wrote: "I am sick and that in a way which makes me completely unfit for any company." This sentence has been construed as further proof of Schubert's having syphilis. However, because this letter was written only three days after the note to Frau Pachler telling of strong headache pains, the sickness probably was a viral infection of the sort common at that time of year. Even on 7 November in a letter to his friend Johann Baptist Jenger, Schubert declined a luncheon invitation from Josef and Karl von Henikstein, bankers and members of the Gesellschaft der Musikfreunde, but agreed to a get-together that evening with Jenger: "Dear friend, I cannot make it to lunch with the Heniksteins, please extend my regrets for me. But I'll certainly show up at 7:30 tonight."

As the fateful year 1828 began, Schubert's financial situation was anything but rosy in spite of the evident success of his Piano Trio in E-flat—which was performed before a large crowd on the occasion of his friend Spaun's engagement to Franziska Röner—and despite the opening he had achieved with a new category of short piano pieces—the so-called *Moments musicaux* (D780) and the *Impromptus* (D899, D935). To do something to solve this problem, Schubert's friends convinced him that he should finally give a public concert of his own. It took place on 26 March 1828, exactly a year after Beethoven's death. This sole grand concert of Schubert's was an overwhelming success and gave him an enormous creative impetus. The last, almost unbelievable period of creative effort that followed was like a flood. The *"Great" C-major*

THE AUTOGRAPH SCORE OF THE BEGINNING OF SCHUBERT'S *"GREAT"* C-MAJOR SYMPHONY, NO. 9 (D944), FINISHED IN 1828.

*Symphony* (D944), begun perhaps in Gastein and Gmunden in 1825, was completed, as well as another group of *Moments musicaux* and *Impromptus* and the beautiful Fantasie in F Minor for four hands (D940). In the summer of 1828, Schubert created the grand Mass in E-flat, which was to be his own requiem and which today is considered one of the greatest in the entire literature of sacred music. As the saying goes, with this wonderful mass, one can die more easily. In the midst of all this activity, Schubert also composed some songs that were later brought together under the title *Schwanengesang* (*Swansong*, D957); among them is the poem *Der Doppelgänger*, by Heinrich Heine, which comes particularly close to Schubert's dual nature in the sense Bauernfeld described it: gaiety and mirth intertwined with a tendency to deep unhappiness.

Considering this overflowing creative activity, we might conclude that Schubert was enjoying the best of health at the time.
But that was not the case.  He was suffering from headaches,
spells of dizziness, and flushes of blood rushing to the head.  For
this reason, his doctor, Dr. Ernst Rinna von Sarenbach, advised a
vacation in the country air.  Not having enough money, Schubert
indefinitely postponed a planned trip to Graz and decided instead on a move to the semi-rural outskirts of Vienna.   On
1 September 1828, his brother took rooms in a house so newly
built that the paint was not yet dry, in the suburb known as Neue
Wieden (now Kettenbrückengasse 6 in Vienna's 4th district), and
Schubert moved in.

It is hard to believe that, in the midst of all the confusion of
moving, Schubert was able to compose the crowning work in his
chamber music oeuvre, the masterful String Quintet in C Major
(D956), with an extra cello in place of the more usual extra viola.
And in this September too he composed his last three great piano
sonatas—in C minor, A major, and B-flat (D958-960)—which, along
with their incomparably lyrical sensitivity, persistently convey an
aching Schubertian plaintiveness.  We feel it particularly in the
slow movement of the last of his sonatas, the one in B-flat, which
can be seen as an attempt to express his deep absorption with the
phenomenon of death.  In addition to all this work, Schubert did
the sketches for three movements of a symphony in D major
(D936a) that were discovered by Ernst Hilmar.  They were committed to paper in the fall of 1828 in only a few weeks' time.  The
production of such a tremendous number of compositions of the
highest quality in such a short period of time is virtually unique in
the history of music.

Schubert was feeling anything but well throughout September.  In the remembrances written by his brother Ferdinand, we
read that Franz was "feeling poorly and doctoring himself with
medicines" at that time.  Later his condition must have improved
somewhat, however, for Ferdinand reports that at the beginning
of October Schubert

> ...in the company of his brother Ferdinand and
> two friends made a little excursion to Unter-
> Waltersdorf [about nine miles north of Eisenstadt],

where he went to visit Joseph Haydn's tomb and lingered there for some time. During these three days underway, he was very moderate in what he ate and drank, but at the same time he was in very good spirits and had a lot of amusing ideas. When he was back in Vienna once more, however, his feeling of being sick grew again.

This is the reason he was not able to accept an invitation to go to Pest for the first performance of Franz Lachner's opera *Die Burgschaft* on 11 October. But at least he had been able to cover the nearly forty-five miles from Vienna to Eisenstadt and Haydn's grave and back, all on foot.

Many biographies suggest that the restlessness which drove Schubert to work at such an inconceivable pace in the last months of his life was rooted in a premonition that he did not have long to live. Such an interpretation runs the risk of using our knowledge of historical events to infer thoughts and ideas in retrospect that have nothing to do with reality. Moreover, there are many reasons to believe that, in those last months of his life in a year filled with so many hopes and plans, Schubert did not anticipate his death and most certainly did not long for it.

## The Mortal Illness

Schubert's death, when it came, was not caused by his venereal disease, but by an illness of a completely different nature. The end snuck up on him "like a thief in the night." The illness that would lead to his death began on 31 October 1828. On that day, Schubert went to supper with his brother Ferdinand at their favorite neighborhood tavern, Zum roten Kreuz. There the fatal sickness made its presence known for the first time, as we read in Ferdinand's memoirs written in 1831:

> On the last evening in October, he was intending to eat some fish when, after taking the first bite, he suddenly threw down his knife and fork and declared the food nauseated him and it was just as though he had taken poison. From this moment

on, Schubert ate almost nothing more and merely took medicines.

On 3 November, Schubert went to the parish church in Hernals to hear a requiem his brother Ferdinand had composed. Afterward, he took a long three-hour walk, hoping to revive the weak, unsteady state of his health by exercise in the fresh air. On the way home, however, he complained of great weariness and fatigue, a feeling that would increase in the days to follow. In spite of it, being moved by his study of Handel's works, he decided to join the pianist Josef Lanz in taking lessons from Simon Sechter, a former pupil of Antonio Salieri and later Anton Bruckner's teacher, with the aim of learning more about the art of fugue. Sechter later reported:

> Not long before his last illness, Schubert came to me with his good friend Josef Lanz to learn counterpoint and fugue, because, as he put it, he could see that he needed help with them. We had only had a single lesson when Herr Lanz showed up alone the next time to tell me that F. Schubert was very sick and now he would take the instruction all by himself.

The joint lesson took place on 4 November; the second hour of instruction probably had been set for 10 November. By that date, however, Schubert's illness had obviously progressed to the point that he not only had given up the idea of continuing the lessons with Simon Sechter, but also had already experienced difficulty staying on his feet. This problem is confirmed in an alarming letter written on 12 November to his friend Schober (who, by the way, never once ventured to visit Schubert before he died, for fear of infection):

> Dear Schober, I am sick. For 11 days now I haven't had anything to eat or drink and I wander, lurching and exhausted, from my chair to my bed and back again. Rinna is treating me. Even if I eat something, then it comes right back up again. So, please do me the favor of helping me in this desperate situation to get something to read. So far I

> have read the following by [James Fenimore] Coo-
> per: "The Last of the Mohicans," "The Spy," "The
> Pilot," and "The Pioneers." Should you perhaps
> have something else by him, then I beseech you
> to leave them with Bogner's wife at the coffee-
> house. My brother, who is reliability personified,
> will most conscientiously bring them to me. Or
> anything else too. Your friend Schubert.

Some thirty years after Schubert's death, Baron Schönstein, to whom the song cycle *Die schöne Müllerin* is dedicated, wrote an account claiming that Schubert "had dined with him and other friends approximately 10 days before his death" and was uproari-ously gay as the result of "having enjoyed a great quantity of wine"; the letter of 12 November from Schubert to Schober re-futes these claims completely.

On 14 November Schubert's weakness finally reached the point that he "sank completely into his sickbed," as Ferdinand said in his reminiscences. His mind remained active, however, as we can see in his request to Schober for reading material. And Joseph von Spaun reported:

> I found him sick in bed, but his condition appeared
> completely innocuous to me. Sitting in bed, he
> corrected what I had copied out, was happy to
> see me, and said: "Actually I have everything I
> need, only I feel so weary I think I'll fall right
> through the bed." A charming thirteen-year-old
> stepsister, whom he praised very highly, was giv-
> ing him the most tender care. I was quite uncon-
> cerned as I left him.

Schubert's last work was making corrections to the second part of his lieder cycle, *Die Winterreise*.

When his personal physician, Dr. Rinna, also fell ill, Dr. Josef von Vering, a former student at Schubert's old boarding-school, took over his care. On 16 November, Dr. Vering consulted with Dr. Johann Baptist Wisgrill, a professor at the Vienna University. According to the account given by Schubert's first biographer, Kreissle von Hellborn: "On the 16th, the doctors held a consultation; it appeared to them that the illness was about to turn into typhoid fever, although hope for recovery was not excluded. Many of his friends came to visit him, but fear of infection held others back." One of the friends who came was Bauernfeld, who said in 1829:

> On 17 November, the author of this report [Bauernfeld] found him weak but resting and still hoping to recover. He also expressed his fervent wish to receive a new opera libretto. On the evening of this same day, however, his delirium, which had affected him only slightly and seldom up to then, was much greater and hardly ever left him after that. The illness had turned into a bad case of nerve [typhoid] fever.

In a newspaper article in 1864, Bauernfeld supplemented his comments:

> The last time I visited Schubert—it was the 17th of November—he was completely exhausted, complained about being weak, with a burning head, still in the afternoon he was completely himself without any sign of delirium, although my friend's mood of depression filled me with dire forebodings. His brother arrived with the doctors—then in the evening, the sick man began to suffer strong hallucinations, never came to himself again—a violent typhoid fever had broken out....Just the week before he had eagerly discussed the opera with me, how splendidly he intended to orchestrate it. Completely new harmonies and rhythms were going through his head, he assured me—and with these, he passed quietly away.

According to this account, then, a state of delirium set in on the evening of 17 November, from which Schubert never completely emerged. Franz Lachner, who must have visited him on the 18th, found him still in this state: "As I went to him in his room, he lay with his face to the wall in a deep feverish delirium." On this day, the feverish delirium appeared to lead into a manic

*Einladung zu FRANZ SCHUBERTS Todtenfeyer*

SCHUBERT DIED ON 19 NOVEMBER 1828. THIS IS THE INVITATION TO THE REQUIEM MASS HELD FOR HIM ON 23 DECEMBER 1828.

phase—in those times, one spoke of a so-called "typhomanie" or *typhus delirium*—for in his confusion, Schubert began to sing over and over again and could be held in bed only with great effort. The care Schubert's brother Ferdinand and his little half-sister Josefa Theresia gave him in these difficult hours and days as he wrestled with death is truly touching. It is scandalous that in recent times film makers have suggested an incestuous relationship between Schubert and his stepsister during his fatal attack of typhoid fever.

In the evening of 18 November, Schubert imagined in his feverish delirium that he was lying in a strange underground room, and no amount of gentle persuasion or calming words could bring him from this delusion. Ferdinand wrote:

> The night before he died, he called his brother to
> his bed with the words, "Ferdinand! Put your ear

to my mouth," and then said very secretly, "Tell me, what's happening with me?" Ferdinand replied: "Dear Franz! Everyone is very anxious to make you better again, and the doctor promises too that you will be well again soon, only you really have to stay in bed!" All day long he wanted to get out of bed and he constantly had the idea he was in a strange room. And half conscious, he whispered again and again in his brother's ear: "I implore you, get me into my room, don't leave me here in this corner under the ground; don't I deserve a place above the ground?" I said to him: "Dear Franz! Be still, do believe your brother Ferdinand who you've always believed and who loves you so much. You are in the room you were always in up to now, and you're lying in your own bed!" And Franz said: "No, it's not true, Beethoven is not lying here."

On 19 November 1828, Franz Schubert lay breathing his last. When the doctor paid his visit that day, Schubert stared at him with unseeing eyes, feebly reached out to the wall, and said, slowly and solemnly: "Here, here is my end." For days he had fought with all his might against the approaching doom—in vain. At three o'clock in the afternoon, "the most lyrical musician there ever was" closed his eyes forever. He was thirty-one years old.

Schubert appears to have resisted any clerical intercession to the very end, which is why, according to the record in the death register of St. Josef's Church in Margareten, he received "only the last sacrament." But surely Arthur Schnabel is right in believing that Franz Schubert "is the composer nearest to God." He was certainly nearer than his father, who made a lifelong show of piety but who, instead of coming to visit the sickroom and death-bed of his brilliant son, preferred to send a letter dripping with sanctimonious phrases to Ferdinand. On 19 November, before Schubert had died, he wrote:

My dear son Ferdinand. The day of sorrow and pain weighs heavily on us. The perilous illness of our beloved Franz painfully affects our feelings.

> Nothing remains for us in these unhappy days but to seek consolation in God, and to bear every suffering which is meted us according to God's wise dispensation with unflinching surrender to His holy Will; and the outcome will convince us of the wisdom of God and of His Goodness and give us peace. Therefore, take heart and put your faith in God; He will strengthen you so that you are not brought down, and, through His blessing, will grant you a happy life to come. Do as much as possible so that our good Franz receives the holy sacraments of the dying without delay, and I live in the consoling hope that God will comfort and receive him.

How different were the words of Schubert's friend Schwind, who wrote from far away to Schober on 25 November 1828: "You know how I loved him, you can also imagine how I could hardly cope with the thought of having lost him....I have wept for him like one of my brothers; I am happy for him now, however, that he died in his greatness and is free of his trouble at last. The more I see now what he was, the more I see what he suffered." With these last remarks, Schwind was alluding certainly to the torment Schubert had suffered ever since he developed syphilis, the fear that every symptom of illness could somehow be related to his chronic affliction. The thought of being threatened by this unpredictable disease must never have fully left him.

After consecration of the body in St. Josef's Church in Margareten, the burial should then have taken place on the afternoon of 21 November in the Matzleinsdorf Cemetery, which served the district of the church. Ferdinand, however, took his dying brother's words—"No, it's not true, Beethoven is not lying here"—as a sign that Schubert wanted his last resting place to be at the side of Beethoven, whom he so admired. In keeping with that wish, Ferdinand arranged the transport of the body to the Währing Cemetery, where Schubert was buried the same day just a few feet from Beethoven's grave. Franz Grillparzer suggested several possible epitaphs to go on Schubert's tombstone; in the fall of 1829, one was finally chosen:

> Music buried a precious treasure here,
> But even more beautiful hopes besides....

Grillparzer himself would later (in 1872) be buried in this same cemetery in Währing, where the bones of Beethoven and Schubert still rested at the time.

Some thirty-five years after Schubert's death, the peace of his grave was disturbed. His body, along with that of Beethoven, was disinterred for the first time on 13 October 1863 "to secure the mortal remains of Beethoven and Schubert against the spreading of further decay." Naturally, the authorities took advantage of the exhumation to address open medical questions, particularly ones about possible syphilitic changes in the bones of the skull and the extremities, through appropriate examination of the skeleton. As already discussed in relation to both Haydn and Beethoven, many people gave credence to the theory of craniology of Franz Joseph Gall, with its idea that specific intellectual abilities and traits of character are located in certain parts of the brain and can be recognized by the external shape of the skull. Accordingly, in connection with Schubert, proponents of the theory actually believed they found "remarkable thickenings of the cranium in the vicinity of the temples," which allegedly indicated an especially well developed auditory center of the brain. Similar notions had already been expressed in relation to Joseph Haydn. It is extraordinary that this nonsensical theory of Gall's craniology was able to persist into the latter part of the 19th century.

More interesting than these wild speculations, however, are the reports of the anatomical examinations of the skeletal system and photographs of Schubert's skull, which may have revealed the typical bony syphilitic alterations of the sort often associated with untreated cases.*

The official medical record of the first disinterment of 13 October 1863 says:

> The well preserved skull, unmarred by any postmortem operative effects, was first visible in its natural position in the coffin and was, in common with all the other parts of the skeleton, conspicuously dark, almost blackish-brown....Around the skull but no longer attached to the cranium was

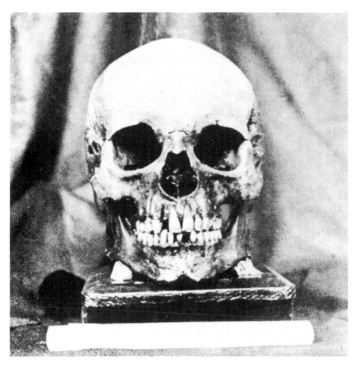

Schubert was initially buried only a few yards from Beethoven. Both were disinterred and buried again in October 1863. This photograph of Schubert's skull was taken at the time of the first disinterment.

still a rather dense cap of thick hair intermingled with moist earth, sawdust that was half rotten, and hundreds of insect larvae..,.The skull's interior and thinner parts, specifically the temporal bones and the nasal bone, were partially disintegrated. The two perfectly fitting jawbones showed a double row of the most healthy and beautiful teeth. One of them, the right upper outside incisor, was already missing; another, the left upper inside incisor, which had come out and been taken for the time being by Andreas Schubert, along with a third...was later put back in place again. —The rest of Schubert's skeleton was decayed, damp,

> brittle, and very much in fragments.  Hardly 4-5
> vertebrae of the backbone could be found, and
> only a few fragments of the ribs.  Not all the bones
> of the hands and feet were present, nor were any
> intact; and of the larger parts, only the long bones
> of the arms and legs.

During the second exhumation, before the transfer of Schubert's
and Beethoven's remains to memorial tombs in Vienna's main
municipal cemetery on 21 June 1888, the skeleton was found to
have disintegrated even more despite reburial in a soldered metal
casket after the first disinterment.  According to a report made to
the anthropological society by Professor Karl Toldt, head of the
anatomical institute of the University of Vienna,

> ...apart from the skull which to all appearances
> was rather well preserved, only the bones of the
> upper arm, the thigh, and the shins were still in-
> tact.  The bones of the upper arm are peculiarly
> small, thin, and delicate, the thigh bone on the
> other hand rather strong, the shinbones also thin,
> with very sharp edges and completely smooth sur-
> faces; all of them indicate only a short body length.
> —Around the skull, whose base was extremely
> brittle (in the grave, the head was sunken forward),
> the left pyramid and most of the petrosal bone,
> the roof of the eyesocket including the adjacent
> parts, as well as lateral sections of the cerebellum
> receptacle are missing; the nasal bones are bro-
> ken off at the bottom end; everything else is there.
> —The skull, moderately large and very regularly
> formed, is light, has barely indented sutures, and
> the sagittal suture along with the adjacent parts of
> the coronal and the lambdoid sutures is indistinct.

For a medical investigator, the most important finding revealed
by the medical reports after the two exhumations is the absence
of any suspicious signs of syphilitic alterations to the bones or the
skull.  It is particularly significant because in many biographies
and medical reviews the headaches that Schubert constantly

mentioned and the pains in his arm that once even kept him temporarily from playing the piano have been rashly attributed to a late stage of syphilis.

Although no medically attested description of the specific symptoms of his disease has come down to us, the documentary sources at our disposal today enable us to make a relatively informed reconstruction of Schubert's case history. There is no question but that his chronic affliction, which had been present from the end of 1822 on, was syphilis, a sexually transmitted disease that had come to Europe from America at the end of the 15th century. The Spaniards who colonized what is today the Dominican Republic and other Antilles islands in 1492 and 1493 under Christopher Columbus became infected through intercourse with the native women. Soon after their glorious return, rumors of a mysterious disease that was passed on especially by soldiers and sailors spread like wildfire. The participation of Spanish soldiers of fortune in driving the French forces from Naples in 1494 resulted not only in the people of Naples becoming infected with this disease, but the French forces as well, and ultimately all of Europe. Because no one knew the cause of this disease, it was viewed—like leprosy and the plague—as a punishment inflicted by God. In some respects, the fate of syphilitics was even harder than that of people with leprosy: they could not be given housing or the use of public baths, doctors were strictly forbidden to treat them, and they could not beg in the streets. These unfortunate souls were driven to sleeping on the streets, in parks, and under bridges, or to living in forests. Even lepers would have nothing to do with syphilitics. This rigorous quarantine from society was only slightly relieved by the establishment in many places of municipal asylums for persons sick with this disease, such as the Blatterhaus in Strasbourg. Because the chances of becoming infected were unknown and the risk of infection was present everywhere, it is hardly surprising that syphilis raged through Europe in the centuries to follow.

These historical considerations set the context for addressing the unfair moralistic judgments associated with Schubert's syphilis. For a young, unmarried man in the early 19th century, the danger of becoming infected through a casual sexual affair was much greater than it is now. If such an infection did occur, the means of treatment were very limited and the disease could hardly be kept hidden from the world. Today antibiotic treatment directed specifically at syphilis makes it possible to cure the disease quickly before it becomes clinically obvious and before the victim's acquaintances know anything about it. With this fact in mind, we should refrain from passing judgment on persons of earlier centuries who had venereal disease or slandering them before posterity, as the moralistic Wilhelm von Chezy, for one, tried to do. Although he was certainly not one of Schubert's intimate friends, Chezy maintained far and wide that Schubert had even bragged of his "mishaps" with women. However, we know from the reports of Schubert's friends that he hardly ever said a word about his sex life.

The broad range of symptoms of syphilis, which affects not only the skin but most of the internal organs and the entire nervous system as well, was difficult to cure in earlier times because of inadequate means of making an early diagnosis and ineffective methods of treatment. These difficulties are unknown to doctors today because this disease can largely be cured before general symptoms develop or damage to internal organs and body structure occurs. It is useful, therefore, before we analyze Schubert's medical history, to sketch briefly the course of an untreated case of syphilis, or of a case treated with only the very limited measures available then, as described in the medical textbooks of the 19th century.

Untreated syphilis typically took the following course: some four weeks after infection, a hard, sharply delimited lesion, a chancre, appeared at the affected location, usually on the penis, and the nearby lymph nodes became hard and swollen. During the next six weeks, the person affected generally experienced no further changes. The secondary stage of syphilis began some six to twenty weeks after infection, often with chills and fever and sharp pains in the muscles and particularly in the bones, the shinbones and the skull being most affected. The most characteristic symptom of this stage, however, was a rash over the surface of the body. Brownish-red spots, as well as pus-containing skin lesions (pustules), occurring frequently at the hairline on the forehead (often referred to as the "Venus wreath"). Frequently the hair would fall out, although it grew in again after recovery. In untreated cases, this secondary stage lasted six months or longer. In the third or tertiary stage, soft, gummy tumors appeared in the most diverse organs of the body. In the 19th century these tumors could not be cured and culminated in death. But even then the third stage of syphilis and its associated life-threatening complications could be prevented more often than not, if suitable treatment was instituted at the very beginning and carried out over a sufficiently long period of time.

It was not possible, however, either to predict or prevent relapses, which were to be expected especially in the first three years after infection, but often occurred many years later as well, especially if the initial treatment had been brief. Mercury was regarded as the medicine of choice for the first and second stages of syphilis. To avoid the serious effects of mercuric poisoning, this treatment with mercury, which had been popularized in Vienna by Gerhard van Swieten, Empress Maria Theresa's personal physician, was followed by a so-called smear treatment: the patient had to take a daily bath, then rub a mercuric ointment into the skin. These treatments were repeated every six months during the first three years and after that once a year, even if no signs of relapse had appeared in the meantime. In this way, even in the 19th century, persons with syphilis could be cured.

## Schubert's Death:
## Some Final Medical Considerations

In researching Schubert's medical history, one is struck right from the start by the fact that the reports available today about the nature and course of his persistent illness do not contain a single mention of a medical diagnosis as such, apart from the veiled allusion, as previously mentioned, to Cellini's syphilis in Bauernfeld's diary. Still, we can conclude with confidence that Schubert contracted syphilis because this diagnosis is supported by both the typical course run by his disease and the verbal testimony of the direct descendants of Schubert's closest friends, from whom O. E. Deutsch received the unanimous assurance that they had heard from their fathers of the syphilitic nature of Schubert's chronic disease. The agreement of these verbal accounts with the medical aspects of Schubert's reconstructed case history is pointed out in the following discussion.

Infection could well have taken place toward the end of 1822. It could be what lay behind the words Schubert chose to write in a friend's guest book on 28 November, "...let each take care where he is and he who's upright, that he doesn't fall," as well as Schober's dark intimation in his New Year's Eve comments that the New Year could be "dismal and grim or perhaps even ruinous." In any case, Schubert must have already contracted an illness by the beginning of 1823, one of such a nature that he did not want to be seen by his nearest friends but chose rather to closet himself with the family of his friend who was infected with the same disease. There the medical care of Drs. Schaeffer and Bernhardt was administered, although we do not know the nature of the treatment. According to his remarks in a letter of 28 February 1823, Schubert was still not up to leaving the house. He must have been fully aware of the seriousness of his illness, however, as we can infer from his poem, *My Prayer*, written in May 1823, which expresses the depth of his despondency and dejection. Then, in the summer of 1823, some improvement in his condition must have occurred, even though the brisk correspondence with his doctor suggests certain symptoms of the disease were still present.

A new attack of the disease in the fall of 1823 must have been serious because Schubert had to be admitted to the Vienna General Hospital for treatment until about the middle of November. While he was in the hospital, he had to have his hair cut off, as we learn from Schwind's letter of 24 December 1823, which is why for some time after his discharge he wore a wig. The reason for cutting off his hair must have been the emergence of a syphilitic skin rash, which tends to show up on the face and neck. Alternatively, he may also have had general hair loss in which the hair may have fallen out in patches, as often happens with syphilis.

By the end of 1823, Schubert's condition had improved substantially. We read in Schwind's letter of 22 February 1824 that Schubert had quit wearing the wig and his head was beginning to show "signs of sweet little curls." A regimen of dieting apparently was the only treatment imposed by his doctors at this time.* In March he had another relapse, and this recurrent appearance and subsidence of his illness caused him once more to fall into deep depression. His discouraged letter of 31 March 1824 to Leopold Kupelwieser shows how near he was to giving up all hope. The precise symptoms accompanying this relapse are not known, but they could have been the pains in the muscles and joints typical of the secondary stage of syphilis. It would be possible, for example, to interpret Schwind's comment of 14 April—to the effect that Schubert was complaining of pains in his left arm that prevented him from playing the piano—in this sense. However, because he was able to go off on his second sojourn to Hungary with the Esterhazy family only two weeks later, obviously once more free of complaints, these pains in the arm more likely were self-limited symptoms caused by overexertion.

Schubert must have been well throughout the summer months of 1824 during his stay at the Esterhazy country estate in Hungary, but remained uneasy in view of his previous relapses, for in August he wrote Schwind, "I am still well, thank God." His recovery must have continued, and Schubert almost certainly told his friend and fellow-sufferer Schober about it. Schober wrote back on 2 December 1824 to say, "How glad I am that you are all well again, soon I will be too." In fact, after the eventful years of 1823 and 1824, we seldom hear any more of Schubert's health problems. The short spell in bed at the turn of the year from 1825 to 1826 and the temporary indisposition mentioned by Bauernfeld in August 1826 could have resulted from some completely banal illness. Schubert frequently suffered from headaches, but in view of his intensive work in writing out his music scores, often by meager candlelight, they almost certainly were caused chiefly by "eyestrain" associated with his nearsightedness.

Analysis of Schubert's case history allows us to assume with ample certainty that Schubert did in fact contract syphilis at the end of 1822 and suffered several recurrences of that disease during the following two years, perhaps as the result of inadequate treatment. Syphilitic skin rashes are the most prominent of the specific disease symptoms, accompanied by a generalized feeling of being unwell. Muscle and joint pains also are prominent symptoms on occasion. Reflection on the later course of Schubert's disease leads us to conjecture that, from 1824 on, his syphilis* could be regarded as healed.

His cure may have been achieved in the spring of 1824 with an innovative treatment involving use of a mercuric salve. On 6 March 1824, Schwind wrote about a "new treatment" carried out by Dr. Bernhardt that consisted of "baths," among other things. Baths were prescribed and normally taken before the mercuric ointment was rubbed in. What was novel about this particular approach, however, was not the use of mercuric ointment in connection with baths, but rather in all likelihood the "drinking of tea by the gallon," as Schwind reported in his letter. In Schubert's case, the tea could have been extracts from the roots of various trees, which were still used in the form of the so-called Zittman decoctions toward the end of the 19th century. Each morning and evening the patient would receive a half liter (about a pint), sometimes more, of a warm "tea," the main effect of which was due entirely to its mercuric content. If Schubert's syphilis had been cured by this method of treatment, his later headaches obviously cannot be attributed to a third stage of syphilis with its characteristic alterations in bone structure. Confirmation for this conclusion is provided by the results of the medical evaluations from the two exhumations, which showed no suspicious changes whatsoever either to the skull or to the skeleton.

The diagnosis of Schubert's final illness, which led to his death in a few weeks' time, is not in doubt. In his remembrances, Ferdinand Schubert said that, soon after moving into the apartment on 1 September 1828, his brother was "feeling poorly and doctoring himself with medicines." Because Schubert was nagged by headaches, spells of dizziness, and hot flashes in the summer of that year, many writers have concluded that a new flare-up of his syphilitic disease had occurred. If that had been the case, however, Schubert's physician, Dr. Rinna, would hardly have promised him that a move to the outskirts of Vienna would bring results. It is much more likely that Schubert's complaints of generally feeling unwell, along with headaches and hot flashes, may have been related to an almost inconceivable volume of creative productivity in these months. Moreover, the idea of a syphilis flare-up is contradicted by the fact that in October Schubert was able to undertake a three-day hike to Eisenstadt and back with friends. In the fall of 1828, Schubert was indeed overworked and generally worn down, but there are no good grounds for believing further clinical manifestations of his syphilis were involved. A critical review of all available documentary sources appears to justify the supposition that the treatments that were begun immediately after infection and evidently repeated frequently may have suppressed any further recurrences of his syphilis after 1826. In all likelihood, he was as completely healed as was his friend and companion in being infected, Franz von Schober, who lived to be more than 80 years old.

There is little doubt that Schubert—like his mother—died of typhoid fever, an infectious disease that was endemic in the unimaginably bad hygienic conditions of Vienna's outlying communities. To enable us to place Schubert's symptoms in the context of typhoid's clinical picture, a brief description of the course of the disease as it was seen by doctors in the 19th century is helpful. Particularly informative is the treatise from the year 1810, *Concerning Infectious Typhoid*, by Dr. Johann Valentin von Hildenbrand.

As the doctors then observed it, two to three weeks after infection, a condition appeared in which "only very slight premonitory symptoms of the disease were noticed while, to all appearances, one still seemed healthy" and it was characterized by "general manifestations of indisposition, quick fatigue following physical activity, sleeplessness, and frequent dizziness." Accompanying these symptoms were a complete lack of appetite and "gastric upsets...which caused stomach problems, nausea, and vomiting." The transition of these early symptoms into the disease itself was so gradual that in retrospect it was only occasionally possible to identify precisely the first day of fever.

With the appearance of fever increasing by stages came a strong feeling of being sick, causing the patient to take to bed. Very often the victims would try to fight off the illness, going on with their usual activities for several days until increasing weariness and exhaustion finally brought them down. Because interpretation is not always correct even in medical pathographies, it is important to note the clinical observation that, in the first two weeks of the disease in most cases, there is usually no diarrhea, but instead an obstinate constipation. For this reason, the absence of diarrhea cannot be taken as an argument against the presence of typhoid fever.*

In the third week of the illness, "the nervous system suffers above all with mental confusion and the raving that goes with it," and in this prolonged state of high fever, an overall feeling of weakness and infirmity continued to increase. The patients became disoriented and restless and began to be delirious, which is why people also used the term "nerve fever" as a synonym for typhoid fever. Occasionally the patients were so agitated in their fever that they became violent, began to thrash about wildly and shriek, or tried to jump out of bed and run out of the room, which meant they had to be constantly watched.

From his own experience of being ill with typhoid, Hildenbrand called this stage "typhomanie" *(typhoid delirium)* and related that he "frequently raved in [his] speech as the result of unrelenting preoccupation with inner impressions. It is strange that such a single prevailing impression and a fantasy or *idée fixe* born of it usually torment the patients throughout the whole time of the fever, and its persistent annoyance tortures and frightens them." For seven days, he himself was "prey to the single thought that an unsightly bit of decoration on [his] oven had to be done away with." Interestingly, he also noted that in cases of *typhoid delirium* one "often observes very logical actions and remarks on the part of the patients, of the sort which, in connection with other kinds of febrile deliria, particularly a true brain fever or encephalitis, one usually does not see."

This infectious disease with its high fevers, which doctors in the early 19th century termed "typhus" or "nerve fever," accords so exactly with the symptoms and progression of typhoid (or intestinal or enteric) fever as it is called today that we can be confident the doctors of Schubert's time were capable of differentiating between it and similar potentially fatal infectious diseases, even though objective proof of the disease-causing organism (discovered in 1880) was not yet possible. Comparing what we know of Schubert's last weeks with the clinical picture of typhoid, we can diagnose an acute case of typhoid fever. The sudden revulsion during supper on 31 October 1828 with nausea and, later, vomiting, the complete loss of appetite in the succeeding days (which he reported on 12 November by saying, "For 11 days now I haven't had anything to eat or drink"), and his increasing lassitude and weakness are characteristic initial symptoms. And as was typical of typhoid victims, Schubert made an effort to overcome this general feeling of weakness in the first days of the disease, taking a walk of several hours on 3 November and going to Simon Sechter's for a composition lesson on 4 November. His fatigue soon increased so much, however, that he was unable to take part in the next hour of instruction on 10 November and from that time on he often had to spend days in bed. On 12 November he wrote: "I wander, lurching and exhausted, from my chair to my bed and back again." It was only on 14 November that he finally went to bed and stayed there, complaining of no particular problems but only a feeling of overwhelming weariness, as is typical of typhoid fever. As he described it to Spaun when he came to visit: "Actually I have everything I need, only I feel so weary I think I'll fall right through the bed."

In the third week, from 16 November on, Schubert was in the grip of a high, persistent fever and he began occasionally to be delirious, prompting the doctor attending him, Dr. Josef von Vering, to call a consultation with Professor Wisgrill. According to Bauernfeld's account, the delirium became continuous on the evening of 17 November, after Schubert only shortly before had discussed his plans for a new opera and new, daring rhythms and harmonies he wanted to use in future compositions. On 18 November, Schubert was already in a deep febrile delirium, as Franz Lachner reports, when he was seized by one of those states of excitement that often appear with untreated cases of typhoid fever: he made wild, violent movements, started to sing loudly, and had to be held in bed by the nurse. In a state quite like the *typhoid delirium* described by Hildenbrand, Schubert began to talk wildly. He could hardly be deflected from the *idée fixe* that he was lying in a strange room and had the illusion that people wanted him to believe Beethoven was lying there. On 19 November 1828, death came finally while he was in a deep coma.

These symptoms of disease, taken from the words of Schubert himself and those of his friends as well as his brother Ferdinand, form a convincing chain of circumstantial evidence that enables doctors, even today after so many years have elapsed, to make the retrospective diagnosis of typhoid fever. The disease that had taken his mother's life caused Schubert's death as well.

The treatment carried out by Drs. Rinna and Vering and Professor Wisgrill is of interest, for we can learn something from a list of expenses dated 6 December 1828 indicating the money spent on doctors, nurses, and medicines during Schubert's final illness. This list shows that particular use was made of mustard powder and of vesicant salves (salves to induce blistering), together with salves not otherwise identified; moreover, Schubert was subjected to one bleeding during the illness. This course of treatment was in line with the normal practice of the time, as we can derive from Dr. Hildenbrand's 1810 treatise on typhoid. Favored therapeutic means were vesicants and emetics, i.e., agents to induce vomiting.*

> Expectations of the splendid effects of these remedies are but seldom disappointed...as long as the doctor knows the proper moment to employ them. And this moment comes actually on the seventh or eighth day of the typhoid fever, with first signs of effects on the nervous system....Following the blistering agents, but especially even during their use, there is no better remedy at this stage of the fever than camphor...ten to twelve grains per day....One or at the most two bloodlettings...are usually sufficient for the worst cases of this kind.

Schubert was obviously given treatment along these lines, but unfortunately not with the results Hildenbrand promised in his textbook: "When it happened in Galicia during the bad typhoid epidemic of 1806 and then again recently in the imperial French military hospitals in Vienna that I had an enormous number of persons sick with typhoid to take care of, I instituted...the following method of treatment, which I describe here...for I did not lose even a tenth of the people."

The full dimensions and significance of the vast work bequeathed to us by Schubert as the legacy of his regrettably brief life came to be understood only after he had died. In 1860, as hitherto unknown compositions by Schubert were still being discovered, the famous music critic Eduard Hanslick appraised

Schubert's impact on later generations in these words: "If his contemporaries were right to look on him in wonder as an inexhaustible composer—what must we who come after say as we ceaselessly experience new works of his. The master has been dead for thirty years, and yet it is as though he were working away unseen—we can hardly keep up with him." Since then, more than a hundred years have passed and we still stand amazed at the great life's work of this composer, who in the final months of his life forged on into new spheres of music, even into spheres whose ultimate secrets he took with him to the grave. Schubert's music is unique in its ability to reach people's innermost feelings, and it has given comfort and peace to untold numbers of persons in pain. Schubert himself expressed this most movingly with his setting of Franz von Schober's poem *An die Musik* (D547), through which he spoke his thanks to his sole passion, music, for all its help in times of his heart's deepest need:

## An die Musik

Du holde Kunst, in wieviel grauen Stunden,
wo mich des Lebens wilder Kreis umstrickt,
hast du mein Herz zu warmer Lieb' entzunden,
hast mich in eine bess're Welt entrückt!

Oft hat ein Seufzer, Deiner Harf' entflossen,
kin süßer heiliger Akkord von Dir,
den Himmel bess'rer Zeiten mir erschlossen,
Du holde Kunst, ich danke Dir dafür!

## To Music

O enchanting art, in how many dull, gray hours,
Caught up in life's interminable rounds,
Have you lighted love's glow in my heart,
Have you raised me, enraptured, to a better world!

How often has a sigh, breathed from your harp,
A dulcet, sacred chord of yours,
Revealed to me a paradise of better times,
O enchanting art, for all this, I thank you!

# Schubert's Doctors

## *Dr. August von Schaeffer (1790-1865)*

Dr. Schaeffer, together with Dr. Josef Bernhardt, was the first doctor to attend Schubert after he had contracted a venereal disease toward the end of 1822.

## *Dr. Ernst Rinna von Sarenbach (1791-1837)*

Dr. Rinna became a doctor to the imperial court in 1824 and was the editor of a two-volume work, *A Compendium of the Most Efficacious Cures, Remedies, and Operating Methods*, published in 1833. Dr. Rinna was Schubert's first doctor at the onset of his mortal illness, but became ill himself and had to ask his colleague, Dr. Josef von Vering, to take over for him.

## *Dr. Josef von Vering (1793-1862)*

He was the son of Dr. Gerhard von Vering who had briefly treated Beethoven in the summer of 1801. Among Dr. Josef von Vering's scientific works, his publications on the treatment of syphilis are particularly prominent: a report from the year 1821, *Concerning the Treatment of Syphilis by Applying a Mercuric Liniment*, and a paper from 1826, *Syphilitic Therapy*. For this reason, some persons have conjectured that Dr. Rinna referred Schubert to Dr. Vering because of his special experience in the field of syphilis—an assumption that seems quite unlikely in view of the fact that from its outset, Schubert's ultimately fatal illness clearly showed symptoms of typhoid fever. Dr. Vering must have quickly recognized the threatening nature of Schubert's illness, for immediately after his first call on his patient he summoned Dr. Wisgrill to a consultation.

Dr. Vering was a follower of humoralism, the pathology of the body's humors or temperaments, whose foremost practitioner was Philipp Carl Hartmann. This approach to medicine was typical of the Vienna school of medicine in those days. In keeping with humoral curriculum, Vering regarded Schubert's hopeless condition as the consequence of an extreme liquation of the blood.

## *Dr. Johann Baptist Wisgrill*

Dr. Wisgrill was a professor at the University of Vienna. He was highly regarded as a physician for, among other things, the publication of his handbook, *Curriculum for the Study of Surgery*, which was completed in 1834. Research by O. E. Deutsch suggests that, as consultant, Dr. Wisgrill must have modified the therapeutic course initiated by Dr. Vering, although details of the modifications are not known.

# *Bibliography*

Music and Medicine:
Reflections on the Historical Relationship

Avicenna: Liber canonis. Venedig 1507. Nachdruck Hildesheim 1964.

Bacon R.: Opus tertium. London 1859. Nachdruck London 1965.

Berendes J.: Musik und Medizin. Wehr:Baden 1961 S, 3314-3344.

Boethius: De institutione musicae libri V. Hrsg. Friedlein G., Leipzig 1867.

Ficino M.: De vita libri tres. Basel 1576.

Frank J. P.: System einer vollständigen medicinischen Polizey, Bd. 1-4, Mannheim 1779-88.

Harburger W.: Die Metalogik. München 1919.

Haschek H.: Musik und Medizin. Wr. Med. Wochenschriften 128, 1 (1978)

Huppmann G. und Strobel W.: Möglichkeiten der Musiktherapie in der inneren Medizin. Med. Klin. 72, 2186 (1977).

Kayser H.: Lehrbuch der Harmonik. Zürich 1950.

Kepler J.: Harmonices mundi libri V. Linz 1619.

Kern E.: Theodor Billroth und die Musik. Zbl. Chriurgie 107, 1408, (1982)

Kircher A.: Musurgia universalis. Rom 1950.

Kümmel W. F.: Musik und Medizin. Freiburg 1977.

Kurth E.: Grundlagen des linearen Kontrapunkts. Berlin 1922.

Lichtenthal P.: Der musikalische Arzt oder Abhandlung von dem Einfluss der Musik auf den Körper und von ihrer Anwendung in gewissen Krankheiten. Wien 1807.

Pontvik A.: Heilen durch Musik. Zürich 1955.

Schadewaldt H.: Musik und Medizin. Ciba Zeitschrift, Basel 1969.

## Joseph Haydn

Artaria F.: Verzeichnis der musikal. Autographien von Joseph Haydn. Wien 1893.

Bartha D.: Joseph Haydn, Gesammelte Briefe und Aufzeichnungen. Budapest - Kassel 1965.

Böhme G.: Medizinische Portraits berühmter Komponisten. Bd. 2: Stuttgart - New York 1987

Botstiber H.: Joseph Haydn. Bd. 3 (Weiterführung der Biographie von Pohl, C. F.). Leipzig 1927.

Carpani G.: Le Haydine. Mailand 1812.

Dies A. Ch.: Biographische Nachrichten von Joseph Haydn. Wien 1810.

Engl J. E.: Haydns handschriftliches Tagebuch des 2. Aufenthaltes in London. Leipzig 1909.

Franken F. H.: Joseph Haydns Leben aus medizinischer Sicht. Wr. klin. Wochenschr. 88, 429, 1976.

Franken F. H.: Krankheit und Tod grosser Komponisten. Baden-Baden - Köln - New York 1979.

Geiringer K.: Joseph Haydn. Mainz 1959.

Griesinger G. A.: Biographische Notizen über Joseph Haydn. Wien 1810. (neu hrsg. von F. Grasberger. Wien 1954).

Huss M.: Joseph Haydn. Wien - Eisenstadt 1983.

Iffland A. W.: Almanach für Theater. Berlin 1811.

Jacob H. E.: Haydn: Seine Kunst, seine Zeit, sein Ruhm. Berlin 1969.

Klampfer G.: Joseph Haydn und die Haydn-Gedenkstätten in Eisenstadt. Offizielle burgenländische Festschrift. Wien 1959.

Landon R.: Joseph Haydn. Wien - München - Zürich - New York 1981.

Nowak L.: Joseph Haydn. 2. Aufl. Wien 1959.

Olleson E.: Georg August Griesingers Korrespondenz mit Breitkopf und Härtel, in: Haydn-Jahrbuch III, 1965.

Pohl C. F.: Joseph Haydn. Bd. 1: Berlin 1875, Bd. 2: Leipzig 1882.

Radant E.: Die Tagebücher von Joseph Karl Rosenbaum 1770-1829, in: Haydn-Jb. V, 1968.

Reich W.: Joseph Haydn: Chronik seines Lebens in Selbstzeugnissen. Zürich 1961.

Reichardt J. F.: Vertraute Briefe geschrieben auf einer Reise nach Wien 1808-1809 (Neuauflage von 1810). München 1915.

Riesbeck J. K.: Briefe eines reisenden Franzosen über Deutschland, 2 Bde. Zürich 1783.

Schnerich A.: Joseph Haydn und seine Sendung. Zürich - Leipzig - Wien 1926.

Somfai L.: Joseph Haydn. Sein Leben in zeitgenössischen Bildern. Kassel - Basel 1966.

Tandler J.: Über den Schädel Haydns. Mitt. Anthrop. Ges. Wien. 39, 1, 1908.

Tenschert R.: Frauen um Haydn. Wien 1946.

### WOLFGANG AMADÉ MOZART

Abert H.: W. A. Mozart. 2 Bde. Neubearbeitete und erweiterte Ausgabe von Otto Jahns *Mozart.* Leipzig 1983.

Bär C.: Mozart: Krankheit, Tod und Begräbnis. Schriftenreihe der Internat. Stiftung Mozarteum, 2. Aufl. Salzburg 1972.

Bär C.: Mozarts Zahnkrankheiten. Acta Mozartiana 3/1963.

Barraud J. A.: A quelle maladie a succombé Mozart? Chron. méd. 12, 737, 1905.

Bauer A., und Deutsch O. E.: Mozart, Briefe und Aufzeichnungen. Bd. I-IV. Kassel - Basel 1962/63.

Belza I.: Mozart und Salieri. Moskau 1953.

Bett W. R.: Mozart: a puzzling case history. Med. Press and Circ., London, 235, 90, 1956.

Blume F.: Requiem und kein Ende. 318, Wissenschaftl. Buchgesellschaft Darmstadt 1977. (Hrsg.: Gerhard Croll)

Bókay J.: The cause of Mozart's death. Orv. hetil. 28, 213, 1906.

Born G.: Mozarts Musiksprache. München 1985.

Bouillaud J. B.: Die Krankheiten des Herzens, 2 Bde. Leipzig 1836.

Braunbehrens V.: Mozart in Wien. München 1986.

Briellmann A.: Mozart und Salieri. Schweiz. Ärztezeitung 66, 615,1985.

Cacchi R.: zitiert nach Rappoport.

Carpani G.: Lettera del sig. G. Carpani in difesa del M. Salieri calunniato dell
avvelenamento del M. Mozzard. *Biblioteca Italiana*, 10. agosto 1824, IX,
Tom XXXV, 262-275.

Carr F.: Mozart und Konstanze. London 1983.

Clein G. P.: Mozart, a study in renal pathology. King's Coll. Hosp. Gaz. 38,
37, 1959.

Cloeter H.: Die Grabstätte W. A. Mozarts. Mozartgemeinde Wien, 1964.

Dalchow I., Duda G., und Kerner D.: Die Dokumentation seines Todes.
Pähl/Obb. 1966.

Daumer G. F.: *Aus der Mansarde*, Heft IV, Mainz 1861.

Davies P. J.: Mozart's illnesses and death. J. of the Royal Soc. of Medicine,
76, 776, 1983.

Deutsch O. E.: Mozart: Die Dokumente seines Lebens. Kassel - Basel 1961.

Deutsch O. E.: Die Legende von Mozarts Vergiftung. Literatur-Eildienst *Roche*
Nr. 3. Basel 1965.

Deutsch O. E.: Die Legende von Mozarts Vergiftung. Mozartjahrbuch 1964.
Internat. Stiftung Mozarteum. Salzburg 1965.

Dibelius U.: Mozart Aspekte. München 1972.

Duda G.: Gewiss, man hat mir Gift gegeben. Pähl/Obb. 1958.

Eichhorst H.: Lehrbuch der praktischen Medizin innerer Krankheiten. Berlin -
Wien 1899.

Einstein A.: Mozart: Sein Charakter - sein Werk. Stockholm 1947.

Engl v. J. E.: Hyrtls Mozartschädel. I. Die geschichtliche Schilderung. Int.
Stiftung Mozarteum. Salzburg 1906.

Esman A. H.: Mozart: a study in genius. Psychoanal. Qu. 20, 603, 1951.

Eyerel J. und Sallaba M. v.: Medicinische Chronik. 4 Bde., Wien 1793/94.

Fog R., und Regeur L.: Did W. A. Mozart suffer from Tourette's Syndrome?
Abstract Internat. Congress of Psychiatry. Vienna 1985.

Franken F. H.: W. A. Mozart: Krankheit und Tod. Med. Monatsschr. 27, 386,
1973.

Franken F. H.: Krankheit und Tod grosser Komponisten. Baden-Baden -
Köln - New York 1979.

Franken F. H.: Mozarts Todeskrankheit. Schriftenreihe der Internat. Stiftung
Mozarteum, 23. Salzburg 1980.

Gerber P. H.: Mozart's Ohr. Deutsch. Med. Wschr. 24, 351,1898.

Greither A.: Mozart und die Ärzte, seine Krankheiten und sein Tod. Deutsch.
Med. Wschr. 81, 121, 1956.

Greither A.: Die Legende von Mozart's Vergiftung. Deutsch. Med. Wschr. 82,
928, 1957.

Greither A.: Die Todeskrankheit Mozarts. Literatur-Eildienst *Roche* Nr. 4
Basel 1967.

Greither A.: Woran ist Mozart gestorben? Schriftenreihe der Internat. Stiftung
Mozarteum 3/4. Salzburg 1971.

Greither A.: Mozart; seine Leidensgeschichte. Heidelberg 1958.

Greither A.: Eine Pathographie Mozarts. Farbenfabriken Bayer AG.

Leverkusen, 1970.

Greither A.: Wolfgang Amadé Mozart. Hrsg. K. Kusenberg. (Reinbek bei Hamburg) 1982.

Gruber G.: Mozart und die Nachwelt. Salzburg 1985.

Gugitz G. : Mozarts Schädel und Dr. Gall. Z. Musikwiss., Wien 1934.

Guitard E. H.: A-t-on empoisonné Mozart au mercure? Rev. Hist. Pharm. (Paris) 47, 16 1959.

Hildesheimer W.: Mozart. Frankfurt am Main 1977.

Holl M. M.: Mozart's Ohr. Mitt. Anthrop. Ges. Wien 21,1,1901.

Holmes F.: Life of Mozart. London 1845.

Holz H.: Mozarts Krankheiten und sein Tod. Inaug. Dissertation. Jena 1939.

Hutchings A. : Mozart: der Mensch. Phonogramm Internat., Baarn. Niederlande 1976.

Jochmann G.: Lehrbuch der Infektionskrankheiten. Berlin 1914.

Juhn B.: Mozarts Leiden und Sterben. Ciba Symposium. Basel, 3, 191, 1956.

Katner W.: Woran ist Mozart gestorben? Mitteilungen der Internat. Stiftung Mozarteum 1, 1967.

Kerner D.: Krankheiten grosser Musiker. 3. Aufl. Stuttgart - New York 1973.

Kraemer U.: Mozarts Pech beim Kartenspiel. *Walsroder Zeitung* 1./2. September/1979.

Landon R.: Mozart and the Masons. London 1982.

Langegger F.: Mozart: Vater und Sohn. Zürich - Freiburg 1978.

Langhans D.: Beschreibung der gefährlichen Krankheiten. Bern 1762.

Littrow C.: Meteorologische Betrachtungen an der k. k. Sternwarte 1750 - 1850. Wien 1860.

Ludendorff M.: Mozarts Leben und gewaltsamer Tod. München 1936.

Marini A.: zitiert nach Rappoport.

Medici N., und Hughes R.: A Mozart Pilgrimage, Travel Diaries of Vincent and Mary Novello. London 1955.

Minnich F.: Hyrtls Mozartschädel. II. Die anatomische Beschreibung. Int. Stiftung Mozarteum, Salzburg 1906.

Moscheles J.: Aus Moscheles Leben. Nach Briefen und Tagebüchern. Hrsg. von seiner Frau. Leipzig 1877.

Mozart und seine Welt: in zeitgenössischen Bildern. Kassel - Basel 1961.

Nettl P.: Musik und Freimaurerei. Esslingen a. N., 1956.

Nettl P.: W. A. Mozart: Als Freimaurer und Mensch. Hamburg 1956.

Niemetschek F. H.: Lebensbeschreibung des k.k. Kapellmeisters Wolfgang Gottlieb Mozart. Prag 1798.

Nissen G. N.: Biographie W. A. Mozarts. Leipzig 1828.

Paton A., Pahor A., und Graham G.: Looking for Mozart's ears. Brit. Med. J. 239, 1622, 1986.

Paumgartner B.: Mozart. Zürich - Freiburg 1967.

Pichler C.: Denkwürdigkeiten aus meinem Leben. Hrsg.: Blümml, E. K., 2 Bde. München 1914.

Pribram A.: Der akute Gelenkrheumatismus. Wien 1899.

Rappoport A. E.: An unique and hitherto unreported theory concerning a genetic pathologic anatomic basis of Mozart's death. Abstract, Internat. Congress of Pathology, Vienna 1986.

Robbins Landon H. C.: 1791 - Mozart's Last Year. New York 1988.

Rosenberg A.: W. A. Mozart: Der verborgene Abgrund. Zürich 1976.

Sallaba M. v.: Historia Naturalis Morborum. Wien 1791.

Schenk E.: Mozart, sein Leben-seine Welt. Wien 1975.

Schiedermair L.: W. A. Mozarts Handschrift in zeitlich geordneten Nachbildungen. Leipzig 1919.

Schlichtegroll F.: Mozarts Leben. Graz 1794. Faksimile-Nachdruck in: Documenta musicologica. Kassel - Basel 1974.

Schneider O., und Algatzy A.: Mozart-Handbuch. Wien o. J.

Sederholm C. G.: Ist Mozart an Morbus Basedow gestorben? Ciba Symposium 5. Basel 1959.

Stoll M.: Heilungsmethode in dem praktischen Krankenhaus zu Wien. 2 Bde. Breslau 1794.

Szametz R.: Hat Mozart eine Psychose durchgemacht? Dissertation. Frankfurt 1936.

Tschitscherin G. W.: Mozart - eine Studie. Leipzig 1975.

Tichy G.: Zur Anthropologie des Genies: Mozarts Schädel. In: Jahrbuch der Universität Salzburg 1989.

Tichy G., Puech P. F.: Identification of a Passing Guest Wolfgang Amadeus Mozart. J. Canadian Soc. Forensic Science, Ottawa 1987.

Voser-Hoesli I.: Der Briefstil. In: Mozart-Aspekte. Hrsg.: Schaller, P., und Kühner H. Olten und Freiburg 1956.

## LUDWIG VAN BEETHOVEN

Bankl H.: Beethoven's Krankheit - Morbus Paget? Pathologie 6, 46, 1985.

Bankl H., und Jesserer H.: Die Krankheiten Ludwig van Beethovens. Wien - München 1987.

Beethoven L. van: Konversationshefte. Hrsg.: K. H. Köhler und G. Herre, 10 Bde. Leipzig 1968.

Bekker P.: Beethoven. Berlin 1912.

Bienenfeld E.: Ertaubte Tondichter. Wiener med. Wschr. 83, 1105, 1933.

Böhme G.: Ludwig van Beethoven. In: Medizinische Porträts berühmter Komponisten. Stuttgart - New York 1979.

Breuning G. v.: Aus dem Schwarzspanierhause, Wien 1874.

Chop M.: Ludwig van Beethovens Symphonien. Leipzig 1910.

Cohn H.: Beethoven's Brillen. Wschr. f. Therapie und Hygiene d. Auges, 5, 5, 1901.

Crohn B., Ginsburg L. und Oppenheimer G.: Regional ileitis. J. A. M. A. 99, 1323, 1932.

Czeizel E.: Murdering Beethoven. Lancet II, 1127, 1977.

Eder M.: Deutung von Beethovens Krankheit und Tod. Münch. med Wschr. 99, 1345, 1957.

Ernest G.: Der kranke Beethoven. Med. Welt 13, 491, 1927.

Fahrländer H.: Persönliche Mitteilung, Basel 23. 4. 1987.

Fischer G.: Des Bonner Bäckermeisters Gottfried Fischers Aufzeichnungen über Beethovens Jugend. Hrsg.: von J. Schmidt-Görg: Schriften zur Beethovenforschung 6. Bonn - München - Duisburg 1971.

Forster W.: Beethovens Krankheiten und ihre Beurteilung. Wiesbaden 1955.

Frank J. P.: Biographie des Dr. Johann Peter Frank, von ihm selbst geschrieben. Wien 1802.

Franken F. H.: Krankheit und Tod grosser Komponisten. Baden-Baden - Köln - New York 1979.

Frimmel Th.: Beethoven-Handbuch. 2 Bde. Leipzig 1926.

Gattner H.: Zu "Beethovens Krankheit und sein Tod." Münch. med. Wschr. 100, 1009, 1958.

Goldschmidt H.: Zu Beethoven: Aufsätze und Annotationen. Beiträge zur Musikwissenschaft. Berlin 1979.

Hawkins C.: Inflammatory bowel diseases, London 1983.

Hess W.: Beethoven. Winterthur 1976.

Hyrtl J.: Vergangenheit und Gegenwart des Museums für menschliche Anatomie an der Universität Wien, Wien 1869.

Jacobsohn L.: L. v. Beethovens Gehörleiden. Deutsch. med. Wschr. 36, 1282, 1910.

Jesserer H. und Bankl H.: Ertaubte Beethoven an einer Paget'schen Krankheit? Bericht über die Auffindung und Untersuchung von Schädelfragmenten L. van Beethovens. Laryng. Rhinol. Otol. 65, 592, 1986.

Kalischer A. Ch.: Beethovens sämtliche Briefe. 5 Bde. Berlin - Leipzig 1906-1908.

Kastner E.: Ludwig van Beethovens sämtliche Briefe. Hrsg. J. Kapp. Leipzig 1923.

Kerner D.: Krankheiten grosser Musiker. Bd. I. Stuttgart 1973.

Kerst F.: Die Erinnerungen an Beethoven. Bd. 1 und 2., 2. Aufl. Stuttgart 1925.

Klapetek J.: Beethovens letzter Arzt. Deutsch. med. Wschr. 93, 368, 1968.

Kobald K.: Beethoven. Wien 1960.

Köhler K. H.: ...tausendmal leben! Konversationen mit Herrn van Beethoven. Leipzig 1978.

Landon R.: Beethoven. Zürich 1970.

Langer v. Edenberg: Die Cranicen dreier musikalischer Koryphäen. Mitt. Anthrop. Ges. Wien XVII, Sitzungsbericht vom 19. 4. 1887.

Larkin E.: Beethoven's illness a likely diagnosis. Proc. R. Soc. Med. 14, 493, 1971.

Laskiewicz A.: Ludwig van Beethovens Tragödie vom audiologischen Standpunkt. Laryngologie 43, 261, 1964.

Leitzmann A.: Ludwig van Beethoven. Berichte der Zeitgenossen. Bd. 2, Leipzig 1921.

Ley S.: Die Ärzte Beethovens. Med. Welt 8, 747, 1934.

Ley S.: An Beethoven's letztem Krankenlager. Med. Welt 10, 1058 und 1094, 1936.

Ley S.: Beethoven. Sein Leben in Selbstzeugnissen, Briefen und Berichten. Wien - Berlin o. J.

London S. J.: Beethoven. Case report of a Titan's last crisis. Arch. Int. Med. 113, 411, 1964.

Magenau C. B.: Beethoven's Gehörleiden und das Heiligenstädter Testament. Zschr. ärztl. Fortbild. 34, 268, 1937.

Magnani L.: Beethovens Konversationshefte. Riccardo Ricciardi, Mailand - Neapel 1962.

Marek G. R.: Ludwig van Beethoven. München 1970.

McCabe B. F.: Beethoven's deafness. Ann. Otol. 67, 192, 1958.

Mercklin A.: Über das Misstrauen und den sog. Verfolgungswahn der .Schwerhörigen. Allg. Zschr. Psychiat. 74, 420, 1918.

Müller E.: Johann und sein grosser Sohn Ludwig van Beethoven. Psychiat.

neurol. Wochr. 41, 323, 1939.

Müller K.: Beethovens Brillen. Klin. Monatsbl. Augenklinik 138, 412, 1961.

Naiken V. S.: Did Beethoven have Paget's disease of bone? Ann. Intern. Med . 74, 995, 1971.

Nettl P.: Beethoven und die Ärzte. Ciba-Symposium 14, 95, 1966.

Neumann H.: Beethoven's Gehörleiden. Wien. med. Wschr. 77, 1015, 1927.

Nohl L.: Beethovens Leben. 4 Bde. 2. Aufl., Berlin 1909.

Nottebohm G.: Beethoven Studien: Leipzig - Winterthur 1873.

Nottebohm G.: Beethovens Unterricht bei J. Haydn, Albrechtsberger und Salieri. Leipzig 1873.

Piroth M.: Beethovens letzte Krankheit auf Grund der zeitgenössischen medizinischen Quellen. Beethoven-Jahrbuch 1959/60. Hrsg. von P. Miss und J. Schmidt-Görg. Bonn 1962.

Rexroth D.: Beethoven. München 1982.

Riemann H.: L. van Beethovens sämtliche Klaviersonaten. Berlin 1917.

Riezler W.: Beethoven. Zürich-Freiburg, 1977.

Rolland R.: Beethoven. Zürich und Stuttgart 1969.

Schering A.: Beethoven in neuer Deutung. Leipzig 1934.

Scherf H.: Die Krankheit Beethovens. München 1977.

Schiedermair L.: Der junge Beethoven. Leipzig 1925.

Schindler A.: Biographie von Ludwig van Beethoven. 3. Aufl. Münster 1860.

Schmidt F. A.: Noch einmal: Beethoven's Gehörleiden und letzte Krankheit. Deutsch. med. Wschr. 54, 284, 1928.

Schmidt-Görg J.: Beethoven. Die Geschichte seiner Familie. Veröffentlichungen des Beethoven-Hauses. Neue Folge. 4. Reihe, Bd. I., Bonn 1964.

Schmidt-Görg J.: Dreizehn unbekannte Briefe an Josefine Gräfin Deym geb. v. Brunsvik (Faksimile) Bonn 1957.

Schultze F.: Die Krankheiten Beethovens. Münch. med. Wschr. 75, 1040, 1928.

Schweisheimer W.: Beethovens Ärzte: Haben sie den Meister richtig behandelt? Medizinische Welt 6, 258, 1959.

Schweisheimer W.: Beethoven's Krankheiten. Münch. med. Wschr. 67, 1473, 1920.

Schweisheimer W.: Beethovens Leiden, ihr Einfluss auf Leben und Schaffen. München 1922.

Solomon M.: Beethoven. München 1979.

Sterba E. und R.: Ludwig van Beethoven und sein Neffe. München 1964.

Sterpellone L.: Pazienti illustrissimi. Roma 1985.

Stevens K. M., Hemenway W. G.: Beethoven's deafness. J. Am. Med. Ass. 213, 434, 1970.

Thayer A. W.: Ludwig van Beethovens Leben. 4 Bde. Deutsche Übers. und Bearb. von H. Deiters. Hrsg.: Hugo Reimann. Leipzig 1907-1923.

Waldegg R.: Sittengèschichte von Wien. Stuttgart 1957.

Wawruch A.: Ärztlicher Rückblick auf L. van Beethoven's letzte Lebensepoche. Allgem. Wiener Musikzeitung II, 218, 1842.

Wegeler F. G., und Ries S.: Biographische Notizen über Ludwig van Beethoven. Coblenz 1838.

Weisbach A., Toldt C. und Neynerth Th.: Mitt. Anthrop. Ges. Wien. XVIII.

Weissenbach A.: Meine Reise zum Kongress. Wien 1816.

Wessling B. W.: Beethoven. Das entfesselte Genie. München 1982.

Zeraschi H.: Das Beethovenporträt von Waldmüller. Musik und Gesellschaft, 21, 630, 1971.

Zobeley F.: Beethoven. Hamburg 1983.

### SCHUBERT

Bauernfeld E. von: Erinnerungen aus Alt-Wien. Wien 1923.

Brown M. J. E.: Schubert. A critical biography. London 1953.

Chezy W. v.: Erinnerungen aus meinem Leben. Schaffhausen 1863.

Dahms W.: Franz Schubert. Berlin - Leipzig 1912.

Deutsch O. E.: Schubert, A documentary biography. London 1946.

Deutsch O. E.: Erinnerungen seiner Freunde, gesammelt und hrsg. von O. E. Deutsch. Wiesbaden 1957.

Deutsch O. E.: Franz Schubert, Briefe und Schriften. 2. Aufl. München 1922.

Deutsch O. E.: Franz Schubert, die Dokumente seines Lebens. Basel - Kassel 1964.

Einstein A.: Schubert. Ein musikalisches Porträt. Zürich 1952.

Eulenberg H.: Schubert und die Frauen. Hellerau bei Dresden 1928.

Feigl R.: Klar um Schubert. Linz 1936.

Fischer-Dieskau D.: Auf den Spuren der Schubert-Lieder. Wiesbaden 1974.

Franken F. H.: Krankheit und Tod grosser Komponisten. Baden-Baden, Köln - New York 1979.

Friedländer M.: Franz Schubert, Skizze seines Lebens und Wirkens. Leipzig 1928.

Fröhlich H. J.: Schubert. München - Wien 1978.

Gal H.: Franz Schubert oder die Melodie. Frankfurt 1970.

Goldschmidt H.: Franz Schubert. Leipzig 1976.

Heischkel E.: Was ist über die Krankheiten und Todesursachen Luthers, Lessings, Mozarts, Schillers und Schuberts bekannt und wissenschaftlich erwiesen? Med. Welt 10, 577, 1936.

Heuberger R.: Schubert, Berlin 1920.

Hilmar E.: Franz Schubert in seiner Zeit. Wien - Köln Graz 1985.

Hitschmann E.: Franz Schuberts Schmerz und Liebe. Internat. Zschr. Psychoanal. Wien, 3, 287, 1915.

Höcker C.: Wege zu Schubert. Regensburg 1940.

Jaspert W.: Franz Schubert. Zeugnisse seines irdischen Daseins. Frankfurt 1941.

Kahl W.: Verzeichnis des Schrifttums über Franz Schubert 1828 bis 1928. Kölner Beiträge zur Musikforschung. Regensburg 1938.

Kerner D.: Der kranke Schubert. Münch. med. Wschr. 100, 977, 1958.

Klein R.: Schubert Stätten. Wien 1972.

Kobald K.: Franz Schubert und seine Zeit. Zürich - Leipzig - Wien 1928.

Kreissle v. Hellborn H.: Franz Schubert, Wien 1865.

Lesky E.: Die Wiener medizinische Schule im 19. Jahrhundert. Graz - Köln 1965.

Lux J. A.: Franz Schubert. Ein Lebensbild aus deutscher Vergangenheit. Berlin 1922.

Mandyczewski E.: Franz Schubert. Leipzig 1897.

Marek G. R.: Schubert. London 1986.

Müller R. F.: Die Körpergrösse Schuberts. Bericht über den internat.

Kongress für Schubertforschung. Augsburg 1929.

Neuberger M.: Das alte medizinische Wien in zeitgenössischen Schilderungen. Wien 1921.

Ofner J.: Franz Schubert und Steyr. Steyr 1973.

Osborne A.: Schubert: Leben in Wien. Königstein/Ts. 1986.

Osterheld H.: Franz Schubert, Schicksal und Persönlichkeit. Stuttgart - Degerloch 1978.

Paumgartner B.: Franz Schubert. Zürich 1947.

Petzoldt E.: Franz Schubert, Leben und Werk. Leipzig 1939.

Rehberg W. und P.: Franz Schubert, sein Leben und Werk. 2. Aufl. Zürich 1947.

Reininghaus R.: Schubert und das Wirtshaus. Wien 1978.

Riezler W.: Schuberts Instrumentalmusik. Zürich - Freiburg 1967.

Franz Schubert. Musik-Konzepte Sonderband. Hrsg. von Metzger H. K., Reihn R., und Pribil H. München 1979.

Franz Schubert. Werkverzeichnis. Der kleine Deutsch. München - Kassel 1983.

Schünemann G.: Erinnerungen an Schubert: J. V. Spauns erste Lebensbeschreibung. Berlin - Zürich 1936.

Schweisheimer W.: Der kranke Schubert. Zeitschr. f. Musikwissenschaft III, 553, 1921.

Silvestrelli A.: Franz Schubert. Das wahre Gesicht seines Lebens. Salzburg - Leipzig 1939.

Toldt C. und Weisbach A.: Mitt. Anthrop. Ges. Wien XVIII, 77, 1888 (Sitzungsbericht zweiter Anhang 4-6, April).

Vetter W.: Der klassische Schubert. Leipzig 1953.

Vorberg G.: War Schubert syphilitisch? Ärztl. Rundschau 35, 165, 1925.

Wechsberg J.: Schubert. München 1978.

Werba R.: Schubert und die Wiener. Wien - München 1978.

Werlé H.: Franz Schubert in seinen Briefen und Aufzeichnungen. Leipzig 1951.

Ziese E.: Schubert's Tod und Begräbnis. Grossdeuten 1933.

# *Sources of Illustrations*

Austrian National Library (Vienna)

Photo Archives of the Institute for Medical History of University of Vienna

Vienna Musical Society

Mozarteum, Salzburg

Beethoven-Haus, Bonn

Mrs. Eva Alberman, London

Radio Times Hulton Picture Library

Public Archives, The Hague

Museum of Military History, Vienna

# Acknowledgments
## for the English Edition

The translator, Bruce Cooper Clarke, is a student of the music of the Viennese classical period and the author of numerous articles, reports, and reviews concerned principally with Mozart. Mr. Clarke is a graduate of Syracuse University and The American University (Washington, D. C.). He and his family live in the foothills of the Austrian Alps, about midway between Salzburg (where Mozart was born) and Vienna (where he died).

The editor, Emily P. McNamara, holds a Bachelor of Arts degree from DePauw University and has more than thirty years' experience as an editor of business, professional, and scientific publications. Today Ms. McNamara is a free-lance editor living in Bloomington, Illinois.

The medical editor, Harold O. Conn, M.D., is a graduate of the University of Michigan School of Medicine; he performed his housestaff training at The Johns Hopkins Hospital and at the Yale-New Haven Medical Center. He was appointed Emeritus Professor of Medicine at Yale University School of Medicine. He is a world-renown hepatologist, educator, and author. He lives in East Haven, Connecticut, with his wife, Marilyn.

# Personal Comments
## by the Medical Editor

What is a nice English-speaking guy like me doing as a medical editor of a book that was written in German? I'm here because I'm probably responsible for this translation project. In April, 1991 I was a guest lecturer at the medical school of the University of Vienna. After the lecture during dinner at the Plaza Hotel with Drs. Alfred Gangl, Herbert Thaler and Peter Ferenci, I was pursuing one of my favorite mysteries—Beethoven's terminal illness. It was clear from the description of Dr. Andreas Wawruch, one of Beethoven's last physicians, that Beethoven had developed decompensated alcoholic cirrhosis with a large accumulation of abdominal fluid (ascites) for which he had required a series of large withdrawals of ascitic fluid that are known as paracenteses or colloquially as "taps". As the physician who first described and named spontaneous bacterial peritonitis (bacterial infection of the ascitic fluid), I have a strong proprietary interest in this syndrome and a low threshold of suspicion for this diagnosis. Since the autopsy had been performed in Vienna, I had hoped to learn more about Beethoven's illness. I asked Dr. Gangl with whom I should speak to get the answers to some of my questions. Without hesitation he replied, "Professor Anton Neumayr is the world's expert on Beethoven and his diseases".

"Who?" I asked. After he explained that Neumayr had written three books on famous composers and their illnesses, he excused himself and left the table. He returned a few minutes later to tell me that Dr. Neumayr had invited Marilyn, my wife, and me to tea at his home the following day.

The next afternoon at the appointed hour, Marilyn and I went to their home where Anton and Nina Neumayr greeted us warmly. We spent a lovely afternoon at their beautiful home. Anton explained that he had two loves—music and medicine— and that he gave equal time to both. It was the year of the Mozart bicentennial and he played portions of several of Mozart's concertos on his magnificent Imperial Bösendorfer concert piano. When the recital started, their boxer, Dagobert, lay down under the piano and listened intently until the music stopped.

During our conversation it became abundantly clear that Dr. Neumayr was, indeed, the world's expert on composer's diseases. In fact, earlier that day I had walked across the plaza from the Sacher Hotel, at which we were staying, to the Opera House Book Store where I saw Dr. Neumayr's book, *Musik und Medizin*, for the first time. Because it had not been translated into English, I bought a copy in German, planning to ask Dr. Neumayr to autograph it for me. Before I had a chance to ask, he gave me a copy of the book that he had already inscribed.

Two items of "business" took place during the afternoon. It was clear that Beethoven had had advanced cirrhosis of the liver and, therefore, I asked Dr. Neumayr if he had considered the possibility that Beethoven may have developed spontaneous bacterial peritonitis. He said flatly "Beethoven did not have bacterial peritonitis." I was surprised, but I did not pursue the conversation.

Second, I explained to Dr. Neumayr that every American doctor considers himself a musicologist and a medical historian with a special interest in composers' illnesses. "Why haven't you translated the book into English?" I asked him. "We Americans need it badly."

He responded by telling me that it was very difficult to get a publisher and to have it translated properly. I assured him that his English was superb and that he could do it easily. He told me that he was too busy to do it in the foreseeable future. "Can you help me find a publisher?" he asked.

I told him that I knew a small publisher that I thought would probably want to publish the book in English, and that I would try to find a translator, too. We shook hands without further discussion.

When I returned to the United States the following day, I contacted Sherlyn Hogenson, the owner of Medi-Ed Press, who had published my two books with Professor Johannes Bircher on Hepatic Encephalopathy and told her what a marvelous opportunity I thought Neumayr's books offered. After a brief period of consideration she agreed, and shortly thereafter signed a contract with Jugend & Volk (J&V), Edition Wien, to publish a translation.

Meanwhile I contacted a cousin who plays trumpet in the Philadelphia Orchestra, many members of which are of German nationality. He suggested several possible translators, who were German-speaking musicians, but neither they, nor their nominees were able to translate especially well the portions of the Mozart chapter that I sent to them as an "audition". Later, on recommendations of J&V and Dr. Neumayr, Medi-Ed Press discovered Bruce Cooper Clarke whose lyrical translation, in my opinion, appears to equal Neumayr's original prose. Of course, I was reading Clarke in English and Neumayr in German. It was decided that I was to be the Medical Editor, to assure that the medical translations were expressed accurately and in modern medical terminology.

As I received each translated chapter of Volume I, I read the manuscript and made the changes I thought necessary. I made lists of medical questions for Dr. Neumayr about observations and concepts concerning the four Viennese composers that weren't clear to me. In addition, I made separate lists of questions for Bruce Clarke about portions of the medical translations. Professor Neumayr encouraged me to make whatever changes I thought would enhance the volume. Consequently, I added short sections to explain medical concepts of the 18th and 19th centuries, in modern terms, to be noted with an asterisk in the text.

Both the author and the translator responded positively and in detail to my many questions and appropriate revisions were made. Ms. Hogenson and the staff at Medi-Ed Press, the publishers with whom it has long been a pleasure to work, integrated this three-way amalgamation.

My interest in Beethoven's terminal illness had been stimulated by a chapter in O. G. Sonneck's book, *Beethoven: Impressions by His Contemporaries*, which describes Wawruch's treatment of Beethoven's cirrhosis. Dr. Wawruch, who was the Director of the Viennese Medical Clinic, was first consulted by Beethoven in December, 1826, after Beethoven had just returned, acutely ill, from Gneixendorf. He had developed jaundice, vomiting, diarrhea, severe fluid retention in his legs and abdomen, severe abdominal pain, fever and chills. This constellations of symptoms and signs which had developed without apparent cause, is characteristic of bacterial infection of the abdominal fluid. I had jumped to the conclusion that he had developed spontaneous bacterial peritonitis (SBP) that had not been described until almost 150 years after Beethoven died. It is a disease now recognized as a common complication of cirrhosis. The appearance of "erysipelas" of the abdominal wall, a phenomenon that I had observed after paracenteses in several patients, convinced me that he had this syndrome. When Professor Neumayr had rejected my suggestion that Beethoven may have had peritonitis, I had been a little offended. In my confidence in my own knowledge, I concluded that although Neumayr is the world's expert on Beethoven's diseases, I am one of the world's experts on SBP. However, after reading the entire medical history of Beethoven and the details of his last illness that had been assembled by Neumayr, I agreed that he may not have had SBP, although it cannot be excluded with absolute certainty. A primary reason for reaching this conclusion is that even today SBP is usually fatal, and Beethoven survived over a month under terribly unsanitary conditions, with repeated "tappings" of the fluid. In fact, if he hadn't had spontaneous bacterial peritonitis, he should have developed secondary (nonspontaneous) peritonitis. In the absence of modern diagnostic bacteriologic and microscopic methodology, it is impossible to exclude these diagnoses.

I have no reservations, however, about Professor Neumayr's spectacular diagnosis of regional ileitis (Crohn's disease) in Beethoven. He had made the diagnosis of a disease that had not been described until 1932, over a century after Beethoven had died, and documented every facet of this complex disorder. Furthermore, his analysis of the difficult differential diagnosis of the cause of Mozart's death is equally impressive, and in my opinion is completely correct.

In all humility about my lack of formal training in music, I feel it essential that I try to justify my role in this volume. My brief formal training in music may have unintentionally contributed to my specializing in the performance of randomized, clinical trials, the area to which I have devoted most of my professional life. It began when I was a young teenager. My mother and her sister had agreed that their sons should learn to play a musical instrument. They conspired with a third sister; her boyfriend, a professional trumpet player, would be the teacher. In short order, an impromptu, controlled investigation was designed. Two boys of similar genetic and environmental background were to be the participants of this study: both were taught by the same teacher, using the same type of trumpet. However, the two experimental subjects were not identical, as they are supposed to be, but, rather, were intrinsically dissimilar in talent and degree of dedication. My cousin had significantly more of both and quickly our courses diverged. He progressed promptly to classical music, musical honors in high school and a scholarship to the Curtis School of Music in Philadelphia. I persisted on the trumpet for four long years and, at best, achieved a recognizable rendition of "My Old Kentucky Home." When Seymour graduated from Curtis he was hired by the St. Louis Symphony Orchestra and, shortly thereafter, he was invited by Eugene Ormandy to join the Philadelphia Orchestra where he played until he retired several years ago. Clearly, I had been the control group.

I believe that this experience in my one involvement in musical education set the stage for my investigative career in medicine and my appreciation of music. Despite my devastating defeat on the trumpet, my cousin and I remained good friends and he nurtured my interest in music. Indeed, during my participation in the translation of this book, I was continually within earshot of the music composed by Haydn, Mozart, Beethoven and Schubert.

Harold O. Conn, M.D.
East Haven, Connecticut

# Medical Editor's Notes

## Mozart

P. 114  The dependence on the occurrence of diarrhea in typhoid fever is still widely and erroneously believed.

p. 184  Erythema nodosum consists of large (1 to 3 centimeters in diameter) red "bull's-eyes" on the trunk, arms and legs. They appear to be an immunologic response to bacteria such as tuberculosis or to sarcoidosis.

p. 186  The acute epidemic gastroenteritis, with accompanying fever and vomiting, could also have been atypical acute viral hepatitis.

p. 200  The concept of "deposito alla testa" (deposit in the head) originated in the second half of the 18th century as part of the humoral explanation of disease which assumed that acute rheumatic arthritis resulted from the deposition of a toxic substance in the joints that caused the inflammation, pain and swelling in that joint. Deposition of this substance in the knee joint induced involvement of the knee joint; its deposition in the elbow joint caused inflammation of that joint. Actually, this concept is quite a rational one, which is probably ultimately correct, even though the nature of the deposit and its mechanism of inducing the abnormal symptoms and signs were not understood. Deposits could also be deposited in the thorax, e.g., on the pleura, where they could cause pleuritic pain and pleural effusions, in the brain where it could cause Sydenham's chorea (St. Vitus dance, i.e., irregular, spasmodic, involuntary movements of the limbs or facial muscles), or death.

"Deposits" have a counterpart in modern histopathology. In the deposition of complexes that consist of streptococcal antigens, the patients' antibodies to the streptococcus and other substances such as complement. Such deposits are visible by electron microscopy.

p. 203  Acute rheumatic fever and acute glomerulonephritis are both delayed, nonsupperative (without pus), inflammatory reactions to streptococcal Group A infections of the throat that almost always occur in children, as Dr. Neumayr stated previously. Such infections, which were in Mozart's time referred to as catarrhs, angina or pharyngitis, are usually referred to now as upper respiratory infections. The subtypes of the bacteria that cause these two types of infections are different; specific antibodies to these two types of bacteria can be detected. It is also probable that the patients who develop acute rheumatic fever have subtly different genetic or histocompatibility characteristics, i.e., different HLA tissue types (Histocompatibility Locus A) that make them more susceptible to develop rheumatic fever rather than glomerulonephritis or to be resistant to both.

Both disorders tend to occur in clusters of cases that follow epidemics of streptococcal throat infections. Both occur more frequently in more primitive countries in which hygiene is poor. Thus, these epidemics were much more common and much more serious in Mozart's time, and caused many more post-streptococcal syndromes than they do now. Furthermore, these bacteria are exquisitely sensitive to penicillin, which is now able to eradicate the bacteria before these abnormal reactions can develop. Penicillin has also prevented the epidemics of streptococcal infections.

Both syndromes are caused by autoimmunologic mechanisms that are not completely understood, but it is clear that the more frequent and severe the infections, the more frequent and severe these post-streptococcal complications are. Rheumatic fever is characterized by arthritis, which causes painful swellings of the joints, especially the knees, elbows, ankles, and wrists. The arthritis may migrate from joint to joint, so that several or, occasionally, all are swollen and extremely tender at the same time. The joint symptoms occur from one to five weeks after the streptococcal infection. These are accompanied by fever, which may be extremely high. At the present time fevers are less common and temperature levels are lower because of the use of aspirin and antibiotic drugs. The arthritis may be preceded by abdominal pain as it was in Mozart's case. The most severe damage caused by rheumatic fever is the injury to the valves of the heart which is its most common complication. Such injury may often cause chronic heart failure and death, years after the initial infection. Unlike the situation in Mozart's time, epidemics of and deaths from acute rheumatic fever are rare at present except in underdeveloped countries.

Acute glomerulonephritis, the other typical post-streptococcal manifestation of streptococcal Group A infections, often follows scarlet fever, which is also a streptococcal infection, as well as after upper-respiratory infections. It almost always occurs in children, at the cooler times of the year, i.e., in the fall or winter. The patients often develop swelling of the face, especially around the eyes, smoky or rust-colored urine and high blood pressure. The patients may appear pale, show swelling (edema) of the feet, legs or scrotum and complain of tiredness, headache, poor appetite and dull back pain. The edema tends to be more severe in adults than in children. Fever, when it occurs, is low grade. These symptoms develop one to three or four weeks after the streptococcal infection.

Microscopic examination of the urine shows the presence of red blood cells and protein that is caused by injury of the glomeruli. These symptoms and signs usually subside spontaneously after a few weeks or months, or may persist (chronic glomerulonephritis). Glomerulonephritis is rarely fatal in the acute stage of the presentation at the present time, but was more frequently fatal in previous centuries. Repeated infections tend to make the kidney disease chronic and more severe.

The disease represents injury, i.e., the deposition of complexes of streptococcal protein and antibodies to it in the glomeruli. The glomeruli are small, spherical collections of blood vessels which are found near the surface of the kidney that filter the blood as it passes through the kidneys. Injury to the glomeruli results in the loss of red blood cells, which causes anemia, and of protein, which leads to the retention of fluid. High blood pressure and kidney failure, which may be fatal many years later, are manifestations of chronic nephritis. In such patients, a sallow, olive complexion may be noted. Patients rarely, if ever, develop both rheumatic fever and glomerulonephritis after streptococcal infection. It is interesting that Mozart appears to have exhibited some characteristics of both types of post-streptococcal illness.

Although the two disorders are different, one can understand how physicians in the 17th and 18th centuries, before these two diseases were delineated, might have confused the two. The swelling of the legs, for example, is easy to confuse in retrospect, when one realizes that descriptions of "swelling of the arms and legs" can represent either the painful inflammatory arthritis in acute rheumatic fever, or painless, soft, edematous swelling in chronic kidney disease. Indeed, this differentiation makes it clear that Mozart's swelling was of the arthritic type and the difficulty in moving his extremities was a consequence of the painful joints, not of massive swelling.

## BEETHOVEN

p. 227 This "inherited disease" was alcohol addiction. It is surprising that addiction to alcohol and the consequent complications of alcohol abuse was recognized so long ago. At present it is widely known that alcohol addiction occurs in families and, indeed, specific genetic abnormalities have been reported in the medical literature. Without doubt such associations occur commonly. Whether these associations are inherited or are environmental is yet to be established.

p. 238 This diagnosis was incorrectly assumed without objective confirmation by a lawyer, B. Springer. It was mentioned in his book, *Die genialen Syphilitiker,* which was published in Berlin in 1926.

p. 272 It is not known even today what the exact cause of the jaundice was. In all probability, it was acute viral hepatitis, although whether it was caused by Hepatitis virus A, B, or C is not clear. The presence of the rheumatic symptoms suggest that Hepatitis B or C was the most likely agent. Tests for Hepatitis virus B became available in about 1970 and for Hepatitis virus C in 1990. Both of these viruses are often associated with abnormal proteins in the blood, i.e., cryoglobulins, that can give rise to muscle or joint pains, especially when the patient is chilled.

p. 290　The treatment of Beethoven's ascites by Dr. Wawruch serves as the basis for the current treatment of intractable ascites. The technique of performing large paracenteses ("taps") as were performed on Beethoven has been shown to be at least as effective, as rapid and as safe, as any other therapy, including the use of diuretic medications to stimulate the increased excretion of urine or of surgery of various types to reduce the abnormally high pressure in the veins of the liver. Dr. Wawruch had performed four large taps on Beethoven between December 1826 and April 1827.

Admittedly, present day paracenteses are performed using sterile techniques and almost always with the intravenous administration of water-retaining substances to prevent a reduction in blood volume caused by internal shifts of body fluids after such procedures. Nevertheless, Dr. Wawruch set the precedent for the performance of serial, large aspirations of ascitic fluid more than one hundred fifty years before this procedure was introduced into the present-day management of massive ascites.

p. 333　Cirrhosis could be a consequence of Hepatitis B or Hepatitis C virus infection, which is indeed a possibility, given the span of several months between the premonitory symptoms of rheumatism in the spring of 1821 and the appearance of jaundice in the summer. Presumably, at that time, Hepatitis B or C virus could have been transmitted as it is now, by exposure to blood or other body fluids such as semen or saliva. It would have been transmittable through sexual intercourse,

## Schubert

p. 399　In syphilis, bony lesions are not always found and six years may not have been long enough for these tertiary lesions to develop.

p. 405　It is now known unequivocally that diet does not affect the course of the disease.

p. 406　Had Schubert lived longer, he might well have developed some of the neurologic complications of syphilis.

p. 408　Despite widespread evidence to the contrary, many physicians today still believe that diarrhea is the hallmark of typhoid fever.

p. 410　Such therapy may well have contributed to dehydration and electrolyte and metabolic disturbances that may eventually have worsened the disease.

# Index of Musical Compositions

Explanation of Abbreviations
—BWV: Bach Werke Verzeichnis (catalog of Bach's works)
—D: Catalog numbers of Schubert's works according to Otto Erich
     Deutsch
—KV: Köchel Verzeichnis (Köchel's catalog of Mozart's works)
—WoO: Werk ohne Opuszahl (work without opus number)

FRANZ VON SUPPÉ

PAUL WRANITZKY

Prepared 26 April 1994
Bruce Cooper Clarke

# Index of Names